INVOLUNTARY UNEMPLOYMENT

The Great Depression of the 1930s with its dramatic unemployment rates was one of the most striking economic events of the past century. It shook economists' belief in the existence of self-adjusting forces and prompted Keynes to write his masterwork, *The General Theory of Employment, Interest and Money* (1936).

Involuntary unemployment was the central concept of Keynes' book. However, after having been considered for decades the sine qua non of macroeconomics, it has gradually disappeared from textbooks and research. This book recounts and ponders this demise, asking is this a manifestation of a defect of economic theory or is it rather that the involuntary unemployment concept is of little use when it comes to economic theory?

In order to disentangle these issues, the author critically examines the different explanations of involuntary unemployment that have been offered, from Keynes up to the end of the 1980s. After a consideration of *The General Theory*, the author studies the works of pioneering macroeconomists such as Hicks, Modigliani, Lange, Leontief, Tobin, Klein and Hansen. A consideration of the 're-appraisal of Keynes' and the disequilibrium school is followed with a discussion of Friedman's and Lucas' anti-Keynesian attack. The final section of the book investigates a series of models purporting to revive the Keynesian project, implicit contract, efficiency wages, insider–outsider, coordination failure and imperfect competition models.

Michel De Vroey is Professor of Economics at the Université catholique de Louvain. His main research interest is the history of macroeconomics. He has held visiting positions at the Université de Paris, Panthéon-Sorbonne, Duke University and the University of Montréal. He has published articles in *Economics and Philosophy*, *Cambridge Journal of Economics* and in the main history of economic thought journals.

ROUTLEDGE FRONTIERS OF POLITICAL ECONOMY

1 EQUILIBRIUM VERSUS UNDERSTANDING
Towards the rehumanization of economics within social theory
Mark Addleson

2 EVOLUTION, ORDER AND COMPLEXITY
Edited by Elias L. Khalil and Kenneth E. Boulding

3 INTERACTIONS IN POLITICAL ECONOMY
Malvern after ten years
Edited by Steven Pressman

4 THE END OF ECONOMICS
Michael Perelman

5 PROBABILITY IN ECONOMICS
Omar F. Hamouda and Robin Rowley

6 CAPITAL CONTROVERSY, POST KEYNESIAN ECONOMICS AND THE HISTORY OF ECONOMICS
Essays in honour of Geoff Harcourt, volume one
Edited by Philip Arestis, Gabriel Palma and Malcolm Sawyer

7 MARKETS, UNEMPLOYMENT AND ECONOMIC POLICY
Essays in honour of Geoff Harcourt, volume two
Edited by Philip Arestis, Gabriel Palma and Malcolm Sawyer

8 SOCIAL ECONOMY
The logic of capitalist development
Clark Everling

9 NEW KEYNESIAN ECONOMICS/POST KEYNESIAN ALTERNATIVES
Edited by Roy J. Rotheim

10 THE REPRESENTATIVE AGENT IN MACROECONOMICS
James E. Hartley

11 BORDERLANDS OF ECONOMICS
Essays in honour of Daniel R. Fusfeld
Edited by Nahid Aslanbeigui and Young Back Choi

12 VALUE, DISTRIBUTION AND CAPITAL
Essays in honour of Pierangelo Garegnani
Edited by Gary Mongiovi and Fabio Petri

13 THE ECONOMICS OF SCIENCE
Methodology and epistemology as if economics really mattered
James R. Wible

14 COMPETITIVENESS, LOCALISED LEARNING AND REGIONAL DEVELOPMENT
Specialisation and prosperity in small open economies
Peter Maskell, Heikki Eskelinen, Ingjaldur Hannibalsson, Anders Malmberg and Eirik Vatne

15 LABOUR MARKET THEORY
A constructive reassessment
Ben J. Fine

16 WOMEN AND EUROPEAN EMPLOYMENT
Jill Rubery, Mark Smith, Colette Fagan, Damian Grimshaw

17 EXPLORATIONS IN ECONOMIC METHODOLOGY
From Lakatos to empirical philosophy of science
Roger Backhouse

18 SUBJECTIVITY IN POLITICAL ECONOMY
Essays on wanting and choosing
David P. Levine

19 THE POLITICAL ECONOMY OF MIDDLE EAST PEACE
The impact of competing trade agendas
Edited by J.W. Wright, Jnr

20 THE ACTIVE CONSUMER
Novelty and surprise in consumer choice
Edited by Marina Bianchi

21 SUBJECTIVISM AND ECONOMIC ANALYSIS
Essays in memory of Ludwig Lachmann
Edited by Roger Koppl and Gary Mongiovi

22 THEMES IN POST-KEYNESIAN ECONOMICS
Essays in honour of Geoff Harcourt, volume three
Edited by Claudio Sardoni and Peter Kriesler

23 THE DYNAMICS OF TECHNOLOGICAL KNOWLEDGE
Cristiano Antonelli

24 THE POLITICAL ECONOMY OF DIET, HEALTH AND FOOD POLICY
Ben J. Fine

25 THE END OF FINANCE
Capital market inflation, financial derivatives and pension fund capitalism
Jan Toporowski

26 POLITICAL ECONOMY AND THE NEW CAPITALISM
Edited by Jan Toporowski

27 GROWTH THEORY
A philosophical perspective
Patricia Northover

28 THE POLITICAL ECONOMY OF THE SMALL FIRM
Edited by Charlie Dannreuther

29 HAHN AND ECONOMIC METHODOLOGY
Edited by Thomas Boylan and Paschal F. O'Gorman

30 GENDER, GROWTH AND TRADE
The miracle economies of the postwar years
David Kucera

31 NORMATIVE POLITICAL ECONOMY
Subjective freedom, the market and the state
David Levine

32 ECONOMIST WITH A PUBLIC PURPOSE
Essays in honour of John Kenneth Galbraith
Edited by Michael Keaney

33 INVOLUNTARY UNEMPLOYMENT
The elusive quest for a theory
Michel De Vroey

34 THE FUNDAMENTAL INSTITUTIONS OF CAPITALISM
Ernesto Screpanti

35 TRANSCENDING TRANSACTION
The search for self-generating markets
Alan Shipman

36 POWER IN BUSINESS AND THE STATE
An historical analysis of its concentration
Frank Bealey

37 EDITING ECONOMICS
Essays in honour of Mark Perlman
Hank Lim, Ungsuh K. Park and Geoff Harcourt

38 MONEY, MACROECONOMICS AND KEYNES
Essays in honour of Victoria Chick, volume one
Philip Arestis, Meghnad Desai and Sheila Dow

39 METHODOLOGY, MICROECONOMICS AND KEYNES
Essays in honour of Victoria Chick, volume two
Philip Arestis, Meghnad Desai and Sheila Dow

40 MARKET DRIVE AND GOVERNANCE
Reexamining the rules for economic and commercial contest
Ralf Boscheck

41 THE VALUE OF MARX
Political economy for contemporary capitalism
Alfredo Saad-Filho

42 ISSUES IN POSITIVE POLITICAL ECONOMY
S. Mansoob Murshed

43 THE ENIGMA OF GLOBALISATION
A journey to a new stage of capitalism
Robert Went

44 THE MARKET
Equilibrium, stability, mythology
S. N. Afriat

45 THE POLITICAL ECONOMY OF RULE EVASION AND POLICY REFORM
Jim Leitzel

46 UNPAID WORK AND THE ECONOMY
Edited by Antonella Picchio

47 DISTRIBUTIONAL JUSTICE
Theory and measurement
Hilde Bojer

48 COGNITIVE DEVELOPMENTS IN ECONOMICS
Edited by Salvatore Rizzello

49 SOCIAL FOUNDATIONS OF MARKETS, MONEY AND CREDIT
Costas Lapavitsas

50 RETHINKING CAPITALIST DEVELOPMENT
Essays on the economics of Josef Steindl
Edited by Tracy Mott and Nina Shapiro

51 AN EVOLUTIONARY APPROACH TO SOCIAL WELFARE
Christian Sartorius

52 KALECKI'S ECONOMICS TODAY
Edited by Zdzislaw L. Sadowski and Adam Szeworski

53 FISCAL POLICY FROM REAGAN TO BLAIR
The Left veers Right
Ravi K. Roy and Arthur T. Denzau

54 THE COGNITIVE MECHANICS OF ECONOMIC DEVELOPMENT AND INSTITUTIONAL CHANGE
Bertin Martens

55 INDIVIDUALISM AND THE SOCIAL ORDER
The social element in liberal thought
Charles R. McCann Jnr.

56 AFFIRMATIVE ACTION IN THE UNITED STATES AND INDIA
A comparative perspective
Thomas E. Weisskopf

57 GLOBAL POLITICAL ECONOMY AND THE WEALTH OF NATIONS
Performance, institutions, problems and policies
Edited by Phillip Anthony O'Hara

58 STRUCTURAL ECONOMICS
Thijs ten Raa

59 MACROECONOMIC THEORY AND ECONOMIC POLICY
Essays in honour of Jean-Paul Fitoussi
Edited by K. Vela Velupillai

INVOLUNTARY UNEMPLOYMENT

The elusive quest for a theory

Michel De Vroey

Routledge
Taylor & Francis Group
LONDON AND NEW YORK

First published 2004
by Routledge
11 New Fetter Lane, London EC4P 4EE

Simultaneously published in the USA and Canada
by Routledge
29 West 35th Street, New York, NY 10001

Routledge is an imprint of the Taylor & Francis Group

Typeset in Baskerville by Wearset Ltd, Boldon, Tyne and Wear
Printed and bound in Great Britain by MPG Books Ltd, Bodmin

British Library Cataloguing in Publication Data
A catalogue record for this book is available from the British Library

Library of Congress Cataloging in Publication Data
A catalog record for this book has been requested

ISBN 0-415-08074-6

TO ANTOINETTE, CHARLOTTE, ORIANE
AND DAMIEN

CONTENTS

FIGURES

TABLES

ACKNOWLEDGEMENTS

During the many years I have been working on this book, I have benefitted from many encouragements and comments. First of all, I wish to express my gratitude to the successive generations of students who attended my History of Macroeconomics Seminar at the Université catholique de Louvain, the Université Paris-I Panthéon-Sorbonne and Duke University. I also benefitted from stimulating oral reactions from the audiences to which I presented the views developed in this book in Aix-en-Provence, Bergamo, Bilbao, Bologna, Bristol, Davis, Dijon, Durham (North Carolina), Durham (UK), Graz, Greensboro, Grenoble, Lausanne, Lille, Louvain-la-neuve, Lyon, Marseilles, Montréal, Nice, Orléans, Paris, Rennes, Rotterdam, Saint-Etienne, Siena, Stirling, Toronto, Tunis and Wake Forest. Several colleagues and friends read and commented on various drafts. Many thanks in particular to Lionel Artige, Jean-Pascal Benassy, Carlo Benetti, Mark Blaug, Pascal Bridel, Mauro Boianovsky, Jean Cartelier, Robert Clower, Antoine d'Autume, Neil de Marchi, Ghislain Deleplace, Franco Donzelli, Rodolphe Dos Santos Ferreira, Jacques Drèze, Jean-François Fagnart, Daniel Hausman, Kevin Hoover, Christophe Lavialle, Philippe Mongin, Antoine Rebeyrol, Michel Rosier, Goulven Rubin, Peter Skott, David Soskice, Philippe Van Parijs, Bruno Van der Linden, Howard Vane. Roger Backhouse, Ludovic Julien and Aude Pommeret read several chapters of the final draft of the book and provided useful advice. Finally, I am especially grateful to Alain Béraud who carefully read and made helpful comments on the whole manuscript.

I also wish to express my gratitude to the publishers of the following journals for their permission to reprint passages from earlier published articles:

The European Journal of the History of Economic Thought ('Involuntary Unemployment. The Missing Piece in Keynes' *The General Theory*', 1997, 4, p. 2, pp. 258–283) http://www.tandf.co.uk.

Journal of Economic Methodology ('Is the Tâtonnement Hypothesis a Good Caricature of Market Forces?', 1998, 5, pp. 201–222) http://www.tandf.co.uk.

Journal of Economic Methodology ('Perfect Information *à la* Walras versus

Perfect Information *à la* Marshall', 2003, 10, pp. 465–492) http://www.tandf.co.uk.

Eastern Economic Journal ('From Labour Rationing to (Involuntary) Unemployment. A Conceptual Elucidation', 1999, 25, pp. 315–330).

Journal of the History of Economic Thought ('Keynes and the Marshall–Walras Divide', 1999, 21, 2, pp. 117–736) http://www.tandf.co.uk.

The Scottish Journal of Political Economy (Blackwell Publishing Ltd) ('The Marshallian Market and the Walrasian Economy. Two Incompatible Bedfellows', 1999, 46, 3, pp. 319–338).

The European Journal of the History of Economic Thought ('Marshall on Equilibrium and Time. A Reconstruction', 2000, 7, pp. 20–44) http://www.tandf.co.uk.

History of Political Economy ('IS-LM "à la Hicks" versus IS-LM "à la Modigliani"', 2000, 32, 2, pp. 293–316). Copyright, 2000, Duke University Press. All rights reserved. Used by permission of the publisher.

Eastern Economic Journal ('Friedman and Lucas on the Phillips Curve: From a Disequilibrium to an Equilibrium Approach", 2001, 27, 2, pp. 127–148).

Cambridge Journal of Economics ('Price Rigidity and Market Clearing. A Conceptual Clarification', 2001, 25, 5, pp. 639–655). By permission of Cambridge Political Economy Society.

Cambridge Journal of Economics ('Lucas on Involuntary Unemployment', 2004, 28, 3, pp. 397–411). By permission of Cambridge Political Economy Society.

European Journal of the History of Economic Thought ('Can Slowly Adjusting Wages Explain Involuntary Unemployment? A Critical re-examination of Patinkin's Theory of Involuntary Unemployment', 2002, 9, pp. 293–307) http://www.tandf.co.uk.

Journal of the History of Economic Thought ('Equilibrium and Disequilibrium in Walrasian and Neo-Walrasian Economics', 24, pp. 405–426).

Figure 13.1, 'Friedman's account of the working of the labour market', is reprinted with permission from *Price Theory* by M. Friedman, p. 266, Copyright © 1962, 1976, by Aldine Publishing Company, New York. Renewed 2004 by Walter de Gruyter Inc. Published by Aldine de Gruyter, Hawthorne, NY.

Figure 16.1, 'Involuntary unemployment in the shirking model', is reproduced from C. Shapiro and J. Stiglitz, 'Equilibrium Unemployment as a Worker Discipline Device', *American Review*, vol. 74, 1984, with the permission of the American Economic Association.

Figures 16.2, 'The distribution of land in Dasgupta and Ray's model' and 16.3, 'Involuntary Unemployment in Dasgupta and Ray's model', reproduced from Dasgupta, P. and D. Ray, 'Inequality and the Determination of Malnutrition and Unemployment Theory', *Economic Journal*, vol. 96, 1986, are reprinted with the permission of Blackwell Publishing Ltd.

Figure 18.1, 'Underemployment in Diamond's search model', is reproduced from Diamond, P. 'Aggregate Demand Management in Search equilibrium', *Journal of Political Economy*, vol. 90, 1992 with the permission of the University of Chicago Press.

Figures 19.1, 'Underemployment in Hart's model' and 19.2, 'Involuntary unemployment according to d'Aspremont, Gérard-Varet and Dos Santos Ferreira' are reproduced from Silvestre, J. 'The Market-Power Foundations of Macroeconomic policy', *Journal of Economic Literature*, vol. 31, 1993 with the permission of the American Economic Association.

Figure 19.3, 'Underemployment in Blanchard and Kiyotaki's model', is reproduced from Blanchard, O. and N. Kiyotaki, 'Monopolistic Competition and the Effects of Aggregate Demand', *American Economic Review*, vol. 77, 1987 with the permission of the American Economic Association.

Finally I express my gratitude to Taylor and Francis and Palgrave Macmillan Publishing Houses for their permission to reprint passages from my contributions to the following collective volumes:

Fontaine, P. and A. Jolink (eds), *Historical Perspectives on Macroeconomics: 60 Years After The General Theory* ('Keynes, Keynesian Programmes and Unemployment', 1998, Routledge, pp. 17–39).

Backhouse, R., D. Hausman, U. Mäki and A. Salanti (eds), *Economics and Methodology: Crossing Boundaries* ('Accounting for Involuntary Unemployment in Neoclassical Theory. Some Lessons from Sixty Years of Uphill Struggle', 1998, Macmillan, pp. 177–224).

1
INTRODUCTION

The Great Depression of the 1930s was one of the most dramatic economic events of the last century. It shook economists' belief in the existence of self-adjusting forces and prompted Keynes to write his masterwork, *The General Theory of Employment, Interest and Money* (1936). His aim in this book was to justify the possibility that the economy might be stuck in a state of underemployment, which he qualified as involuntary unemployment and which, he claimed, could be remedied only through state interventions.

A large majority of economists soon rallied to Keynes' views and praised his enterprise as a success. Nobody objected to the involuntary unemployment concept because, in the wake of the Great Depression, it looked evident that the prevailing mass unemployment was involuntary. It took economists several decades to realise that important stumbling blocks were standing in the way of the integration of this concept into neoclassical theory. At the end of the 1960s and in the 1970s Milton Friedman and, later, Robert Lucas and his new classical colleagues launched a scathing criticism of Keynesian theory bearing on both its conceptual consistency and the efficiency of its policy prescriptions. Involuntary unemployment was not the central target of their attack, yet it became a collateral victim. So-called New Keynesian economists reacted by constructing new involuntary unemployment models built on stronger microfoundations. However, while still claiming that the functioning of the market system could be marred by market failures, they gradually ceased to put the defence of involuntary unemployment on top of the agenda, thereby implicitly giving in to the Lucasian criticism that theoretical conversations would lose nothing by dispensing with it. The aim of my book is to recount and ponder this demise.

Why devote a whole book to a concept that to all appearances has failed? Several justifications can be offered. First of all, the possibility cannot be discounted that, in spite of its present disrepute, involuntary unemployment will return to prominence in the future. Moreover, involuntary unemployment has played a central role in the development of macroeconomics – it was once deemed to be the *sine qua non* of macroeconomics. Hence its study may constitute a powerful angle of attack for the understanding of the broader evolution of macroeconomics. Finally, this concept has been the object of heated debates, defended and attacked by prominent economists with equal vehemence. Witness the following two quotations from Mancur Olson and Robert Lucas:

> There are, of course, large numbers of people who voluntarily choose not to work for pay (such as the voluntarily retired, the idle rich, those who prefer handouts to working at jobs, those who stay at home full time to care for children, and so on) and, given the way unemployment statistics are gathered in the United States and other countries, no doubt some of these show up in the unemployment statistics. Yet common sense and the observations and experiences of literally hundred of millions of people testify that there is also involuntary unemployment and that it is by no means an isolated or rare phenomenon . . . Only a madman – or an economist with both 'trained incapacity' and doctrinal passion – could deny the reality of involuntary unemployment.
>
> (Olson 1982: 195)

> Involuntary unemployment is not a fact or a phenomenon which it is the task of theorists to explain . . . It does not appear possible, even in principle, to classify individual unemployed people as either voluntary or involuntarily unemployed depending on the characteristics of the decision problem they face. One cannot, even conceptually, arrive at a usable definition of full employment as a state in which no involuntary unemployment exists.
>
> (Lucas 1978: 315)

A concept that gives rise to such trenchant views must be of some interest!

To the layperson, the expression 'involuntary unemployment' raises no eyebrow. Perhaps the usefulness of the 'involuntary' modifier could be questioned because of its redundancy – leaving aside a small proportion of profiteers, unemployment seems involuntary by definition. A philosopher might have a different attitude, realising that a basic philosophical issue, freedom, is hidden behind this modifier – a theme on which Aristotle pondered in his *Nichomachean Ethics*, on which I will reflect in Chapter 14. Turning to economics, it is clear that theorising involuntary unemployment proved to be more difficult than expected.[1] Is this difficulty due to a defect of economic theory or is it rather that, in spite of its *prima facie* plausibility, the involuntary unemployment concept is of little use when it comes to economic theory?

Unfortunately, no compelling answer can be given to this question. Let me just point out a few factors that are responsible for the complexity of the problem. First, for better or worse, economic theory is about human choice. It is predicated on the optimising rationality assumption: economic agents are depicted as making constrained optimising choices. The question then arises of how a theory which is premised on such an assumption might be left with non-chosen results. Another factor is that involuntary unemployment was only one element within Keynes' broader programme. Hence the challenge facing Keynesian authors was not just to demonstrate involuntary unemployment. Such a demonstration had also to prove to be congruent with the other facets of Keynes' programme. As will be seen, several decades had to pass before involuntary unemployment models saw the light of day, at which juncture it turned out that their success occurred at the expense of other elements of his programme. This in turn raises the question as to whether it is worthwhile to give priority to the involuntary unemployment aim over the others. Finally, involuntary unemployment is a value-laden concept. Most of the authors who have set forth the task of demonstrating it wanted to bring out something deeper, a flaw in the functioning of the capitalist economy. Actually, to them, involuntary unemployment seemed to be the market failure *par excellence.* Involuntary unemployment thus carries a symbolic charge and constitutes a rallying banner for those who do not believe in laissez-faire. The opposite is true for its opponents, their rejection usually going hand-in-hand with an endorsement of the free market.

In order to disentangle these issues, I will critically examine the different explanations of involuntary unemployment that have been offered, starting with Keynes' *The General Theory* and ending with New Keynesian developments up to the end of the 1980s, as well as the criticisms that have been levelled against them. My investigation does not claim to comprehensiveness. Instead of trying to cover the whole range of models that have been proposed, my attention will be limited to seminal contributions.[2]

Most of my book will follow a historical thread except for the three chapters forming Part I of the book. Written in a retrospective spirit, they pursue the twofold aim of clarifying the concepts that will be used subsequently and of constructing the benchmarks against which my historical analysis will proceed.

In Chapter 2, I compare different definitions of involuntary unemployment and justify my endorsement of the 'breaching the reservation wage principle' definition. I also emphasise the need to make a distinction between involuntary unemployment and underemployment. Finally, I bring to the fore the ambiguity of the notion of full employment, of which no less than six different meanings are shown to be possible.

In most of the models that will be surveyed, labour market rationing and involuntary unemployment are considered synonymous. This is also the definitional line that I shall adopt. Chapter 3, 'From labour rationing to (involuntary) unemployment', stands as an exception in this respect since it explores the consequences of drawing a distinction between labour rationing and unemployment. That is, labour rationing exists when a given labour market features an excess supply of labour while unemployment refers to the specific activity of job searching. The former can be viewed as a necessary yet insufficient condition for the latter. Hence the need to study agents' post-rationing trajectories, of which voluntary and involuntary unemployment are two conceivable end-results amongst others. By bringing out the conditions under which labour rationing can result in involuntary unemployment, I show that Lucas' assertion above as to the impossibility of making sense of the opposition between voluntary and involuntary unemployment can be overturned.

While my work was in progress, I gradually realised that I needed to tackle some broader topics. The first is the working of markets or what, following Clower, I shall call trade technology or trade organisation, i.e. the institutional assumptions that are necessary in order that a logically existing equilibrium may come into effective existence as the result of economic agents' interactions. The second is the relationship between the Marshallian and the Walrasian approaches, both of them broadly understood as encompassing neo-Marshallian as well as neo-Walrasian models. The standard view is that the Marshallian and the Walrasian approaches are complements, the former being supposedly concerned with partial equilibrium, the latter with general equilibrium. I have been led to question this view and to argue instead that they are alternative research programmes. The models that will be studied can be classified as belonging either to the Walrasian or the Marshallian line. It then occurred to me that the stumbling block impeding the attainment of the involuntary unemployment result were different according to which approach was taken. In short, in the Walrasian framework the obstacle relates to trade organisation, in particular the auctioneer hypothesis, while in the Marshallian approach it lies in the specifically Marshallian perfect information assumption upon which the working of markets rests.

These views are expounded in Chapter 4. I start by drawing the reader's attention to the difference between centralised and decentralised markets. Although most real-world markets are decentralised, for better or worse, economic theory, be it Marshallian or Walrasian, usually assumes that markets function in a centralised way. An essential feature of the centralised market is that exchanges are confined within well-defined trade rounds. Hicks' week device, with exchanges taking place exclusively on Mondays, turns out to be the proper time framework both for Marshallian and Walrasian models. Next, I examine the trade organisation assumptions underpinning the Walrasian and Marshallian approaches, a rather easy task for the Walrasian, a more complicated one when it comes to the Marshallian stream. In a further step, I bring out the two stumbling blocks mentioned above. Chapter 4 ends with a critical reflection on the meaning on the notions of rigidity, flexibility and slow adjustment.

Part II investigates Keynes' attempt to give a foundation to involuntary unemployment in his *The General Theory*. The purpose of Chapter 5 is to delineate the theoretical project that Keynes set forth in this book. In my reconstruction it comprises four linked objectives: demonstrating the existence of involuntary unemployment; demonstrating that wage rigidity can be exonerated as a cause of the phenomenon; explaining involuntary unemployment in a market interdependency perspective while assuming perfect competition; demonstrating that demand stimulation is its remedy.

Chapter 6 probes into the inaugural chapters of *The General Theory*. While few works have been as much dissected, I nonetheless believe that I am able to say something original about it. This is due to my following Clower and Leijonhufvud in taking in earnest the premise that *The General Theory* ought to be read against the background of Marshallian theory. Two main lines of argumentation are developed by Keynes. The first concerns the working of the labour market. Keynes' claim in this respect is that wage-earners are unable to fix the market-clearing real wage in spite of their ability to fix the nominal wage. Market non-clearing supposedly ensues. Keynes' second line of argumentation consists of claiming that involuntary unemployment is caused by a deficiency in effective demand. After an in-depth examination of these two claims, I come to the conclusion that neither of them stands up. I also elucidate why the contrary has long been held true. In my view this has to do with the ambiguity of the full employment concept and a confusion between involuntary unemployment and underemployment. Finally, I also consider the claim developed by Keynes in Chapter 19 of *The General Theory* that the wage-rigidity assumption can be removed without harm for his earlier conclusions, and show that it is flawed. In sum, no valid explanation of involuntary unemployment remains after Keynes' reasoning errors have been straightened out.

My concern in Part III is the first generation of Keynesian economists. In Chapters 7 and 8, I study the rise of the IS-LM model, Chapter 7 dealing with Hicks, Chapter 8 with Modigliani. My claim in these chapters is that, although Hicks invented the IS-LM model, it is Modigliani who gave it lasting form. In Hicks' model, involuntary unemployment exists both in the classical and the Keynesian regime, the result of nominal wage rigidity. The contrast between the two regimes is a matter of policy effectiveness. An increase in monetary supply is able to counteract the effects of wage rigidity in the classical regime, yet it fails to do so in the Keynesian regime, due to the preference for liquidity. In contrast, in Modigliani's model, market clearing prevails in the classical regime while involuntary unemployment, still resulting from wage rigidity, characterises only the Keynesian regime. Money activation is now the proper remedy. Chapter 9 critically examines the contributions of other pioneering Keynesian economists, Lange, Leontief, Tobin, Klein and Hansen. Finally, in Chapter 10, I examine the account of involuntary unemployment to be found in a few macroeconomics textbooks of the 1960s during the heyday of Keynesian economics. I show that these textbooks mark no progress on *The General Theory* for what concerns the vindication of involuntary unemployment. Their basic flaw is a confusion between underemployment and involuntary unemployment: while macroeconomists were claiming that their models were about involuntary unemployment, their actual object of analysis was underemployment in its most trivial form.

Gradually, the weakness of standard Keynesian theory became better perceived. This led to two distinct developments. First, as I show in Part IV, a few authors, who were initially known under the 'disequilibrium school' label, became aware of the need to give Keynesian theory better microfoundations. Chapter 11 examines the pioneering works of Patinkin, Clower and Leijonhufvud, Chapter 12 the models of Barro-Grossman, Drèze, Malinvaud and Benassy. I show that the link between these authors is thinner than usually claimed. Patinkin and Leijonhufvud are criticised on the ground of their willingness to explain involuntary unemployment as the result of slow adjustment, a claim that I have discounted in Chapter 4. The ambiguities of Clower's celebrated 'Keynesian Counter-revolution' article (1965) are brought to the fore, and I show that none of its possible interpretations stand up to scrutiny. As for the authors of the second generation, I endorse Lucas' criticism that the price rigidity assumption comes on a collision course with the Walrasian trade technology hypothesis. Eventually, the lesson to be drawn from the disequilibrium episode is that Keynes and Walras are indeed incompatible bedfellows.

While the authors studied in Part IV were trying to salvage Keynes, the contrary is true for the other reaction to standard Keynesianism that I study in Part V of the book, entitled 'The anti-Keynesian offensive'. It arose at the end of the 1960s and the beginning of the 1970s. In a context where the upsurge of stagflation suggested the failure of traditional Keynesian demand-activation policy, economists who did not share the Keynesian viewpoint as to the role of the state in the economy started to become more outspoken and to break away from the earlier existing consensus. Partly responsible for this move was Milton Friedman. His influential 1967 Presidential Address to the American Economic Association, introducing the expectations-augmented Phillips Curve, was a powerful first step in the dismissal of the too-hastily endorsed Phillips Curve apparatus. But the decisive blow was struck by Lucas. In his ground-breaking 1972 'Expectations and the Neutrality of Money' article, he demonstrated the ineffectiveness of monetary policy in a more rigorous way than Friedman. From a broader perspective, Lucas' blunt view on Keynesian theory was that it was to be disposed of. Macroeconomics, he claimed, needed to abide by the discipline imposed by equilibrium, and to rest on the twin postulates of optimising behaviour and market clearing.

Chapter 11 provides an in-depth – and again, I think, original – analysis of Friedman's 1967 Presidential Address. I show that it must be read against the background of Marshallian theory to make sense. However, Friedman failed to be a fully consistent Marshallian economist. In particular, his famous notion of the natural rate of unemployment comprises two features which I find contradictory, the matching of supply of and demand for labour, on the one hand, and the existence of unemployment, on the other. The former implies market clearing, the latter market non-clearing. How could they be combined? Hence my claim that the proper object of analysis of Friedman's model is the natural rate of *employment* rather than the natural rate of *unemployment*. When this line is taken, it turns out that Friedman's model is about market clearing departures from the natural rate of employment taking the exclusive form of either under- or over-employment. No resorting to involuntary unemployment is needed.

In Chapter 12, I discuss Lucas' views. First, I take on his claim that Keynes betrayed what Lucas calls the 'equilibrium discipline'. In my opinion, Keynes has been unable to achieve his project of demonstrating what I shall call states of individual disequilibrium. Nor have most subsequent Keynesians fared batter in this respect. However, I disagree with Lucas' indictment that such a project runs counter to first principles. Second, I assess Lucas' three arguments against the involuntary unemployment concept: first, that there is no rationale for drawing a distinction between two sorts of unemployment; second, that every economic outcome features both voluntary and involuntary options jointly; and, third, that alternatives to unemployment are always present. My conclusion is that while Lucas must be credited for having spotted the flaws of Keynesian theory, his criticism is nonetheless less compelling than often believed. Be that as it may, he and his associates won the battle. They were able to change the agenda of macroeconomics, shifting its subject matter from the malfunctioning of the market system to fluctuations and growth without market failures.

Of course, this is not the end of the story. In Part VI, I study the reaction of New Keynesian economists to the new classical offensive. To speak of a New Keynesian school is certainly an exaggeration since quite different research strategies are co-existing under the single New Keynesian label. Moreover, the meaning of the 'Keynesian' modifier has become blurred. Earlier, it designated the conjunction of a Keynesian apparatus, the IS-LM model, and of a Keynesian motivation, i.e. bringing out market failures that required demand activation as their remedy. In the present context, these two dimensions are disjoined. The conceptual apparatus used by New Keynesians has nothing specifically Keynesian about it. What remains is the motivation of denouncing market failures although these are no longer necessarily related to demand deficiencies. For what concerns the subject of my inquiry, the main divide is between models aiming at demonstrating involuntary unemployment and those purporting to vindicate underemployment. In Chapter 15, I examine Azariadis' implicit contract model, in Chapter 16, Shapiro and Stiglitz's special brand of efficiency wage model, the shirking model, and in Chapter 17 Lindbeck and Snower's insider–outsider theory. As far as the shirking model is concerned, I claim that it displays a paradoxical state of affairs: true, it demonstrates involuntary unemployment in the 'breaching the reservation wage' meaning, yet no real progress of the Keynesian cause goes along. First, other elements of Keynes' programme, the interdependency perspective and demand activation, are sacrificed. Second, contrary to what is usually asserted, its involuntary unemployment result is efficient. Thus, its success has a pyrrhic victory flavour. My assessment of the insider–outsider model is also original. According to Lindbeck and Snower, involuntary unemployment exists as soon as outsiders have a reason for being jealous of insiders. I show that this definition has the odd implication that some agents need to be considered involuntarily unemployed in spite of their having a job!

Chapters 18 and 19 deal with coordination failures and imperfectly competitive general equilibrium theory. In Chapter 18, three models are examined, Diamond's search equilibrium model, Howitt's transaction costs model and Roberts' coordination failure model. The first two have, to all intents and purposes, foregone the involuntary unemployment concept in favour of the study of the underemployment concept. The positive counterpart of such a retreat is that they fare better with respect to the other elements of Keynes' programme. Roberts' model confirms my view about the decisive role played by trade organisations: his involuntary unemployment result springs from his dispensing with the Walrasian trade technology. Chapter 19 is mainly concerned with Hart's model on the one hand, and Blanchard and Kiyotaki's on the other. Both models witness the same shift from involuntary unemployment to underemployment as Diamond's and Howitt's models. Yet Blanchard and Kiyotaki's is considered more Keynesian, especially because of its rebuttal of the ineffectiveness of the monetary policy claim.

Chapter 20 offers concluding remarks. I show that, for all the headway made by Keynesian theory, to date, almost seven decades after the publication of *The General Theory*, Keynes' programme still remains unfulfilled. There is thus a strong presumption that it is unfeasible. Which of its elements should then be foregone? Should it be involuntary unemployment?

More precisely, should economists with a Keynesian motivation keep fighting for the involuntary unemployment concept or should they focus on underemployment results? No compelling answer can be given to these questions. I will nonetheless endorse the view that, in the present state of economic theory, Keynesian economists have some good reasons for putting aside the involuntary unemployment objective. They are not those invoked by Lucas – that the 'thing' to be explained does not exist or that a concept like involuntary unemployment falls outside of the 'equilibrium discipline'. It is rather that the few models that have succeeded in demonstrating involuntary unemployment are disappointing with respect to the other elements of Keynes' programme. Moreover, the root of the problem may lie deeper: what is lacking is a broader theory as to the functioning of markets wherein market clearing would cease to be a foregone conclusion.

The above considerations will suffice to indicate to the reader what sort of book mine is. It is a study in the history of modern economic analysis – and for that matter macroeconomics. Its methodological ingredients are internal (rather than external) history, rational reconstruction and the retrospective method. It is also a book that does not eschew semantic issues. A lot of time will be devoted to discussing the meaning of concepts, to drawing distinctions and building up taxonomies, the result of my belief that the very reason debates over involuntary unemployment have ended up in an impasse is that semantic issues have been dodged.[3]

Finally, the target audience of my book consists of macroeconomists as well as historians of economics. At present, the gulf between economic theorists and historians of economic thought has yawned wider than ever. Different factors, on which I cannot comment, may explain it. Let me just say that I deeply regret this state of affairs. I am of the opinion that, in our age of widespread division of labour, which has turned economists into specialists of narrow fields of knowledge, historians of economics have a new role to play, to bring theorists the broader historical and critical perspective that they are usually lacking when left on their own. To use an analogy, historians of art are often better able to grasp the evolution of a given artistic domain than the artists who shaped it. The same can be stated, I think, of historians of economics with respect to economists. My hope is that this book will contribute to bridging the gap.[4]

Part I

CONCEPTUAL PREREQUISITES

2
DEFINING INVOLUNTARY UNEMPLOYMENT

Anybody interested in studying what economic theory has to say about involuntary unemployment will soon discover to their dismay that all economists using the term 'involuntary unemployment' hardly share the same definition of it. Several definitions co-exist, most of which claim to have a lineage in Keynes' *The General Theory*. The task set forth in this chapter is to disentangle this unfortunate conceptual confusion.

Alternative definitions of involuntary unemployment

At least four main definitions of involuntary unemployment can be separated. They can be regrouped into two broader categories, each of which has a lineage in *The General Theory*: the 'breaching the reservation wage principle' and the underemployment definitions.

The 'breaching the reservation wage principle' definitional line

According to standard microeconomic theory, the fact that an economic agent is not participating in the labour market has nothing incongruous to it. Simply, it must be the case that the prevailing wage is lower than or equal to his reservation wage (i.e. the highest value of the real wage such that the demand for leisure is equal to the total time endowment of the agent concerned).[1] Call this the 'reservation wage principle'. The existence of involuntary unemployment can then be seen as its violation. It occurs if agents are observed as non-trading despite the fact that the market wage exceeds their reservation wage. According to the first order condition of their decision problem – i.e. the equalisation of the marginal rate of substitution between consumption and leisure with the real wage rate – they should be participating, yet they are not. Nonetheless trading, instead of an adjustment in the wage rate, is occurring. Put differently, at the real wage/employment mix characterising effective trading, some suppliers are 'off their supply curve' and rationed. Market non-clearing and the breaching of the reservation wage principle are thus two faces of the same coin.

This definition can be traced back to Chapter 2 of *The General Theory*, where it is pinpointed by Keynes as a violation of the second classical postulate. It has also been the most accepted definition. The following quotations illustrate:

> It is assumed [in conventional discussions] that individuals may work as many hours as they wish at a known wage rate. Suppose now that this latter assumption is false and that there is some upper limit on the number of hours that a consumer-worker can sell to his employer or to any other employers he can find. A worker is then defined as involuntarily unemployed if the number of hours he would otherwise choose to sell is greater than the number of hours he can sell. By this definition a worker who is involuntarily unemployed is forced to consume more non-market time than he would prefer and, consequently, a smaller bundle of commodities. Alternatively, a worker who is involuntarily unemployed cannot work as much as he would prefer and thus cannot purchase as large a bundle of commodities as he would prefer.
>
> (Ashenfelter 1978: 136)

> From the economist's point of view, there is involuntary unemployment whenever, for any substantial number of workers, the marginal (consumption) value of leisure is less than the going real wage in occupations for which they are qualified.
>
> (Solow 1986: S 33)

> For Keynes a worker is involuntarily unemployed if the market wage for his labour exceeds his shadow wage. The shadow wage is that wage at which a worker would be indifferent between not accepting and accepting an offer of work.
>
> (Hahn 1987: 1)

> For Keynes, a worker is involuntarily unemployed when he is willing to work at the same wage received by workers like him in every respect, yet the employer will not hire him.
>
> (Hoover 1988: 58)

The 'breaching the reservation wage principle' definition has the merit of giving a micro-founded definition of involuntary unemployment. It succeeds in locating exactly wherein the departure from standard microeconomic theory has to be rooted, i.e. the reservation wage principle.

Even detractors of the involuntary unemployment result should admit it as an apposite definition. Moreover, it brings about the fact that unemployment is a phenomenon of disparity, marked by a split between the employed and the unemployed. It exists when total employment is unequally distributed across agents, as it affects a proportion of the active population – the unemployed – while leaving the employed agents undamaged. Although every valid unemployment theory should display this disparity feature, this is far from always being the case, as will be seen.

With hindsight, it has turned out that the reservation wage principle definition can be understood in two distinct meanings: a narrow and a broad one. The former may be called the 'individual disequilibrium' definition, the latter the 'frustration' definition. Clearly, the former implies the latter while the converse does not hold.

To give a foundation to the individual disequilibrium meaning, it is necessary to reflect on the notion of equilibrium. Authors such as Hayek and Patinkin may be taken as our guides. As to Hayek, he wrote:

> I have long felt that the concept of equilibrium itself and the methods which we employ in pure analysis have a clear meaning only when confined to the analysis of the action of a single person and that we are really passing into a different sphere and silently introducing a new element of altogether different character when we apply it to the explanation of the interactions of a number of different individuals.
>
> (Hayek [1937] 1948: 35)

The same insight is to be found from Patinkin's pen when drawing a distinction between individual experiments and market experiments (1965: 11–12; 387–392). Patinkin's distinction has been aptly summarised by Yeager in the following way:

> An individual experiment involves discovering, at least conceptually, the desired behaviour of an individual person, of a small or large group of individuals, or even of all individuals in the community, acting in certain capacities, under certain specified circumstances. Whether these circumstances are compatible with other economic conditions and whether they can in fact prevail (whether they are genuinely or even conceptually attainable, to use the Chicago terminology) is beside the point: it is not the purpose of an individual experiment, by itself, to describe the economic equilibrium that will tend to emerge ... This other type of analysis, which pulls together the results of various individual experiments, examines the conditions under which the plans of various persons would and would not mesh, and describes the

> processes at work when plans fail to mesh, and describes the equilibrium position, is what Patinkin means by market experiments.
> (Yeager 1960: 59)

Elaborating on Hayek's and Patinkin's views, I suggest to separate the notions of optimal plan and optimising behaviour. Optimal plan then refers to an agent's solution to the choice-theoretical problem being considered. It is formed before the opening of trading. As stated by Patinkin:

> We can consider the individual – with his given indifference map and initial endowment – to be a 'utility-computer' into whom we 'feed' a sequence of market prices and from whom we obtain a corresponding sequence of 'solutions' in the form of specified optimum positions.
> (Patinkin 1965: 7)

Agents' optimal plans become expressed in their individual supply or demand (or excess demand) schedules. In contrast, optimising behaviour refers to what is observable after trading has started. Thus, optimising behaviour implies that the optimal plan has come through. The gist of the above quotations is that optimal choice and optimising behaviour need to be logically separated – finding out a solution to a choice problem and having it implemented are not one and the same thing.

To follow Hayek ([1937] 1948: 37), individual equilibrium exists whenever the action of a given agent during a given trade round turns out to be the execution of his or her individual optimising plan as decided at the beginning of the trade round. Individual disequilibrium refers to a case where this is untrue. Individual disequilibrium thus means the inability of some agents to transform their optimal plan into optimising behaviour.

What is usually understood by equilibrium *tout court* is actually an interactive equilibrium, i.e. a state where optimal plans have been made compatible. Thus, interactive equilibrium implies generalised individual equilibrium. In Hayek's terms:

> Equilibrium in this connection exists if the actions of all members of society over a period are all executions of their respective individual plans on which each decided at the beginning of the period.
> (Hayek [1937] 1948: 37)

The interactive disequilibrium notion follows, as referring to a state of incompatibility across individual plans. Its counterpart at the individual level is that at least some agents are in a state of individual disequilibrium.

Returning to the definition of involuntary unemployment, the spontaneous interpretation is to view it as a typical case of individual disequilibrium. In this line, involuntary unemployment ought to be understood as 'forced leisure', as opposed to 'chosen leisure'. The unemployed, the argument runs, are deprived of the capacity normally attached to every economic agent to participate in the interactive process through which market outcomes are generated. Excluded from the opportunity to work, they are left aside by the market system through no fault of their own.[2] Therefore, the 'involuntary' modifier seems perfectly appropriate.

The problem with this understanding of the "breaching the reservation wage principle" definition is that constructing models able to demonstrate this has proven to be a most daunting task. True, a straight way to get such a result exists. It consists of assuming an exogenous nominal wage. A mandatory nominal wage floor, imposed by the state, will do. Involuntary unemployment results as soon as supply and demand match a nominal wage that is lower than the wage floor. In this case, some agents must become rationed, without their responsibility being involved. However, the wage-floor assumption has little to recommend it. Either the wage floor is instituted for some good reason, and then the existence of involuntary unemployment is the price to be paid for it. Or it would suffice to eliminate the floor to get rid of unemployment.[3] As will be seen, trying to give a rationale for rigidity, thereby removing the contrived character of the wage-floor idea, has been an important research track. As long as wage rigidity is not vindicated, in one way or another, any explanation of involuntary unemployment resting on it must be considered trivial.

With the unfolding of economic theory, a softer version of the 'breaching the reservation wage principle' definition has emerged. This emergence, and the types of models in which it became embedded, will be studied in Chapters 15 and 16. Here, we still find the feature that the agent wishes to be working (or to be working more) at the ongoing wage. A mismatch between supply of and demand for labour (market non-clearing) also remains present. Yet the individual disequilibrium characterisation is no longer valid. On the contrary, the breaching of the reservation wage principle now goes along with individual equilibrium. For example, in Azariadis' implicit contract models (1975), a lottery allocates the risk-averse members of a firm's labour pool in two sub-groups: those who work and those who do not. It is assumed that the lottery offers them a favourable bet. After it has taken place, the losers are frustrated, being jealous of those who, having won, are working. Nonetheless, theirs is a position of individual equilibrium, since it was optimising behaviour to enter into the lottery. In this context, the 'involuntary' modifier must be understood in a milder sense, as simply meaning that agents are frustrated. Its infringement on freedom connotation is lost.[4]

The underemployment definitional line

According to the second definitional line, to which I now come, involuntary unemployment designates cases where the employment level endogenously reached by the economy is deemed to be inferior in welfare or efficiency terms with respect to some higher level, attainable only through exogenous action. In other words, amongst the conceivable employment levels, that which endogenously prevails is not that which allows the most utility to agents. To every agent, it is optimal in the sense that it results from constrained optimising decision-making. Thus, the reservation wage principle is satisfied and supply of and demand for labour are matching. Nonetheless, a higher utility would be reached if a greater employment level could be arrived at. The wedge between the optimal and the effective level of employment is then called involuntary unemployment. Here, the 'involuntary' modifier makes sense only in a loose way as referring to some inability to achieve a welfare-dominating higher level of employment.

This conception of involuntary unemployment is to be found in the writings of several authors. Its gist was captured by Haavelmo long ago:

> Consider a situation with given technological constraints and a prevailing system [i.e. 'the totality of rules – adopted collectively, either explicitly or by silent agreement – under which the individual groups must operate] S', leading to a market point x'. Let S'' be an alternative system under the same technological constraints, and let x'' be the corresponding market point [i.e. the value of an economic variable]. Suppose that if the two situations (S', x') and (S'', x'') were presented for collective decision, the decision would be in favour of (S'', x''). In that case we shall say that the society is involuntarily operating under the system S' . . .Why should one call the maintenance of system S' involuntary if the system is not in fact discarded in favour of S''? Should not this be called 'irrational' rather than 'involuntary'? The crucial point here is the following. Each group operating under the system S', may, from that group's point of view, be acting in the most rational and consistent fashion. The eventual decision to change the system S' is of an entirely different nature. It requires collective action. The posing of the alternative S'' for collective action requires a way of thinking and a power to act which are outside the functional sphere of any individual group as such.
>
> (Haavelmo 1950: 3)

The notion of involuntary economic decision, of which the Keynesian definition of involuntary unemployment is an example, is – stated generally – that a market point x' entails involuntary action

> to the extent that it differs from another 'more desirable' market point x'' ... The 'involuntariness' consists in maintaining S' when S'' would be collectively preferred.
>
> (Haavelmo 1950: 5)

Several present-day authors have followed Haavelmo's footsteps, probably unwittingly. Darity and co-authors (Darity and Horn 1983; Darity and Horn 1987–1988; Lawlor, Darity and Horn 1987; Darity and Goldsmith 1995) characterise involuntary unemployment as the opposite of full employment, viewed as the maximum feasible level of employment. It 'is reached when the elasticity of employment with respect to an increase in the effective demand reaches zero' (Darity and Horn 1983: 722). Borrowing from *The General Theory*'s Chapter 3, they note that 'as long as an expansion in effective demand could continue to raise output or employment, Keynes' involuntary unemployment would exist' (Darity and Horn 1983: 724). In this conception, employment can increase without a concomitant increase in real wage. What is now called involuntary unemployment is perfectly compatible with market clearing.

This definition, these authors argue, permits the de-emphasising of the role of rigid wages as an explanatory factor of involuntary unemployment and, for that matter, at 'getting labour markets out of the way'.[5] Thereby, they come close to defending a radical or quasi-Marxian line of thought. It amounts to asserting that the labour market should not be considered as a market, i.e. characterised by the confrontation of two 'forces' to be put on the same footing – supply and demand. Rather, it should be viewed as the locus of some unequal social relationship between members of two opposite social classes, the capitalists and the workers. It is assumed that workers are in a position of subordination and dependence with respect to capitalists, the latter deciding unilaterally on employment.

Allan Meltzer is another economist having adopted the sub-maximum level of employment definition (yet without the above connotation). According to him:

> Keynes' involuntary unemployment is the difference between maximum unemployment and equilibrium employment.
>
> (Meltzer 1988: 118)

> My definition of involuntary unemployment does not depend on whether the labour supply curve is horizontal at the given money wage until full employment or is generally upward sloping, as suggested by Keynes' rejection of the reverse-L-shaped curve. Involuntary unemployment is the difference between the point at which the supply curve of labour becomes vertical and any *equilibrium* position at a lower level of employment. At full employment,

> the supply of output – output supplied as a function of the price level – becomes inelastic and involuntary unemployment is zero.
>
> (Meltzer 1988: 166)

Finally, this definition is also sometimes to be found in the coordination failure literature, as the following extract from Drazen (1987) makes clear:

> For inefficiency to be present (which is what the notion of 'involuntarity' is attempting to capture), there must exist another equilibrium, which for the same tastes and technology (but perhaps a different level of government activity), has a higher level of employment. Hence, models of involuntary unemployment are often ones with multiple equilibria.
>
> (Drazen 1987: 437)

The 'less-than-maximum' definition of involuntary unemployment faces a serious ambiguity. The point is that one should be interested in the optimal level of employment rather than in the maximum feasible level, and often they will fail to coincide. Three cases are conceivable:

1 they coincide;
2 the maximum level is one among several optimal levels;
3 the maximum level is not optimal.

Evidently, the optimality criterion must have the upper hand. Therefore a distinction must be drawn between two types of underemployment: 'dominated underemployment', on the one hand, and 'efficient underemployment', on the other. The former pertains to cases where the existing level of employment is non-maximum and sub-optimal – it is welfare-dominated by one or several higher levels. The latter will designate cases where the existing level of employment is non-maximum yet optimal – reaching a higher level of employment does not increase agents' utility.

Models that demonstrate efficient underemployment should cut no ice, this result being uninteresting and trivial. Of course, we are not going to find models that declare explicitly that they demonstrate a state of underemployment that is less-than-maximum yet optimal. However, to all intents and purposes, such models have existed and have played an important role. The very fact of a lack of distinction between dominated and efficient underemployment has allowed the belief that a case of less-than-optimal employment had been demonstrated. The most striking example is models based on the inverse-L-shaped supply of labour. In these models it is declared that involuntary unemployment exists whenever the demand for labour intersects the supply on its horizontal section, the extent of involuntary unemployment being measured by the distance between this intersection and the kink of the supply curve. This is wanting because agents utility remains unchanged over this distance. No increase in utility results from moving towards full employment. Thus, we have a situation of less-than-maximum employment that is nonetheless optimal.[6]

Involuntary unemployment in the dominated underemployment sense captures an idea that must certainly have been relevant to Keynes and is still so to Keynesian economists. It suggests that underemployment ought to be related to a systemic flaw associated with the decentralised nature of the decision-making process in capitalist economies rather than to wage rigidity or too-high wages. However, its drawback is that it is not ambitious enough. Models demonstrating involuntary unemployment in this sense fail to come to grips with the unequal distribution of total employment across agents, deemed to be a central feature of unemployment. In these models, every agent wanting to participate in the labour market does so in an optimising way – no individual disequilibrium is present. It is just that their participation can be increased through exogenous actions. So what is called involuntary unemployment has nothing to do with joblessness – i.e. people who are totally out of work – while the very motivation of the theory was to give a theoretical account of this phenomenon. In short, we have an alleged theory of involuntary unemployment from which unemployment, strictly understood, is absent.

The connections between the four definitions

Four meanings of involuntary unemployment have been identified:

1 involuntary unemployment in the reservation wage sense

   a with the individual disequilibrium connotation
   b without the individual disequilibrium connotation

2 involuntary unemployment in the underemployment sense

   a dominated underemployment
   b efficient underemployment.

This list of definitions of involuntary unemployment is hardly exhaustive. For example, it will be seen that the insider–outsider model does not enter my taxonomy. Moreover, other definitions exist. One of them, to be found in the writings of French interpreters of Keynes (Benetti 1998; Dos Santos Ferreira 2000; Rivot 2001; Rosier 2002), consists of adding a supplementary criterion to the individual disequilibrium definition, namely that unemployment cannot be trimmed as the result of a decrease in wages. Only at this condition, these authors claim, can one can speak of involuntary unemployment.[7]

These four definitions can be viewed as distinct branches of a conceptual tree spanning different sub-types of the general notion of underemployment, as shown in Figure 2.1.

At the risk of repetition, let me underline the contrast between the two main branches of this tree. The left-hand branch exhibits two important features, a breaching of the reservation wage principle and an unequal allocation of total employment across labour suppliers (i.e. unemployment properly speaking). This goes along with market non-clearing. All these features are absent from the right-hand branch of the tree. Therefore, contrary to the practice adopted by several authors, the concepts of involuntary unemployment and underemployment cannot be considered synonymous. 'Involuntary unemployment' may well be a sub-category of 'underemployment in general' yet it must be separated from 'underemployment' *tout court.*

It will be seen in the course of my analysis that, somewhat oddly, involuntary unemployment is not necessarily an inefficient result. Thus, the efficient/dominated divide can also be applied to the left branch of my tree.

Further reflecting on the links between these definitions, it may be observed that whenever the criterion for involuntary unemployment in the first meaning (individual disequilibrium) is satisfied, involuntary unemployment in its second meaning (frustration) will also be present. Likewise, whenever the criterion for the third definition (less than optimal employment) is satisfied, the fourth (less than maximum employment) will also be verified. In contrast, the existence of involuntary unemployment according to the second definition does not imply involuntary unemployment according to the first definition. Nor does the existence of involuntary unemployment according to the fourth definition imply involuntary unemployment according to the third definition.

In the next chapter I will adopt the 'breaching the reservation wage principle' definition. That is, involuntary unemployment implies the

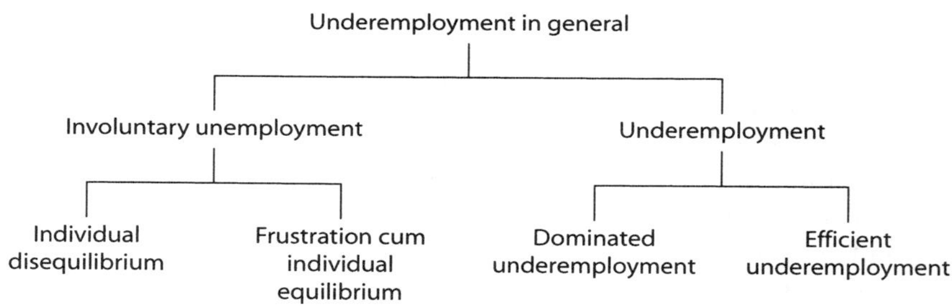

Figure 2.1 The four definitions of involuntary unemployment.

breaching of the reservation wage, the existence of unemployment as defined above, and the existence of market non-clearing (this term will be taken as synonymous to market rationing). I will not follow the authors who take the underemployment definitional line, and will call 'underemployment' what they call 'involuntary unemployment'.

Full employment

Hitherto, no reference has been made to the concept of full employment. While I believe that theoretical discussions would lose nothing from dispensing with it, it cannot be left aside, since it has been abundantly used in the literature, on top of having found an important place in ordinary language, be it political discourses, newspapers articles or daily-life opinions. Full employment, understood as the minimum feasible rate of unemployment, is viewed as a target for economic policy, and a criterion against which governments are gauged. Unemployment in turn amounts to the total active labour force minus the employed labour force. As it is deemed an evil, any decrease of it is judged to be good news, even if it is admitted that some uncompressible level exists.

The problem is that at least six different definitions of full employment can be found in the literature.

According to a first definition, full employment is any point on the supply of labour curve. This definition, which can be found in Patinkin's *Money, Interest and Prices* (1965), has an undeniable choice-theoretical foundation as it considers the choice problem of a given economic agent who envisages participating in the labour market.[8]

According to a second definition, full employment is selfsame to market clearing. This definition, which refers to a sub-set of the first one, comes more spontaneously to mind. It is to be found, for example, in Robinson (1947).[9] Whenever this definition is adopted, the converse of full employment is involuntary unemployment in the reservation wage sense. Yet it faces two problems. First, if full employment means market clearing, why have two concepts for a single result? Second, semantic confusion arises as soon as it is admitted, as it is standard in the Marshallian approach, that a distinction must be drawn between market equilibrium and normal equilibrium. It is possible to have, at the same time, full employment (i.e. market clearing) and underemployment (i.e. the market level of employment being lower than the normal level), definitely an awkward state of affairs.

The third definition takes care of this drawback. It consists of making full employment selfsame to normal equilibrium. Here market clearing becomes a necessary yet insufficient condition for full employment, the latter term then coinciding with the notion of the natural rate of employment.[10]

The fourth definition arises when multiple equilibria are considered in coordination with failure models. In this case full employment refers to the employment level that generates the highest social welfare.

The fifth definition pertains to general equilibrium models with imperfect competition. Here full employment designates the employment level that would exist if perfect competition rather than imperfect competition prevail.

Finally, according to a sixth definition, full employment can be equated with maximum employment. While this definition fits the common-sense understanding, its integration into economic theory is troublesome. What counts is an assessment of the optimal employment level, yet maximum and optimal employment will coincide only under special assumptions.

This profusion of definitions cannot but generate a semantic mess. The main issue, however, concerns the confusion between the second definition (full employment as market clearing) and the last one (full employment as maximum employment). In Chapter 6, I will claim that this confusion is present in Keynes' *The General Theory*. The most striking example of this confusion is to be found in models adopting the inverse-L-shaped supply of labour curve evoked above. In Figure 2.2 below, full employment arises at point A according to the market clearing definition, and at point B according to the maximum employment definition. For all its common-sense validity, the latter should yield to the former.[11]

Unfortunately, many economists have scarcely even been aware of the need to differentiate between these two main definitions of full employment. Let me illustrate their difference by comparing two possible accounts of the labour market, illustrated in Figure 2.3. Assume, on the

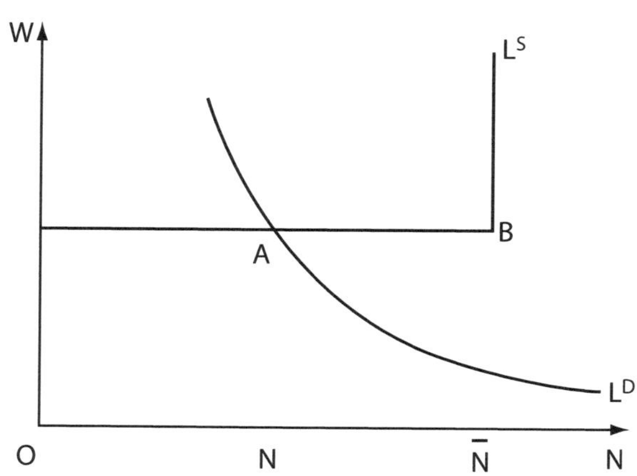

Figure 2.2 The labour market with an inverse-L-shaped supply of labour.

one hand, a Keynesian economist adopting the less-than-maximum definition of involuntary unemployment and resting his or her case on the inverse-L-shaped supply of labour (panel a) and, on the other hand, a standard neoclassical economist reasoning in terms of an upwards sloping supply of labour, and taking the stance that full employment equates market clearing (panel b). They will interpret the effect of a decrease in the demand curve in two distinct ways. Referring to panel a and assuming that full employment (according to the maximum employment definition) is not achieved to begin with, the Keynesian economist will claim that the decrease in demand moves the economy farther away from full employment and hence increases involuntary unemployment. In contrast, the neoclassical economist will argue that the decrease in demand for labour merely leads to a shift from one full employment level to another one, if the full employment term is to be used at all. To this economist, the decrease in employment does not go along with an increase in unemployment. Actually there is no reason to evoke unemployment since market clearing is prevailing both before and after the change.

Underpinning this difference in interpretation lies the fact that, in reference to the real world, the concepts of employment and unemployment are usually considered converse. That is, it is taken for granted that any increase in employment means a decrease in unemployment, and vice versa. But this assertion is false for what concerns standard neoclassical theory. Market clearing is a constant result in elementary Marshallian and

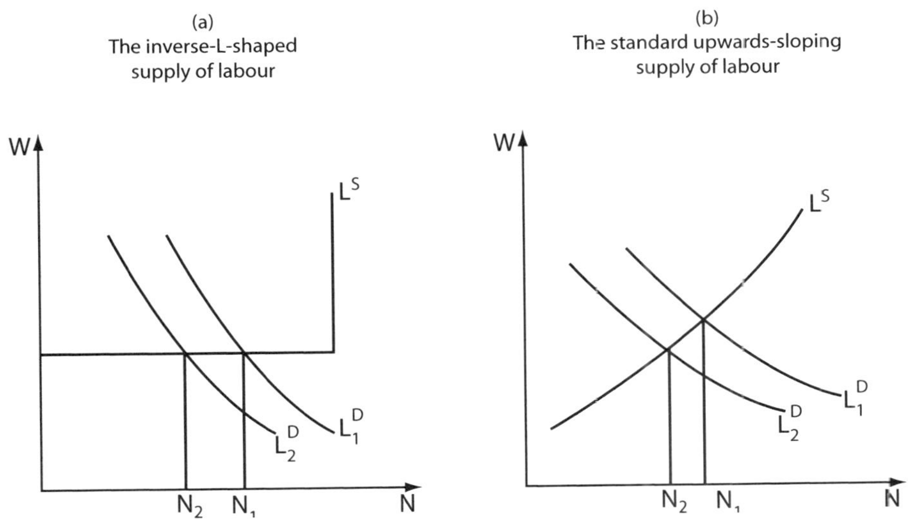

Figure 2.3 Two accounts of the labour market.

Walrasian theory, as I shall argue in Chapter 4. In these theories, the converse of changes in employment are changes in chosen leisure, the unemployment category remaining empty whatever the employment level.

Frictional or search unemployment

Up to now no mention has been made of what used to be called frictional unemployment (in more modern terms, search unemployment).[12] Should it be brought into the picture, by stating for example that, when involuntary unemployment (or underemployment) arises, it comes on top of frictional unemployment? This was Keynes' stance. To me, however, this is not the right way of putting the matter. I would rather keep involuntary unemployment and underemployment models separate from search models.

The reason for this is that they are underpinned by alternative assumptions about the organisation of trade (more on this in Chapter 4). Search unemployment involves a highly decentralised trading set-up. First, markets are seen as functioning continuously, with labour suppliers visiting firms in sequence. In this context, queuing is a normal feature. Second, the unicity of wages is dismissed. Third, trade occurs in a bilateral way. No preliminary market-wide equilibrium conditions are required for trading to start. In this framework, all existing unemployment, however big, should be put under the mantle of search unemployment. Periods of high unemployment are characterised by the fact that search is longer than normal. Thus, there is no need for introducing another category of unemployment. Reference could be made to involuntarity in its common-sense meaning. If somebody's offer to work with a firm is refused, their remaining in the pool of the unemployed is, it can be stated, involuntary. If, on the other hand, an individual refuses a job proposal, remaining unemployed would be voluntary. Yet there would be no involuntary unemployment distinct from frictional unemployment. Moreover, the 'involuntary' modifier would now become trivialised.

Semantic pitfalls

Theoretical discussions about involuntary unemployment are marred with semantic confusion. This is no surprise in view of the co-existence of the above definitions. To give just an example, the distinction between underemployment and unemployment is scarcely made. A compounding factor, to be analysed in more depth in the next chapter, is the fact that labour market rationing and unemployment are corollaries only if the assumption of a single labour market is made. Actually, economic theory may well discuss unemployment, yet its real object of analysis is market rationing.

Another semantic problem is that the common-sense and the theoretical meanings of either involuntary unemployment or voluntary unemployment are often on a collision course. Consider the involuntary unemployment notion. Either it means what the terminology suggests, and then its integration into economic theory faces formidable obstacles. Or it receives the softer, counter-intuitive meaning of frustration, and the question must be raised of why misleading terminology is retained. In contrast, in common-sense language, the involuntary nature of unemployment is *grosso modo* taken for granted, to the effect that the 'involuntary' modifier looks redundant.

Consider now voluntary unemployment. When this concept is used in the theoretical discourse, it refers to chosen leisure, an optimising refusal of participation in the labour market. However, such a terminology is awkward. While the 'voluntary' modifier may well be fitting, the 'unemployment' substantive is inadequate, in view of the fact that it normally applies to job-searchers while here we have people who do not want to participate in the labour market. On the other hand, in common-sense speech, the idea of voluntary unemployment makes sense in two different ways. It can, for example, refer to those who prefer to keep looking for jobs corresponding to their skill levels rather than accepting jobs for which they would be over-qualified. Yet it may also designate people who pretend to be searching for a job in order to get unemployment benefits without doing it in earnest.

3

FROM LABOUR RATIONING TO (INVOLUNTARY) UNEMPLOYMENT

The previous chapter has established that the semantics of involuntary unemployment are far from simple. In this chapter, I want to draw attention to a compounding factor: Is the object of analysis of unemployment theory really unemployment as this term is understood in common language? The answer is no. Most of the models that will be studied below, while allegedly dealing with unemployment, are concerned with a narrower subject matter, labour rationing. They just presume that labour rationing results in unemployment while this is true only under restrictive conditions.

A distinction must then be drawn between labour rationing and unemployment. Labour rationing refers to a specific market outcome, the occurrence of excess supply in a given labour market. Unemployment in turn pertains to a typology of the active population, where people are classified according to the sort of activity they are engaged in. The category of unemployment applies to those agents whose specific activity is job searching. They have, it is supposed, experienced labour rationing in their preferred labour market and remain in a waiting position with the hope of participating in a later trading round, instead of engaging in non-wage activities or taking a job in some less preferred labour market at once. Obviously, labour rationing and unemployment are linked, as the former is a necessary condition for the latter. Yet labour rationing is not a sufficient condition for unemployment. It is not necessarily true that individuals who are rationed in their preferred labour market will end up unemployed.

The task set forth in this chapter is to explore the steps leading from labour rationing to unemployment. Two aims will be pursued. First, I will examine the transition from labour rationing to unemployment by assessing rationed agents' possible post-rationing trajectories (including unemployment). Imagine a violinist who fails to be hired in an orchestra, e.g. because of insider–outsider factors. Let the violinist be considered rationed. Which paths are open to him or her – to go on the dole, to give private violin lessons (with the risk of losing the chance of being hired later on), to drop the violin and start another occupation, to emigrate? To raise comparative issues, would a low skilled manual worker face the same choice set as the violinist? Or, take two violinists, both rationed in their preferred job (to play in an orchestra). They are identically able violinists but one is wealthy and the other poor. How does this influence their lot? These are the sorts of questions that I will address. Second, I will discuss the issue of whether the involuntary unemployment concept – the emphasis on involuntary – makes sense once unemployment is understood as a post-rationing activity rather than as synonymous to rationing.

A taxonomy of post-rationing activity possibilities

In this section, I present a taxonomy of the social forms in which economic activities can be embedded. The notion of an economic activity choice set (in short, choice set) will be introduced to capture the idea that distinct social forms are available to agents for their economic activities. Before, however, a few methodological points must be settled. First, certain sections of the population, namely the young, the old and the disabled, are left aside. Second, for the sake of keeping things simple, I do not enter into the issue of the intra-household distribution of activities. Third, the notion of social form of economic activities ought to be separated out from that of occupation. For example, occupations as different as being an engineer or a lorry driver can be grouped in the same category, in as far as they are exercised in the same social form, i.e. as an employee. On the other hand, two plumbers who technically speaking are doing the same work, ought to be classified differently in social relationship terms if one of them is an employee whilst the other is self-employed. Fourth and finally, some boundaries must be assigned to the choice set. There are activities individuals are entitled not to envisage entering into. That is, the choice set should comprise only 'decent' activities allowing normal social integration whilst those expressing or prompting social exclusion, should be excluded, for example, entering into illegal activities. The same will be the case for activities such as begging, washing car windows at street corners, etc. More delicate is the matter of whether emigrating or moving down the skill ladder should be viewed as belonging to, or excluded from, the choice set. Evidently, the choice set will be wider or narrower according to the stance taken on these issues. Here, to simplify, I will exclude emigration but retain lower-skill activities. That is, an agent refusing to relocate still qualifies for the involuntary unemployment classification, while an agent refusing a job in his or her residential area because of over-qualification is excluded from it.

In Table 3.1, I give a general typology of conceivable forms of economic activities *prior to any rationing*. It is built on very simple criteria, as it follows from asking two questions: are agents participating in the product

Table 3.1 A taxonomy of social forms of economic activities

		Participation in goods market		
		Lack of participation	*Participation in demand yet not in supply*	*Participation in supply and demand*
	Lack of participation	the autarkical activity	the rentier activity	the self-employment activity
Participation in the labour market	*Participation in supply*		the wage-earning activity	
	Participation in demand			the capitalist activity

and/or labour markets? And second, if they are, are they sellers, purchasers or both?[1]

Five main categories of activities emerge.[2] The first one is the autarkical activity. It pertains to agents engaged in self-production and consumption. They function entirely outside the market sphere (or, to put it the other way, entirely within the domestic sphere). Whenever this mode of subsistence is an effective possibility, it means that agents are able to survive without trading. As this activity is borderline, it will not be considered. The rentier activity, concerns individuals who live on unearned income. They act as purchasers in the product market without participating in the labour market. They are full-time 'leisure choosers' and hold this activity either on a definitive or a temporary basis. In order to belong to this category, an obvious condition is that agents are endowed with enough non-labour resources to ensure subsistence without working.

Agents will differ widely with respect to the activities open to them. The broadest conceivable set will include all the different types of activities, the narrowest being the wage-earning activity as any individual's labour power is his or her smallest endowment.[3] Agents whose activity choice set comprises only this activity will be dubbed as 'wage-dependent'. Wage dependency thus encapsulates the old idea that some agents may have no alternative to wage labour in order to earn their subsistence. In Marx's term, they are 'proletarians'.[4]

Think of two individuals, alike in terms of occupation and skill as well as other professional features and who are both wage-earners, yet differ in terms of their personal wealth. As a result, one of them is wage-dependent whilst the other has an extended choice set and could have taken up a non-wage activity if desired. The second agent enjoys a wider scope of freedom and is less vulnerable to economic adversities than the wage-dependent one; were both of them to become rationed, their prospects would be different. In the same vein, take the case of wage-dependent agents belonging to the same occupation but at different levels of skill. One can argue that the higher skilled have a broader scope of freedom than the lower skilled. Were they rationed in their own market, i.e. the market corresponding to their skill, they would still have the possibility of participating in lower-skill markets. Such a recourse is obviously lacking for those whose own market corresponds to the lowest skill.

The labour market structure

For the purpose of my argument, a unique labour market cannot be assumed. Instead, it is necessary to identify the relationship between markets in a simplified way. Some assumptions ought to be made about agents' mobility possibilities across labour markets. It is also necessary to be more specific about the organisation of trade.

To begin, I assume that the amount of labour markets depends on the occupation-skill structure. Assume that m different occupations i (i.e. $i = 1 \ldots m$) exist, each sub-divided into the same amount n of skill-levels j ($j = 1 \ldots n$). Moreover, assume there exists one further category, z, the unskilled type, to which no specific occupation is attached. The occupation-skill structure is the array consisting of $(m \times n) + 1$ elements. Supposing that one specific labour market is attached to each of them, we thus have $(m \times n) + 1$ different labour markets.

Table 3.2 describes the occupation-skill structures. x^{ij} is the market for workers of occcupation i and whose skill level if j. Skills are decreasing from left to right, i.e. x^{11} is a market with a higher skill than x^{12}. The market corresponding to a given agent's skill-occupation will be called the normal market, which is also the preferred market for labour participation. Occupations and skills are given. It is further assumed that mobility across occupations is impossible, even from a higher to a lower skill level (e.g. from x^{11} to x^{22}), and that people cannot be employed above their

Table 3.2 The structure of markets

		Skills 1	....	j	....	n
	1	x^{11}	....	x	....	x^{1n}
	⋮	⋮		⋮		⋮
Occupations	i	x^{i1}	....	x^{ij}	....	x^{im}
	⋮	⋮		⋮		⋮
	m	x^{m1}	....	x^{mj}	....	x^{mn}

skill within their occupation. As a result, the only form of mobility is downwards intra-occupational mobility.[5] Take the case of agent h^{ij} whose skill-occupation characteristic is *ij*. If the agent is rationed in his or her normal market x^{ij}, all lower-skill markets in his or her occupation plus the unskilled market remain feasible. Thus, the agent's labour market participation opportunities amount to $(n - j) + 1$.

Finally, some additional assumptions about the organisation of trade must be made. Let us assume that the economy consists of a sequence of self-contained trade rounds. My interest here is in what arises in one of them rather than in their intertemporal dynamics. Assume that each self-contained round is sub-divided into two phases, input markets taking place in advance of goods markets (the only input I am actually concerned with is labour). Wages are set instantaneously. Assume moreover that there is a sequential order within the operation of labour markets: they open in decreasing order of skill. As each occupation is sub-divided into the same number of skill levels, trade occurs in parallel across occupations down the skill ladder. The first decision an individual therefore has to make concerns his participation in his normal labour market. Labour rationing is considered to be a possible outcome within each labour market and rationed agents are allowed to participate in lower markets within their occupation. As a result, two types of labour suppliers can be encountered in each labour market (excluding the highest skill ones): downwardly mobile agents, i.e. people rationed in higher markets, as well as those agents for whom the market in question is their normal market.

Unemployment as an element of the post-rationing activity choice set

Let me now sketch out the possible trajectory of a skilled agent who has experienced rationing in his or her normal market. The activity choice set, as described above, needs to be modified and replaced by a post-rationing activity choice set. The very fact that the agent made a trade offer in the market from which he or she was excluded means that the different elements comprising this new choice-set are all second-best outcomes. The post-rationing activity choice set contains two additional differences from the first-best activity choice set: first, participation in other labour markets may still be possible; second, a new activity enters the picture, namely unemployment.

More precisely, the agent in question potentially faces a threefold choice (its effectiveness depending on the content of the agent's choice set): first, accepting the downward-mobility solution, i.e. supplying labour service in a lower-skill market; second, dropping labor participation and engaging in one of the non-wage activities referred to in Table 3.1 and, third, opting for the unemployment solution.[6] I suggest subsuming the first two alternatives under the new term 'misemployment'. The prefix indicates the second best character of such an outcome, whereas the suffix 'employment' is meant to indicate that they have chosen whatever activity except unemployment.[7] The upshot of rationing is either misemployment of different forms or unemployment. To illustrate, let me go back to the violinist example. Assume there is a correspondence between the ranking of the orchestra and the musicians' skill. Were the violinist not to be hired by an orchestra corresponding to his or her skill, he or she might (a) apply to a lower-ranking orchestra, (b) become a self-employed violin teacher or, were he or she wealthy, commence living as a rentier or, finally, (c) prefer to be registered as unemployed thereby declaring his or her aim to apply to orchestras corresponding of his or her skill-level at the next trade round.

Whenever the agent chooses either unemployment or the non-wage activity, the course of his or her post-rationing trajectory ends. However, if the downward mobility solution is taken, the trajectory continues, as in the lower market the agent may either be employed or encounter rationing again. Possibly, the agent may end up in the unskilled labour market, while at each step retaining the possibility of foregoing labour market participation. Assume that eventually the agent ends up in the unskilled market and again becomes rationed. Even now, selection is still available as the agent may either register as unemployed or decide to take up another social form of activity, other than the wage-earning activity. The choice concept remains relevant as there is still more than one element in the choice set. This reasoning is illustrated in Figure 3.1 below which, for the sake of simplicity, considers one specific occupation i and assumes there is just one skill-level, $j = 1$. There are thus two ordered labour markets to consider: the skilled and the unskilled labour market.

The conditions for involuntary unemployment

For my purpose, the most interesting question is to know whether involuntary unemployment is conceivable. Recall that here my object of analysis is different from what it was in Chapter 2. There, by 'involuntary unemployment', I meant 'labour rationing'. Here I am interested in post-rationing activities, and unemployment means what it means vernacularly, i.e. looking for a job, wanting to participate in the labour market. But still the question arises, can unemployment so understood be involuntary? If yes, under which conditions?

Take case I of unemployment in Figure 3.1. For sure, the agents involved cannot be considered involuntarily unemployed since an agent who happens to be rationed in the skilled market always has the possibility to supply his or her services in lower markets. Hence, they ought to be

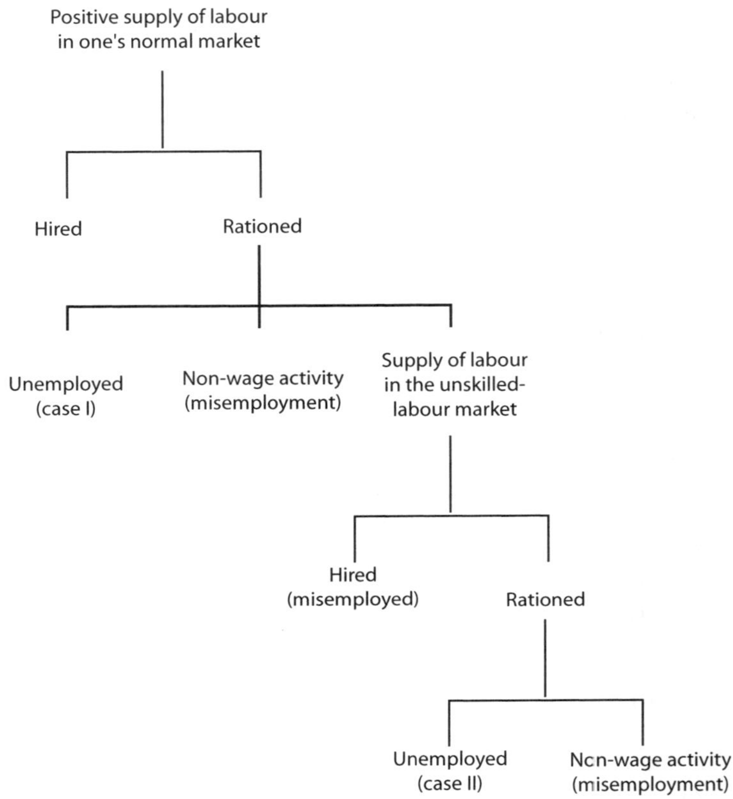

Figure 3.1 An example of post-rationing choice trajectory.

classified as voluntarily unemployed. A first necessary condition for involuntary unemployment then emerges, namely that rationing must arise in the unskilled labour market. An additional condition is that the rationed agent has to be wage-dependent as his or her choice set then turns out to be a singleton: it comprises no other possibility than the unemployment status. Only when this is the case, can his or her status no longer be considered chosen. In contrast, as soon as a non-wage activity alternative exists, any unemployment position should be considered as chosen.

It could be argued that even if an agent's choice comprises only one element, this element might be the option they would have chosen anyhow even if alternatives were available. This objection leads to an issue which has not been considered up to now, namely the moral hazard effects of unemployment benefits. Evidently, their existence may prompt some people to prefer to withdraw from labour market participation, in as far as the difference between wage and benefits does not compensate for labour disutility. Since unemployment benefits are normally conditional to job search, these people may have to pretend they are searching, whereas in fact they are moonlighting or living as temporary insurance-financed (small-scale) rentiers. Hence the need to draw a distinction between two sorts of labour rationing separating those agents who are true victims of rationing from those who are not. A further condition should then be added, namely that the agents considered are not 'pseudo-rationed'.

In total, three conditions ought to be fulfilled for the existence of involuntary unemployment:

1 the national agents experience labour rationing in the unskilled labour market,
2 the rationed agents ought to be wage-dependent,
3 the rationed agents are not pseudo-rationed agents.

At this point, it may be worth giving neater definitions of the different concepts introduced above. They run as follows:

1 *Labour rationing*: An individual is labour rationed when the market real wage rate exceeds his reservation wage, yet he is not participating in labour trade. A skilled individual may successively enter into lower-skill markets and be rationed each time.
2 *Unemployment*: Unemployment is a social category regrouping individuals (i) who have encountered labour market rationing, (ii) who neither take up a job in lower-skill markets nor take up a non-wage activity, and (iii) who still want to participate in the specific market from which they have been rationed at the first possible opportunity.
3 *Voluntary unemployment*: Voluntary unemployment refers to individuals who, after being rationed in their specific labour market, prefer to remain jobless during the trade round under consideration in order to preserve their chances of being hired in this market in further trade rounds, rather than either supplying their labour service in a lower-skill market or taking up some available non-wage activity.
4 *Involuntary unemployment*: Involuntary unemployment refers to individuals who face rationing in the unskilled labour market and who, moreover, lack any non-wage activity possibility.
5 *Misemployment*: Misemployment is the alternative to unemployment when somebody is rationed. It refers to individuals who have succeeded in taking up a second-best activity position, either by participating in a lower-skill labour market or by adopting a non-wage activity.

I believe that these definitions constitute notable progress in the phrasing of the issue. In particular, drawing a distinction between labour rationing and unemployment permits an important clarification. In addition, my classifications suggest that the current understanding of voluntary/involuntary unemployment should be replaced by a more complex set of relationships. Three observations are worth making in this respect. First, the voluntary unemployment category is too heterogeneous. To many authors, it means chosen leisure. In my view, leisure requires a category on its own – the rentier activity – and should not be considered as belonging to the sphere of unemployment. Even leaving the rentier activity aside, the voluntary unemployment label remains ambiguous as it groups together two cases which should be separated out: workers preferring the job-seeking activity to misemployment and the pseudo-rationed agents pretending to be looking for a job. Things would be clearer if voluntary unemployment designated only the first of these two types.[8] Second, voluntary unemployment (narrowly understood) should not be viewed in a pejorative way. Voluntary unemployment is better than misemployment in many cases. Finally, the voluntarily unemployed and the involuntarily unemployed categories should be viewed as two sub-types of the broader job-searcher category rather than as being polar opposites. The only difference between them pertains to agents' scope of freedom. Involuntary unemployment implies that some agents have less freedom than assumed in economic theory. When rationed, they have less scope to manoeuvre than better endowed agents. Hence, whenever involuntary unemployment yields ground to voluntary unemployment, this should be hailed as good news!

Social embedding

To expand on the above definitions, it is worth reflecting on the social context in which they may become embedded. Clearly, my classifications apply best to a developed economy or 'welfare state economy', where unemployment benefits have become a pervasive social institution. Moreover, it should be realised that the unemployment concept is not universal. It emerged only gradually, not having its present-day meaning initially. The following observation by Piore, in his review of Salais *et al.*'s, *L'invention du chômage*, and Keyssar's *Out of Work: The First Century of Unemployment in Massachusetts*, brings the point home:

> In the early nineteenth century, unemployment as we know it today does not seem to have existed as a category, at least in the modern sense of the term. The word was widely used, but it referred mainly to 'those who were simply "not employed", who were idle or not working'. It thus included small children, who were never engaged in productive labor and grown men who had taken the day off to go fishing. By the end of the century, however, it had come to be understood exclusively in the modern

> sense of 'involuntary idleness', wanting a job but being unable to find one.
>
> (Piore 1987: 1838)[9]

The autonomisation of unemployment as an effective social category followed the emergence of unemployment benefits. In Piore's terms, it might have been the case 'that workers have been induced to behave as unemployed by the fact that they thereby become eligible for unemployment insurance payments' (1987: 1837). Thereby it became possible to drive a wedge between rationing and poverty, for without this wedge, the threat of falling into poverty loomed large on rationed agents.[10]

These brief remarks may help to explain why the unemployment category is not found in the writings of the first generation of classical political economists. Adam Smith is an enlightening example. If, at his time, one were to look at the activity choice set of agents populating the wage-earning category then, without doubt, the overwhelming majority of them would belong to the wage-dependent group. As stated by Smith, propertyless labourers 'stand in need of a master to advance them the material of their work' (Smith [1776] 1976: 83). Actually, in this context, nobody having a choice would take up waged labour, because such jobs were unattractive, low skilled and badly paid. Labour rationing was then an issue affecting only wage-dependent agents, whereas misemployment was of marginal importance. What was strikingly absent, however, was the unemployment outcome. The following extract is from his *Wealth of Nations* chapter on wages witnesses:

> But it would be otherwise in a country where the funds for the maintenance of labour were sensibly decaying. Every year the demand for servants and labourers would, in all the different classes of employment, be less than it had been the years before. Many who had been bred in the superior classes, not being able to find employment in their own business, would be glad to seek it in the lowest. The lowest class being not only overstocked with its own workmen, but with the overflowings of other classes, the competition for employment would be so great in it, as to reduce the wages of labour to the most miserable and scanty subsistence of the labourer. Many would not be able to find employment even upon these hard terms, but would either starve, or be driven to seek subsistence either by begging, or by the perpetration perhaps of the greatest enormities. Want, famine and mortality would immediately prevail in that class, and from thence extend themselves to all the superior classes, till the number of inhabitants in the country was reduced to what could easily be maintained by the revenue and stock which remained in it.
>
> (Smith [1776] 1976: 90–91)

Smith's account is telling. Excess supply triggers downward mobility (mis-employment), with people moving from superior to lower markets. As a result, the wage rate decreases and reaches the subsistence floor, before being able to absorb the excess supply. Rationed agents would then, one might think, become unemployed. However, this will rarely be the case because, in the Smithian framework, rationed agents barely have the means to survive without working: 'Many workmen could not subsist a week, few could subsist a month, and scarce any a year without employment' ([1776] 1976: 84). Thus, unemployment can have only a fugitive existence. Either people are able to leave it quickly or they slide into poverty. There is, as it were, a short-cut from labour rationing to disenfranchisement, with the unemployment stage being skipped. Labour rationing, according to Smith's argument, is the antechamber of poverty and starvation – a dramatic yet effective way of radically solving the excess labour supply issue.

Concluding remarks

In this chapter I have examined the neglected issue of post-rationing occupational trajectories. Its basic purpose was to make more explicit the mediating elements that need to be considered in order to link labour rationing and involuntary unemployment. I have brought out the conditions under which rationing can lead to involuntary unemployment. The coincidence between market rationing and unemployment arises only in models with a single labour market and wherein self-employment and other alternative activities are assumed away. Otherwise unemployment theory should be viewed as distinct from labour rationing theory, its concern being the issue of how and why rationed agents end up unemployed.

The broader lesson to be drawn from this chapter and the previous one is that the subject of involuntary unemployment needs to be tackled with subtlety. Any straightforward definitional stance cannot stand up to scrutiny. To give an example, my colleague Professor Alain Béraud from the University of Cergy-Pontoise, who was kind enough to comment on my manuscript, wrote to me that, to him, unemployment was involuntary by definition. Hence one should not speak of involuntary unemployment but only of unemployment *tout court*. While at first many will concur with him, upon reflection, the matter turns out to be more complicated. Béraud may well be right whenever the topic I have discussed in this chapter is left aside (i.e. no distinction is drawn between labour rationing and unemployment). In that case, the 'involuntary' modifier is effectively redundant in so far as it is accepted that the voluntary unemployment terminology should be refused for designating chosen leisure. Still a distinction should be made between two types of unemployment according to whether they carry the individual disequilibrium or only the frustration connotation. However, this standpoint is no longer valid whenever rationing and unemployment are considered separate. In this new context, the distinction between voluntary and involuntary unemployment makes perfect sense, as argued above.

Be that as it may, most of the models that will be studied do not consider the distinction between labour rationing and unemployment. They assume that only one labour market exist and that no alternative activities are possible. As a result, rationing automatically ends up in unemployment. Such an approach can be criticised for its incompleteness. However, this criticism must be mitigated by the admission that demonstrating labour rationing is the most challenging part of the programme. Hence, it is understandable that it receives the most attention.

The definitions of labour rationing, unemployment, voluntary unemployment, involuntary unemployment and misemployment given above are the right ones to me. Nonetheless, for the rest of this book, I will abide by the standard terminology and call 'involuntary unemployment' what, strictly speaking, should be called 'labour rationing', i.e. a breaching of the reservation wage principle. I could have adopted a narrower definition by considering that involuntary unemployment is a breaching of the reservation wage principle manifesting individual disequilibrium. Instead I have opted for a somewhat wider definition where involuntary unemployment covers both the individual disequilibrium and the frustration cases.

4

TRADE ORGANISATION

As the rest of this book will amply demonstrate, giving involuntary unemployment its theoretical credentials has proved to be a daunting task. It took several decades after Keynes' *The General Theory* to be achieved, and then still in an unsatisfactory way. The aim of this chapter is to explain with hindsight why this has been the case. What, in other words, is (are) the stumbling block(s) standing in the way of getting at a robust theory of involuntary unemployment in the individual disequilibrium meaning?

Answering this question will take me on a long journey. My starting point will be the basic distinction between the determination and the formation of equilibrium. Its consideration will allow me to introduce the notion of trade technology that will be central to my argumentation. Next, I will draw a contrast between the centralised and the decentralised market organisation, and claim that the notion of trade round is an essential ingredient of the centralised trade technology. Tracing back the presence of the trade round in Marshallian and Walrasian theory, I will further contend that, though present in the two approaches, the trade round is organised differently in either of them. In Walras, the driving force of the formation of equilibrium is the market secretary while in Marshall it is agents' perfect information (rather than haggling and bargaining as it is usually claimed). At this juncture, I will be able to answer my initial question: the basic stumbling block to involuntary unemployment viewed as an individual disequilibrium phenomenon lies in the assumption of a centralised market. In effect, adopting this assumption makes market clearing a foregone conclusion, at least in canonical models. Finally, to close the chapter, I engage in a minute examination of the meaning of the notions of rigidity and flexibility as well as of the linked notion of slow adjustment.

The difference between the determination and the formation of equilibrium

Let me start with recalling a basic distinction that should never be sidestepped when discussing equilibrium, the distinction between the determination and the formation of equilibrium.[1] The issue of the determination of equilibrium consists of assessing whether an allocation making agents optimising plans compatible exists logically. The issue of the formation of equilibrium pertains to the effective coming into existence of the equilibrium solution – how the equilibrium values calculated by the theoretician can effectively be attained as the result of agents' interactions.[2] It comprises an institutional dimension related to the organisation of trade or 'trade technology' enabling the equilibrium outcome to be arrived at. If 'a market is an institution for the consummation of transactions', as Stigler once stated ([1957] 1965: 245), this institutional dimension cannot be shelved.

Centralised versus decentralised markets

A straightforward observation to be made about the real-world market economy is that the market notion does not cover a single reality. Many sorts of markets co-exist. For the sake of my inquiry, let me regroup them in two *ideal types*: the 'centralised' and the 'decentralised' markets.

The centralised market – is characterised by the fact that trading takes place within well-defined, self-contained trade rounds, whose boundaries pertain to time, space, the type of good or service traded and the agents participating in trading.[3] It may also feature the presence of an institutional price-setting mechanism, eliciting a single final price. In many centralised markets – and certainly in those where a market secretary of some sort is present – effective trading takes place only after the determination of equilibrium. Such an arrangement insures that agents' optimising plans are made compatible.

In contrast, decentralised markets lack precise boundaries. This is certainly true for what concerns time and space. On the one hand, there are no well-delineated trade rounds. Trade is ongoing, sometimes around the clock. On the other, the spatial boundaries of a market are imprecise. Product delineation is vague as well. In short, it is hard to assess where one market stops and another begins. The trade round category makes no sense in such a context. For sure, no auctioneer is present. Agents are no longer simultaneously interconnected, as in the centralised set-up. Sellers post prices, while potential purchasers visit them sequentially.[4] In this framework it is plausible to have some agents being rationed, without any opportunity of over-bidding, simply because inventories were already depleted when they visited suppliers, the system working on a 'first come, first served' basis.

A centralised market is directly observable. Its operations and results are visible to everyone interested. In contrast, in the case of decentralised markets, the only observable reality is a myriad of bilateral monetary exchanges. The 'market for good x' exists only as an intellectual reconstruction undertaken by economists and statisticians, the result of complex data processing. Assuming that statistics could be obtained about the different trades that occurred in a given time-span, it would be observed that the same product has been sold at different prices.[5]

Both types of markets co-exist in the real world, yet most commentators would agree that the second type, the decentralised market, is overwhelmingly dominant. Surprisingly enough, when it comes to economic theory, it is the other way round. Most economic models are based on the assumption that markets function in a centralised way, search models being the important exception. It is straightforward to see that this statement is true in relation to Walrasian theory, yet it is also valid for Marshallian theory.[6]

The trade round in the Walrasian approach

The Walrasian economy, the object of analysis of Walrasian theory, constitutes a single centralised market, encompassing every agent and every good and service. Its cornerstone is the auctioneer whose main task consists of using the price system in order to bring the economy into equilibrium. To this end, he announces price vectors to which agents react by naming the optimal quantity they wish to trade. General equilibrium (at which every market excess demand is nil or negative, in which case the price is equal to zero) will be arrived at through changes in prices. Actual transactions remain suspended until the equilibrium price vector is arrived at. The duration needed for the price formation mechanism to come to an end matters little in this context. Therefore, making use of Occam's razor, it can as well be assumed that equilibrium is formed instantaneously, i.e. in logical time. Every auctioneer-led tâtonnement process is associated with a giving trade round, itself viewed as being a point-in-time.

All this is well-known.[7] A less noted feature of the auctioneer-led economy is its democratic character. The very fact that the market solution will make agents' plans compatible means that this outcome can come through only if no agent is left out, their optimising program remaining unfulfilled. Thus, whatever agents' endowment, they hold a veto power on the decision to decree the closing of the price formation process. Put differently, the corollary of agents' participation in tâtonnement is their right to optimal trade. Agents are supposed to participate freely in this set-up while every agent's participation is needed for the deal to be struck. This amounts to a unanimity decision-making process. As a result, it is inconceivable that trade might occur with non-consenting agents in a tâtonnement context. Whenever an economic agent is observed as non-trading, the conclusion must be drawn that such a lack of participation is the outcome of his or her optimising choice.

The idea that the auctioneer hypothesis is a central ingredient of the

Walrasian research programme (broadly defined so as to encompass neo-Walrasian models) will play a central role in my analysis. I am well aware that many, if not most, general equilibrium theorists recognise the role of the tâtonnement hypothesis only grudgingly, and openly declare their dislike of it.[8] Yet, it remains that, whenever the question of the institutional procedure through which a Walrasian equilibrium might effectively be realised is raised, the only available answer is the auctioneer led-tâtonnement.

The trade round in the Marshallian approach

I must start with a brief reminder of the Marshallian conception of equilibrium. It rests on two equilibrium concepts; market-day (in short market equilibrium) and normal equilibrium, respectively.[9] Theirs is a relationship of hierarchy with normal equilibrium being the higher or more fundamental concept and market equilibrium the lower or less fundamental concept.[10] Normal equilibrium exists whenever the market outcome in a given branch is such that firms lack incentives to change their behaviour (Marshall's attention focusing more on firms than on households). Yet another definition of normal equilibrium is that it consists of a matching between *normal* supply and demand. Market equilibrium concerns a given trade round in which exchanges take place, and is equivalent to market clearing, i.e. the equality between *market* supply and demand.

Three outcomes are *a priori* conceivable. The first is full equilibrium – the combination of market and normal equilibrium, arising whenever the values associate with market equilibrium coincide with those characterising normal equilibrium. Full disequilibrium is the converse case featuring both market disequilibrium and normal disequilibrium. The third outcome is when market equilibrium (the matching of market supply and demand) and normal disequilibrium (a mismatch between normal supply and demand) are combined. I will shortly claim that full disequilibrium is absent from Marshall's analysis. As a result, the third outcome can be called disequilibrium without ambiguity. Yet it must then be kept in mind that disequilibrium means the non-attainment of normal equilibrium and goes along with market clearing.

Let me now delve into the functioning of the market-day, Marshall's specific trade round.[11] It is well delineated in terms of space, time and product. It is implicitly assumed that all potential participants are present from the start of the trading process until the end. As a result, any phenomenon of the 'first come, first served' kind, with the risk of rationing it puts on latecomers, is excluded. However, the auctioneer figure is absent, and the market equilibrium is supposed to result from agents' price-making behaviour. Perfect competition is assumed to be present. The issue to be addressed is the formation of market equilibrium – how agents' actions will end up in making effective the equilibrium values calculated by the external economist.

Two explanatory factors are to be found in Marshall's analysis. The first is the bargaining that takes place between agents: 'And in like manners, buyers will fence, and pretend to be less eager than they really are. So the price may be tossed hither and thither like a shuttlecock, as one side or the other gets the better in the "haggling and bargaining" of the market' (1920: 333). The second is the assumption that economic agents hold perfect information about every data necessary for the calculation of equilibrium: 'The price of 36s. has thus some claim to be called the true equilibrium price: because ... every dealer *who has a perfect knowledge of the market* expects that price to be established' (Marshall 1920: 333; my emphasis).

Interpreters usually adopt the first of these explanations while shelving the latter, probably because it conveys the appealing vision of a bazaar-like market place. However, upon scrutiny it appears that no clue is given as to how haggling and bargaining can lead to the realisation of the equilibrium price and quantity values calculated by the omniscient economist. On the other hand, perfect information suffices for getting such a result. Therefore Marshall's argument reminds me of Voltaire's parable about the possibility of killing a goat through black magic, the sufficient condition for such an outcome being to combine magic with a little dose of poison. In Marshall's reasoning, bargaining is the witchcraft and perfect information the poison.[12]

Perfect information *à la* Marshall means that agents know as much about the market as the outside economist. As a result, they can mentally reconstruct supply and demand functions and calculate equilibrium values. Note that perfect information *à la* Marshall's is stronger than perfect information *à la* Walras, since in the latter agents are not supposed to be knowledgeable about market supply and demand functions, and their underpinnings.[13] Returning to Marshallian theory, the very fact that everybody has perfect foresight about the equilibrium price will insure that trading will take place only at this price. But there is no need for bargaining if all agents know this price from the onset. Marshall's bargaining argument turns out to be just window dressing, leaving the less appealing assumption of perfect information in the shadows.[14]

Although Marshall devoted some attention to the particularities of the demand for, and the supply of, labour, he never claimed that they impinged on the working of the labour market. The latter should then be viewed as operating on the same principles as the corn market, and the labour market would be no exception to the market clearing principle.[15]

The 'Week' device was proposed by Hicks in *Value and Capital* in order to structure the temporal dimension of Walrasian theory. Time is subdivided in discrete periods, the day constituting the unit period. Trade takes place every Monday, the rest of the week being devoted to the execution of contracts. Thus, the notions of trade round and Mondays are equated. In the light of my above considerations, it turn out that this device fits Marshallian theory as well. The conclusion drawn above when discussing the Walrasian approach, that the duration required for the formation of market equilibrium, then applies also to Marshallian theory. Any Monday equilibrium can be arrived at fast or slowly, yet this should have no impact, since the implementation of decisions made on Mondays starts only on Tuesdays. It must be considered as arising in logical time, i.e. instantaneously. On the other hand, were it accepted that the adjustment process could still be unfinished by Monday midnight, the 'week' framework would collapse.

Two broad conclusions surface. First, although Marshall is usually hailed for having given a more realistic account of the working of markets than Walras, I have shown that both accounts are based on a *deus ex machina*, perfect information in one case, the auctioneer in the other. Perfect information is no less a betrayal of the alleged theoretical *explanandum*, a decentralised trading system, than the auctioneer, because the hallmark of a decentralised economy is that private data will not become public. As aptly perceived by Hayek, the underlying flaw is that two levels of knowledge, which should have been kept separate – the knowledge of the outside omniscient economist and that of the economic agent – have become blurred.

The second conclusion is that the point made above about the Walrasian model – that the market system functions in a democratic way, to the effect that no market outcome will effectively emerge without the assent of all participants in the market – applies to the Marshallian model as well. Market clearing, i.e. the matching of market supply and demand, is always realised in Marshallian value analysis as it is in Walrasian theory. That is, neither frictional nor involuntary unemployment has any room within it.

In both cases, the explanatory factor is the centralised market assumption, and in particular the trade round assumption, i.e. the fact that trade is confined to, say, Mondays. Whenever the Monday trade assumption is combined with the auctioneer, in one case, with agents' omniscience, in the other, market clearing becomes a compelling result. Conversely, it may be wondered whether the market clearing notion makes any sense in a decentralised framework, because of the absence of its prerequisite, the trade round. Market demand and supply become elusive concepts, the same being true for the notion of their matching.[16] Put differently, there exists only one context within which raising the question as to whether market clearing is present makes sense, the centralised market, yet in this context market cleaning is a foregone conclusion. In contrast, the concept of market clearing seems useless against the decentralised market framework.

Justifying the centralised market assumption

Most real-world markets function in a decentralised way. Why is it that, with a few exceptions, economic theory has nonetheless adopted the opposite assumption? Let me answer this question in reference to the Marshallian framework.

Tractability is certainly a possible explanation. The trade round assumption distorts reality yet it makes things easier. In contrast, constructing a theory aiming at explaining the functioning of truly decentralised markets has proved to be a daunting task. Two other arguments can be evoked. The first is benign neglect. It amounts to claiming that the issue of how exchanges take place concretely is of secondary importance relative to the issue of the formation of normal equilibrium. In other words, competition is viewed as bearing on more basic adjustments than those governing individual trade rounds. This line of thinking is long-lived, going all the way back to Adam Smith. Smith was interested in the formation of natural prices and only dealt offhandedly with market prices. Likewise, to Marshall normal equilibrium was the important equilibrium concept. Likewise, it may be presumed that Marshall would have found it inadmissible to discard the possibility of disequilibrium as a departure from normal equilibrium, while having no qualms about discarding departures from market equilibrium. The second argument has to do with the divide that existed within Marshallian theory between value theory and business cycle and money theory. Marshall did not deny the existence of unemployment and surely aimed to explain it, as well as relieving it. But then, Marshall's was a split personality. On the one hand, as seen, no room existed for market rationing in his value theory. Yet, on the other hand, this was deemed of little consequence because unemployment had full right of abode in business cycle theory. The latter was deemed, as it were, an annexe of value theory – what could not be generated in value theory, like unemployment, would find a place in business cycle theory.

Rigidity

Rigidity and its converse, flexibility, are central to the literature that will be surveyed later in this book. Yet their meaning should not be taken for granted.

Rigidity concerns the behaviour of prices and wages over a given time-span. It exists whenever a price or wage that should be changing does not do so, the result of some externally imposed impediment to the formation of equilibrium. In turn, flexibility is said to prevail when no such impediment is present. Sluggishness or stickiness or still slow adjustment will designate cases where a change in a price or wage is observed, yet not to the full extent required.[17]

The main distinction made about rigidity, especially in reference to wages, is between nominal and real rigidity. Nominal rigidity concerns a monetary economy and raises no special problems. Real rigidity is more troublesome, because it can be used in two different contexts. The first is Walrasian general equilibrium theory. Here, since money is absent, at least from elementary models, the only rigidity concept that can be considered is real rigidity. It indicates the blocking of the price vector, a fact that will obviously impede the formation of equilibrium (except if by chance it is blocked at the equilibrium value).[18] The second context is the study of bilateral relations between employers and employees as, e.g. in the efficiency wage model. Now it makes sense to distinguish monetary and real values. It is usually claimed that this model's hallmark is real rigidity. However, if my definition is accepted, such a characterization is inappropriate. In effect, nothing in this model impedes the formation of equilibrium. A lack of reaction to a mismatch between supply and demand does not imply rigidity in the impediment meaning. Hence, contrary to the usual characterisation, wages should be considered flexible rather than rigid in efficiency wage models. If the contrary is believed true, it is because of the mistaken view that only rigidity can explain market rationing.

Another pitfall that should be avoided consists of representing wage rigidity under the form of a specially-shaped labour supply curve. To me, this account is off the mark, as I will show in Chapter 8, when discussing Modigliani's theory.

Finally, the rigidity term should be understood differently according to whether it is used in statements aimed at describing real-world processes or in statements pertaining to the theoretical universe. In the first case, the attention focuses on the evolution of a given price or wage index over a conventionally defined span of time, say, one year, this index being constructed through some complex data processing. Rigidity will be said to exist if no change in the index is observed in spite of the fact that reasons exist for such a change. Whenever the discussion bears on abstract theoretical models, the matter is different as soon as it is accepted that these models, be they Marshallian or Walrasian, are based on the specific temporal framework of the Hicksian 'week'. As a result, any possible market rationing outcome must happen on a given Monday.

If this analysis is accepted, the popular view that market rationing can be caused by slow adjustment, should be rejected. To make this point, let me resort to the well-known cobweb example. Figure 4.1 illustrates.

Let me assume a time-to-build factor: it takes two trade rounds to change the quantity produced. Producers have adaptive expectations – supply at a given trade round is a function of the price that prevailed at the previous one. Start from a state of normal equilibrium at price p^*, and assume that a shift in normal demand occurs at t_1, moving the normal demand schedule from D_N^* to D_N^{**} (where N stands for normal). The normal supply function

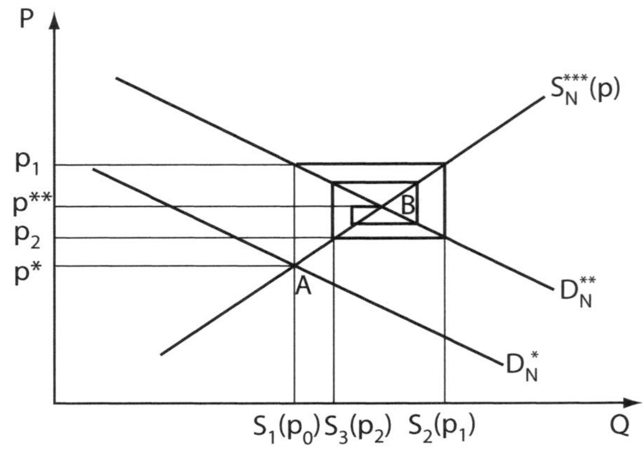

Figure 4.1 The cobweb case.

is assumed to remain unchanged. The earlier normal equilibrium is A, the new one is *B*. At t_1, market supply equals $S_1(p_0)$, and the market equilibrium price is p_1. At t_2, market supply equals $S_2(p_1)$, and the market equilibrium price is p_2. Eventually, point B will be reached where the new equilibrium is established at p^{**}.

Two features stand out. First, the formation of normal equilibrium takes time. In other words, slow adjustment is present. Second, during the interval separating the two normal equilibria, the market exhibits disequilibrium. Yet, this is a disequilibrium against normal equilibrium and not against market equilibrium. Actually, it co-exists with market clearing. That is, at each trading round, market demand and market supply (vertical lines starting from $S_1(p_0)$, etc.) match. As it stands, the graph suggests a reccession of states of excess supply until B is reached. This assessment is correct, of course, yet it must be realised that the mismatch in point concerns *normal* supply and demand instead of *market* demand and supply.

To conclude, while slow adjustment explains disequilibrium, i.e. the delayed attainment of normal equilibrium, it nonetheless generates no market rationing since the latter is a matter of non-attainment of market equilibrium.

Unfortunately, this point has been recurrently passed over. Let me give two examples. The first is Blinder's following statement, which he presents as a central tenet of Keynesian economics:

> Keynesians believe that goods markets and, especially, labour markets respond only sluggishly to shocks, i.e. that prices and wages do not move quickly to clear markets.
>
> (Blinder [1988] 1997: 111)[19]

The question must be raised as to whether Blinder's statement pertains to the real or the model economy. As far as the first is concerned, as stated above, any reference to market clearing is misplaced because real world markets are decentralised. Be that as it may, Blinder's statement cannot be accepted as far as the model economy is concerned. In the latter, there is no room for stickiness. Trade rounds operating in logical time, wages are either flexible or rigid. Sluggishness can only characterise adjustment across trade rounds.

My second example is Hahn and Solow's following definition of flexibility:

> Nominal-wage rates are flexible if they rise pretty promptly and rapidly when there is excess demand for labour and fall pretty promptly and rapidly when there is excess supply of labour.
>
> (Hahn and Solow 1986: 1)

This definition is unsatisfactory when gauged against my above remarks. Its first flaw is the vagueness of the rapid adjustment idea. No distinction is made between trade round adjustment and adjustment across trade rounds. Because of their lack of attention to the trade round notion, and its requirements, Hahn and Solow miss my point that slow adjustment cannot cause market rationing. Second, it follows from their definition that a price or a wage is rigid whenever it does not adjust in case of excess supply or excess demand. This definition is in accord with the usual characterisation of efficiency wage models. Yet, as claimed above, it is inadequate because it comes on a collision course with what seems to me to be the basic feature of rigidity, namely its being an impediment to the formation of equilibrium.

Concluding remarks

In this chapter I have studied the institutional assumptions underpinning the Marshallian and the Walrasian approaches, and clarified some related concepts. The following observations have been made:

1 In both approaches exchanges take place in a centralised way. They are confined within trade rounds, contrary to what is the case for decentralised markets. The operation of trade rounds must be conceived of as taking place in logical time.

2 Any market rationing outcome must be explained within the trade round framework.

3 The auctioneer is the *modus operandus* of the Walrasian trade round. He is absent from the Marshallian trade round. In the latter the automatic formation of market equilibrium is due to the assumption of agents' omniscience.

4 The auctioneer, in the Walrasian approach, or the agents' omniscience assumption in the Marshallian approach are the two stumbling blocks impeding the success of the involuntary unemployment programme since their very presence guarantees market clearing. As long as they remain, this programme is doomed to fail.

Two main lines can be envisaged in order to achieve the project of demonstrating involuntary unemployment: breaking away from the auctioneer trade organisation whenever the Walrasian approach is adopted; removing the perfect information assumption whenever the analytical framework is Marshallian.[20] Evidently, these are retrospective prescriptions. As will be seen, it took economists a long time to engage with either of them, due to both their lack of awareness as to the nature of the stumbling blocks and the genuine difficulty of the task at hand.

Part II

INVOLUNTARY UNEMPLOYMENT IN KEYNES' *THE GENERAL THEORY*

5

KEYNES' PROGRAMME

A reconstruction

Keynes wrote *The General Theory* (1936) with both a political and a theoretical motivation. Whereas the policy dimension remained somewhat implicit, it nevertheless stands to reason that Keynes wanted his book to be more than just a theoretical work. To him, it had to serve a policy purpose – positively, a justification for government intervention in the economy and, negatively, a dismissal of wage deflation policy. His targeted readership, however, was academic, which resulted from his perception that these policy recommendations faced a theoretical hurdle. Economists, he recognised, were torn between their 'flair and instinct' (Keynes [1934] 1973: 486) and their analytical tools. Their flair prompted them to believe that mass unemployment resulted from a system failure and was to be corrected accordingly, whereas their theoretical reasoning compelled them to trace it back to wage-earners' unwillingness to accept a fall in wages.[1] Something thus had to be done in the field of theory, in order to unravel the existing deadlock and give the new policy its missing intellectual credentials.

From the theoretical viewpoint, *The General Theory* is a complex book, mixing different objectives. Looking for what Keynes intended to do when undertaking to write his book, we may turn to his 1931 Chicago Lectures, where he discussed the issue of whether decreases in wages could be viewed as a remedy for unemployment, and answered in the negative (Keynes 1973: 355–372). It can then be argued that the purpose of *The General Theory* was to provide theoretical foundations for this view. This assessment is plausible when considering Keynes' initial intention. However, finished works do not necessarily achieve the programme their authors had in mind when starting to write them. While the adjustment dimension does not fully disappear from Keynes' book, it nonetheless takes the back seat with respect to the aim of demonstrating the logical existence of involuntary unemployment, independently from any adjustment problem.

A radical or a reformist strategy?

A preliminary issue to be tackled is to ask, to put it in a crude way, whether *The General Theory* should be viewed as neoclassical or anti-neoclassical. Favereau (1985) argues that when starting to write *The General Theory*, Keynes was wavering between two lines of thought, a radical and a reformist one, to finally opt for the latter. Underlying the radical research strategy is the conviction that, without the consideration of a series of factors – such as radical uncertainty, money, real time, asymmetry between firms and workers – the involuntary unemployment claim cannot win the day. Given that the existing theory is impervious to them, a thorough change in paradigm is deemed to be needed. On the contrary, the reformist strategy rests on the opinion that the integration of the hitherto excluded concept can be achieved with only minimal changes in economic theory as it exists.[2]

Keynes himself would probably have refused to be locked into having to choose between the two strategies that Favereau attributed to him. Assuming that he would recognise their difference, he would probably have avoided seeing them as antagonistic. Actually, his discourse was either radical or reformist, depending on the occasion.

So, both trends appear in Keynes' work. They can partly be disentangled by drawing a distinction between the bare model it contains and that part of it which consists of meta-theoretical commentaries about the model. The most popular view is that Hicks' IS-LM model aptly captures the gist of *The General Theory*. Its meta-theoretical part would then consist of the passages falling outside of this model, as well as Keynes' statements of purpose, polemical passages, earlier and posterior expositions of his main insights, etc. If this line is taken, the impression prevails that, as far as model is concerned, Keynes' work ought to be put under the mantle of the reformist strategy. Keynes' claim to offer a generalisation of classical theory, his desire to change only one postulate whilst keeping the other ones testify to such a strategy.

However, taken alone, this argument cannot win the day. The problem is that the model contained in *The General Theory* is in prose, and several alternative interpretations as to its features are possible. While the IS-LM model is a plausible reading, it is certainly not the only one. Moreover, it would be an exaggeration to state that all radical elements of Keynes' work belong to its 'sub-text'. For example, the drafts of the first chapters should be considered as more than commentaries.[3] On the other hand, the very fact that they were dropped is indicative of a shift from the radical towards the reformist strategy. Assuming that, at an initial stage of his writing, Keynes found the radical programme more appealing intellectually, it might have dawned on him that the pragmatic programme had the advantage of being easier to 'sell' to fellow economists. In view of the urgency of the policy issues underlying the debate, this would have been a crucial argument to him. Yet, he did not fully renounce the radical viewpoint, as his 1937 *Quarterly Journal of Economics* demonstrates.

Be this as it may, in this book my interest will be limited to Keynes' reformist strategy. The issue to be addressed can then be described as follows: granting that, at a certain stage of theoretical development, a given concept (involuntary unemployment) is absent from the theory, what are the smallest possible changes in assumptions that are required in order to allow its integration in a 'methodologically correct' way?

Keynes' programme

My reconstruction of Keynes' research programme pursued in *The General Theory* consists of the constellation of the following four elements.[4]

First of all, Keynes pursued the objective of demonstrating the theoretical existence of involuntary unemployment. Beyond doubt, he had in mind involuntary unemployment in the individual disequilibrium meaning. He reckoned it as a phenomenon whose real-world existence was compelling yet for which economic theory could find no room. Bridging this gulf was the task he set himself.

Second, Keynes' interest in involuntary unemployment followed from the presumption that it expressed some system failure, a malfunctioning of the decentralised economy.[5] Its existence had to temper, if not upset, the optimistic interpretation of this system put forward by economists since Adam Smith. In particular, he wanted to link it with a deficiency in aggregate demand for the output as a whole, itself associated with some leakage from the productive towards the financial sector.

The claim that involuntary unemployment follows from some system failure affects the type of analysis which emerges. The common explanation in the time of Keynes was that unemployment was the result of wage levels being too high. Such an explanation is part of a Marshallian analysis in which one market, here the labour market, is considered in isolation from the rest of the economy. Keynes wished to escape this framework in a twofold way. On the one hand, he wanted to exonerate too high wages from any responsibility in the existence of involuntary unemployment. On the other hand, he believed that its explanation had to be looked for outside the labour market. As Meltzer puts it, 'the problem is manifested in the labour market, but it does not arise in the labour market' (1988: 197).[6] What he was actually striving for was to move the analysis of unemployment from a partial to a general equilibrium framework (although this terminology was non-existent at this time).[7] Yet, such a willingness to adopt an interdependency perspective should not be interpreted as an adhesion to the Walrasian general equilibrium approach. In Keynes' time, Walras' views were hardly appreciated in Cambridge and, for better or worse, Keynes did not think that Walras' theory could be of any help to his own project.[8] To him, the route to be taken was to generalise Marshallian analysis, by taking into account the interdependency across markets.[9]

On the other hand, Keynes did not want to join the imperfect competition line of argument which was emerging at the time in Cambridge. He wanted to put his argument in terms of perfect competition, – possibly because he associated imperfect competition with collusion, unions, etc. His concern was to bring to the fore something deeper, namely that unemployment could be possible even when the labour market was functioning in a perfectly competitive way without either frictions or market power.[10]

The third objective concerns policy. Keynes believed that a remedy existed for the flaw in the economic system that he had strived to display, and that was different from lowering wages. While Keynes held the insight that the government had an active role to play, it received no precise content in *The General Theory*. For all Keynes' evasiveness on this matter, the interpretation, which quickly became popular, that the appropriate remedy was state-induced demand stimulation, seems appropriate.[11] The rationale for this view is that demand activation follows from the diagnosis Keynes is positing, namely that involuntary unemployment results from aggregate demand deficiency. The latter implies demand activation as its remedy!

The above analysis can be summarised by stating that Keynes' research programme consisted of four items:

1. the phenomenon to be explained is involuntary unemployment in the individual disequilibrium meaning;
2. demonstrating that wage rigidity can be exonerated as its cause;
3. giving a general equilibrium explanation of the phenomenon within a perfect competition framework;
4. demonstrating that demand stimulation is the proper remedy to be taken for solving the problem.

The aim of my book is to assess whether this programme has been met with success, first in Keynes' *The General Theory*, and second, in subsequent Keynesian models.

The broader context: Keynes as a Marshallian economist

A basic intuition guiding my interpretation of Keynes is that he was a Marshallian as opposed to a Walrasian economist, as forcefully argued by Clower and Leijonhufvud (e.g. [1975] 1984). Therefore, no correct assessment of Keynes' contribution can be made without positing it in reference to Marshallian theory. In this light, three aspects are worth insisting on.

The first has already been touched upon. Keynes should be considered the creator of a nascent Marshallian general equilibrium perspective, having little to do with Walrasian general equilibrium theory. However, if he initiated such a move, it was hardly for the mere sake of it, but rather because it was a prerequisite to a new explanation of unemployment. As a result, two tasks were to be tackled – first, to boost a transformation within the standard Marshallian approach (that is, a shift from partial to general equilibrium analysis) and, second, to drive a wedge within this recast standard theory by replacing its normal market-clearing result with involuntary unemployment.

A second way of characterising Keynes' enterprise in contrast to the standard Marshallian approach is to view it as an attempt to move the unemployment category away from business cycle into value theory. I have claimed in Chapter 4 that, in the Marshallian tradition, business cycle theory rather than value theory was deemed to be the proper place for a subject matter like unemployment. Against this background, Keynes' aim in *The General Theory* can be recast as consisting of trying to transfer involuntary unemployment from business cycle to value theory. Put differently, the originality of Keynes' project turns out to lie in his attempt to generate labour-market rationing in a value-theory framework. Until then it had been absent from this framework, while its existence in a business cycle theory framework was taken for granted.

Finally, a third way in which Keynes' project marks a departure from standard Marshallian theory relates to equilibrium. The Marshallian conception of equilibrium has been sketched out in Chapter 4. Two distinct outcomes can arise in Marshallian analysis. Let me call them the 'equilibrium triad' and the 'disequilibrium triad'. The former is the combination of individual equilibrium, market clearing, and normal equilibrium, the latter the combination of individual equilibrium, market clearing and 'normal disequilibrium' (i.e. a departure from normal equilibrium). This disequilibrium triad is considered a perfectly plausible outcome and as theoretically correct as the equilibrium triad.

Against this background, Keynes' aim in *The General Theory* can be reconstructed as the replacement of the 'Marshallian disequilibrium triad' with the 'Keynesian triad', i.e. a combination of individual disequilibrium, market non-clearing and normal equilibrium. Table 5.1 illustrates the involuntarily unemployed would be in a state of individual disequilibrium, and the labour market would close with a mismatch between market-day supply and demand. Such a state of affairs should nonetheless be considered as a normal equilibrium (or standstill situation).

At the time Keynes was writing, no basic methodological objections were levelled against his overall project. Microeconomics was insufficiently developed to bring out the difficulties involved. Moreover, the fact that unemployment was massive was seen as an indication of the fact that it was

Table 5.1 Keynes' triad against Marshall's two triads

The Marshallian equilibrium triad	optimising behaviour	market clearing	normal equilibrium
The Marshallian disequilibrium triad	optimising behaviour	market clearing	normal disequilibrium
The Keynesian triad	individual disequilibrium	market non-clearing	normal equilibrium

involuntary. Finally, the view that some system failure was present, which needed state interventions as a cure, was hardly revolutionary. Against the Great Depression context, the majority of English economists were opposed to wage-cuts and advocated public works against unemployment.[12] It is only with the unfolding of time that the daunting character of Keynes's programme was gradually to surface.

The real world versus the theoretical universe

Following Marshall's footsteps, Keynes' methodological stance was that theory should be as close as possible to reality. Therefore, he felt allowed to jump back and forth from theoretical to empirical statements. To him, economic reasoning might well have consisted of models, yet the latter were only present implicitly – they were still in prose and far from what this notion came to mean. Soon after *The General Theory*, things began to change and a new, more formalised, style of theorising emerged, gradually taking the upper hand. Hicks' IS-LM model, which transformed the impressionistic mode of reasoning of Keynes' book into a simultaneous equations equilibrium model, was a benchmark in this respect.

Once formal modelling becomes predominant, the rules of the game change. To borrow from Lucas, models deal with artificial, fictitious economies created by economists for the sake of reasoning in a demonstrative way. They need to be non-realistic even if they draw their inspiration from reality. Modelisation has it advantages – and they are compelling – yet it also bears a price. In particular, a sharp line must be drawn between propositions that pertain to the real world and propositions valid for the fictitious theoretical universe. One cannot move freely from the real world to the fictitious theoretical world. Take involuntary unemployment. In the context of the Great Depression, most economists would have endorsed the view that the unemployment they were observing was involuntary. The problem, however, is whether real-world existence is sufficient to make the phenomenon theoretically admissible. To all intents and purpose, Keynes' answer was positive. Yet, to me, his viewpoint, which is still often held today, is wrong. The 'real world' and the fictitious universe of economic theory should not be amalgamated.[13] One may prove able to put forward solid arguments for the empirical existence of the involuntary unemployment category, whilst being unable to succeed in making it theoretically acceptable. Conversely, a cogent demonstration of the unacceptability of involuntary unemployment in the theoretical parable does not allow that this category is irrelevant for characterising reality. Real-world existence may serve as a motivation for attempting to introduce the corresponding concept in economic theory. Yet, the 'authority of reality', i.e. the undisputed existence of a phenomenon in the real world, cannot by itself warrant the theoretical acceptability of the concept that is meant to represent it.

6

INVOLUNTARY UNEMPLOYMENT IN KEYNES' *THE GENERAL THEORY*

One way of recasting the objective pursued by Keynes in his *The General Theory* is to state that he purported to demonstrate the possible existence of involuntary unemployment within a neoclassical framework. Starting from the realisation that this concept had no place in neoclassical theory – he, for one, was speaking of 'classical' theory – his aim was to elicit which minimal change in hypotheses could reverse such a state of affairs. Quite sanguinely, Keynes believed that he had achieved this. This was also the prevailing opinion in the years which followed the publication of *The General Theory*. From the 1970s onwards, however, this view has been strongly questioned. As a result, at present most economists rather think that Keynes failed in his enterprise, which in turn raises the question of why people believed the contrary earlier.

This chapter comprises four sections. In the first, I critically examine Keynes' definition of involuntary unemployment. In the second, I discuss Keynes' account of the working of the labour market, in particular his claim as to the existence of a wedge between the nominal and the real wage. In the third section, I assess his other claim that the cause of involuntary unemployment lies in an effective-demand deficiency. Finally, in the fourth section I examine Keynes' claim that his earlier wage-rigidity assumption can be removed without harm for his earlier conclusions (Chapter 19 of *The General Theory*). My final conclusion is that no valid explanation of involuntary unemployment remains after Keynes' reasoning errors have been straightened out.

Keynes' definition of involuntary unemployment

Keynes did not invent the concept of involuntary unemployment. It can, for example, be found in Pigou's short book, *Unemployment* (1914) and Dennis Robertson's *A Study of Industrial Fluctuations* (1915).[1] However, he gave it a more central role. As stated above, he aimed at introducing it into the core of economic theory, i.e. value, theory rather than letting it exist only in its confines, i.e. business cycle theory.

Moreover, he may be credited for having identified the basic microeconomic proposition which had to be modified in order to introduce the involuntary unemployment notion. What was needed, he stated, was a removal of what he called the 'second classical postulate', according to which the 'utility of the wage when a given amount of labour is employed is equal to the marginal disutility of that amount of employment' (1936: 5). The following graph *à la* Jevons illustrates what Keynes had in mind.

Involuntary unemployment exists whenever the quantity of labour that is traded is lower than the equilibrium quantity. For any such lower quantity the marginal utility drawn from consuming the wage income exceeds the marginal disutility of labour. In modern terms, this statement is tantamount to the reservation wage definition of involuntary unemployment analysed in Chapter 2. Moreover, to Keynes, the 'involuntary' modifier was definitely to be understood in its common-sense meaning. Thus, to him, involuntary unemployment was selfsame to individual disequilibrium.

Keynes was right in stating that demonstrating involuntary unemployment was a matter of removing a postulate from the canonical model. Yet he was unable to identify properly the postulate that needed to be withdrawn. In effect, the equality between the marginal disutility of labour and the marginal utility of income cannot be a postulate, rather it stems from some upstream choice-theoretical or trade organisation premise.[2] Identifying the latter is the task which he should have set for himself.

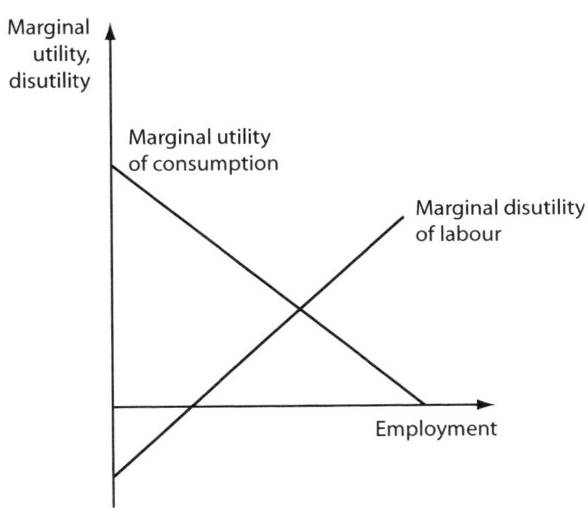

Figure 6.1 The second classical postulate.

Keynes also insisted on giving the involuntary unemployment notion a narrow meaning. As noted by Leijonhufvud:

> It is extremely important to be clear on three things: (a) how very widely Keynes defined 'voluntary' unemployment; (b) that his own concern was entirely with the residual category of 'involuntary' unemployment and that it is with this unemployment that his theory of employment deals; (c) that his policy recommendations and remarks on the relative efficacy of fiscal and monetary policy measures refer specifically to the task of relieving 'involuntary' unemployment, so that his judgements of the usefulness of monetary policy, for example, apply to such situations and not in general.
>
> (Leijonhufvud 1968: 92)

To Keynes, other forms of unemployment should be considered voluntary:

> In addition to frictional unemployment, the postulate is also compatible with 'voluntary unemployment' due to the refusal or inability of a unit of labour, as a result of legislation or social practices or of combination for collective bargaining or of slow response to change or of mere human obstinacy, to accept a reward corresponding to the value of the product attributable to its marginal productivity.
>
> (Keynes 1936: 6)

Any unemployment resulting from the existence of unions or imperfect competition should be considered as voluntary. The same is true, of course, for chosen leisure.[3] All this is fine. However, I disagree with Keynes on his assertion that any unemployment resulting from the existence of a legally imposed wage floor must be considered voluntary. Here Keynes' criterion for involuntary unemployment, the violation of the second postulate, is met. Therefore, it would have been better to have stated that he was not interested in this type of involuntary unemployment instead of denying that it was involuntary unemployment!

A further step should be taken. Accept, first, that the category of frictional unemployment has no room at the level of abstraction at which the analysis in *The General Theory* is evolving; second, that perfect competition is present and, third, that 'chosen leisure' should not be labelled 'unemployment'. Under these conditions, if any unemployment is present in Keynes' model, it must be involuntary unemployment. Put differently, as long as, first, it is admitted that chosen leisure should not be called voluntary unemployment and, second, the issue of post-rationing trajectories analysed in Chapter 3 is put aside, the 'involuntary' modifier can be considered redundant, and unemployment can be equated with labour market rationing.

Correctly defining the involuntary unemployment concept is an indispensable task, yet it is hardly sufficient to make involuntary unemployment theoretically acceptable. There is a gulf between correctly defining a concept and generating it in a methodologically correct way (i.e. to provide a causal explanation of it whilst respecting the basic premises of neoclassical theory). New classicists could agree about Keynes' definition whilst refusing to integrate his concept into the theoretical discourse.

As far as Keynes' attempt to give a foundation to involuntary unemployment is concerned, two distinct arguments can be disentangled. The main one is indirect. It bears on the possibility of an effective-demand deficiency of which involuntary unemployment is deemed to be the result. This line dominates the scene from Chapter 3 of *The General Theory* onwards. However, in Chapter 2, Keynes presents a more direct argumentation related to the working of the labour market. In particular, in his famous second observation, he claims that involuntary unemployment is caused by wage-earners' inability to bargain over the determination of the real wage. I need to scrutinise these two streams, and will start with the second.

Involuntary unemployment and the labour market[4]

Keynes' second observation

One difficulty in interpreting Keynes' passages on the labour market in Chapter 2 of *The General Theory*, is his lack of explicitness. Keynes seemingly took for granted that there existed a well-established standard view as to the functioning of the labour market, from which he had just to depart. This is hardly true. First, as claimed above, the Marshallian approach is plagued with a basic ambiguity on this issue of the functioning of markets. Recall that Marshall claimed that the market-day equilibrium was the outcome of agents' 'haggling and bargaining' while, actually, there was no theory to support these words. While the rhetoric was about bargaining, the effective driving force behind the formation of equilibrium was agent's omniscience – their ability to reconstruct mentally the market equilibrium. Second, to compound the matter, the commonly accepted view, that the labour market equilibrium is a matter of real wage adjustment, ought to be questioned.

This is the background against which Keynes' second observation, which he considered as fundamental, ought to be examined. It states that involuntary unemployment originates in the fact that wage earners bargain in monetary terms rather than in real terms. In other words, the logically existing real wage rate that would equate the demand for, and the supply of labour cannot be reached endogenously. The following quotation summarises his claim:

> The traditional theory maintains, in short, *that the wage bargain between the entrepreneurs and the workers determine the real wage*; so that, assuming free competition amongst employers and no restrictive combination amongst workers, the latter can, if they wish, bring their real wages into conformity with the marginal disutility of the amount of employment offered by the employers at that wage. If this is not true, then there is no longer any reason to expect a tendency towards equality between the real wage and the marginal disutility of labour
>
> (Keynes 1936: 11)[5]

Unfortunately, Keynes' statement does not stand up to scrutiny. To make this point, I must delve into the institutional set-up wherein the adjustment flaw is supposed to occur, namely what I have suggested to call a 'Marshallian economy', the only set-up in which Keynes' reasoning makes sense (De Vroey 1999b). It can be characterised in a threefold way. First, each market is a separated locus of equilibrium formation. Second, it is a monetary economy. Third, it comprises a two-stage sequential trade procedure, with factors being traded before final goods.

Keynes considers that in the standard Marshallian vision the real wage is a magnitude whose value is determined within the labour market: 'the traditional theory maintains in short, that the wage bargain between the entrepreneurs and the workers determine the real wage' (1936: 11). Most economists will agree with such a statement. To give one of many examples of contemporary re-formulations of this viewpoint, consider the following statement by Gerrard: 'In classical theory the real wage and employment are determined simultaneously in an allocative process in the labour market' (1995: 448). To me, however, while this statement is true in reference to a Walrasian economy, it is false with respect to a Marshallian economy. The correct formulation should rather run as follows (following the pattern of Gerrard's statement): 'In classical theory – now understood as meaning the Marshallian approach – the *nominal* wage and employment are determined simultaneously in an allocative process in the labour market. The *real* wage, an index purporting to measure the purchasing power of the nominal wage, can be determined only afterwards at the closure of goods markets'.

The basic principle is that the labour market adjusts through changes in the nominal wage. No conclusion of monetary illusion should, however, be drawn. When households supply their labour they must develop expectations about the general price level that will prevail when they enter the goods markets, as it will determine the purchasing power of the income drawn from hiring out their labour services. Hence there is no contradiction between the assertion that markets function in a monetary way and the assertion that agents reason in real terms. In other words, and assuming a single final good, the supply of labour should be expressed as

$$L^S = f(w; p^e_w)$$

rather than as

$$L^S = f(w/p)$$

where w is the money wage, p the price of the final good and p^e_w workers' expectations about p.[6]

Whenever workers are assumed to hold perfect information, this wedge between the formation of the money and the real wage is of no practical consequence. While it remains true that the nominal wage is fixed before the real wage, this gap is just formal since no surprise will arise as to the value of the real wage.[7] As a result, economists may feel authorised to make the short-cut of putting the real wage on the vertical axis of their labour market graphs. However, the wedge should be kept in mind as a matter of principle. Note, for example, that the mere statement that such graphs having the real wage on the ordinate describes a labour market outcome is misleading, since it actually collates the labour market and the goods market results. Be that as it may, as soon as perfect information is removed, the short-cut becomes invalid.

At this juncture, the important point is whether this wedge can be the cause of involuntary unemployment, as claimed by Keynes. My answer is 'no'. Assume, as will be the case in Friedman's Phillips Curve model (to be studied in Chapter 13), that workers hold imperfect information about the price of consumer goods. Surprises can then arise at the end of the market-day. The possibility of a nominal/real wage wedge now turns out to be a wedge between the expected and the realised real wage. Suppose that (contrary to what is the case in Friedman's model) wage-earners receive a real wage higher than expected. This is the very situation described by Keynes when writing that 'a decline in employment, although necessarily associated with labour *receiving* a wage equal in value to a larger quantity of wage-goods, is not necessarily due to labour's *demanding* a larger quantity of wage-goods' (1936: 18). Thus, the wedge can cause a positive or negative discrepancy between the expected and the real wage. Yet – and this is the central point – it generates no involuntary unemployment. The latter must arise inside the labour market as a result affecting the formation of the market-day equilibrium. Note that this formation (or the lack thereof) is a matter of having the right (or the false) nominal wage, and not a matter of getting the right (or the false) real wage. Once the money wage is formed – that is, as soon as the labour market has come to a close – what exists is either market clearing or market rationing. At this stage, the matter is already sealed. In other words, if involuntary unemployment is present, it must have come into existence before the determination of the real wage. Labour market rationing and the formation of the real wage are two distinct issues. The former is a labour market outcome, the latter a goods market outcome, these two outcomes occurring sequentially.

To understand Keynes' mistake, reference can be made to Patinkin's distinction between individual and market experiments evoked in chapter 2. As far as the individual experiment aspect is concerned, the formation of agents' optimising plans is a matter of confronting the utility provided by consuming the real wage with that of enjoying leisure. Here the real wage is indeed the relevant variable. Yet it is wrong to conclude from this that the real wage remains so when it comes to the market experiment, the functioning of the labour market. As far as the latter is concerned, the relevant variable is the nominal wage.

Hitherto my analysis is based on the assumption that what is going on in the labour market has no impact on the goods market result. It can be posited that Keynes had the opposite in mind. Let me therefore examine the interrelationship between the labour and the goods market, as illustrated in Figure 6.2. $L^S(w; \overline{P}^e_w)$ is the labour supply, a function of the nominal wage with workers' expectations about the goods price as a parameter. $L^D(w; \overline{P}^e_f)$ is the demand for labour, a function of the nominal wage with firms' expectations about the goods price as a parameter. $G^D(p; \overline{w})$ is the demand for goods, a function of their price with the wage as a parameter. $G^S(p; \overline{w})$ is the supply of goods, a function of their price with the wage as a parameter. Consider the nominal adjustment process in the labour market and compare two out-of-equilibrium nominal wages W_1 and W_2, both supposedly above the market-clearing wage, with $W_1 > W_2$. Going from W_1 to W_2, the argument runs, has an impact on what goes on in the goods market, where the supply and demand functions are supposed to comprise the nominal wage as a parameter. As a result, the transition from W_1 to W_2 would displace both the supply of goods and the demand for goods – the former to the right (from G^S_1 $(P; \overline{W}_1)$ to G^S_2 $(P; \overline{W}_2)$), the latter to the left (G^D_1 $(P; \overline{W}_1)$ to G^D_2 $(P; \overline{W}_2)$). A possible outcome is that the equilibrium quantity of the goods remains the same while the price will fall. Hence the possibility that $W_1/P_1 = W_2/P_2$. As in Keynes' argument, the decrease in the nominal wage is unaccompanied by a decrease in the real wage. Of course, the story should not end here, since a change in price expectations will in turn displace the labour market functions, which will have a further impact on the conjectured goods market outcome, etc. However, my above reasoning remains valid. Only two occurrences are

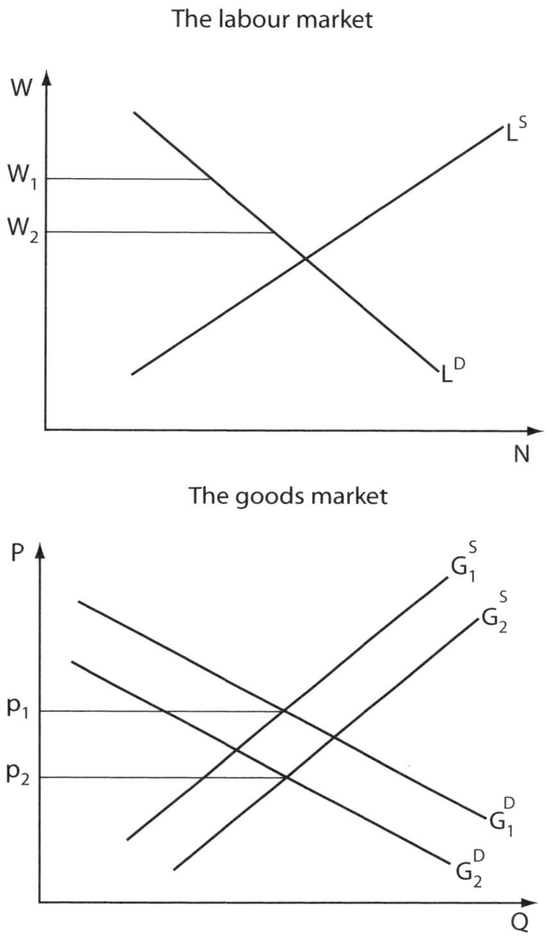

Figure 6.2 The interrelationship between the labour and the goods market.

conceivable. Either, a joint equilibrium in the two markets logically exists, in which case agents will be able to discover it, due to the perfect information assumption. Or it does not exist, in which case we are in the dark as to what is going to happen. Salvaging Keynes' observation by viewing it as pointing to this last possibility – that involuntary unemployment exists because no compatible labour market and goods market equilibria exist – seems difficult to accept.

The conclusion to be drawn is that whenever perfect information is assumed, the real wage is de facto known at the closure of the labour market. Accepting to use the 'bargaining' terminology for a while, it could be stated that wage-earners are able to bargain the nominal and the real wage in one stroke. In contrast, in an imperfect information context, it is possible that workers are unable to bargain the real wage. Friedman's expectations-augmented Phillips Curve model is an example. Still, Keynes' second observation remains of little interest. As argued, it cannot explain the emergence of involuntary unemployment. Moreover, it is unsatisfactory, less because of its falseness than its triviality. It just brings to the fore a general feature of a Marshallian economy with imperfect foresight, characterising all factors which are used extensively.[8] For example, it could be stated that imperfectly informed oil owners are unable to bargain the real price of oil when participating in the oil market.

Keynes' first observation

Let me now turn to Keynes' first observation, which Keynes found less fundamental than the second. He describes it as follows:

> A fall in real wages due to a rise in prices, with money-wages unaltered, does not, as a rule cause the supply of available labour on offer at the current wage to fall, below the amount actually employed prior to the rise of prices.
>
> (Keynes 1936: 12)

The main comment to be made about Keynes' observation is that it provides no causal explanation of involuntary unemployment but a mere test for its existence. As Keynes' money wage–real wage paraphernalia is now considered as invalid, his claim can be recast with no damage as pertaining to a fall in the money wage. Keynes had in mind a real-world observation, but again he was too prone to jump back and forth from the real-world to the fictitious universe of theory. My own reasoning refers exclusively to the latter. Look at a given market-day result, at the very instant when the market has come to a close and trading has not started yet. Assume that for some reason, an outside regulatory agency steps in at this very moment and impedes the occurrence of trading. Starting to play the auctioneer's role, it announces a new price, lower than the previously prevailing one, and gathers agents' new trade proposals. The normal result, presuming that the market has adjusted to its market equilibrium – which is the right presumption to be made because it would not have closed otherwise – is that disequilibrium will ensue. That is, the quantity supplied will decrease, the quantity demanded increase, and excess demand will emerge. Were trade to occur under these conditions and a short side-rule adopted, the quantity traded would be lower than before the agency's intervention. To have the contrary result, the market under discussion must have been in a state of market non-clearing before, in which case this intervention would have corrected the previous state of imbalance, and the quantity traded would in effect increase. Thus, whenever such an experiment results in an increase rather than a decrease in trade, it can be concluded that market rationing was existing beforehand. This is the import of Keynes' observation.

In section IV Chapter 2 of *The General Theory* Keynes gives the following definition of involuntary unemployment:

> My definition is therefore as follows: *Men are involuntarily unemployed if, in the event of a small rise in the price of wage-goods relatively to the money-wage, both the aggregate supply of labour willing to work for the current money-wage and the aggregate demand for it at that wage would be greater than the existing volume of employment* ... It follows from this definition that the equality of the real wage to the marginal disutility of employment proposed by the second postulate, realistically interpreted, corresponds to the absence of 'involuntary unemployment'.
>
> (Keynes 1936: 15; his emphasis)[9]

This definition is hardly different from Keynes' first observation. Hence it should similarly be interpreted as an existence test rather than as a definition, *strictu sensu* Leijonhufvud (1968: 94). For the latter purpose the statement that the reservation wage principle is breached suffices. Thus, I would have inverted Keynes' sentence order. I would have begun with writing the last sentence of the above quotation, which he presented as a result of the definition, and call its converse the proper definition of involuntary unemployment while ending up with introducing his formal definition as an existence test.

Workers' resistance to a cut in nominal wages

Keynes stated that any unemployment due to workers resistance to a wage must be characterised as voluntary. He also admitted that workers' resistance to a cut in nominal wage was a recurrent real-world occurrence. The nominal/real wage wedge provided him with a way out from this corner. The refusal of a decrease in nominal wage, which he explained in terms of agents' preoccupation with relative wages, posed no threat for his argument, he declared, as long as it went along with workers' disposition to accept a decrease in real wage coming along through a different route – that is, whenever the price level increased alongside an unchanged nominal wage. 'Whilst workers will usually resist a reduction of money-wages, it is not their practice to withdraw their labour whenever there is a rise in the price of wage-goods' (Keynes 1936: 9).[10]

There are several reasons explaining why Keynes' argument cannot prevail. First, it runs counter to my above claim that any labour market rationing must be a matter of the malfunctioning of the labour market with the nominal wage functioning as the adjustment variable. Second, the standpoint taken by Keynes here is hard to reconcile with his second observation, suggesting that workers are ready to take a lower nominal wage yet are unable to transform any decreased nominal wage into a decreased real wage. Third, one wonders what 'workers' resistance to a cut in nominal wage' exactly means? It is an odd expression in reference to economic theory, because, in any standard account of the working of markets, agents' choice bears on a price/quantity mix, rather than on the price alone. If refusing 'a cut in nominal wage' is simply tantamount to a refusal to trade the same quantity of labour for a lower wage, it is hardly subversive – it just expresses the upwards sloping of the supply of labour curve. We find here in a nascent way a mistaken interpretation of the rigidity concept that will be encountered again and again in the subsequent literature. While rigidity should characterise the functioning of the labour market, it is often mistakenly represented as a trait of the supply of labour. Market rationing must be attached to the former and not to the latter.[11]

In sum, Keynes' observation on workers' resistance to a cut in money wage serves only the purpose of discarding an objection that should not have been surfaced to begin with. Be this what it may, Keynes decides to adopt the assumption of a rigid nominal wage. In section II of Chapter 3, he notes:

> In this summary we shall assume that the money-wage and other factors costs are constant per unit of labour employed. But this simplification, with which we shall dispense later, is introduced solely to facilitate the exposition.
>
> (Keynes 1936: 27)

Contrary to what this quotation suggests, this assumption of constancy is not limited to Keynes' summary of his view. He keeps it until Chapter 19. However, Keynes claims that its removal at the latter juncture will hardly imperil the demonstration made earlier. As to the meaning of constancy, I take it as meaning that the nominal wage is considered fixed. Yet, at which level? It would be nice for Keynes' enterprise to have it fixed at the level insuring market clearing, since wages could then be definitively exempted from being the cause of market rationing. But the possibility that the wage is fixed at a superior level cannot be excluded, in which case it is hard to avoid the conclusion that it indeed plays a causal role.

The effective-demand deficiency explanation of involuntary unemployment

From involuntary unemployment to effective-demand deficiency: the claim of equivalence

As it has often been noticed, a breach of continuity exists between Chapter 2 and Chapter 3 of *The General Theory*. In the former, the existence of involuntary unemployment is attached to some malfunctioning of the labour market, summarised in Keynes' second observation. In the latter, the labour market takes the back seat and another explanatory line is taken, involuntary unemployment now being viewed as the result of a deficiency in effective-demand.

To Keynes, effective-demand designates the intersection between the aggregate supply and the aggregate demand functions. This intersection, he argues, can occur at different employment levels, full employment being only one of them (1936: 25). Effective-demand deficiency arises whenever the level of employment needed to produce the amount of output corresponding to the matching of aggregate demand and supply in the goods market falls short of full employment.[12] It can be overcome (and employment increased) by autonomous increases in aggregate demand.

> It follows, therefore, that, given what we shall call the community's propensity to consume, the equilibrium level of employment, *i.e.* the level at which there is no inducements to employers as a whole either to expand or to contract employment, will depend on the amount of current investment ... Thus, given the propensity to consume and the rate of new investment, there will be only one level of employment consistent with equilibrium ... There is no reason for expecting it to be equal to full employment.
>
> (Keynes 1936: 27–28)

Keynes seems to claim that his theory is able to demonstrate a case where only one market, namely the labour market, features rationing. What he calls the 'equilibrium level of employment' to all intents and purposes describes the equilibrium in the goods markets. He goes on to state the possibility that no state of full employment may correspond to the goods market equilibrium. If lack of full employment is understood as equivalent to involuntary unemployment in its reservation wage definition, one may conclude that the labour market features market non-clearing. Nothing is stated about the bonds and the money market. They can thus be considered in balance.[13]

Attention ought to be given at this juncture to Keynes' use of the full employment notion. In Chapter 2, it is posited in contradistinction to involuntary unemployment. In other words, it corresponds to my 'full employment equals market clearing' definition. However, in Chapter 3, Keynes gives another definition of full employment, which, he claims, is selfsame to the first. Here, full employment is seen as the point where demand expansion has no longer any quantitative effects (at a given wage). So understood, full employment is lacking whenever there is a gap between the maximum and the effective level of employment. This is my 'full employment equals maximum employment' definition. In Keynes' words:

> In the previous chapter we have given a definition of full employment in terms of the behaviour of labour. *An alternative, though equivalent,* criterion is that at which we have now arrived, namely a situation in which aggregate employment is inelastic in response to an increase in the effective demand for its output.
>
> (Keynes 1936: 26; my emphasis)

This quotation suggests that involuntary unemployment and effective demand deficiency are selfsame. There could be no involuntary unemployment without effective demand deficiency and vice versa. They constitute the same occurrence, approached from two distinct angles. Let me call this the 'claim of equivalence'.

Although Keynes does not voice this claim explicitly, its presence is evidenced by the narrative thread of *The General Theory*. Keynes regularly skips between the themes of involuntary unemployment and demand deficiency, as if they were twins. In Chapter 2, Keynes devotes five sections to the subject of involuntary unemployment before, quite abruptly, broaching aggregate demand in his criticism of Say's Law in section VI. Eventually, the two threads are brought together in section VII, in which the equivalence of involuntary unemployment and effective-demand deficiency is proclaimed.[14] Afterwards, i.e. from Chapter 3 onwards, the involuntary unemployment theme gradually fades away whereas the twin notions of lack of full employment and effective-demand deficiency come to the fore.[15] In the subsequent chapters, involuntary unemployment intervenes only incidentally (1936: 274, 284, 289) and then just as the corollary of the claim made about effective demand.

At first sign, the claim of equivalence looks plausible enough. Obviously, involuntary unemployment is a case of non-maximum employment. Moreover, no reason for thinking that demand activation could fail to remedy it seems to exist. Hence, falling back on Keynes' test of the existence of involuntary unemployment discussed earlier, one is easily tempted to assess the existence of effective demand deficiency through an experiment of the style 'the proof of the pudding is in the eating': if the employment level can be increased exogenously, involuntary unemployment must have been existing beforehand.

At Keynes' time, the validity of the claim of equivalence was an open question. At present, however, this is no longer true. With hindsight, it is clear that it is wanting. It is invalidated as soon as it proves possible to demonstrate cases of involuntary unemployment unaccompanied by a deficiency in effective-demand, or the inverse. This is precisely what modern Keynesian theory has been witness to. As will be seen, in those models which have succeeded in demonstrating involuntary unemployment – e.g. efficiency wage models – demand deficiency is conspicuous by its absence, whereas, on the contrary, models exist that feature a demand deficiency result without involuntary unemployment, such as coordination failure models. Thus, contrary to what Keynes assumed, involuntary unemployment and demand-deficiency do not fall and stand together and do not logically involve each other.

The widespread acceptance of the effective demand-deficiency explanation

Before entering the task of examining whether Keynes succeeded in demonstrating his claim that involuntary unemployment was caused by a deficiency in effective demand, I want to document its widespread acceptance. A great many Keynesian economists seem to have believed that this claim is indeed the centre piece of *The General Theory*, and, moreover, that Keynes succeeded in demonstrating it. The following quotations, spanning forty years of commentaries and ranged in chronological order, illustrate:

> Classical economics, in Keynes' view, assumes that the marginal disutility of labour is equal to the real wage. Against this postulate, Keynes contends that involuntary unemployment generally prevails, a condition associated with an excess of the real wage over the marginal disutility of labour. *Involuntary unemployment prevails when demand is deficient.*
>
> (Harris 1947: 551–552; my emphasis)

> Whenever unemployment could be reduced by expansion of aggregate demand, Keynes regarded it as involuntary.
>
> (Tobin 1972: 3)

> Keynesian involuntary unemployment is defined, of course, as the situation in which unemployed workers are willing to accept employment at currently prevailing real wages (or slightly lower wages) *or* as the situation in which employment can be increased by increasing effective demand with an unchanged level of real wages.
>
> (Negishi 1979: 27; my emphasis)

On this view, the Keynes characterisation of involuntary unemployment is to be regarded as a test for the existence of deficient aggregate demand, and is inseparably and simultaneously linked both to the theory of effective demand and the determination of the level of employment and output and to the policy of demand management.

(Hines 1980: 145)

His [Keynes] 'involuntary' unemployment is the result of *effective demand failures.*

(Leijonhufvud 1983: 195–196)

In a Keynesian world, on the other hand, involuntary unemployment is due to an insufficiency or lack of effective demand.

(Davidson 1984: 364)

In chapter 2, and throughout *The General Theory*, Keynes stressed that the tools of traditional theory need not be rejected completely, but just one axiom: That axiom is the second classical postulate. The revolution in economics was complicated by the fact that the offending axiom was enunciated differently in different theories. While the second postulate was the form dominant when Keynes wrote, he argued that the equality of demand and supply price for output as a whole at all levels of output expressed as Say's law was formally equivalent. He thus found it necessary to provide a separate argument for each of the two forms of the axiom: one on the level of individual decision in the labour market (in chapter 2), and another (in chapter 3) in terms of aggregate supply and demand price for output as a whole. Since Keynes considered the most general expression of the axiom as the absence of involuntary unemployment, he also had to provide two definitions of involuntary unemployment, one for the 'classical' labour market version and another for the aggregate Say's law version of the axiom.

(Kregel 1987: 135)

The main argument of *The General Theory*, namely, that it is income that adjusts to bring savings and investment into equality and persistent involuntary unemployment occurs through the lack of effective demand.

(McCombie 1987–1988: 205)

Whether or not unemployment is to any great extent involuntary has enormous implications for policy. If it is, if there is 'system

> failure', an increase in aggregate demand is called for; but if not, if there is simply labour market failure, the remedy lies in adjustment of prices and wages.
>
> (Collard 1990: 334)

> Keynes used the term [involuntary unemployment] intentionally to take the blame for mass unemployment away from labour – organised or not – and on to the economic system itself.
>
> (Corry 1996: 21)

Keynes' argumentation

I now turn to Keynes' Chapter 3 argumentation as to involuntary unemployment being caused by a deficiency in effective demand. As argued by Clower (1989), Keynes' reasoning is less original than it appears at first sight. His discussion of aggregate demand and supply for output is actually a mere extrapolation of Marshall's short-period equilibrium analysis of individual markets.

The point I shall try to make can be summarised as follows. A contrast can be drawn between 'effective demand *à la* Marshall' and 'effective demand *à la* Keynes'. The former states that variations in the aggregate demand for goods generate variations in the employment level, from one market clearing position to another. For example, a decrease in aggregate demand results in a lower level of employment. However, as explained in Chapter 2, no unemployment phenomenon ensues, the counterpart of the decrease in employment being an increase in leisure. 'Effective demand *à la* Keynes' claims that involuntary unemployment results from a deficiency in aggregate demand. Any decrease in aggregate demand has the joint effect of decreasing the employment level and of creating (if full employment was prevailing before) or increasing unemployment. Here, the converse of employment is unemployment. I will claim that 'effective demand *à la* Keynes' is wanting on two grounds: first, the only rationale that it can receive is nominal wage rigidity, and, second, it rests on a confusion between two definitions of full employment.

Let me begin by pondering upon Marshall's discussion of short-period equilibrium in Book V, Chapter 5 of the *Principles*, where his concern is the firms' supply behaviour in the final goods markets. This is a partial equilibrium analysis, yet it comprises an element of interdependency, as firms decide jointly about the supply of outputs and the demand for factors. When they establish their supply curve (their marginal cost function) they need to make a conjecture about the cost of their input, associated with varying levels of demand for it. As stated by Marshall, 'a cloth manufacturer would need to calculate the expenses of producing all the different things required for making clothes with reference to the amounts of each of them that would be wanted' (1920: 364). In this chapter, Marshall goes to some length to explain the factors which may intervene in this calculation. Although he does not state this explicitly, what he describes is the experiment through which firms construct the whereabouts of the determination of equilibrium in the different inputs markets which are of concern to them. Therefore one must conclude that the wage rate (to limit myself to this input) which firms will embody in the mental construction of their supply function is a market-clearing value. Put differently, expected market-clearing values in inputs markets is part of the formation of market clearing in the goods markets. Again, we need to fall back on the assumption of perfect information. Marshall's main concern is the logical existence of equilibrium. Yet it is also implicitly assumed that the logically existing equilibrium may become effective (that is, be achieved rather than just being a centre of gravitation).[16] Reflecting on how such an equilibrium may be attained and discarding the auctioneer hypothesis, the only conceivable procedure is to assume that firms are able to conjecture rightly the outcomes of the different markets they are participating in and pre-compute equilibrium values. In short, they must be omniscient. Before the starting of the economy, they must have calculated the equilibrium values in every market having bearing on their own decisions. In other words, the determination of normal equilibrium in a given branch, as illustrated in Frisch's graphs (1950: 501), first occurs as a thought-experiment in the minds of firms' managers to become implemented as an objective observable market experiment only later.

Keynes' reasoning in Chapter 3 of *The General Theory* does not depart from Marshall on the matter of perfect information.[17] When reading the first pages of this chapter against the background of my account of Marshallian theory, it turns out that the formation of effective demand is accounted for along the same line as the formation of the representative firm's equilibrium values. It occurs firstly in entrepreneurs' minds as the result of a thought-experiment on markets outcomes. They forge conjectures about the aggregate supply price and the aggregate demand price functions and derive effective demand as their intersection. This exercise, it should be noticed, bears on the whole economy as well as the part played by each firm within it. As in Marshall, no problem of realisation is evoked. In other words, it is implicitly assumed that these conjectured values actually unfold once the economy starts to operate. All this could not happen if entrepreneurs did not have perfect information.

The departure of 'effective demand *à la* Keynes' from 'effective demand *à la* Marshall' must thus lie elsewhere. The only possibility that I see is as follows. The element of the Marshallian reasoning which Keynes abandons is the view that the aggregate supply price function incorporates inputs' costs at their market clearing values, at least as far as labour is concerned. Instead, it is assumed that the wage rate upon which firms elaborate their supply price function is a 'false' (i.e. market non-clearing) wage. Therefore, all the claims to the contrary notwithstanding, it is difficult to escape the view that Keynes' effective demand reasoning is based on a fixed wage hypothesis. Effective demand becomes a specific Keynesian argument only because it is no longer true that firms make the thought experiment leading to their production decision by conjecturing a market clearing wage rate.

Turning to the issue of what might explain why firms enter a false wage in their decision-making process, two lines are conceivable yet neither is convincing. Either, the story could run, firms are mistaken or unable to make the right conjecture. Their estimate of what will be market clearing wage will turn out to be mistaken, hence their incorporating of a false wage in their cost function. This scenario may explain bad surprises, e.g. that firms' profitability will be different from what it would otherwise have been, but not why market clearing will fail to arise once the labour market is opened. In the alternative story, firms are aware when making their thought experiments that something will happen in the labour market preventing market clearing. They take this into account when devising their supply price function. As a result, they are conscious of incorporating a false (i.e. non-market-clearing) wage in their cost function. But the reason for unemployment then lies in the labour market, and no fuss should be made about effective demand as being its cause. Unemployment logically precedes the determination of effective demand rather than the other way round. Moreover, no explanation of the false wage is available, except the exogenous wage floor type of explanation. Nor can the argument of sluggishness adjustment be brought in here, for in Chapter 3 of *The General Theory* Keynes implicitly assumes that the adjustments towards market outcomes occur instantaneously.

Conceptual pitfalls

Keynes was probably right in believing that the remedy for mass unemployment as it existed at the time he was writing lay in increasing aggregate demand – and thus that its cause was an aggregate demand deficiency. However, one can be right factually while being unable to make a robust theoretical demonstration.[18] It is also possible that some argumentation may look strong at a given juncture while turning out to be weak with hindsight. In Keynes' case, conceptual looseness played a decisive role in hiding the flaws in his reasoning.

When Keynes' argumentation is gauged against the background of my taxonomy of forms of underemployment (Figure 1.1), it surfaces that he implicitly assumed that the underemployment category was empty or, in other words, that involuntary unemployment was the only possible form of 'underemployment in general'. Hence a lack of realisation that unemployment and underemployment were two different occurrences. The same lack of perception of the need for sharper concepts surfaces when pondering Keynes' use of the full employment concept. As stated above, in Chapter 2 of *The General Theory*, full employment designates market clearing, and is an endogenous variable varying with market conditions, while in Chapter 3, it refers to maximum employment, and is a single, exogenous magnitude. Keynes claims that these definitions are equivalent, without realising that they belong to two different conceptual worlds, standard Marshallian value theory, on the one hand, and a more descriptive account of the economy, on the other. If the discussion takes place in the first of these frameworks, the equivalence assumed by Keynes is verified only if agents decide for no leisure, clearly an exceptional outcome. Otherwise, full employment in the market clearing sense will co-exist with lack of full employment in the maximum employment sense.

Consider 'effective demand à la Marshall'. Starting from a situation of equilibrium, assume a decrease in demand in the market for bonds going along with an increase in the demand for goods. An increase in the demand for labour ensues. A new equilibrium is established in the labour market, with an augmented quantity of labour traded. Obviously, the level of employment has increased, yet semantics are treacherous here. The change that is occurring is a shift from a given market-clearing level of employment to another higher one or, looking at the matter against the market-clearing definition of full employment, a shift from one level of full employment to another. Since the unemployment category is absent, it makes no sense to state that unemployment has decreased. It is leisure that has decreased.

When the same evolution is interpreted against the less-than-maximum definition of full employment, a different interpretation surfaces. It will now be asserted that a progress towards full employment has taken place, with the connotation that social welfare has improved. The concepts of employment and unemployment being viewed as converse, it will be claimed that unemployment has decreased.

However, no good reason exists for using this second definition in a Marshallian theoretical context. Why should an absolute increase in labour market participation have an automatic welfare implication? We are so impregnated with the common-sense view, that more employment is better than less, that we tend spontaneously to transpose it in the world of theory, where it is definitely false.

Finally, look at Keynes' own pinpointing of the essence of *The General Theory* in his Chapter 3 proposition (5):

> (5) The volume of employment in equilibrium depends on (i) the aggregate supply function (ii) the propensity to consume and (iii) the volume of investment. This is the essence of the General theory of Employment
>
> (Keynes 1936: 29)

Keynes argues that this proposition stands in sharp contrast to the classical position. Yet, this is untrue. On the contrary, it is perfectly congruent with it. To bring about the contrast between Keynes' and the classical viewpoints, proposition (5), which pertains to employment, must be transformed into a proposition pertaining to unemployment. Consider then proposition (5') where I have substituted 'unemployment' for 'employment':

> (5') The volume of unemployment in equilibrium depends on (i) the aggregate supply function (ii) the propensity to consume and (iii) the volume of investment. This is the essence of The General Theory of Employment.

Here, the contrast between the two viewpoints comes out. To Keynes, this proposition is equivalent to proposition (5), since to him employment and unemployment are opposite concepts. Things are different from a Marshallian value theory point of view. While proposition (5) is acceptable, this is not so as far as proposition (5') is concerned since the unemployment category is absent from this theory, at least from its kind of canonical model to which Keynes was confronted

Any salvation from chapter 19?

Involuntary unemployment can be studied either as an end-state or as a process occurrence.[19] Hitherto I have been concerned with the first type of analysis. As seen, while Keynes' initial motivation was to explain involuntary unemployment, in terms of a flaw in the self-adjustment capacity of the economic system, he ended up with presenting a claim as to the logical existence of involuntary unemployment at one point in time. However, in Chapter 19 of *The General Theory* he returned to the topic of adjustment. The relationship of this chapter to the rest of the book needs therefore to be examined.

To Patinkin, an eminent Keynes scholar, it constitutes its apex:

> Thus chapter 19 is the climax of *The General Theory*. And it is clear from it that, the many contentions to the contrary notwithstanding, the analysis of this book does not depend on the assumption of absolutely rigid money wages.
>
> (Patinkin 1987: 28)

Patinkin follows suit with Keynes in believing that the distinct task performed in Chapter 19 consists of removing the wage rigidity assumption provisionally made before, thereby prompting the rebuttal of the indictment that 'it all hinges on wage rigidity'.[20] This is the last point I need to examine in this chapter – is it true that Chapter 19 allows to get rid of the wage rigidity assumption? My answer is 'no'.

To begin, note that Keynes' procedure is rather odd. If wage rigidity is not the cause of involuntary unemployment, why introduce it to begin with? Be that as it may, the issue addressed by Keynes in Chapter 13 is 'what effect on unemployment will a reduction in money-wage have' (1936: 260)? Unfortunately, this question is awkward. A twofold clarification is needed. First, we need to make clear whether this question relates to the real world or the fictitious theoretical universe. As to the issue of whether decreases in nominal wages have succeeded to decrease mass unemployment during the Great Depression, many economists will concur that it did not. Yet the aim is to generate this result in the theoretical model. Second, it is necessary to separate adjustment as pertaining to a given trade round ('point in time adjustment') and adjustment across trade rounds ('intertemporal adjustment'). As discussed in Chapter 4, when speaking of adjustment it must always be made clear which of these is of concern. Whenever the discussion bears on involuntary unemployment, a flaw in the first of these two adjustment processes must be demonstrated. The rigidity factor in need of removal in order to substantiate Keynes' and Patinkin's claim pertains to adjustment at a given trade round. That is, the alleged removal must consist in a replacement of the 'point-in-time rigidity' by 'point-in-time flexibility' assumption.

Against this background, it turns out that a trick is at work in Chapter 19. Outward claims to the contrary notwithstanding, Keynes' reasoning is not concerned with this replacement. His discussion bears on a different topic, namely intertemporal rigidity, point-in-time rigidity remaining assumed. His subject-matter is variations over time of the exogenous rigid wage. In other words, the question addressed is: will employment increase if an exogenous wage-floor decreases from t_0 to t_1, an exogenously rigid wage being assumed at each trading round, yet possibly a different one at each round? Keynes may well have clinched a point when stating that intertemporally rigid wages might be more desirable than intertemporally flexible wages, yet this is hardly tantamount to removing the point-in-time rigidity assumption, his alleged claim. So, contrary to what Keynes, Patinkin and the others have claimed, the rigid wage assumption is not abandoned for what concerns the trade round analysis, the proper context in which the arising of involuntary unemployment must be dealt with.

Part III

IS-LM MACROECONOMICS

7

HICKS' 'MR KEYNES AND THE "CLASSICS"'

When Keynes' *The General Theory* was published in 1936, the first reaction it elicited was perplexity. Pigou, who admittedly had reasons to be prejudiced against it, found it 'barely intelligible' ([1936] 1983: 21). Yet he was scarcely alone in holding this opinion. Many of those who were to become fully-fledged Keynesians shared it. As noted by Young:

> The majority of 'working economists', however, seemingly did not know how to digest Keynes' new book and remained in a state of what may be called 'conceptual inertia' until the IS-LM approach was expounded in the papers of Harrod, Hicks and Meade.
>
> (Young 1987: 17)[1]

However, this state of affairs changed swiftly. In their contributions to the 1936 Oxford meeting of the Econometric Society, the three authors mentioned by Young were able to recast Keynes' arcane and kaleidoscopic piece into a tractable model. Although their contributions were quite similar, Hicks' piece, which became his 'Mr. Keynes and the "Classics"' article (1967), has by far been the most influential. It constitutes the subject-matter of the present chapter.

Hicks' appraisal of Keynes' *The General Theory*

Before discussing Hicks' article, it is worth pausing on his recounting of Keynes' theoretical project. There is plenty of material in this respect, for 'Hicks has gone on reviewing it [*The General Theory*] throughout his career' (Coddington 1983: 66).[2] Hicks' appraisal can be acccunted for under three headings. First, he interprets Keynes' argumentation as geared towards criticising the old 'neutrality of money' viewpoint. Second, he praises Keynes for having generated a shift in the main subject-matter of economic analysis, from the long-period to the short-period perspective. Third, to him, one of the central features of Keynes' theory is its fixed wage assumption.

Keynesian theory as monetary theory

In Hicks' eyes, there was no doubt that *The General Theory* belonged to the field of monetary theory. According to him, the main issue it addressed was whether changes in money supply could have real effects and, thus, whether monetary expansion could be used as a policy tool when the economy was slack. Keynes' real target when attacking classical theory, Hicks claimed, was not Pigou but a much older viewpoint to be traced back to the writings of authors such as Hume, Ricardo and Mills. Their bone of contention was the effectiveness of money supply activation. As Hicks puts it:

> Would it be true, even in a world where all borrowing and lending was long-term borrowing and lending (for that, at the least, must be assumed if we are to have no credit), that interest rates will be entirely determined by saving and investment, that the level of activity will be solely determined by the real factors in the system, and that the quantity of money will solely act upon the level of prices?
>
> (Hicks 1967: 159)[3]

A short-period analysis

To Hicks, the main originality and interest of Keynes' theory lay in the shift it operated about the time period under which the analysis was led, from the long-period – the classical economists' main subject of interest – to the short-period. This assertion is one of the most recurrent themes in Hicks' commentary of Keynes. Here is how he put it in what was to be his last book, *A Market Theory of Money* (1989):

> What is the essence of the 'Keynesian revolution'? I would now state it in the following way. It had been a common assumption of his predecessors that the economy under study had a 'long-term equilibrium' about which it would indeed fluctuate, but the fluctuations would be limited and by wise policy their amplitude could be damped. I think I can show that this was in their day a defensible position; in the days of the old Gold Standard it made a good deal of sense. By the time Keynes was writing his *The General Theory* that standard was being abandoned; by his 'persuasions' he had contributed to its abandonment, especially the abandonment of its old authority; he had no desire to go back to anything so rigid, so firm. Thus the only equilibrium which survives in his theory is a short-term equilibrium with no sheet-anchor to hold it.
>
> (Hicks 1989: 1)

Hicks did not object to the classical conclusions as far as the long-period was concerned. In his words, 'the classical *long-period* theory is *full-equilibrium* theory' (1967: 149). Rather, his point was that a change in emphasis from the long- to the short-period was overdue. According to him, classicists admitted that 'in the short period, while the supply of money is increasing, the increase can be a real stimulus' (1967: 161). Yet they refrained from uttering their views on this, for fear of the consequences it might have.[4]

By characterising the Keynesian revolution in such a way Hicks allowed himself to claim co-paternity over it. Keynes and himself, he recounted, started independently to build up a short-period model. Before the publication of *The General Theory*, Hicks had already begun to tread the short-period route in his 'Equilibrium and the Cycle' paper (1982). His temporary equilibrium model, a central piece of his *Value and Capital*, stemmed from the same purpose.[5] His very interest in Keynes' theory sprung from the discovery of this similarity. Hence, his suggestion that the revolution towards short-term period analysis was a case of 'parallel discovery'.

Keynes as the initiator of the fixprice method

In *Value and Capital*, Hicks stated that 'Mr Keynes goes as far as to make the rigidity of wage-rates the corner-stone of his system' (1946: 266). More generally, he praised Keynes for having laid the groundwork for a shift from the flexible to the fixed price method.

> To pass from the one pure method to the other is quite a revolution. It is a revolution that is mixed up with the so-called 'Keynesian revolution'; but I do not think that it is accurate to identify them ... There is, however, no question that, as between his two works, Keynes was moving in the direction of the new method; and it is in the work of his interpreters and successors that the clearest examples of the new method are to be found.
>
> (Hicks 1965: 77)

Terms of truce

Finally, as to Hicks' broader appraisal of the role played by *The General Theory* in the development of economics, a contrasting picture emerges. On the one hand, he concurred with Harrod and Meade in believing that Keynes' claim as to its revolutionary character – in particular, his claim that his theory was more general than the classical – did not stand up to scrutiny. However, such a belittling of Keynes' theoretical contribution went along with an opposed judgement concerning policy. Leijonhufvud and Coddington aptly captured the whereabouts of the ensuing terms of truce:

> The terms of the truce between the two factions comprise two broad propositions: (1) the model which Keynes had the gall to call his 'general theory' is but a special case of the Classical theory, obtained by imposing certain restrictive assumptions on the latter; and (2) the Keynesian 'special case' while theoretically trivial, is nonetheless important because it so happens that it is better guide in the real world than is the general (equilibrium) theory. Together the two propositions make a compromise that both parties can accept, since one of them has been more interested in having the policy-relevance of its view recognised, and the other in carrying off the theoretical honours.
>
> (Leijonhufvud 1968: 7)

> His [Hicks'] verdict is that Keynes was misguided in presenting his own theory as an attack on and as in conflict with the 'classical' system . . . Keynes' method of associating, on the one hand, national income determination with saving and investment decisions and, on the other hand, interest rate determination with asset-holding decisions (as between money and bonds), is demonstrated by Hicks to be not a new theory but rather an alternative analytical procedure which, properly handled, leads to the same results as the previously-adopted procedure . . . [But] despite his analytical verdict's being so uncompromisingly harsh, Hicks's attitude to *The General Theory* was (after some early wavering) unambiguously favourable: indeed he regarded himself as a convert to Keynes's way of thinking.
>
> (Coddington 1983: 89–90)

'Mr Keynes and the "Classics"' revisited[6]

The labour market

A common feature of Keynes' *The General Theory* and Hicks' 'Mr Keynes and the "Classics"' is their lack of giving an explicit account of how the labour market functions and which state it happens to end up in. The only information Hicks' reader gets is that the per capita rate of money-wages is given and that the employment level can be increased both in the classical and in the Keynesian model (1967: 128).

The reason why Hicks offered no explicit vindication for the assumption of money-wage rigidity is that he had no qualms about it. To him, its adoption was simply a matter of empirical relevance. As stated in his subsequent article, 'The "Classics" Again':

> This [price rigidity] is a special assumption that can be incorporated into any theory. Certainly the economists of the past cannot be criticised for not making it, for in their time it would quite clearly, not have been true. This is not a matter on which there can be any theoretical contradiction; it is the kind of change in the exposition of the theory which we ought to be making, all the time, in response to changing facts.
>
> (Hicks 1967: 147)

However, as far as the cause of wage rigidity was concerned, Hicks had an explanation of his own, emphasising the role of fairness – a theme which runs through all his writings. Here is how he put it in *Value and Capital*:

> The most important class of prices subject to such rigidities are wage-rates . . . They are particularly likely to be affected by ethical notions, since the wage-contract is very much a personal contract, and will only proceed smoothly if it is regarded as 'fair' by both parties.
>
> (Hicks 1946: 265)[7]

The fairness argument was an original and quite modern line of explanation for wage rigidity, making Hicks a forerunner of Bewley's views (Bewley 1999). However, when it came to depicting its impact on the working of the labour market, Hicks' reasoning was anything but original In fact, he did not conceive it differently from an exogenous wage floor, with its effect of disallowing the realisation of market clearing. As a result, the Hicksian labour market can be assessed as featuring involuntary unemployment in the reservation wage definition caused by the existence of an exogenous wage floor. Oddly enough, Hicks did not mention the term 'involuntary unemployment' in his article. Nor is it to be found in Hicks' other works.[8]

If facts of life can be considered as compelling, both the classical and the Keynesian models should adopt the same assumption about wages in as far as they purport to enlighten the same real-world phenomena. Hence Hicks' similarity of treatment of the labour market in the two models – the fixed money wage is present in both cases. Had he believed that the labour market was different in the Keynesian and the classical model, he would have stated it. Thus, unlike the case of modern textbook IS-LM models, it cannot be asserted that market clearing is present in the classical model whilst lacking in the Keynesian model. In both of them the labour market is supposed to be in the same state of market non-clearing.

A comparative exercise in policy effectiveness

At stake in Hicks' article is a confrontation of what the classicists and Keynes had to say on the subject of the short-period real effects of monetary expansion in a context of money-wage rigidity. In short, Hicks' endeavours to make a comparative exercise in policy effectiveness. His particular interest is to study the effects of an increase in the inducement to invest in employment and the interest rate respectively. Table 7.1 below summarises the argument.

The solution for what concerns the classical model is straightforward. The effect of monetary expansion is to increase the level of employment and to decrease the interest rate.[9] An increase in the inducement to invest (i.e. a rightward movement of the schedule of the marginal efficiency of capital) always elicits a rise in the interest rate. However, its effect on the employment level depends on the elasticity of supply in the two sectors of production considered.[10]

Let me now turn to the Keynesian outcome. According to Hicks, a preliminary distinction ought to be drawn between Keynes' 'special' and 'general' models. In the former it is assumed that the demand for money function has a single argument, the interest rate. This amounts to considering that the only motive for demanding money is speculative or, conversely, that no transaction demand for money is present. Hicks believed that such a position, on top of being untenable, was not to be found in *The General Theory*. He rather regarded Keynes as taking a more orthodox line by also considering the transaction motive in addition to the speculative motive. This is Keynes' 'general' model. Only the latter, Hicks argued, should be taken into account when drawing a contrast with classical theory. To compound the matter, two versions of the Keynesian general model ought to be distinguished, each depending on how liquidity preference is characterised, the 'standard Keynesian general model' and the 'liquidity trap Keynesian general model'.[11] In the latter, the liquidity preference schedule has a section where the demand for money exhibits perfect-interest elasticity.

Looking at the 'standard Keynesian general model', both an increase in the supply of money and an increase in the inducement to invest will have the same effects as in the classical model. As far as the second of these factors is concerned, Hicks observes that:

> A rise in the marginal-efficiency-of-capital schedule must raise the curve IS; and, therefore, although it will raise income and employment, it will also raise the rate of interest.
>
> (Hicks 1967: 135)

Table 7.1 A comparative exercise in policy effectiveness. A summary of the argument

	Exogenous increase in money supply		*Exogenous increase in the inducement to invest*	
	Effect on employment	*Effect on the interest rate*	*Effect on employment*	*Effect on the interest rate*
1 The classical model	$N_1 > N_0$	$r_1 < r_0$	$N_1 \gtreqqless N_0$	$r_1 > r_0$
2 The Keynesian general model				
2.1 The 'standard Keynesian general model'	$N_1 > N_0$	$r_1 < r_0$	$N_1 > N_0$	$r_1 > r_0$
2.2 The 'liquidity trap Keynesian general model'				
2.2.1 The IS curve intersects the LL curve on its horizontal section	$N_1 = N_0$	$r_1 = r_0$	$N_1 > N_0$	$r_1 = r_0$
2.2.2 The IS curve intersects the LL curve on its upwards-sloping section	$N_1 > N_0$	$r_1 < r_0$	$N_1 > N_0$	$r_1 > r_0$
2.2.3 The IS curve intersects the LL curve on its vertical section	$N_1 > N_0$	$r_1 < r_0$	$N_1 = N_0$	$r_1 > r_0$

Note
N_0, r_0 (N_1, r_1) are the magnitudes prevailing before (after) the exogenous increase in the independent variable.

Thus, no basic difference between the two models exists. The only difference is in the reasoning procedure.[12] However, this conclusion should be amended as soon as the liquidity trap assumption is made, the case where the LM curve has an horizontal section.[13] A specifically Keynesian outcome can now arise, hinging on where the initial intersection between the IS and the LM curves is located. Consider first the case where the IS curve intersects with the LM curve on its horizontal section. Here, a rise in the money supply affects neither the interest rate nor employment since only the positively-sloped section of the LM curve will shift to the right, whereas its horizontal section will remain unchanged. In contrast, an increase in the inducement to invest, eliciting a rightwards move of the IS curve, boosts employment without changing the interest rate. Next, consider the case where the IS curve intersects with the LM curve on its upwards sloping section. Here, an expansion either of the money supply or of the inducement to invest will increase employment. But these factors will exert an asymmetric effect on the interest rate: monetary expansion results in a decreased interest rate whereas a shift in the IS curve raises it. Finally, consider the case where the IS curve intersects with the LM curve on its vertical section. The result of monetary expansion is the same as in the earlier case, whereas the change in the inducement to invest has no impact on employment but does increase the interest rate.

In sum, the Keynesian model is fully at odds with the classical model only when the liquidity trap assumption is made and when it is furthermore assumed that the intersection between the IS and LM curves lies on the horizontal section of the latter. Then, but only then, is the Keynesian system 'completely out of touch with the classical world' (1967: 136), as it displays both a stumbling-block to the traditional monetary recommendation (the liquidity trap) and an alternative remedy (acting upon IS through fiscal policy). In this case, the classical and the Keynesian models exhibit differences in policy effectiveness. The Keynesian model is characterised by the inefficiency of monetary policy, contrary to what is possible in the classical model.

Concluding remarks

When Hicks' model is gauged against Keynes' programme, the following result comes out. As far as involuntary unemployment is concerned, the first thing to be noted is that this term is absent from Hicks' article. However, this does not mean that the occurrence it usually designates – a market rationing phenomenon underpinned by a breaching of the reservation wage principle – is absent. I have claimed that the contrary is true. Involuntary unemployment in the reservation wage sense is present in Hicks' model, the result of the existence of a false wage. In Hicks' model the latter is postulated, probably because his main interest is in the policy issue. But hints of what may explain it are to be found in *Value and Capital*. In particular, he stresses an interesting aspect, the fairness element. However, failing to perceive that it requires a theoretical demonstration of its own, to all intents and purposes he assimilates its impact with that of an exogenous wage floor.

Hicks' approach thus differs from that of Keynes by the fact that he admits without qualms that nominal wage rigidity is the cause of unemployment. As he feels no need to look for its explanation in some systemic flaw, no reference is made to effective-demand deficiency.

Another interesting conclusion bears on the relationship between Hicks' model and subsequent IS-LM models. Here, it turns out that the lineage between Hicks' model and subsequent IS-LM is less direct than usually believed. First, in Hicks' account, involuntary unemployment exists both in the classical and the Keynesian model. This is no longer true in the textbook account of IS-LM, where only the Keynesian model is supposed to exhibit involuntary unemployment. Second, in Hicks' article, monetary expansion has real effects in the classical model, whereas this is not necessarily the case in the Keynesian model. In contrast, in the textbook account the inefficiency of monetary expansion is the hallmark of the classical model, the opposite being true for the Keynesian model.[14]

Therefore, the standard view about the supposedly direct relationship between Hicks' own model and the IS-LM model as it was to stand in macroeconomics textbooks must be challenged. The transition from Keynes' economics to Keynesian economics is actually a two-step process, of which Hicks' models constitutes the first stage. Its second stage concerns the shift from Hicks' use of the IS-LM framework to its modern understanding. It will be seen in the next chapter that Modigliani's article, 'Liquidity Preference and the Theory of Interest and Money' (1944) played the decisive role in this transformation. It is Modigliani's and not Hicks' version that underlies the standard models.

8

IS-LM *À LA* MODIGLIANI

In Hicks' account the specificity of the Keynesian model hinges on the liquidity trap argument. No difference between the Keynesian and the classical model would remain were this argument proven to be weak or flawed. Now, this is precisely what happened with the emergence of the 'real-balance effect', put forward by Pigou (1943).[1] Eventually, the only bequest from the Keynesian revolution was a rudimentary pragmatic general equilibrium model, the IS-LM apparatus, devoid of any specific Keynesian trait. Clearly, Keynesians were in need of finding a new way of contrasting the Keynesian and the classical models.

Modigliani's explanation of involuntary unemployment

Modigliani's role (Modigliani 1944) in the unfolding of the debate was both destructive and constructive. From the former viewpoint he argued for the dismissal of liquidity preference – to him, it was just a curiosity. From the latter, he put forward a new account of the contrast between the classical and the Keynesian models. In sharp contrast to Hicks, Modigliani's claim was that the Keynesian model was characterised less by a lack of investment than by a maladjustment between the quantity of money and the money-wage, the latter being too high relative to the quantity of money.

> It is usually considered as one of the most important achievements of the Keynesian theory that it explains the consistency of economic equilibrium with the presence of involuntary unemployment. It is, however, not sufficiently recognised that, except as a limiting case to be considered later, this result is due entirely to the assumption of 'rigid wages' and not to the Keynesian liquidity preference. . . . The monetary conditions are sufficient to determine money income and under fixed wages and technical conditions, to each money income there corresponds a definite equilibrium level of employment. This equilibrium level does not tend to coincide with full employment except by mere chance,

> since there is no economic mechanism that insures this coincidence. There may be unemployment in the sense that more people would be willing to work at the current real wage rate than actually employed; but in a free capitalist economy production is guided by prices and not by desires and since the money wage rate is rigid, this desire fails to be translated into an economic stimulus.
>
> (Modigliani 1944: 66)

According to Modigliani, the distinctive feature of Keynes' theory is that it contains a particular supply of labour: it has a perfectly elastic section up to a kink from which it becomes upwards sloping.[2] The employment level corresponding to the kink is called 'full employment'.[3] And, 'unless there is "full employment", the wage rate is not really a variable of the system but a datum, a result of "history" or of "economic policy" or of both' (Modigliani 1944: 47). Whenever the demand for labour intersects the supply schedule on its horizontal section, involuntary unemployment supposedly exists.

The contrast between Hicks' and Modigliani's approaches can now easily be drawn. It is synthesised in Table 8.1 below. As seen, Hicks' classical model is characterised, first, by the existence of a false wage and its ensuing lack of market clearing and, second, by the effectiveness of monetary expansion in increasing employment, on the other. Modigliani's Keynesian model takes up these two traits, which, in contrast, are absent from the classical model. The latter refers to a new configuration, characterised by wage flexibility and labour market clearing on the one hand, and ineffectiveness of monetary policy on the other. Modigliani's recasting of the classical/Keynesian divide will become the accepted view, dethroning Hicks' initial contrast.

An assessment

In Modigliani's model, the existence of involuntary unemployment exclusively depends upon the particularity of the labour supply schedule, i.e. its incorporating a horizontal section. At first, this interpretation may look appealing, if only because it echoes Keynes' remarks on the sociological factors giving the labour market its specificity. However, upon scrutiny, it turns out to be flawed. Two objections can be levelled against it. First, no involuntary unemployment in the reservation wage sense is present. This result surfaces as soon as the choice-theoretical foundation of the inverse-L-shaped labour supply is made explicit. The case at hand is underemployment, and even worse, efficient underemployment. Second, attributing a special shape to the labour supply is an incorrect way of capturing wage rigidity.

Table 8.1 IS-LM '*à la* Hicks' and IS-LM '*à la* Modigliani'

	The labour market		*The money market*		*Policy effectiveness*	
	The classical model	*The Keynesian model*	*The classical model*	*The Keynesian model*	*The classical model*	*The Keynesian model*
Hicks	fixed money wage resulting in involuntary unemployment	fixed money wage resulting in involuntary unemployment	normally shaped liquidity preference curve	'liquidity trap'	monetary expansion increases employment	monetary expansion may fail to have real effects
Modigliani	market clearing	particular supply of labour function possibly resulting in underemployment	normally shaped liquidity preference curve	the existence of the liquidity trap is possible but not necessary	monetary expansion has no effects on employment	monetary expansion increases employment

The choice-theoretical foundation of the inverse-L labour supply

First of all, a discrepancy exists between Modigliani's model, or more precisely its labour supply component, and his meta-theoretical commentary about it. He states that the horizontal section of the labour supply schedule expresses a 'datum, a result of "history" or of "economic policy" or both' (1994: 47), which suggests that workers' volition is not involved. This is wrong. A supply function (as well of course as a demand function) expresses agents' optimising trading dispositions, and nothing else. To Modigliani, the supply of labour curve is supposed to express two different realities according to which of its two sections is considered: before the kink it is meant to embody a datum alien to workers' volition while, beyond it, it is supposed to regain its standard status of expressing optimising behaviour. This is an odd and ultimately indefensible account.

Modigliani claims that involuntary unemployment exists whenever the demand for labour intersects with the supply of labour along its horizontal section. Its magnitude is equal to the distance between the kink and the intersection (AB in the upper panel of Figure 8.1). An exogenous increase in the demand for labour can absorb it, assuming additionally that productive capacity is available. Clearly, underemployment of some sort is present. However, when assessing it against the typology put forward in Chapter 2, it turns out that it coincides with my efficient underemployment category, the uninteresting case! Involuntary unemployment in the reservation wage sense is absent, and so is involuntary unemployment in the dominated underemployment sense.

Reaching the highest possible employment level – i.e. going up to the kink – would give agents no higher utility when compared to the other employment levels belonging to the horizontal section of the supply schedule. When the choice-theoretical foundation underlying the inverse-L supply curve is reconstructed, consumption and leisure turn out to be perfect substitutes. The agent's indifference 'curves' are linear. Except when the expected real wage is equal to the absolute value of the slope of the indifference lines, such cases usually result in corner solutions (cf. the lower panel of Figure 8.1). This exception is exactly what happens at the wage magnitude corresponding to the horizontal section of the supply curve all levels of employment are indifferent to him at this wage. Hence, any increase in employment along the horizontal section does not affect utility. In the quotation given above, Modigliani states that 'more people would be willing to work at the current real wage rate than actually employed'. His model does not verify this statement – its representative worker is indifferent towards working either more or less at the existing wage.

What explains the fact that Modigliani's mistake has passed unseen, with only few exceptions?[4] The main reason probably lies in a lack of

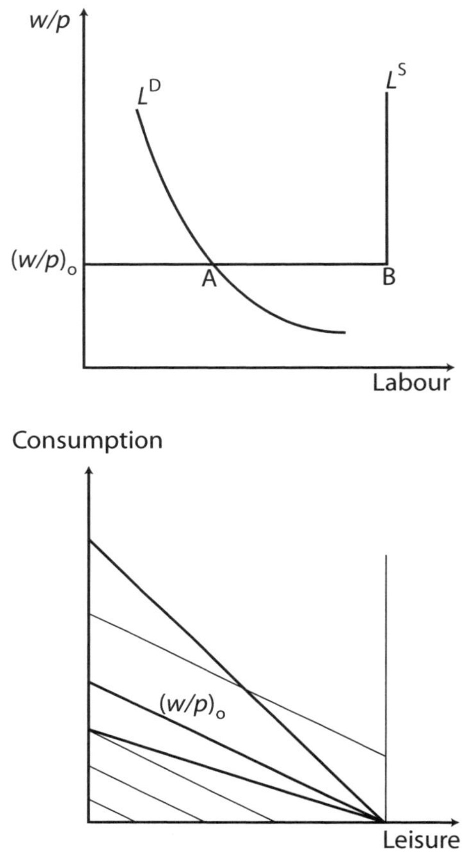

Figure 8.1 The inverse-L supply of labour and its choice-theoretical foundation.

reflection on the meaning of the involuntary unemployment and full employment concepts. Moreover, the labour supply curve *à la* Modigliani hides a twofold pitfall. First, as stated, the maximum level of employment gives the agent the same utility as less than maximum employment levels. Thus, it deserves no prominence. Obviously, looking at standard IS-LM models that have adopted Modigliani's viewpoint (cf. Chapter 9), this principle is hardly respected. On the contrary, it is erroneously taken for granted that more employment is always better. For all its possible truth with respect to real-world economies, this proposition cannot be transposed to the theoretical universe. In the second place, whenever a standard upwards sloping labour supply is assumed, a growth in employment at the same wage level is normally inconceivable, except if rationing is present. Hence, any demonstration that employment can increase without a decrease in wage would indicate the existence of rationing. But a small step is then needed to extend this 'proof of the pudding is in its eating' argument to the case of a Modigliani-type supply of labour. Yet what is valid for the standard labour supply is not so for Modigliani's. Apropos the latter, a change in employment along the horizontal section of labour supply amounts only to passing from one full employment point (in the market clearing sense) to another.

Can wage rigidity be expressed in a specially-shaped supply curve?

Modigliani's claim that involuntary unemployment is due to the special shape of the labour supply is flawed in a second way because it rests on a semantic confusion between rigidity as a feature of the supply function and rigidity as characterising the functioning of the market. At stake here is the meaning of the wage rigidity notion, a point already discussed in Chapter 4. That this notion plays a central role in Modigliani's reasoning is obvious. What escaped his attention is that the type of rigidity he should be concerned with must affect the working of the market, i.e. be an impediment to the formation of the market equilibrium, rather than being a characteristic of either supply or demand. The supply function may be such that it can be called rigid – in that it comprises an infinitely elastic section, as in Modigliani – yet rigidity so understood causes no market rationing. The fact that one of the two blades of the scissors has a special shape does not prevent their intersection. To put the matter in Patinkin's terminology, referred to in Chapter 2, rigidity needs to be grasped as a market experiment rather than as an individual experiment. Rigidity viewed as an individual experiment means that a given agent does not change his or her optimal quantity choice across different prices. Rigidity viewed as a market-experiment means that an impediment to price variations is present. Modigliani's mistake is to have failed to perceive this distinction and to have believed that labour market rigidity could be equated with a labour supply curve of a special shape.[5]

Concluding remarks

Modigliani's model departs from Keynes' programme on three scores. First, involuntary unemployment in the reservation wage sense is absent. Second, he evidently parts company with Keynes' programme for what concerns the aim of discharging wage rigidity from playing any role in the existence unemployment. Finally, consider the policy dimension. True, increasing money supply will result in a higher employment level. However, such an increase in employment cannot be really viewed as a remedy, since there is no failure to remedy!

9

LANGE, LEONTIEF, TOBIN, KLEIN AND HANSEN

My aim in this chapter is to complete my previous analysis by examining how involuntary unemployment is accounted for in the works of other outstanding first-generation interpreters of Keynes.[1]

Lange

Oskar Lange's conception powerfully illustrates how little unanimity on the meaning of the involuntary unemployment existed in the post-war period. At the beginning of his Cowles Commission monograph, *Price Flexibility and Employment* (1944), Lange devotes a lengthy footnote to the subject of involuntary unemployment:

> Underemployment, having been defined by us as excess supply of a factor production, implies thus the existence of excess demand somewhere else in the economy. This treatment of underemployment differs from the 'involuntary unemployment' as defined by Lord Keynes. 'Involuntary unemployment' is not an excess supply of labour but an *equilibrium position* obtained by intersection of a demand and a supply curve, the supply of labour curve, however, being infinitely elastic over a wide range with respect to money wages, the point of intersection being to the left of the region where elasticity of supply of labour with respect to money wages becomes finite. Thus 'involuntary unemployment' in the Keynesian sense, does not imply excess demand for cash balances, or for other goods, or for both. Demand and supply for cash balances as well as for all other goods are supposed to be in equilibrium in the Keynesian theory. The difference is shown in the adjoining diagram [see below Figure 9.1]. *D* is the demand curve and *S* is the supply curve of the factor. In our treatment 'underemployment' consist in the excess supply *AB* (*PQ*), while Lord Keynes considers the line *CQS* as the supply curve, *P* as an equilibrium point and *PQ* (= *AB*) as involuntary unemployment.
>
> (Lange 1944: 6)

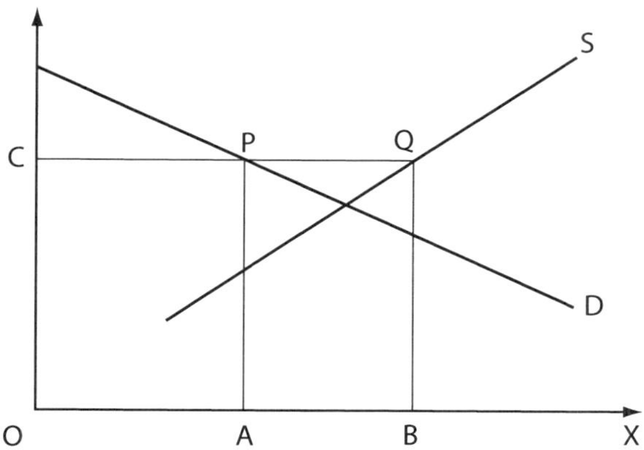

Figure 9.1 Underemployment and involuntary unemployment according to Lange.

Figure 9.1, drawn from Lange (1944: 6), illustrates.

In contrast to most of the authors studied, Lange is aware of the divide between underemployment and involuntary unemployment yet he defines them very differently to the way I have. While it is hard to see which textual evidence from *The General Theory* may support his definitional stance, its underlying rationale can be reconstructed as follows. As seen in Chapter 6, Keynes claimed that involuntary unemployment was an equilibrium outcome. He envisaged it as a result where a single market, the labour market, featured disequilibrium while market clearing was prevailing in the other ones. To Lange, this was an inconceivable result as it violated Walras' Law. Thus, he felt that either the labour market mismatch or the idea that involuntary unemployment was an equilibrium phenomenon needed to be foregone. He chose to dispose with the former and keep the latter.

Leontief

Like most, if not all, of his contemporaries, Wassily Leontief was convinced of the real-world existence of involuntary unemployment. If the latter had no place in theoretical models, the model was at fault or, more precisely, its premises were:

> The orthodox theory proves that involuntary unemployment cannot exist, but we know that it actually does exist. Since the formal logic of the orthodox proof is essentially correct, the fault must be sought in its choice of the basic empirical premises.
>
> (Leontief 1947 242)

His own solution was hardly original, as it amounted to assuming the existence of an outside mandatory wage floor. In his contribution to the Seymour Harris volume (1947), he claimed that this was the only plausible reading of Keynes' theory.[2] Apparently, he had no qualms about the fact that Keynes' views thereby ceased to be different from those of classical economists. Nor was he interested in textual exegesis, contenting himself in this respect with a vague reference to the spirit of *The General Theory*:

> Much more in keeping with the spirit of *The General Theory* is an interpretation which ascribes the monetary bias of the Keynesian supply curve of labour to the influence of some outside factor, that is, factors clearly distinguishable from the preference system of the workers. A minimum wage offers a good example of such an outside factor.
>
> (Leontief 1947: 236)

As a result, the normal functioning of the labour market is disturbed, at least in so far as the market clearing nominal wage is lower than the wage floor. Figure 9.2, drawn from Leontief (1947: 236), illustrates. Whenever the equilibrium wage is below the wage floor, the labour supply schedule (S_1) becomes ineffective over some section of its domain and labour transactions are fixed by the intersection of labour demand and the horizontal line amounting to the wage floor (at point *B*).

Leontief suggests that the wage floor idea should be understood in a broad sense, covering the idea that wages are historically determined. By this, he seems to mean that, as soon as a given money wage has been granted, it becomes impossible to reduce it for some sociological or hysteresis-type reason.[3] As a result, at each new point in time, the earlier

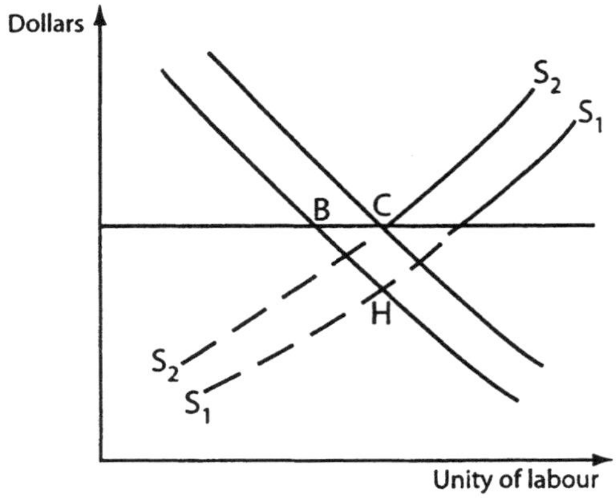

Figure 9.2 Leontief's wage floor.

money wage acts as the wage floor. This means that any necessary decrease in nominal wage, as in an economic depression, will be impeded.

Leontief departs from Modigliani by emphasising the existence of an outside factor impeding the attainment of market equilibrium instead of the shape of labour supply.[4] However, he follows Modigliani as far as policy is concerned by endorsing monetary policy.[5] Start from a situation in which involuntary unemployment exists as the result of the wage floor and assume a general rise of all prices whilst keeping the wage floor unchanged. Both the monetary demand and supply curve shift upwards. The eventual result will be a decrease or an elimination of involuntary unemployment (point *C* in Figure 9.2). Further inflation would make the supply of labour effective again. Note that such a policy would not work if the floor was conceived of in real terms.

In sum, Leontief's views come close to Modigliani's, except for his substituting an exogenously fixed wage to Modigliani's inverse-L labour supply. This represents some progress – contrary to the special labour supply schedule, the wage floor can cause involuntary unemployment in the reservation wage sense, albeit in a trivial and contrived way.

Tobin

At the time, economists did not object as they do at present against the view that workers supplied their labour services against the consideration of the nominal rather than the real wage. Such behaviour was interpreted as money illusion, yet the latter was considered an empirically plausible assumption.[6] James Tobin, then a Harvard Junior Fellow, was one of the defenders of this line of thinking. In one of his first articles, also published in the Harris *New Economics* (1947) volume, he admitted that involuntary unemployment could not exist without workers' irrationality and money illusion.

> Clearly one of Keynes basic assumptions – Leontief calls it *the* fundamental assumption – is that 'money illusion' occurs in the labour supply function. Labour does attach importance to the money wage rate *per se*, and more labour will be supplied at the same real wage the higher the money wage. This assertion concerning the behaviour of wage-earners is indispensable to Keynes in establishing the existence of involuntary unemployment.
>
> (Tobin 1947: 580)

> Wage-earners are the only inhabitants of the Keynesian economy who are so foolish or so smart, as the case may be, as to act under the spell of the 'money illusion'. They are under its spell only in their capacity as suppliers of labour. The 'homogeneity postulate'

> is denied for the labour supply function; for all other demand and supply functions it is retained.
>
> (Tobin 1947: 581–582)

Basically, Tobin's defence of the money illusion hypothesis is that it is a realistic assumption. The four reasons he gives in favour of the 'non-rational' behaviour of labour are all related to presumed 'real-life' behaviour – high money wages is the target pursed by union leaders; wage-earners have obligations fixed in terms of money; labour has inelastic price expectations; and labour may genuinely be ignorant of the course of prices. All of which lead him to conclude that:

> Altogether, the support for Keynes' assumption in regard to the supply of labour is convincing; his denial of the 'homogeneity postulate' for the labour supply function constitutes a belated theoretical recognition of the facts of economic life.
>
> (Tobin 1947: 581)

How times have changed! While Tobin's argumentation raised no eyebrows in 1947, at present almost nobody would dare to endorse it.[7]

While Tobin followed Leontief's 1936 interpretation of *The General Theory*, ironically enough, Leontief dismissed his earlier view in the same Harris volume, observing that the Keynesian supply of labour function, as based on money illusion:

> would include, among the ultimate constituents of an individual's preference varieties, not only the physical quantities of (future and present) commodities and services but also the money prices of at least some of them. In particular the *money* wage rate would be considered as entering directly the worker's utility function: confronted with a choice between two or more situations in both of which his real income and his real effort are the same, but in one of which both the money wage rates (and, consequently, also the prices of consumers' goods) are higher than in the other, he would show a definite preference for the former. A classical *homo economicus* would find neither of the two alternatives to be more attractive than the other.
>
> (Leontief 1947: 235)

Thus, to Leontief in 1947, money illusion represented some odd preference structure characterised with a fetishist attitude towards monetary magnitudes. Furthermore, Leontief claimed that it missed its target:

> It deprives Keynes' unemployment concept of its principal attribute. Why should any given rate of employment or unemploy-

> ment be called 'involuntary', if it is determined through conscious preference for higher money wage as against larger real income?
>
> (Leontief 1947: 236)

Two objections must be levelled against the money illusion argument. First, that agents are to some extent victims of it when it comes to describe the real world is beyond doubt. Yet the same could be stated for example about rationality. The question is whether these real-world refutations of the strict truth of these assumptions warrant their being removed, and the answer to this question is 'no'. Second, Tobin takes it for granted that money illusion is a sufficient condition for market non-clearance, yet this claim receives no justification. The existence of money illusion may well lead to a market result different from the result that would have prevailed without it, yet it would still be a market-clearing result, as illustrated by Friedman's expectations-augmented Phillips Curve model, to be studied in Chapter 13. Why, in other words, would there be a causal link between money illusion and involuntary unemployment?

Klein

Another important interpretation of Keynes' views is to be found in Lawrence Klein's *The Keynesian Revolution* (1948), a book in which Klein tries to distance himself from the standard interpretations according to which either the liquidity trap or rigid money wages as the central contribution of *The General Theory*.[8]

Klein admits that Keynes' theory comprises a twofold change with respect to the supply of labour. First, the real wage is replaced by the nominal wage as the argument of the supply of labour function. Second, a change in shape occurs, with the supply of labour being portrayed as perfectly elastic at the going wage up to the full employment level. In this respect, Klein follows suit with Modigliani. However, to him, these changes cannot be considered as the core of Keynes' contribution. Even without them, he claims, Keynesian theory would keep its basic originality:

> It hardly seems possible that Keynes could say that his major contribution to economic theory was to point out a money illusion on the part of workers as a cause of unemployment.
>
> (Klein 1948: 80–81)

Moreover, if true, workers would be responsible for unemployment, whereas 'Keynes consistently worked against these theories which blamed the depression on labour' (1948: 46). In fact, according to Klein, Keynes' emphasis on wage rigidity as well as his definition of involuntary unemployment testify to his own lack of understanding of the views he was putting forward![9] To him, Keynes central contribution lies instead in his alteration of the savings–investment equation from its classical formulation:

> Keynes' real contribution has been to show that if savings are not offset by legitimate investment outlets, failures to generate a high level of employment will follow. *Even if the Keynesian supply curve of labour is replaced by the classical supply curve in terms of real wages, there remains the problem of making savings pass into investment.*
>
> (Klein 1948: 81; his emphasis)

According to Klein, the non-existence of a general equilibrium is a perfectly plausible outcome. The underlying reason is an inconsistency between the savings and investment schedules, due to their possible interest-inelasticity. As a result, it is quite conceivable that there exists no positive rate of interest allowing for an equality between saving and investment:

> The classical theory of interest assumes that savings decisions and investment decisions both respond sensitively to changes in the rate of interest. But Keynesian economics assumes that both functions are interest-inelastic. Under these conditions there may be no solution ($r>0$) to the above equation [$S=I$] when Y_w [the income level with the wage taken as *numeraire*] is at a full-employment level. In order for the equation to hold something must give way, either r or Y_w. Obviously r cannot give way because it is bounded by the restriction $r>0$. But (Y_w) can change. If Y_w falls we may be able to get savings equal to investment. In fact, Y_w will fall until S and I adjust to an equilibrium.
>
> (Klein 1948: 202–203)

Central to Klein's reasoning is the idea that some 'giving in' process is present. First, income yields, this going along with a decrease in employment. The latter is possible only because of a second 'giving in', that of workers with respect to employers. The underlying reason is that firms and wage-earners are in an asymmetrical power relationship.

> If there is ever any conflict between the demand and supply of labour in the perfectly competitive case like the one we are considering (e.g. one of no trade-union influence), we can be certain that a short demand will dominate a long supply.
>
> (Klein 1948: 203)

The same point was made with an even more radical overtone in Klein's 1947 article where he viewed involuntary unemployment as a manifestation of the capitalist nature of the economy, namely the subordination of workers to capitalists:

> The essence of capitalism is that there exists a definite legal respect for private ownership of the means of production. The owners of the means of production, the capitalists, make all the final decisions with regard to the use of the means of productions. The workers have nothing to say about the amount of employment that will be forthcoming at any point of time. Either the entire concept of the supply curve of labour must be dropped, or the supply curve of labour must become a curve of *virtual* points on which observations do not occur.
>
> (Klein 1947: 116)

The problem with Klein's argumentation is its contrived character. To begin, the savings- and investment-inelasticity assumption looks ad hoc. Moreover, there is a sharp contrast between Klein's claim that Keynes' theory represents a revolution with respect to traditional theory and the fact that the only difference which really matters concerns the shape of two functions. Klein's dismissive remark apropos money illusion could be returned to him: Keynesian theory turns out to be just a special case of classical theory, nothing revolutionary is present.

As far as Klein's 'workers' giving in' argument is concerned, the question is whether there is room for it within neoclassical theory. It amounts to stating that the labour market cannot be conceived of on the same pattern as normal markets, in the way economists envisage them in their theory. As stated in Chapter 4, according to the standard account, all participants in the market, however small, have their say in its final outcome. Any agent might prevent the closure of the market and the starting of trading, were his or her right to optimising trading infringed. This feature, Klein claims, does not hold for the labour market. The latter should rather be viewed as based on a relationship of subordination between capitalists and wage-earners. In particular, the decision to create employment is exclusively bestowed on the former. Such a unilateral decision-making process is much stronger than monopoly power. As the monopolist always chooses a point on the market demand schedule, it does not run counter to the optimising plan of demands. On the contrary, if employers set employment off the labour supply curve, this comes on a collision course with suppliers' optimising behaviour. Thus, we are in a Kaleckian–Marxian, world.[10] As put by Sebastiani:

> They [capitalists] are 'masters of their fate'. As a result – and this is the most relevant political implication – the responsibility of unemployment is thrown back on capitalists.
>
> (Sebastiani 1994: 95)

Hansen

Alvin Hansen is an important figure in the development of Keynesian economics. His *Monetary Theory and Fiscal Policy* (1949) popularised the IS-LM analysis and the income–expenditure interpretation of Keynesian theory. His *Guide to Keynes* (1953) is said to have shaped the thinking of an entire generation of American economists (Lawlor, Darity and Horn 1987: 526). In contrast to Modigliani, Hansen believes that the originality of the Keynesian approach lies in its emphasis in income: 'It is the volume of expenditures, not the quantity of money, to which primary attention must be given' (1949: 83).

Hansen seems to have been unaware of the need to delve into definitional matters. He draws no distinction between involuntary unemployment and underemployment. Actually, when scrutinising the two books mentioned above, involuntary unemployment turns out to be conspicuous by its absence. Instead, the full employment/less-than-full employment divide comes to the forefront. Unfortunately, for its overwhelming presence, the notion of full employment is never defined. Likewise, the working of the labour market is hardly broached. The analysis is concerned with the formation of the IS and LM curves and their intersection. Any income magnitude obtained as the result of the intersection of IS and LM is gauged against an implicit 'employment index', having the full employment as its benchmark. Whenever full employment fails to be reached, 'underemployment equilibrium' is said to exist.

Hansen claims that 'given the wage rate, employment is fairly uniquely determined by the volume of aggregate output' (1949: 119). This statement, encapsulating the gist of Keynes' effective demand theory criticised above, will pervade the Keynesian literature. It is hardly mentioned that it stands in sharp contrast to the canonical microeconomic way of positing wage determination. According to the latter, employment and wage are co-determined. In contrast, Hansen posits that employment and wages are determined separately without giving any justification for this view.

Finally, Hansen claims that Keynes' theory is not dependent upon wage rigidity:

> Some writers have maintained that Keynes's underemployment equilibrium is based on the assumption of wage rigidity. Accordingly, it is held that in this respect there is really no difference between Keynes and the Classicals. The Classicals and the neoclassicals had always held that, given rigid wages, unemployment would result from any falling off in demand. If, however, wage rates were flexible (so they believed) there could be only short-run unemployment, and this would be due to frictions and lags in

> the adjustment process. It is, however, not correct to say that Keynes' analysis of underemployment assumes wage rigidity. Keynes in fact made a thorough analysis of employment assuming the condition of flexible wage rates. He did not regard this assumption as realistic, but he was prepared to make it in order to see whether in fact wage cuts could be an effective remedy for unemployment. But his conclusion is not (as with the Classicals) that under flexible wages the economy must tend toward full employment.
>
> (Hansen 1949: 122)

The crucial sentence in this passage is Hansen's statement that Keynes gave a thorough analysis of underemployment under wage flexibility. Above I have shown that this is not the case. As a result, Hansen's claim turns out to lack any justification.

Concluding remarks

The first generation of Keynesians set themselves the task of clarifying Keynes's somewhat confused ideas at a time where no frontal attack against the validity of the involuntary unemployment notion was on the agenda. Table 9.1 summarises my analysis of the meaning of involuntary unemployment in their writings.

A first conclusion to be drawn from the examination of these attempts is that they present no single explanation. Wage rigidity, money illusion, the liquidity trap, the inconsistency of savings and investment at full employment, the special form of labour supply have all been presented as alternative causes of involuntary unemployment. However, as shown, these factors should not be put on the same footing.

The liquidity trap argument must be disposed with because it explains only the persistence of unemployment, and not its emergence – on top of the fact that it rests on a *curiosum*, the special shape of the LM schedule. Another two of these factors have proved to be wanting, the special shape of the labour supply and money illusion. Even when they are present, no causal link exists between either of them and labour market non-clearing. In other words, they may explain over- or underemployment yet not involuntary unemployment. Moreover, as far as the inverse-L-shaped supply curve is concerned, I have shown that the widely held view, initiated by Modigliani and according to which the shape of the labour supply is a fine way of encapsulating the wage rigidity idea, is wanting. Finally, as far as the remaining two factors are concerned, the inconsistency of savings and investment at full employment, as put forward by Klein, and nominal wage rigidity, as put forward by Leontief, neither is very convincing. For what concerns Klein's standpoint, it suffers from two flaws. First it is too easy an

Table 9.1 The explanation of involuntary unemployment according to the first generation of Keynesian economists

Author	*Definition of involuntary unemployment*	*Emphasis on effective demand deficiency or on the working of the labour market*	*Insufficiencies*
Hicks (1973)	Reservation wage definition	No mention of effective-demand deficiency; no explicit mentioning of the labour market, yet it is implicitly assumed to feature market non-clearing	His model is concerned with the persistence of involuntary unemployment rather than with its emergence The distinctness of the Keynesian model is fragile
Modigliani (1944)	Less than maximum employment	Emphasis on the labour market, characterised with a special supply of labour	Wage rigidity takes the form of a particularly shaped labour supply curve
Lange (1944)	Less than maximum employment		Inversion of underemployment and involuntary unemployment
Leontief (1947)	Reservation wage definition	Emphasis on the labour market	The exogenous nominal wage floor is a contrived and unoriginal explanation of involuntary unemployment
Tobin (1947)	Unspecified	Emphasis on the labour market and money illusion perspective	Why would workers lack rationality just in the labour market? Money illusion is not a necessary condition for market non-clearing
Klein (1947, 1948)	Reservation wage definition	Emphasis on the labour market	His argument rests on (i) the special elasticities of the investment and savings function and (ii) his 'giving in' assumption
Hansen (1949, 1953)	Less than maximum employment	Effective-demand deficiency perspective	Confusion between underemployment and involuntary unemployment Vernacular understanding of full employment

escape to claim that the general equilibrium solution is non-existing. Second, the 'giving in' explanation is *ad hoc.* Leontief's position is trivial and unoriginal. However, a way out can be conceived of, as hinted at by Leontief himself. It consists of stating that wage rigidity may result from other causes than a genuine mandatory wage floor. For some sociological reason, possibly linked to the specificity of the labour market, nominal wages cannot be trimmed. Therefore the trade round starts with a predetermined wage that acts as a mandatory wage floor without really being one. Hysteresis and staggering contracts models have followed up this insight.

This combination of Leontief and Modigliani is the line that most Keynesian authors have taken. At every trade round the nominal wage is supposedly given. If it happens to be higher than the market-clearing wage, involuntary unemployment ensues. The action to be taken to correct this malfunctioning is for the central bank to increase the money supply.

10

INVOLUNTARY UNEMPLOYMENT IN MACROECONOMIC TEXTBOOKS

The previous chapters have shown that most Keynesian economists of the first generation were unaware of the need for a precise definition of the concept of involuntary unemployment. As a result, they usually failed to draw a distinction between involuntary unemployment and underemployment. They were also prone to understand the notion of full employment in its common-sense, instead of its theoretical, meaning. The aim of this chapter is to verify whether these flaws are also discernible in the macroeconomic textbooks that gradually came to flourish. Being unable to engage in a systematic study of a large number of textbooks, I will content myself with a small sample of them. It consists of Ackley's *Macroeconomic Theory* (1961), Dernburg and McDougall's *Macroeconomics* (1963) and Allen's *Macroeconomic Theory* (1967).

Ackley's *Macroeconomic Theory*

Ackley displays an eclectic position as he is upholding three arguments at the same time, wage rigidity, the liquidity trap, and the inconsistency between the saving and investment schedule at full employment, not counting slow adjustment. According to him, 'we do not have to choose one among these competing views as correct, rejecting the others. They are matter of emphasis, and of degree' (1961: 406).

To Ackley, involuntary unemployment is a case of breaching the reservation wage principle (although he does not use such terminology) or off-the-labour-supply curve trading. Actually, he writes about unemployment *tout court*, without referring to the 'involuntary' modifier. However, the ambiguity as to the meaning of full employment, so often to be found, is absent from his analysis. Full employment is equated to the quantity of labour traded at the market clearing wage.

His analysis of unemployment starts with emphasising the nominal wage rigidity assumption:

> Keynes' treatment assumed the money wage level to be dependent upon institutional and historical forces, subject to some influence also by the state of the economy. Money wages at any point in time are at the level where they are mostly because it is close to where they have recently been. To be sure, they may have recently risen or fallen somewhat in response to institutional pressures, such as minimum wage laws, or through the efforts of trade unions, or public opinion.
>
> (Ackley 1961: 380)

> But at any given time and place the money wage rate level was, more or less, a matter 'autonomously' determined.
>
> (Ackley 1961: 381)

According to Ackley, rigid nominal wages result in the fact that a logically-existing position of general equilibrium will fail to be reached while it would have if wages had been flexible. This position is the exact same as Leontief's. However, while Ackley could have stopped here, he makes a step towards Klein's insight by considering the possibility that the equilibrium result can be logically non-existent even with flexible wages because of the investment schedule's insensitivity to the interest rate. That is, no positive interest rate exists that can equalise saving and investment at full employment. Although he does not use Klein's 'labour giving in' expression, this is what Ackley's argument amounts to. In this new context, 'rigid wages, he claims, are not the cause of unemployment' (1961: 405). Its cause lies rather in the non-existence of a full-employment general equilibrium. Furthermore, under such circumstances, wage rigidity is beneficial because it prevents 'unemployment from creating a painful, largely useless, even bottomless deflation' (1961: 405).

Finally, the adjustment slowness argument is also to be found under Ackley's pen:

> This concept of the money wage level is a very different one from the 'flexible' wage level assumed by Classical writers. If the wage level is truly flexible, it falls continuously and without limit, whenever there is any unemployment, and is stable only if all workers seeking jobs can find them.
>
> (Ackley 1961: 381)

> The flatter the speculative demand schedule (even though it never becomes infinitely elastic), and the steeper the investment schedule (even though it is not vertical), the greater is the necessary fall in wages and prices. So great a fall may be impossible to accomplish in any reasonable period of time. Thus wage flexibility

> may be a theoretical but not a meaningful or practicable solution to unemployment.
>
> (Ackley 1961: 385)

Ackley's flaw here is to fail to make explicit the trade technology assumption underpinning his reasoning. Whenever the 'week' device is adopted, as I advocate, the adjustment towards market clearing operates on the Monday following the shock, whatever the size of the needed adjustment. In this context wages will not start to fall after unemployment has begun contrary to what Ackley suggests. Instead, they will fall before the actual emergence of unemployment, their very fall serving the purpose of preventing it. In contrast, Ackley's view is that a fall in wages may fail to make unemployment disappear. Thus, he takes it for granted that unemployment exists prior to the fall in wages. In other words, the question he awkwardly addresses is that of the adjustment across trade rounds – how can such adjustment correct a labour market rationing result that occurred on a given trade round, due to exogenous rigidity? No explanation as to the trade-round emergence of rationing is provided.

Dernburg and McDougall's *Macroeconomics*

Dernburg and McDougall seem to adhere to the reservation wage definition, stating that 'when more workers are willing to work at the going real wage rate than business is ready to hire, we have involuntary unemployment' (1963: 144). However, they also endorse Modigliani's inverse-L-shaped labour supply curve, defining involuntary unemployment as the distance between the kink in the supply curve and the intersection of supply and demand on the horizontal section of the supply:

> The distance $N^* - N_0$ measures involuntary unemployment – the number of people willing to work at the existing level of real wages that do not find employment.
>
> (Dernburg and McDougall 1963: 149)

Clearly, they are unaware of the contradiction that is involved in bringing these two definitions together. Nor do they feel the need to separate involuntary unemployment in the reservation sense from involuntary unemployment as less-than-maximum employment. Moreover, whether they view involuntary unemployment as an equilibrium or a disequilibrium phenomenon is unfathomable. They begin their chapter by suggesting that it refers to disequilibrium:

> The IS-LM intersection is a position at which the market for goods and services and the money market are simultaneously

> cleared. But the level of production that is implied by this intersection may require the use of less labour than is willing to work at the existing rate of remuneration. In other words, equilibrium in the product and money markets may be accompanied by disequilibrium – specifically, excess supply – in the market for labour services.
>
> (Dernburg and McDougall 1963: 142–143)

Yet a few pages later, they declare that Keynesian theory is about 'underemployment equilibrium' (1963: 155).

Allen's *Macroeconomic Theory*

Chapter 7 of Allen's *Macroeconomic Theory*, entitled 'Keynesian Models', contains two distinct theories, the first bearing on 'equilibrium unemployment', the second on 'disequilibrium unemployment', his own appellations.

His first theory combines money illusion and the inverse-L-shaped labour supply.[1] As discussed, none of them, taken in isolation, can solve the problem. Putting them together brings no improvement.

When Allen is read against the conceptual distinctions drawn in Chapter 2, it becomes clear that his understanding of full employment is wanting. On p. 103, in reference to the classical model, he declares that full employment is realised whenever the demand for labour equals the supply. In contrast, when studying the Keynesian model, his reasoning rests on its less-than-maximum employment definition. Endorsing a labour supply function *à la* Modigliani, he states that full employment is achieved whenever trade takes place on or beyond the kink on the supply (1967: 126). Whenever the demand for labour intersects labour supply on its 'rigid' section, 'unemployment equilibrium', he declares, is prevailing. Clearly, he is enmeshed in a confusion between involuntary unemployment and underemployment. Moreover, like Modigliani, he confuses wage rigidity and a specially shaped labour supply.

This is Allen's theory of unemployment equilibrium. After having expounded it, he goes on to say that there is more to the problem of unemployment and introduces what he calls the disequilibrium unemployment theory. The latter is nothing more than Klein's insight. It can happen, Allen notes, that 'the range of variation of investment (e.g. when investment is interest-inelastic) is so narrow that no r exists' (1967: 130). As in Klein, the way out consists in abandoning one equilibrium condition:

> The way out is to drop an equilibrium condition, to allow for disequilibrium ... We have a choice of which market to take for

> disequilibrium and the obvious selection is the labour market, keeping the demand based on marginal productivity but dropping the supply function as a longer-run concept.
>
> (Allen 1967: 130)

Here, the outcome is involuntary unemployment according to the reservation wage definition with trading taking place off the labour supply curve. But Allen seems to be unaware of the fact that this unemployment concept is not the same as that which he used in his first theory.

Concluding remarks

A first lesson to be drawn from my brief exploration of macroeconomic textbooks is that their authors have evidently followed in the footsteps of the earlier Keynesian authors. They depart little from the works of Keynes' first interpreters. They adopt the same explanations – money illusion, wage rigidity (without any distinction being made between an exogenously fixed wage and a special supply of labour schedule), preference for liquidity and, finally, inconsistency between saving and investment at full employment. They often resort to a combination of them as though they think that one alone is insufficient. They also differ in terms of consistency, because, as seen, not all the factors put forward by the pioneering authors are compatible. Of the three authors analysed, Ackley's account is probably the most consistent one. Therefore its wide recognition seems well deserved.

A second conclusion is that the conceptual framework of these texts remains coarse. The need to draw a distinction between the concepts of unemployment and underemployment is hardly perceived. That the concepts of wage rigidity and the shape of the labour supply curve are unrelated phenomena fails to be perceived. The same is true for the link between money illusion and market non-clearing. The concept of full employment remains undefined, except by Ackley, with the risk of surreptitiously jumping from one to another of its possible definitions.

A third conclusion is that the authors of these textbooks do not insist much on the concept of involuntary unemployment and hardly bother to explicitly define it. Nonetheless, its theoretical legitimacy is taken for granted.

Finally, these authors have in common the will to keep theory closely tied in to facts. In a more critical vein, they make the same mistake as Keynes of not drawing a sufficiently sharp divide between the theoretical universe, necessarily an artificial one, and the 'real world'.

Part IV

RECONSTRUCTING KEYNESIAN ECONOMICS

The disequilibrium approach

11

THE FORERUNNERS

Patinkin, Clower and Leijonhufvud

This chapter and the subsequent one are concerned with the so-called disequilibrium approach. Its starting point is Chapters XIII and XIV of Patinkin's *Money, Interest and Prices* (1965). Patinkin's views received a new impetus in Clower's Keynesian Counter-revolution article (1965) and Leijonhufvud's book *On Keynesian Economics and the Economics of Keynes* (1968). Patinkin and Clower's views were synthesised by Barro and Grossman in their 1971 article and 1976 book. While Barro and Grossman were soon to recant the line they had opened, their work sparked important developments. Benassy, Malinvaud, Drèze, Grandmont, Laroque, Younes, Muellbauer and Portes were amongst the main proponents of the new approach. The latter took off fast yet its success was short-lived, as most of the economists who rallied it gradually shifted their attention to other research themes.[1]

Disequilibrium authors share several common features, which are worth explaining before starting to examine their specific contributions.[2] First, they were all educated as microeconomists – more precisely Walrasian general equilibrium theorists – at a time when the contrast between macroeconomics and microeconomics was still sharp. Therefore they are more sensitive to micro-foundations requirements than standard macroeconomists. While their base camp is Walrasian theory (Walras' *Elements of Pure Economics*) and neo-Walrasian theory (the Arrow-Debreu model), their very aim is to depart from the Walrasian canon by producing a rationing result. Hence the non-Walrasian label attached to their models.[3] Second, they share the same basic insight that the cause of involuntary unemployment ought to be looked for in the phenomenon of wage stickiness. In fact, their justification for its introduction into economic theory rests on the view that it is an important 'fact of life', which cannot be sidestepped. Third, their Keynesianism is mostly a matter of spirit and policy motivation. While they hardly bother to take up Keynes' own insights and concepts, they nonetheless buttress to a 'Keynesian motivation', in that they want to vindicate the view that free competition is insufficient to nurture socially optimal outcomes. As a result, their models are geared towards supporting active state interventions in the market economy.

In this chapter, I examine the views held by the founders of the approach: Patinkin, Clower and Leijonhufvud. The contributions of Barro and Grossman, Drèze, Benassy and Malinvaud will be the subject-matter of the next chapter.

Patinkin's *Money, Interest and Prices*

The overriding aim of Patinkin's celebrated book *Money, Interest and Prices* is to study the integration of monetary and value theory in a general equilibrium framework. To his own testimony, its main contribution concerns the real-balance effect and its implications on monetary theory (1989: XVI). However, he broaches the theme of involuntary unemployment in Chapters XIII and XIV, which were the eventual outcome of a reflection started when writing his doctorate dissertation.[4]

Patinkin took it for granted that the corpus within which his work's integration had to take place was Walrasian theory. However, he was also aware of the difficulty that was involved in making involuntary unemployment acceptable within the Walrasian paradigm. He did not question its non-acceptability as long as the analysis was confined to the domain of the existence of equilibrium (1965: 315). This could have solved the issue for some, but not for Patinkin. The existence of equilibrium route being blocked, he laid claim to what seemed to him the only other alternative – that involuntary unemployment existed as a disequilibrium phenomenon. That is, its existence was limited to the re-equilibration process separating two successive equilibrium positions, its occurrence hinging on the slowness of the adjustment process. Patinkin adamantly defended this claim from his first writings at the end of 1940s until his death in 1995.

> It is within the foregoing framework of dynamic disequilibrium ... that we must study the problem of involuntary unemployment ... The essence of dynamic analysis is involuntariness: its domain consists only of positions *off* the demand or supply curves. Indeed, it is this very departure from these curves, and the resulting striving of individuals to return to the optimum behaviour which they represent, which provides the motive power of the dynamic process itself.
>
> (Patinkin 1965: 323)

Patinkin's theoretical scenario

Patinkin gives no model of involuntary unemployment, in the strict sense of the term. Rather he tells his readers a reasoned story, a sort of theoretical scenario, about its existence. Starting from a state of equilibrium, an increase in the demand for bonds is supposed to have occurred, resulting in a decrease in the demand for commodities. Its effects are studied in two alternative contexts. In the first, the adjustment process in the goods market is supposed to operate quickly. As a result, a new equilibrium is rapidly established. In the second context, the proper domain of involuntary unemployment according to Patinkin, this adjustment process is assumed to occur at a slower pace. The proximate effect of the decrease in demand for goods is that its supply exceeds its demand. Firms' first reaction is to pile up inventories. However, after a while, when inventories become too important, they have no choice but to decrease production. As a result, their demand for labour also diminishes – that is, the 'notional' demand for labour, to use later terminology, ceases to be operative. Trading in the labour market takes place off the supply curve, what is tantamount to involuntary unemployment.

Patinkin insists on the fact that prices are sluggish rather than rigid in his story. To him, the state of involuntary unemployment so created should not be viewed as a position of equilibrium susceptible to perpetuating itself. On the contrary, he thinks that its very existence automatically calls into operation corrective forces, which will ultimately eliminate it, as the decrease in the price of the goods exerts a positive effect on demand through the real-balance effect. So, any instance of involuntary unemployment is transitory. Clearly, this is a significant retreat from Keynes' own standpoint.[5] To Patinkin it is the price to be paid for making involuntary unemployment acceptable within economic theory.

Patinkin's story is lent credibility by its realism. Unfortunately, it does not stand up to scrutiny. The reason for this has to do with the trade organisation dimension. Patinkin's flaw in this respect is to surreptitiously make an arbitrary twist in the trade technology assumption from his microeconomics to his macroeconomics analysis.[6] No involuntary unemployment result ensues without it.

Trade technology in Patinkin's microeconomics and macroeconomics

In Chapter III, Section 3, Patinkin makes it clear that he adopts the tâtonnement or auctioneer assumption, including its recontracting component. 'It is by this continuous groping – *tâtonnement* – that the economy ultimately finds it way to the equilibrium position' (1965: 39). This amounts to assuming a centralised market structure, with the formation of equilibrium proceeding instantaneously. Several passages bear witness to Patinkin's awareness of the fact that disequilibrium states have a virtual rather than real existence, the corollary of offers to trade not being binding.[7] He also treads in Hicks' footsteps by adopting the 'week' device with trading taking place on every Monday (Patinkin 1965: 11).

At this juncture, the only difference between Patinkin's view of the formation of temporary equilibrium and mine relates to time. To him, it is a time-consuming phenomenon. It can work quickly or slowly. In contrast, as claimed above, I think that the duration of formation of equilibrium is of anecdotal importance for the 'week' device. It makes no difference whether Monday's equilibrium is attained quickly or slowly.

One would expect Patinkin to keep the same basic assumptions in the macroeconomics part of his book. After all, to him, macroeconomics is just a pragmatic version of the more complex general equilibrium model. At first sight, this is the case since Patinkin continues to refer to tâtonnement in his Keynesian analysis:

> The very existence of disequilibrium anywhere in the economy automatically calls into operation corrective forces, which ultimately eliminate it. Conversely, once the equilibrium position is reached, the generation of market forces making for further changes ceases. That is the process of *tâtonnement* by which the market successfully gropes its way toward the solution of the system of equations of the preceding section.
>
> (Patinkin 1965: 234)

However, it turns out that the earlier institutional set-up is *de facto* abandoned.

Abandoning the 'no false trading' assumption

Actually, Patinkin already has it all wrong when describing the quick adjustment case, in which, he claims, no involuntary unemployment arises. First, he states that, under the standard adjustment assumption, the economy would 'quickly return to a full employment position at a lower level of wages, prices, and interest' (1965: 318). In other words, to him, involuntary unemployment will fail to arise whenever adjustment forces proceed quickly. However, casting the issue in this way is misleading. As argued above, in a Walrasian economy the formation of prices should be considered as taking place instantaneously. 'Instantaneous' and 'quick' are not the same thing. Second, Patinkin declares on the same page that 'throughout this period of adjustment there will exist a state of excess supply in the commodity market. But due to the assumed shortness of this period, producers will react to their temporary inability to sell by simply permitting their inventories to build up' (1965: 318). For all its descriptive appeal, this assertion hardly fits the Walrasian trade technology. Patinkin takes it for granted that firms' inability to sell is a definite fact, to which they have to react in a specific way, for example by letting their inventories pile up. Yet, this view runs counter to the basic feature of the tâtonnement process that states of excess supply have only a virtual existence. It is true by definition that, if excess supply prevails, sellers are unable to sell all that they want to. Still, the auctioneer's very job is to correct any mismatch. Hence the only thing firms must do is to let him complete his job rather than to take any action themselves. In short, a virtual excess supply cannot be confused with an actual excess supply.

Abolishing the 'no false trading' rule turns out to be a crucial move and one would have expected Patinkin to make it explicit, which he fails to do. Assume, however, that he did. Chapter XIII of *Money, Interest and Prices* could then be described as providing a non-tâtonnement model *avant la lettre*, anticipating the works of authors such as Hahn or Negishi. Nonetheless Patinkin's model would still be flawed, because of its discarding income effects. In the microeconomic part of the book, as well as in its appendix on tâtonnement, Patinkin correctly states that the rationale for the recontracting assumption is to permit that the equilibrium values reached at the end of the adjustment process coincide with those arrived at when studying the logical existence of equilibrium. Introducing false trading prompts the formation of a different allocation. Oddly enough, he loses sight of this point in his involuntary unemployment discussion, and income effects are brushed aside.

To all intents and purposes, in this discussion Patinkin seems to have totally forgotten the 'week' framework he adopted at the beginning of his book. Hence the reader is at a loss to understand which trade technology is underpinning it. Patinkin's intention was probably just to amend the Walrasian trade technology assumption. Consistency would then have dictated that the slow adjustment related to the attainment of equilibrium on a given Monday. Yet Patinkin's story is about 'change in production and long drawn-out modifications' which cannot be viewed as taking place within the Monday time span. Patinkin's Mondays may last for months, if not years! Clearly, the change involved is more important than the mere replacement of quick by slow adjustment in an otherwise unchanged scenario. However, while the 'week' set-up has disappeared, the new trade technology assumption replacing it remains totally unspecified.

Process disequilibrium versus end-state disequilibrium

Patinkin's central claim is not that prices are rigid but that they adjust slowly. In his model involuntary unemployment has only a temporary existence since the real-balance effect prompts forces which will restore equilibrium. He admits, however, that if either the wage rate or the price level is absolutely rigid, 'the system will remain in a state of unemployment disequilibrium' (1965: 328), since the real-balance effect will cease to work. To Patinkin this is only an extraneous consideration. But a semantic twist now crops up. To Patinkin, disequilibrium states exist whenever the end-state of some adjustment process has not yet been reached. However, whenever prices and wages are absolutely rigid, to the effect that the system remains indefinitely in disequilibrium, involuntary unemployment becomes a case of end-state disequilibrium rather than of process disequilibrium. Patinkin seems to have been unaware of this shift in meaning of the disequilibrium concept.

Most subsequent authors, disequilibrium theoreticians of the second generation, have substituted price rigidity for price slugglishness, as will be seen in the next chapter. A change in the meaning of disequilibrium ensues, since it now refers to market non-clearing viewed as an end-state outcome existing after adjustment has come to a close – something quite different from what Patinkin had in mind. At the same time, these authors still mean to defend Patinkin's insight by claiming that the fixprice assumption underpinning their theoretical models is a proxy for real-world sluggish prices. In Tobin's words:

> The 'fixprice' method used in many textbooks was a convenient device for expounding the Keynesian calculus of adjustment of quantities to quantities and to interest rates. It was carried to extreme in modern formal 'disequilibrium theory'. The method is misleading when it conveys the impression that Keynesian economics assumes price rigidity and indeed is defined by that assumption. It is especially misleading if it gives the idea that that such an assumption is necessary. This impression of Keynesian theory, whether the result of caricatures by its enemies or careless exposition by its friends, appears to be a source of the defection of many economists. Consider a spectrum of the degree of nominal price flexibility from complete flexibility at one extreme to complete rigidity at the other. Complete flexibility means instantaneous adjustment, so that prices are always clearing markets, jumping sufficiently to absorb all demand or supply shocks. Complete rigidity means that nominal prices do not change at all during the period of analysis. In between are various speeds of price adjustment, various lengths of time during which markets are not clearing . . . Any degree of stickiness that prevents complete price adjustment at once has the same qualitative implications, and can even be treated by the fixprice method on an 'as if' basis.
>
> (Tobin [1993] 1997: 145)

Tobin's viewpoint cannot be accepted because it falls prey to the criticism made in Chapter 4. Either it is admitted that the week device is the proper time framework to be adopted. In this case the idea of slow adjustment must be discarded at once as far as the formation of market equilibrium is concerned. Or, alternatively, this device is refused but then the issue is as to which alternative trade organisation is proposed. When reading Tobin, one is at a loss to see what it may consist of.

Clower's 'Keynesian Counter-revolution' article

Clower's article 'The Keynesian Counter-revolution' ([1965] 1984) is the second keystone of the disequilibrium approach. Like Patinkin, Clower aims at demonstrating the possibility of involuntary unemployment in the reservation wage sense. Yet adjustment slowness is no longer summoned.

The underlying story is as follows. Households are unable to sell the quantity of labour they wish to trade at the ongoing wage. As a result, their demand on the goods market is smaller than what it would have been otherwise. In other words, the quantity of labour effectively traded replaces the notional quantity of labour in their budget constraint. In Clower's model, the goods markets end up in a state that could be qualified as a 'pseudo equilibrium', where firms' notional supply of goods matches households' effective demand for goods rather than their notional demand. The price and quantity emerging at this pseudo equilibrium differ from the Walrasian magnitudes, and are sub-optimal with respect to them. Walras' Law is violated because only one market, the labour market, features market non-clearance.

Clower's argumentation can be reconstructed in two main alternative ways. According to the first, it is assumed that markets operate sequentially with the factor markets taking place in advance of goods markets. It is moreover assumed that market clearing fails to take place in one of the factors markets, the labour market. No explanation for its occurrence is given.[8] This is the context in which his dual decision hypothesis makes sense. Rather than having the standard choice structure where agents decide on all their trades in one stroke, decisions about the trading of inputs are made first, with decisions about the trading of consumers goods being made second. Note that this first reconstruction hardly fits Walrasian theory, since the latter has no room for a sequential operation of the economy. Moreover, it has the drawback of falling back on the exogenous wage rigidity explanation of rationing.

According to the second reconstruction, Clower's article pursues the aim of amending Walrasian theory. Here, the labour market mismatch 'observed' by households has initially no effective existence, in so far as tâtonnement has not yet come to an end when they are making this observation. Rather, they only conjecture such a mismatch. The particularity of Clower's scenario is that, although prices are flexible, the signalling process that should trigger their change is defective. 'As a result, excess demand may fail to appear anywhere in the economy' ([1965] 1984: 53). The tâtonnement institution is not working as it should, and the false *numéraire* wage underpinning households' observation is not removed by the auctioneer because he fails to notice it. Eventually, what was initially pessimistic conjecture becomes an effective reality.

This second reconstruction is more appealing than the first because it displays the coordination failure idea. Involuntary unemployment turns out to be the result of a defect in signalling, a phenomenon of self-fulfilling predictions locking the economy into inefficient states. Moreover, it has the advantage of having nothing to do with rigidity, as Clower wanted.[9] Yet, the dual decision hypothesis must be abandoned.

To assess its validity, we need to gauge whether the departures from the standard tâtonnement hypothesis introduced by Clower are justifiable. First, it must be assumed that the auctioneer must announce a price for every good except the *numéraire*. This condition raises no problems. If the excess demand for all goods except the *numéraire* is nil, market clearing will also prevail for the *numéraire* good. Second, it must be assumed that labour plays the role of *numéraire*. Thus, in reference to Clower's two-goods example, the auctioneer contents himself with watching the excess demand for the commodity. This is of course a totally *ad hoc* assumption. Although hardly made explicit, it underpins Clower's reasoning. Otherwise the auctioneer would be able to notice the labour market mismatch and react to it. Had the good been used as *numéraire* instead of labour, he would have noticed the excess demand for labour and have changed the price ratio.[10] The third change in assumption is that agents move from a standard to a modified budget constraint, the result of their conjecture about the existence of a labour market mismatch. The question to be raised is how such a conjecture can arise. In a tâtonnement framework, agents have no way of becoming aware of the existence of any mismatch, since they have no knowledge of the economy until equilibrium is obtained. It then turns out that the assumption of their pessimistic conjecture falls from the blue and runs counter to the well-functioning of a tâtonnement economy implies that agents react to the auctioneer's questionnaire on the assumption that no rationing will eventually exist. In other words, the right way to avoid rationing is to have agents expressing their standard budget constraints. Moreover, the assumption that agents might be able to observe a mismatch between supply and demand is odd in a Walrasian universe because agents are supposed to have no knowledge at all of market supply and demand functions.[11]

Thus, the assumptions underpinning Clower's reasoning (at least the last two) prove to be contrived. A possible radical conclusion to be drawn from this observation is that the very stumbling-block impeding the involuntary unemployment result is the tâtonnement hypothesis itself. This is the line that Clower, jointly with Leijonhufvud, was to take afterwards. While his

1965 article can be viewed as a reformist attempt within the Walrasian approach, his later writings manifest a clear recantation of this strategy. Clower and Leijonhufvud ([1975] 1984), Clower (1975] 1984) bring to the fore the incompatibility between the Walrasian approach and Keynes' objectives, while indicting Keynesian economics for its Walrasian drift. In Clower's terms:

> The history of the Keynesian Revolution – more particularly the reasons why it effectively fizzled out – can be fully appreciated, therefore, only by viewing it as an episode within a broader and ultimately more influential series of developments which, for reasons that will soon become evident, I shall refer to as the *neo-Walrasian Revolution* ... Keynes did not view his analysis of the *General Theory* as 'Variations on a Theme of Walras'. How is it possible, then, to maintain that developments set in motion by the publication of the *General Theory* can be fully appreciated only by viewing them as part and parcel of a neo-Walrasian revival?
>
> (Clower [1975] 1984: 189–190)[12]

Positively, Clower and Leijonhufvud's aim was to construct a Marshallian 'general process analysis', proposing a theory of the decentralised economy, which should have the following features:

> (1) lacks a central information-processing and bill-collecting agency; (2) has, instead, middlemen trying to coordinate production and consumption activities in each output market separately; (3) makes the management of stocks of inventories essential to the coordination of these activities; and (4) has the system potentially subject to commercial crises associated with expansions and contractions of the volume of bank and nonbank credit. All this might be J.S. Mill or Alfred Marshall.
>
> (Clower and Leijonhufvud [1975] 1984: 217)

Unfortunately, it proved highly difficult to Clower and Leijonhufvud to develop their views beyond the blueprint stage. To date, the scenario of a decentralised economy with money as a social link, in which private merchants substitute the auctioneer and in which multiple disequilibria could be the norm, has hardly been transformed into a full-fledged theory.

Before leaving Clower, another interpretation of his 1965 article, to be found in Jean Cartelier (1993, 1995) and Carlo Benetti (1998), is worth considering. It pulls Clower's views in a Marxian-Kaleckian direction, thus treading in Klein's footsteps. The dual decision hypothesis is now interpreted as reflecting an asymmetrical power position between firms and workers, with firms taking employment decisions unilaterally. In contrast, workers are in a subordinated, passive position. As a result, the labour market must be viewed as falling outside the scope of the *stricter sense* market category. Of course, a labour market is formally existing in that its basic ingredients, a supply and a demand function, are present. However, the hallmark of the market set-up, namely the existence of a process through which some market result emerges to make demand and supply compatible, is decreed to be absent. This impinges on the scope of Walras' Law. It is now claimed that it bears on all transactions except labour trading. Walras' Law in its standard formulation remains valid for this restricted trade space. However, whenever labour trading is added to it, Clower's claim that its equality sign should be replaced by the ≤ sign is verified as soon firms' employment decisions are such that excess labour supply exists. Hence Clower's claim is rescued.

This radical interpretation has, in its favour that asymmetry in decision-making, in particular when employment decisions are concerned, may well be a central feature of capitalist economies. Nonetheless it can be criticised on several grounds. First, its assumption of a polarised distribution of endowments across agents, with the majority of them having their labour power as their exclusive endowment is very restrictive. Second, wage-dependency is hardly a sufficient condition for arguing that the labour market is not a real market. Third and finally, one may wonder whether it makes sense to import a subordination perspective within the Walrasian system considering that the latter is, in essence, a democratic system functioning on an unanimity rule.

Leijonhufvud's *On Keynesian Economics and the Economics of Keynes*

Leijonhuvfud's name has been evoked in relationship to his attempt to develop general process analysis, in collaboration with Clower. My aim here is to assess his renowned book *On Keynesian Economics and the Economics of Keynes* (1968). Its main claim is encapsulated in its title: according to Leijonhufvud, Keynes' theory is quite distinct from Keynesian economics (1968: 8).[13] To him, Keynesian economics completely misrepresents Keynes' main insights for at least two reasons: its adoption of the wage rigidity assumption and its neglect of the role of money. What is needed is to return to basics; Keynes' *The General Theory*. Moreover, while most of the interpreters of Keynes' book have ended up viewing it as a kaleidoscope, mingling incompatible theoretical claims – a point of view that I share – in contrast, Leijonhufvud is firmly convinced that the different components of *The General Theory* are all pieces of the same jigsaw puzzle.

Disequilibrium à la *Patinkin rather than* à la *Clower*

It is beyond doubt that Clower's views play an important role in Leijonhufvud's reasoning. Nonetheless, his filiation to Patinkin should not be overlooked. What unites them is the central role they give to the adjustment process and its slow character. This feature marks them apart, non only from Clower but also from the other disequilibrium theoreticians, who all hold end-state models.[14]

> The real question is why, in the Keynesian unemployment state, the forces tending to bring the system back to full employment are so weak.
>
> (Leijonhufvud 1969: 22, note 1)

> The subject of his work [Keynes's *The General Theory*] is not 'unemployment equilibrium' but the nature of the macroeconomic process of *adjustment* to a disequilibrating disturbance.
>
> (Leijonhufvud 1968: 50)[15]

However, Leijonhufvud departs from Patinkin on one central point. Patinkin claims that his Keynesian model belongs to the Walrasian research programme, while, as noted, it hardly respects the Walrasian trade technology. Leijonhufvud is more lucid in this respect. To him, Keynesian theory must be anchored in Marshallian theory. Realising that Walrasian theory and the auctioneer hypothesis are part and parcel, he draws the right conclusion that, as soon as this hypothesis is adopted, no room is left for those very features which Keynes wanted to demonstrate. So, the one thing Leijonhufvud is sure of is that the auctioneer figure must be disposed of in order to give Keynes' insights any chance of being vindicated:

> To make the transition from Walras' world to Keynes's world, it is thus sufficient to dispense with the assumed *tâtonnement* mechanism. The removal of the auctioneer simply means that the generation of information needed to co-ordinate economic activities in a large system where decision making is decentralized will take time and will involve economic cost.
>
> (Leijonhufvud 1967: 404)[16]

The claim of a reversal in adjustment speeds

Like Patinkin, Leijonhufvud believes that the assumption of wage rigidity is unnecessary for the involuntary unemployment result. What must be foregone is the instantaneous price-adjustment assumption, and it needs to be replaced by the imperfectly flexible prices and wages assumption. His original contribution is to have put this assumption in a broader context, by stating that Keynes' reversed Marshall's ranking of the price and output adjustment speeds.

> In the Keynesian macrosystem the Marshallian ranking of price- and quantity-adjustment speeds is reversed: In the shortest period flow quantities are freely variable, but one or more prices are given, and the admissible range of variations for the rest of prices is thereby limited. The 'revolutionary' element in the *The General Theory* can perhaps not be stated in simpler terms.
>
> (Leijonhufvud 1968: 52)

> In Marshall, roughly speaking, prices are assumed to adjust 'very fast' relative to the speed of output adjustments ... In Keynes, rates of output (and employment) are the first to 'give' when a disturbance occurs, and prices (especially wages) lag behind.
>
> (Leijonhufvud 1969: 29)[17]

This claim of a reversal in the ranking of speeds of adjustment has been very popular. However, I am not inclined towards it. To begin with, I disagree with Leijonhufvud's statement that the ranking of speeds of adjustment is a significant characterisation of Marshallian value theory. As a result, the idea that Keynes reverted it loses its impact.

Is there a ranking of speeds of adjustment in Marshallian theory?

As stated above, the most consistent account of the time structure underpinning the Marshallian theory of value is to consider that trading takes place within trade rounds that are separated by time intervals during which no trade is occurring. Therefore Hicks' 'week' device, where trading takes place every Monday while the execution of contracts takes place during the rest of the week, fits Marshall's conception. Let me use it as my frame of reference. Figure 11.1, freely drawn from Marshall's *Principles* (1920: 346, Figure 19), illustrates.

The formation of market-day equilibrium (the matching of market-day supply and demand) is assumed to occur instantaneously. Consider for the sake of simplicity the market for a perishable good and let the discussion bear on short-period normal equilibrium. The latter, corresponding to *A*, is supposedly existing at t_0. Assume an increase in normal demand (*ND*) occurring at t_1 and prompting the representative firm to change its variable capital while leaving its fixed capital unchanged. Assume, moreover, a time-to-build element – say, that changing production requires a two-week interval. That is, any decision to increase output made at t_1 will become effective only at t_3. At t_1 and t_2 the market is in disequilibrium (point B), with market-day equilibrium differing from normal equilibrium. In other words, at t_1 and t_2 the market supply (*MS*) is different from what it should ideally be, i.e. q_3. This is so at t_1 because this is the trade round where the change in normal demand occurs, and at t_2 because of the time-to-build factor. Nonetheless market-day supply and demand

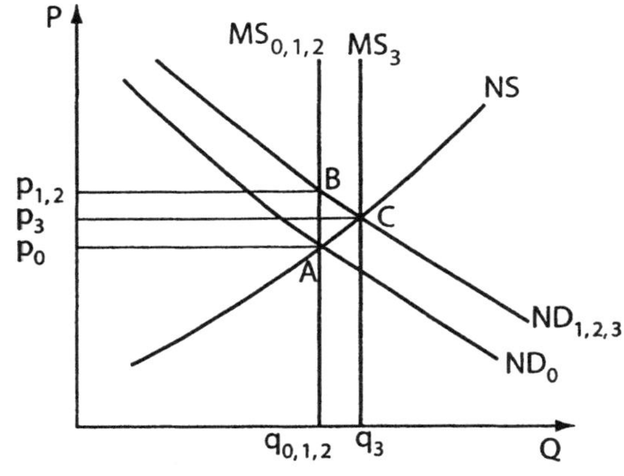

Figure 11.1 The impact of an increase in normal demand in Marshallian value theory.

match. The new normal equilibrium (*C*) arises at t_3, when market-day values and normal values coincide. The same reasoning can of course be made for the case of a decrease in demand.

Does this standard characterisation of Marshallian theory exhibit any difference in speed of adjustment? A new market-day equilibrium price is established every Monday, while it takes several weeks to finalise a change in output. Hence it can be stated that prices adjust faster than output. However, there is nothing profound in this assertion. Recall that a correct understanding of Marshallian theory requires a strict distinction being drawn between market and normal equilibrium and, concomitantly, between market supply and demand and normal supply and demand. Leijonhufvud's claim is that the formation of the equilibrium price arises faster than that of the equilibrium output (one week versus three weeks). However, the snag is that this formulation fails to specify whether he is referring to the market equilibrium or to the short-run equilibrium. Once this point is clarified, the claim of a difference in speed of adjustment turns out to be hollow.

Every Monday a market-day equilibrium arises. It consists of a price-quantity mix. By definition, they are formed jointly. Hence they must have the same speed of adjustment. As to the formation of the short-period normal equilibrium, its implementation takes two weeks by assumption. It occurs at t_3, with prices having first moved to p_1 at t_1 and remaining there at t_2, to eventually arrive at p_3, while output has remained constant at t_1 and t_2, moving to its equilibrium value at t_3. So, in total two weeks were required for both price and output to reach their new short period equilibrium value. Again, there is no difference in speed of adjustment. The formations of the short-period quantity and the short-period price arise over the same time span.

Thus, Leijonhufvud's assertion makes sense only when the price adjustment towards market equilibrium is confronted with the quantity adjustment towards short-period equilibrium. It is true that the former is faster than the latter, yet no fuss should be made about this feature. Whenever the speeds of adjustment of prices and quantities are compared within the context of a single adjustment process, either towards market equilibrium or normal equilibrium, they are identical. In other words, Leijonhufvud's claim of a difference in speed of adjustment boils down to the proposition that the short-term period is longer than the market-day period or, put differently, that adjustment over time takes more time than point-in-time adjustment!

Keynes' alleged reversal in ranking

According to Leijonhufvud, the idea of a reversal in adjustment speeds – that is, that quantities might move faster than prices – is the cornerstone of Keynes' message. Its validity is better assessed by studying the impact of a decrease in normal demand. Figure 11.2 below illustrates.

Retaining the above assumptions, assume price flexibility (the upper panel of Figure 11.2). The decrease in normal demand will generate a move from the initial short-run normal equilibrium (*A*) prevailing at t_0 to the new normal equilibrium (*C*) at t_3. In the meantime, however – that is, at t_1 and t_2 – point *B* prevails. Here, we observe that a change in price has already occured at t_1 while for a change in quantities, one has to wait until t_3.[18] This is the so-called Marshallian difference in speed of adjustment.

What would its reversal be like? Assume a downwards rigid price, due to the existence of a price-floor, $\bar{p}$ (the lower panel of Figure 11.2). Assume, moreover, that the equilibrium price and the price-floor happen to coincide at t_0 ($p_0 = \bar{p}$) so that the floor is ineffective. Yet it will come into play after the decrease in demand. The market outcome at t_1 is now *D* rather than *B* – that is, supply is rationed. Since the good is perishable, $q_0 - \bar{q}_1$ is wasted. The same is true at t_2. Taking the existence of the price floor in account, the firm will decide to restrain its production to the quantity corresponding to *D*, a decision that will become effective only at t_3. Since production has now decreased, rationing has come to an end. Yet *D* is not a normal equilibrium point, since it is off the normal supply curve (although, I repeat, it is a market equilibrium). Can this situation be pinpointed as a reversal in adjustment speed? That is, do quantities adjust faster than prices? Again, the answer is 'yes, but in a trivial way'! True, a change in quantity will start and finish before any change in price, yet this is due only to the fact that no change in price has been allowed to occur. Why resort to the reversal of the speed of adjustment argument if the stumbling block is merely price rigidity?[19]

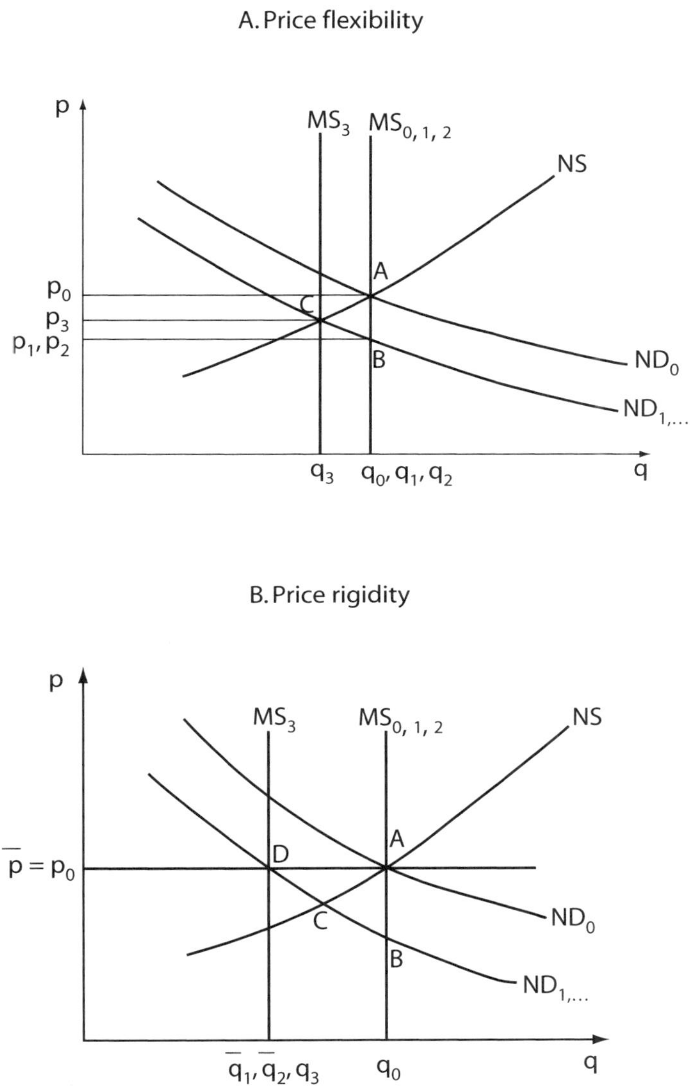

Figure 11.2 The impact of a decrease in demand in a price flexibility and price rigidity context.

The cause of involuntary unemployment: a false interest rate rather than a false wage?

One of the main reasons for Leijonhufvud's rejection of standard Keynesian economics lies in the fact that it rests on the assumption that wages are rigid.

> The emphasis on the 'rigidity' of wages, which one finds in the 'new economics', reveals the judgement that wages did not fall enough in the early thirties. Keynes, in contrast, judged that they declined too much by far. It has been noted before that, to Keynes, wage rigidity was a policy recommendation and not a behavioural assumption.
>
> (Leijonhufvud 1967: 229)

To Leijonhufvud, wage rigidity assumption is a betrayal of Keynes' project – a view on which I agree in so far as Keynes' intentions are concerned. The problem of course lies in their implementation. We have just seen that the reversal of the speed of adjustment argument cannot do because it is just rigidity in disguise. Yet Leijonhufvud has another iron in the fire. Faithfully to Keynes, he argues that involuntary unemployment, although manifesting itself in the labour market, originates in the financial sector, more precisely it is due to the existence of an intertemporal failure, the inability of the rate of interest to coordinate saving and investment. The false price governing the malfunctioning of the system is the long-term interest rate.

> The essence of Keynes's diagnosis of depression is this: the actual disequilibrium price vector initiating the contraction differs from the appropriate, hypothetical equilibrium vector in one major respect – the general level of long-term asset prices is lower than warranted.
>
> (Leijonhufvud 1968: 335)

Again, this brings Leijonhufvud close to Patinkin. The latter claimed (1965: 340) that involuntary unemployment was compatible with the Walrasian real wage, a claim which Barro and Grossman were to take up and which will be examined in the next chapter. In the Marshallian context adopted by Leijonhufvud, substantiating this claim amounts to demonstrating that involuntary unemployment co-exists with the nominal wage that equates the supply of, and the demand for, labour:

> Although the most eye-catching symptom of maladjustment is that of great excess supply in labour markets, *money wages rates may very well be 'correct', i.e. roughly equal to the money wages that the system*

> *would have at equilibrium.* Once demand prices for augmentable assets have moved to 'too low' a level, the pressure of excess supply in the productive sectors of the economy will rapidly be transferred back to the labour market over the whole front. Although this has been allowed to occur, the burden of adjustment should not be thrown on this market. Asset prices are 'wrong' and it is to asset markets that the cure should, if possible, be applied.
>
> (Leijonhufvud 1968: 336; my emphasis)

Unfortunately, Leijonhufvud simply asserts the possibility of a co-existence beween involuntary unemployment and the equilibrium money wage (in the sentence in italics) without giving any hint of a demonstration. Thus, we have an assertion lacking any justification.

Concluding remarks

To Leijonhufvud, the central explanatory factor of involuntary unemployment is slow adjustment. Thus, we fall back on Patinkin! And unfortunately, we reach the same conclusion. For all its outward appeal, the claim that slow adjustment causes market rationing is not vindicated. As soon as the trade round framework is adopted, the issue is sealed. Slow adjustment may well explain why normal equilibrium is not attained at once yet it cannot explain market rationing. Any argumentation as to a reversal in speeds of adjustment hardly improves on this state of affairs.

12

THE SECOND GENERATION

Barro and Grossman, Drèze, Benassy and Malinvaud

The Barro-Grossman model

Barro and Grossman's aim in their 1971 paper and 1976 book was to synthesise and generalise Patinkin's and Clower's models.[1] To work out this synthesis, they had to do violence to both Patinkin and Clower. They abandoned Patinkin's governing-idea, that involuntary unemployment could only exist during the process of price formation, to replace it by an end-state analysis of the existence of equilibrium. Fixed prices were thus substituted to slowly adjusting prices. Clower for his part attributed the sub-optimal end-result of his model to a signalling defect occurring in a context of perfectly flexible prices. This claim also vanished from their synthesis.

Barro and Grossman reason in terms of a simplified general equilibrium model, comprising only three goods: labour, a commodity and a non-produced good (which they inappropriately call money). Prices are formed under the *aegis* of the auctioneer. It is assumed, however, that the Walrasian equilibrium price vector does not come through. This departure of the effective price vector from Walrasian equilibrium prices can be rationalised as a blocking of the tâtonnement process. It is as if nothing could occur after the auctioneer had cried out a first price vector, resulting in prices being stuck at this initial vector. Most plausibly, it will be a 'false price' vector.

The gist of their model is the generalisation of the spill-over effects already present in Clower's and Patinkin's models. They propose a typology of the possible configurations of the economy according to the characteristics of the false price vector, i.e. the direction and size of its departure from the equilibrium vector. No less than nine configurations are sorted out in Barro and Grossman's book (compared to three in the article). The most outstanding of them is 'Keynesian unemployment'. Arising as the result of combining Clower's and Patinkin's insights, it exhibits excess supply in both the labour and the goods markets. I will return to it in my discussion of Malinvaud.

Drèze

The aim of Drèze's paper (1975) is to show that an economy in which prices are rigid still possesses an equilibrium solution, making agents' optimising plans compatible. While Drèze leaves the issue of the underlying institutional set-up untouched, most commentators (e.g. Donzelli 1989; Picard 1993; d'Autume 1985; Grandmont 1977; Guerrien 1989) have nonetheless interpreted his model as requiring the auctioneer assumption.

The economy studied by Drèze is a Walrasian exchange economy where the price vector is blocked. Every agent is supposed to know these prices. The difference from the standard Walrasian case is that a quantity tâtonnement leading to a fix-price equilibrium substitutes for the usual price tâtonnement. The auctioneer sends agents individual quantity signals – that is, a limit to the quantities they can sell or buy. Every agent must express his or her trading offers taking this new constraint into account. Whenever the auctioneer observes a non-zero excess demand, he or she changes the quantity constraint. Equilibrium – that is, an array of trades making agents' plans compatible – is obtained when the excess demand for every good is zero. Any fixed point of this tâtonnement in quantity is an equilibrium in Drèze's sense. It satisfies three conditions: net trades maximise utility under quantity constraints; they are mutually compatible; supply and demand for a given good are not simultaneously rationed. This result can be considered a non-Walrasian equilibrium – it is an *equilibrium* in that it makes agents' plans compatible, it is *non-Walrasian* in that it differs from the equilibrium price and net trade vector that would have occurred had the price system been working.[2]

Benassy

Benassy's distinctive feature with respect to the other disequilibrium authors is to have taken Clower's dual-decision hypothesis seriously. It constitutes the leitmotiv of Benassy's model while, to all intents and purposes, it is put aside by most other authors. Benassy also claims a stronger departure from Walrasian theory. The institutional set-up he evokes is poles apart from the Walrasian trade technology. The economy is monetary, and composed of independently organised and decentralised markets. No auctioneer is present, so that agents set prices. While the economy gropes towards its equilibrium position, this is the result of agents' ability to perceive market signals and to adjust accordingly. Thus, the comment made in the previous chapter about Leijonhufvud – that he identified the Walrasian trade technology as constituting the main stumbling-block to involuntary unemployment, applies to Benassy as well.[3]

The originality of Benassy's institutional set-up rests on two elements. First, he takes up Clower's concept of effective demand:

> Following Clower and Leijonhufvud, we shall call effective demand for good *h* the exchange the agent wishes to realize on market *h* to maximize his utility, taking into account the exchanges he perceives as feasible on the other markets (while the neoclassical demand function implicitly assumes that the individual can realize whatever exchange he wants on the other markets).
>
> (Benassy 1975: 507–508)[4]

The gist of this definition is an asymmetry in agents' perception as to the existence of a quantity constraint on their exchanges. It is asserted that they perceive a quantity constraint for every good in the economy except for the good being currently traded.

Second, Benassy strives at explaining the functioning of markets without resorting to the auctioneer hypothesis. His model depicts a process where agents learn from and react to market signals, which in turn permits the economy to arrive gradually at its equilibrium point. According to several commentators, e.g. Picard (1993), this feature makes his model appealing, since it amounts to taking a very decentralised system as its object of analysis.

In order to display the underlying working of markets, and following Benassy's lead, I start by focusing my attention on a particular goods market while making the assumption that the labour market has ended up earlier with market non-clearing. The scenario is thus sequential. Households first sell their labour service. The income obtained is spent on purchasing goods in a second stage. In spite of their being rationed in the labour market, it is assumed that households enter the goods market without envisaging the possibility of their being rationed therein as well. Clearly, we fall back on the first reconstruction of Clower's model, and its dual-decision hypothesis. However, Benassy makes the further step of dispensing with the auctioneer. Not surprisingly, the level of information supposedly held by agents as well as their calculation ability must be stronger than in the Walrasian model.

The analysis bears on a given trade round and pertains to a particular good. It is assumed that the participants in the market are well identified. It is also assumed that they are connected within a single communication network. Each in turn, agents express their effective demand. Thereby trading offers become common knowledge. Moreover, it is supposed that every agent is able to calculate the effective market excess demand by adding up individual effective excess demands. Agents know that individual plans are incompatible as long as the effective market excess demand is different from zero. It is furthermore assumed that they have agreed on some non-manipulable rationing scheme. Every agent then revises his or her effective demand, according to the size of the market excess demand and the rationing scheme. The equilibrium of the market arises as soon as it is no longer necessary to modify the market excess demand, trade remaining suspended until then. Picard's following quotation summarises:

> Effective demands are expressed independently on each market and they do not depend on the rationing constraint perceived on that market. They only depend on the constraints perceived on the other markets. Effective demands may be incompatible and therefore are different from the *ex post* trades. The incompatibility of effective demands makes agents perceive quantity constraints that limit the possible exchanges and these perceived constraints allow to define new effective demands. A Benassy equilibrium (hereafter a K-equilibrium) is reached when these new effective demands coincide with the previous ones. It is a fixed point of the compound mapping: effective demands → perceived constraints → effective demands.
>
> (Picard 1993: 21)

The end-result of this adjustment process is a non-Walrasian equilibrium, as in Drèze's model.[5]

Malinvaud

In their 1971 article, Barro and Grossman introduced the categories of classical unemployment, Keynesian unemployment and repressed inflation, as in passing. Malinvaud's contribution is to have delved into their respective characteristics. Their combination, he showed, was neatly captured in the following two-entry table (Table 12.1).

The Keynesian unemployment result must be music to Keynesian economists' ears. It gives an interdependency explanation of involuntary

Table 12.1 A typology of disequilibrium states

		Goods markets	
		Excess supply	*Excess demand*
Labour market	Excess supply	Keynesian unemployment	Classical unemployment
	Excess demand	—	Repressed inflation

unemployment. It abides by the reservation wage definition of involuntary unemployment. It also supports the Keynesian policy of exogenous demand stimulation. Moreover, as in Patinkin, involuntary unemployment co-exists with the Walrasian real wage. Thereby the objection that involuntary unemployment results from too high wages, is rebutted.

According to Malinvaud, the Keynesian revolution is characterised as 'a shift of emphasis from one type of short-run equilibrium [classical unemployment] to another type [Keynesian unemployment] as providing the appropriate theory for actual unemployment situations' (1977: 29). He also claims that this contrast has an immediate practical bearing. 'Keynesian unemployment, he claims, is much more frequent than classical unemployment. Casual observation shows this to be a fact' (1977: 77). On the other hand, the policy to be undertaken is radically different depending on whether the unemployment is of the classical or of the Keynesian type.

> To cure Keynesian unemployment, one should lower prices or raise wages. To cure classical unemployment, one should do precisely the reverse. This explains why debates on economic policy were so heated in the thirties, when most economists were more or less consciously thinking in classical terms, whereas a few others were already 'Keynesians' without knowing it.
>
> (Malinvaud 1977: 66)

Finally, the contrast drawn between the two concepts allows for the establishment of some truce between the Keynesian and the classical points of views. It is not denied that, under specific circumstances, the classics are right in their diagnosis. The classical remedy of a decrease in wages is counter-indicated only if unemployment is not of the classical type.

An assessment

While the works reviewed in the previous chapter look like blueprints for a theory, those examined here consist of fully-fledged formalised models. Therefore they mark an undeniable progress. But the point is to see whether they have fulfilled the programme set forth by the pioneering authors.

The incongruity of the rigidity assumption within the Walrasian institutional set-up

Barro and Grossman must be credited for having generalised Patinkin's and Clower's models. The two separate spill-over effects that were present in them are now brought together. As a result, a general equilibrium framework is arrived at. However, at this juncture the Achilles heel of the whole enterprise surfaces, i.e. the incongruity of trying to conciliate the assumption of rigidity and the auctioneer hypothesis, the institutional set-up intrinsic to the Walrasian research programme.[6]

This is Lucas' very criticism in his book *Models of Business Cycles* (1987). Why resort to the theoretical artefact of the auctioneer, he claims, if it is only to arbitrarily prevent them from doing the job for which he was created?

> It is common, particularly in macroeconomic discussions, to summarize the inadequacies of models based on the Walrasian scenario by saying that they 'assume cleared markets' and, of course, they do. But this way of stating the problem has had the unfortunate consequence of suggesting to many that better models, models without these inadequacies, can be obtained simply by dropping the assumption of market clearing while retaining all other aspects of the Walras auction scenario. In these 'fix-price' models, agents continue to submit sell orders for their labour services to the impersonal market just as they do in an equilibrium model. Terms like employer, employee, quits and fires continue to have no counterpart in the theory. The *only* difference is that the auction terminates, and trading occurs, at some price vector *other* than the ones that clears the market. The theory, so modified, loses whatever ability it had to account for wage and employment determination in terms of preference and technology . . . The fix-price model cannot help us get past the limits of the Walrasian scenario, on which the equilibriums model rest because it, too, accepts the Walrasian abstraction from any kind of continuing relationship between buyers and sellers, or between firms and employees. What we mean, in ordinary usage, by 'unemployment' is exactly disruptions in, or difficulties in forming, employer-employees relationships. Simply hamstringing the auctioneer in a Walrasian framework that assigns no role at all to such a relationship is not going to give us the understanding we want. If we are serious about obtaining a theory of unemployment, we want a theory about unemployed people, not unemployed 'hours of labour service'; about people who look for jobs, hold them, lose them, people with all the attending feelings that go along with these events. Walras's powerfully simple scenario, at least with the most obvious choice of 'commodity space' cannot give us this, with cleared markets or without them.
>
> (Lucas 1987: 52–53)

Lucas' criticism is clever. It amounts to disarming the disequilibrium theorists, who are all pledging allegiance to the Walrasian approach, by lecturing them on its limitations and indicting them for not taking these into account. This approach, Lucas insists, is unable to conceptualise notions such as an employment relationship, a job or unemployment, owing to the fact that it rests on the tâtonnement trade technology. If it has no room for unemployment, *a fortiori* there is none for involuntary unemployment.[7]

A related criticism bears on the notion of voluntary exchange. All disequilibrium authors have argued that short-side trading takes place as soon as market rationing exists.[8] Such a result is usually rationalised by recurring to the principle of voluntary exchange. In Barro and Grossman's terms:

> Voluntary exchange is synonymous with the institution of free markets. Voluntary exchange means that no transactor can be forced to buy more than he demands or sell more than he supplies. Thus voluntary exchange suggests that actual total transactions of any good will equal the smaller of the quantities supplied and demanded.
>
> (Barro and Grossman 1976: 39–40)

To these authors – prior to their recanting their earlier view – the case of somebody working more than planned was unacceptable because it contradicted the voluntarity principle, whereas the converse case of somebody selling (buying) less than his supply (demand) raised no objection. Graphically, in reference to a standard labour market graph, trading off the supply curve on its left is accepted yet trading off the supply curve on its right is excluded.

This account is wanting because it runs counter to the democratic character of the tâtonnement process. At stake is the question of the agents' right to optimal trading. Any agent facing the possibility of being rationed should express an 'optimal trading or nothing' stance: either an optimal outcome is arrived at, in which case he or she will sign up for the closure of tâtonnement or, if not, he or she will refuse to sign up, thereby impeding the start of trading.[9]

Upon reflection, it thus appears that a notion such as short-side trading has been accepted too swiftly. Contrary to what disequilibrium authors assume, any trading off the curve, be it on its left or on its right, must be excluded. Patinkin's assertion, that we should 'free ourselves of the mental habit – long ingrained by the methods of static analysis – of seeing only points *on* the demand or supply curve' (1965: 323) has no foundation, at least in a Walrasian perspective. Implications are devastating since any market rationing result becomes inconceivable.

The underlying methodological debate: Malinvaud against Lucas

From the beginning, the driving force of disequilibrium theorists has been their firm belief that involuntary unemployment was a recurrent real-world phenomenon. As it was lacking in Walrasian general equilibrium theory, their preferred type of economic theory, their programme was straightforward: to make this fact-of-life enter Walrasian theory.[10]

Yet, is such a programme valid when due account is taken of the methodological principles upon which Walrasian theory is based? To address this issue, let me narrow the discussion to a confrontation between Malinvaud, the disequilibrium theoretician most alert to methodological issues, and Lucas, heralded as the 'the master of methodology' by Prescott (Snowdon and Vane 1999: 264). Let me start with Malinvaud's viewpoint as expressed in his *Mass Unemployment* book (1984), where he takes on the new classical approach.

First of all, Malinvaud adopts the view that I have criticised in Chapter 4, that slow adjustment is the cause of market rationing. After depicting how the law of supply and demand operates in the determination of temporary equilibrium, according to new classicists, he states that

> It is clear that the labour market does not operate in this way. Wages are not flexible in the short term in the way assumed by this form of the law of supply and demand. They are not completely insensitive to pressure on the labour market, but they adjust much less than would be required for permanent market clearing.
>
> (Malinvaud 1984: 18–19)

He does not deny that the law of supply and demand is at work in the labour market. Rather, he believes that it cannot exert its full effects in the short period:

> To conclude, let me say that the law of supply and demand is not completely inactive in the labour market, but that its influence is slow and, therefore, quite limited in the short term. Large quantity adjustments then have to occur: hours of work are changed, recruitments are accelerated or stopped, or lay-offs of greater or lesser members of workers decided upon.
>
> (Malinvaud 1984: 20)

While admitting that a good explanation of wage rigidity is still unavailable, Malinvaud (writing in 1984) nonetheless believes that it should be integrated in theoretical models at once, since it is a compelling observable phenomenon:

> Economics is therefore not at fault in considering the consequences of wage rigidity if this rigidity has been proved to exist. Of course, explanations of it are (or would be) useful for subsequent scientific progress, but even if they are (or were) lacking, it would still be wrong to overlook the observed facts.
>
> (Malinvaud 1984: 21)

The basic discord between Malinvaud and Lucas relates to the epistemological status of equilibrium in Walrasian theory. Malinvaud takes the common-sense stance that equilibrium and disequilibrium are features of reality. Hence, to him, investigating whether a given market (or economy) is in equilibrium is a sensible task to pursue. Evidently, more often than not, the result of such an inquiry will be negative. Malinvaud furthermore thinks that Lucas agrees with him on this way of putting the issue. According to Malinvaud, the difference between them is that Lucas defends a different factual result by claiming that real-world markets always feature equilibrium, a claim that to him is definitely non-verified.

The point, however, is whether Lucas is actually taking such a stance. Look at what he stated in an interview with Snowdon and Vane:

> I think general discussions, especially by non-economists, of whether the system is in equilibrium or not are almost entirely nonsense. You can't look out of this window and ask whether New Orleans is in equilibrium. What does that mean? Equilibrium is a property of the way we look at things, not a property of reality.
>
> (Snowdon and Vane 1998: 127)[11]

Lucas' assertion amounts to radically shifting the terrain of discussion. If equilibrium is not a feature of reality but a property of the way we look at it, Malinvaud's indictment is circumvented. Lucas' statement amounts to taking an agnostic stance about whether markets effectively clear in reality – either this point simply cannot be assessed (my own viewpoint, as defended in Chapter 4) or market non-clearing, although an effective reality, can be overlooked when it comes to constructing a theory such as Walrasian general equilibrium theory. In other words, market clearing is adopted as a matter of postulate. The validity of such a methodological stance hinges on how 'productive' models based on it are. If this is true, Malinvaud's insisting on the lack of existence of market clearing is hardly biting.[12]

The present discussion must be related to the distinction between the centralised and the decentralised market assumption make in Chapter 4. Malinvaud's claim amounts to stating that the labour market is a decentralised market. Therefore, it comes as no surprise that it features queues and slow adjustment. However, for better or worse, Walrasian theory is based on the opposite assumption, the centralised market assumption. Market clearing and instantaneous adjustment arise as corollaries. Does it make sense to try to introduce the very features that qualifies a market as decentralised into the centralised market hypothesis? I do not believe so. I rather think that disequilibrium theorists are attempting to squeeze a circle by wanting to make a real-world phenomenon acceptable within the Walrasian approach without recognising the incongruity of such an attempt. The reason why Lucas got the upper hand over Malinvaud and the other disequilibrium economists is simply that he had the easier task of sticking to the logic of the Walrasian system.

An assessment of Benassy

I have just argued that trying to introduce the categories of rigidity and unemployment in the Walrasian framework is a dead end. The immediate conclusion that comes to mind is that what is needed is to remove the Walrasian trade technology. As seen, this is the route Clower and Leijonhufvud decided to take, with a twofold departure from earlier thinking – a shift from the Walrasian to the Marshallian approach, on the one hand, and from the study of the logical existence of equilibrium to that of the equilibration, on the other. Benassy's aim was to follow suit, yet in a less radical way.[13] While he must be praised for his attempt, his analysis testifies to the difficulty of the enterprise.

In my above account of Benassy's theory, I have limited myself to presenting his effective demand theory with respect to a single market, that is, in a partial equilibrium context. As long as this is the case, no objection is to be levelled against his adoption of Clower's dual-decision hypothesis. Moreover, Benassy improves upon it by conceiving a process of formation of equilibrium without auctioneer. However, in Benassy's mind, the single market analysis is just a pedagogical preliminary to his main objective of constructing a general equilibrium model. And here comes the twist: the sequentialism assumption is swept under the rug, it now being assumed that trading over all goods takes place concomitantly. In his 1982 book Benassy admits that the underlying rationale for dropping the sequentialist approach is tractability:

> In Part I we studied the microeconomic theory of individual agents and markets . . . On this basis, it would be possible in principle to construct dynamic models of the whole economy by having the set of agents interacting in this way in a sequence of markets. However, the model obtained would be fairly cumbersome, as one would have to specify such things as the order in which agents visit markets, or short-run expectations formation,

> and our knowledge of such factors is not strong enough for the results to be at all robust.
>
> (Benassy 1982: 61)

Benassy does not seem to be aware of the implications of this passage to general equilibrium. In particular he fails to realise that his earlier institutional set-up becomes contrived and, ultimately, unnecessary. While his conception of effective demand with its underlying idea of asymmetry in perception makes sense in a sequential framework, it ceases to do so in a system where trading takes place simultaneously. In the sequential scheme it is easy to understand why agents perceive the existence of rationing in those markets which closed earlier – it is simply that rationing is an objective fact. This is no longer true in the general equilibrium framework. Here, there is no reason to assume an asymmetry in perception any longer. Instead, it must be assumed that, if agents perceive the possibility of rationing, this must be the case for every market, including the market for the good under trade. As a result, the effective demand definition ought to be understood as meaning that agents, although perceiving a quantity constraint for the good under trade, nonetheless deliberately neglect it and express a trade offer in violation of it. I can see no rationale for such a behaviour, except Benassy's will to remain faithful to Clower's insight and to stick to the effective demand concept developed in his partial equilibrium analysis.

The end result is frustrating since it turns out that the very features, which made Benassy's partial equilibrium analysis original, became contrived and at bottom unnecessary when it comes to a general equilibrium analysis. As stated by Donzelli:

> The equilibrium rationed net trades, *indirectly* generated by the equilibrium trade offers through the rationing mechanism, are exactly the same as the equilibrium trades that the agents would be able to determine *directly*, if only they were allowed to maximize their preferences subject to *all* the quantity constraints they are supposed to perceive in equilibrium. In other words, under the above assumptions, the equilibrium trades obtained in an indirect manner by following the entangled procedure suggested by Benassy would precisely be the same equilibrium trades as would be obtained in a direct manner by following Drèze's procedure.
>
> (Donzelli 1989: 296; his emphasis)

From individual disequilibrium to individual equilibrium

To Keynes, involuntary unemployment was a case of individual disequilibrium, i.e. the inability of a given agent to realise his optimising plan.

Whenever involuntary unemployment, so understood, exists at the level of a given individual, interactive disequilibrium – an incompatibility across agents' plans – is present at the level of the economy as a whole. An optimising plan must always be defined with respect to a budget constraint. In the canonical model, it comprises two elements that are considered as given by the agent, his endowments, on the one hand, and prices, on the other. However, things are different in the models studied here since the standard budget constraint is modified with the inclusion of an element that was absent earlier, namely a bound on sales or purchases.

A taxonomic problem ensues. Involuntary unemployment is present in Drèze's and Benassy's model in so far as the standard, unmodified budget constraint remains the reference. In contrast, whenever the existence of a rationing scheme is taken into account, agents must be viewed as having realised their optimising plans in so far as these are defined with respect to the modified budget constraint. But in this case the individual disequilibrium idea (and hence the involuntary unemployment idea) vanishes! The diagnosis made about the result of the model turns out to hinge on a definitional choice, a pure matter of convention, which is rather embarrassing.

Be this as it may, it is clear that Drèze's and Benassy's models belong to an equilibrium perspective. The aim of these authors differs from that of the initiators of the approach. It consists of bringing to the fore the logical possibility of equilibrium, a state of mutual compatibility of plans, as well as its effective existence, the result of a tâtonnement over quantities, in spite of the existence of rigidity. In contrast, the early authors wanted to show that rigidity led to disequilibrium. It is as if Drèze and Benassy set it as their objective to salvage the notion of equilibrium in the presence of such a strong impediment to it as price rigidity. The role assigned to the rationing schemes is then to reconcile price rigidity and optimising behaviour. The shift in label from disequilibrium theory towards a theory of non-Walrasian equilibria rightly expresses this change in objective.[14]

Concluding remarks

A first result of my examination of the disequilibrium approach is that it should be de-homogenised. While the different authors have engaged in much cross-quotations and often presented their views as being unified, my investigation has shown that the differences between them are significant. Some authors defend the view that involuntary unemployment can exist only during the adjustment process. This is true with regard to Patinkin and Leijonhufvud (joined later by Clower). Yet it can hardly be claimed that these authors are therefore fully on the same wave-length, since Patinkin reasons against a Walrasian background while Clower and Leijonhufvud embed their claim in a Marshallian framework. The other authors have taken end-states of the economy as their exclusive object.

How have these contributions fared with respect to the aim of attempts at introducing involuntary unemployment into economic theory? The answer is mitigated. Restricting myself to the second-generation authors, they have succeeded in producing an involuntary unemployment result that fits Keynes' project. In particular, they have dispensed with the earlier view that too high a wage (in their case a *numéraire* wage, i.e. at bottom a real wage) is responsible for involuntary unemployment. Involuntary unemployment can co-exist with the Walrasian wage rate. Increasing the latter may even be the remedy. However, its cause is still an exogenous rigid price vector (i.e. other components of the price vector are false). Moreover – and now more than before – this assumption looks contrived as it comes on a collision course with the institutional set-up proper to the Walrasian approach. But it was probably necessary to try seriously to integrate involuntary unemployment within a neo-Walrasian model to make it plain that involuntary unemployment and the Walrasian research programme are indeed incompatible bedfellows.

Part V

THE ANTI-KEYNESIAN OFFENSIVE

13

FRIEDMAN

My aim in this chapter is to study Friedman's role in the dismissal of Keynesian theory, and in particular of the involuntary unemployment concept.[1] His two most interesting writings in this respect are his 1967 Presidential Address to the American Economic Association (Friedman 1968), and *A Theoretical Framework for Monetary Analysis* (1974a, 1974b).

Although on scrutiny Friedman's Address turns out to be a muddy text The well-functioning of a tâtonnement economy implies that agents react to the auctioneer's questionnaire on the assumption that no rationing will eventually exist. In other words, the right way to avoid rationing is to have agents expressing their standard budget constraints. Moreover, the assumption that agents might be able to observe a mismatch between supply and demand is odd in a Walrasian universe because agents are supposed to have no knowledge at all of market supply and demand functions.

(De Vroey 2001b), it exerted a tremendous influence, paving the way for the eventual demise of Keynesian macroeconomics.[2] Its purpose was to attack the view that the downwards-sloping character of the Phillips curve allowed for using monetary policy in order to decrease unemployment at the expense of some increase in inflation. It was also an attempt to defend the classical sub-model of the IS-LM model. Contrary to subsequent new classical economists, Friedman raised no objections of principle against the IS-LM model – at the least, he was ready to discuss his views within its framework.[3] However, he considered that only its classical regime was valid, rejecting the Keynesian regime on the grounds of its ad hoc wage rigidity assumption. The hallmark of the classical regime was that monetary expansion exerted only nominal effects. The problem confronting Friedman was that the real world seemed to be on the side of Keynesians since casual observation suggested that monetary expansion led to real effects, what in turn suggested that the economy was in a state of underemployment beforehand. The task that Friedman then set himself was to reassess the validity of the classical version of the IS-LM model against contrary evidence. To this end, he needed to re-introduce the short-long period divide, which the IS-LM tradition had thrown overboard by concentrating the attention exclusively on the short period. Against this background, he argued that, while money expansion had indeed real effects, these were temporary, reversible and due to a surprise or misperception effect.

As to Friedman's *A Theoretical Framework for Monetary Analysis* (1974a, 1974b), its aim was to address the request of his critics and commentators that he should make explicit the broader theoretical framework underlying his quantity theory of money. However, as an aside, he used this opportunity for confronting his views with those of Keynes.[4]

I will start by discussing Friedman's misperception on expectations – augmented Phillips Curve model presented in his Presidential Address. Next, I will reflect on his criticism of the Keynesian approach. Friedman was not radically opposed to the Keynesian methodology because to him Keynes had the great merit of being a Marshallian (as opposed to a Walrasian) economist. Instead of launching an all-out attack against Keynesian theory, he chose to co-opt Keynesian tools – the Phillips Curve, the IS-LM model – while transforming them into weapons against Keynesian policy prescriptions. Similarly, Friedman did not frontally attack the involuntary unemployment concept, apparently preferring to ignore it, thereby implicitly demonstrating its lack of relevance. I will also show that Friedman's framework permits a subversive alternative interpretation of some of Keynes' key propositions. In a third stage, I will assess whether Friedman's expectations-augmented Phillips Curve model succeeds in demonstrating policy inefficiency and will show that it does not. Finally, I will ponder upon Friedman's 'Marshallianism'. In particular, I will claim that his views mark a return to the Marshallian conception of equilibrium, from which IS-LM models had departed.

Friedman's misperception model

The gist of Friedman's claim is that non-neutrality follows from workers' misperception.

> Because selling prices of products typically respond to an unanticipated rise in nominal demand faster than prices of factors of production, real wages received have gone down – though real wages anticipated by employees went up, since the employees implicitly evaluated the wages offered at the earlier price level. Indeed, the simultaneous fall *ex post* in real wages to employers and rise *ex ante* in real wages to employees is what enabled employment to increase.
>
> (Friedman 1968: 10)

Friedman's analysis starts from a state of equilibrium where the natural rate prevails. He assumes that the government nonetheless wishes to increase employment and therefore orders the central bank to engage in monetary expansion. Were agents without money illusion, the government's attempt would fail because agents would not respond to such a purely monetary shock. However, Friedman needs them to react positively for the sake of getting a theoretical result supporting the empirical observation of a downwards-sloping Phillips Curve. To this effect, he introduces two assumptions. First, monetary expansion must spill over differently in the goods and labour markets, so that nominal wages increase by less than average prices. Second, firms' and workers' expectations are asymmetrical. While workers hold adaptive expectations about the goods prices, firms have perfect foresight. Under these conditions monetary expansion results in workers and firms agreeing to trade a higher quantity of labour for a higher nominal wage. At the end of the trade round, a trade-off between inflation and unemployment surfaces, confirming a downwards-sloping Phillips Curve. However, as Friedman warns us, this is only half of the story:

> But this situation is temporary: let the higher rate of growth of aggregate nominal demand and of prices continue, and perceptions will adjust to reality. When they do, the initial effect will disappear, and then even be reversed for a time as workers and employers find themselves locked into inappropriate contracts. Ultimately, employment will be back at the level that prevailed before the assumed unanticipated acceleration in aggregate nominal demand.
>
> (Friedman 1977: 14)

When goods markets come to a close, workers realise that their expectations about their real wage were wrong. Were the monetary expansion a one-shot move, the labour market would quickly return to its normal equilibrium. To keep the higher level of employment, monetary expansion must continue at an increased rate. The lesson is clear: a departure from the natural rate is possible only if inflation is unexpected. Moreover, maintaining it requires an unsustainable permanent acceleration of the inflation rate. In other words, the labour market cannot permanently depart from the natural rate of unemployment.

Friedman's argumentation in his 1968 article is rather cryptic and he later gave a more explicit account in his price theory textbook (1976a: 221 ff.). It comprises a graph depicting the labour market and is taken up below as Figure 13.1.

Whenever inflation is absent, everything is assumed to proceed smoothly. The natural rate of employment (E_0) prevails.[5] Consider now the first trading round at which the impact of monetary expansion becomes effective in the labour market. At this juncture, the goods market

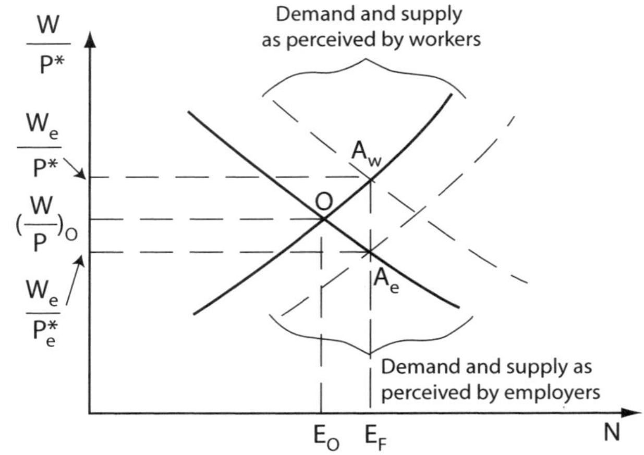

Figure 13.1 Friedman's account of the working of the labour market.

has not yet opened. Expectations about its future price now become crucial. Friedman's account of what is going on in workers' minds is as follows:

> To them [the workers], the real wage that matters is their nominal wage divided by a price index of the goods and service they buy. As yet they have no reason to suppose a change in the price level, hence they have no reason to change their supply function. It will remain the solid supply curve on Figure 12.6 [Figure 13.1 above], if we interpret P^* as the price level *perceived* or *anticipated* by workers. To them, it will appear as if the demand for labour had shifted to the right, to the dashed demand curve. At each nominal wage rate (also real wage as perceived by them), employers are seeking to hire more workers.
>
> (Friedman 1976a: 224; his emphasis)

Workers falsely conjecture that the market demand for labour has autonomously increased with respect to the previous trading round. Yet, they view no reason to change their supply schedule, the result of their lack of anticipation of a rise in the goods price. On the basis of this twofold conjecture, they mentally construe the new market equilibrium position (point A_w), at the intersection of the new perceived demand curve and the unchanged supply curve.

Turning to firms, Friedman notes that:

> Employers faced with an increased nominal demand for their products will count on being able to get a higher price or the equivalent. The same nominal wage means a lower real wage in terms of that higher price of his product. For employers as whole, it will appear as if the supply curve had shifted to the right to the dashed supply curve.
>
> (Friedman 1976a: 224)

Firms are endowed with the same capacity to reconstruct market schedules as workers. They realise two facts, that each firm's demand for labour function remains unchanged and that the market supply of labour, as based on the real wage, shifts to the right. This is a correct assessment since workers' misperception is tantamount in its effects to a change in their preferences. Hence firms are ready to go down their demand curve to the point A_e, where the unchanged demand for labour curve intersects with the shifted supply curve.

Having these conjectures in mind, workers and firms come to the market with an exchange proposal that happens to involve the same increased amount of labour traded (E_F) and the same nominal wage, W_E ($W_E > W_0$). Exchange on this basis is possible and will take place.

I find Friedman's graphical account of working of the labour market wanting on two points. First, it does not show the nominal wage (W_E) that allows the matching of supply and demand. Second, it blurs two results that should be kept separate because of their sequential occurrences, the market-day equilibrium result (E_F, W_E) and the determination of the real wage (W_E/p). Actually, the latter arises only later, when the goods markets come to a close. In other words, his graph collides the result of two markets (the labour market and the goods market) instead of depicting the labour market result alone.[6]

Beyond doubt, Friedman's model fits the Marshallian perspective. Its only difference with the Marshallian canonical model lies in the fact that it grafts the misperception insight onto it. Friedman's natural rate of employment is nothing more than the quantity component of Marshallian normal equilibrium. The result described in Figure 13.1 can be viewed as a standard case of Marshallian disequilibrium, featuring a deviation of the market-day equilibrium values (E_F, W_E) from their normal equilibrium values (E_0, W_0). The existence of market clearing needs to be underlined – the market-day quantity of labour supplied and demanded are equal and amount to 0–E_F. Every agent realises his optimising plan.[7]

A natural rate of unemployment or a natural rate of employment?

As stated, Friedman's Presidential Address exerted a tremendous influence. In particular, it introduced the notion of the natural rate of unemployment that was to play a key role in further theoretical developments. The irony, however, is that strictly speaking there is no room for this notion in Friedman's model.

The conundrum surfaces when reflecting on the standard way in which the natural rate of unemployment is defined. Friedman's definition is as follows:

> My definition of the natural rate of unemployment is that rate at which demand and supply are equal so there is no excess supply or demand and in which people's expectations are satisfied.
>
> (Snowdon and Vane 1999: 130)[8]

The genuine problem I have with this definitional stance is that if supply and demand are equal, no rationing, and hence no unemployment, are present. How can market rationing and zero excess demand co-exist? Friedman's graph confirms this. Nothing in it points to the existence of unemployment, be it involuntary or frictional unemployment.

It will be objected that the natural rate of unemployment is underpinned by frictional or search unemployment. I have already claimed, in Chapter 4, that these categories have no room in the Marshallian value analysis.[9] The same is true for what concerns Friedman's model. As stated by Hahn, 'Traditional search theory finds no *formal* representation of the economy in macro theories of the natural rate. It is referred to, or better appealed to, but it is not connected with the theory proposed' (1995: 52).[10]

Again, we witness here a blurring of the descriptive and the theoretical levels. Santamero and Seater are evidently right when writing that 'because of market frictions and structural changes, unemployment always is positive'. Yet, such a statement does not fit the theoretical universe of Friedman's model.[11] Therefore, the passages about unemployment in Friedman's article – for example, he refers to the 'unemployed who now take jobs at the former nominal wage' (1968: 10) – should be considered as inappropriate meta-theoretical commentaries rather than as belonging to the model contained in his article. Since the model should prevail over the narrative or meta-theoretical commentary, the elements that are present in the narrative yet absent from the model ought to be put aside. Departures from the natural rate of *employment* rather than from the natural rate of *unemployment* turn out to be the real object of Friedman's model. The issue under consideration is the possibility of variations in employment rather than variations in unemployment. Assuming identical agents, the notion of a natural rate of employment indicates their normal equilibrium level of participation in the labour market as grounded in traditional microfoundations. In this context, a departure from the natural rate of employment indicates a level of activity below or in excess of this rate, that is either under- or overemployment.[12] Recall the distinction made in Chapter 2 between unemployment, an unequal distribution of total employment, and underemployment, an equally distributed employment lack. Terminology to the contrary notwithstanding, Friedman's model, when correctly recast, is based on the second of these concepts.

A related point is that, while disequilibrium is present in Friedman's model, it should not be made tantamount to market non-clearing. It is disequilibrium in the Marshallian sense, as analysed in Chapter 4, i.e. a departure from the normal equilibrium values going along with market clearing. Many authors have failed to perceive this point as the following quotations from Hoover and Carlin and Soskice illustrate:

> Even Friedman, who with his natural rate hypothesis asserted the dominance of frictional unemployment interpreted as a consequence of voluntary actions, did not deny that involuntary unemployment was real.
>
> (Hoover 1988: 36)

> He [Friedman] skillfully captured the mainstream by proposing that, while markets clear in the long run where classical results obtain, they do not necessarily clear at full employment in the short run because of a lack of perfect information on the part of all agents.
>
> (Carlin and Soskice 1990: 74)

Hoover takes it for granted that the category of involuntary unemployment is conceivable in Friedman's reasoning while I have argued to the contrary. Carlin and Soskice's mistake is to take it for granted that any departure from the natural rate amounts to market non-clearing.[13]

Friedman's criticism of Keynes

While Friedman's work was aimed at destabilising Keynesian policy views, he was nonetheless far from launching an all-on attack, as Lucas and Sargent were to do ten years later (1978). To wit, in the introduction of his address Friedman characterised Keynes's analysis as 'rigorous and sophisticated' (1968: 1). The only target of his criticism, he claimed, was 'simple-minded Keynesianism' (1968: 5).[14] Two factors may explain his moderate tone. First, Friedman was clever enough to understand that too stern a stance would have been counter-productive. At the time, the Keynesian citadel was still strong. Hence his more subtle strategy of apparently embracing the viewpoint of his opponents just to turn it upside down and make it serve opposing conclusions.[15] On the other hand, there was a real intellectual proximity between Keynes and Friedman related to their style of theorising and their common ties to Marshallian theory.[16] Friedman praised Keynes for being 'a true Marshallian in method' and for adopting the Marshallian instead of the Walrasian framework (1974a: 18).[17]

To Friedman, Keynes' basic challenge to orthodoxy consisted of three propositions:

> 1 As a purely *theoretical* matter, there need not exist, even if all prices are flexible, a *long-run equilibrium* position characterised by 'full employment' of resources.
> 2 As an *empirical* matter, prices can be considered as rigid – an institutional datum – for *short-run economic fluctuations* . . .
> 3 The demand function for money has a particular empirical form – corresponding to absolute liquidity preference – that makes velocity highly unstable much of the time, so that changes in the quantity of money would, in the main, simply produce changes in V in the opposite direction.
>
> (Friedman 1974a: 15; his emphasis)

Proposition 1 and 3 hold together. Proposition 1 is denied by Friedman because of the existence of the real-balance effect. The latter, he claims, 'undermines Keynes' key theoretical proposition, that even in a world of flexible prices, a position of equilibrium at full employment might not exist' (1968: 3). Therefore, any position departing from the natural rate of employment must be temporary. Proposition 2 is assimilated by Friedman to the reversal in speeds of adjustment underlined by Leijonhufvud. While, unlike myself, Friedman does not object to Leijonhufvud's claim that the difference in speeds of adjustment is the hallmark of Marshallian theory, he refuses the idea of its reversal, which he finds arbitrary:

> He [Keynes] rationalised the assumption [of a reversal in speeds of adjustment] in terms of wage rigidity arising partly from money illusion, partly from the strength of trade unions. And at a still deeper level, he rationalised wage rigidity by proposition (1) [of the above quotation]: under conditions when there was no full-employment equilibrium, there was no equilibrium nominal price level; something had to be brought in from outside to fix the price level; it might as well be institutional wage rigidity. Put differently flexible nominal wages under such circumstances had

> no economic function to perform; hence they might as well be made rigid.
>
> (Friedman 1974a: 18–19)

To Friedman, Keynes' stance is unacceptable because it amounts to treating prices as institutional data determined outside the economic sphere. In his words, 'the rigid price assumption of Keynes is, in this sense, much more arbitrary. It is entirely a *deus ex machina* with no underpinning in economic theory' (1974a: 44).[18]

Friedman's criticism of Keynes' theory makes reference neither to involuntary unemployment nor to market non-clearing. To the best of my knowledge, these terms are absent from his vocabulary. He rather proceeds in terms of a opposition between the more general terms of underemployment and full employment, the modifier 'full' often being put in inverted commas.[19] Yet, such a benign neglect is in a sense more potent than an all-out criticism as it amounts to showing that economic theory is able to explain phenomena that, it was earlier believed, needed the involuntary unemployment concept.

Friedman could have pushed his advantage against Keynes further, had he been wanting to enter into conceptual discussions. In effect, certain passages of Chapter 2 of *The General Theory* prove perfectly amenable to a Friedmanian reading – that is, they support Friedman's claim as much as the standard Keynesian interpretation. Let me give two examples, Keynes' definition of involuntary unemployment, on the one hand, and his second observation as to wage-earners being unable to bargain real wages, on the other.

As claimed above, Keynes' formal definition of the involuntary unemployment concept might be seen as a test of its existence. Assume a situation where the money wage is fixed yet the general price level increases as the result of a monetary expansion. If employment increases, it can be inferred, Keynes argues, that involuntary unemployment must have been present previously. If labour supply and demand were matching before the intervention, the falling real wage would have led to a decrease in labour supply and the observed increase in employment would have been impossible. The very existence of some increase in employment is then interpreted as manifesting a return towards market clearing, starting from an initial situation of rationing. Friedman's model offers an alternative explanation. Far from witnessing the correction of some earlier state of market non-clearing, the observed *ex post* decrease in real wage and increase in employment now becomes interpreted as the manifestation of a newly created disequilibrium grafted onto a previous equilibrium state and occasioned by an unwarranted monetary expansion. To Friedman, this expansion elicits a disequilibrium, the exact opposite of the Keynesian insight that it corrects a disequilibrium!

My second example is Keynes' second observation (about workers' inability to determine the real wage). It turns out that Friedman could readily endorse it as an apt account of his own theory. Remember what Keynes wrote in support of his observation:

> A decline in employment, although necessarily associated with labor *receiving* a wage equal in value to a larger quantity of wage-goods, is not necessarily due to labour's *demanding* a larger quantity of wage-goods.
>
> (Keynes 1936: 18)

Friedman's reasoning comes close to Keynes' statement, except that it bears on the opposite case of an increase in employment. In his model, workers accept an increase in their participation in the labour market because they expect an increase in the real wages to be forthcoming as the result of a nominal wage increase. Yet, they end up having a lower real wage. Thus, in analogy to Keynes' assertion, the increase in employment is due to labour expecting to get a larger quantity of wage-goods yet not receiving it. Keynes' second observation could be recast to Friedman's taste as follows:

> The increase in employment, although associated with labour receiving a wage equal in value to a lower quantity of wage-goods, is due to labour's expecting to get a larger quantity of wage-goods

Keynes advanced his second observation as an argument in favour of the existence of involuntary unemployment. Now it turns out that this observation is vindicated by Friedman's model as illustrating agents' misperception and the ensuing state of Marshallian disequilibrium without any need for resorting to the involuntary unemployment concept.

Policy ineffectiveness

Friedman's address claimed that any attempts by the government to exploit the trade-off implied by the downwards-sloping Phillips Curve in order to decrease unemployment would lead to displacements of the curve. This prediction became verified in the 1970s, leading Lucas to claim that for once a theory has been verified through real-life experimentation.[20]

Later such a conclusion became questioned. Yet my aim is not to analyse the much-discussed empirical dimension of the Phillips Curve.[21] Instead, the question that I want to address is theoretical: did Friedman's policy ineffectiveness claim really provide a theoretical rebuttal of Keynesian policy prescriptions?

True, Friedman put forward a theoretical scenario where the fact that monetary expansion had real effects no longer meant that some market failure was pre-existing. Thus, Keynesians ceased to have an interpretative monopoly on the topic of the real effects of monetary changes. Moreover, Friedman made his point by using the Phillips Curve that Keynesians had too hastily claimed to be part of their paradigm.

The reason why Keynesians adopted the Phillips Curve with such enthusiasm has to do with its supplying the so-called missing equation of the IS-LM model. However, with hindsight it appears that they should have been more circumspect. In fact, Phillips' observations were congruent neither with the Keynesian nor with the classical model. While the latter implied a vertical Phillips relationship, the former would have needed the opposite, a horizontal Phillips relationship, coinciding with the abscissa, at least for that part of unemployment which is in excess of the natural rate. Had Keynesians been more alert, they would have been less prone to let the Phillips Curve feature in their models. The story, if any, they advanced in order to conciliate the empirical form of the Phillips Curve and their theoretical framework was that the different labour markets might witness to different states of employment, so that some had already reached full employment while other were still experiencing underemployment. Hence the combination of price and real effects.[22] To me this is a rather poor explanation. What was needed was a theoretical explanation within the framework adopted when constructing IS-LM models – that is, without removing the assumption of a single labour market. Keynesians hardly addressed this challenge. As a result, when Friedman proposed his own explanation reconciling the short-term negatively slope of Phillips Curve with its long-term verticality, and thereby dismissing the claim of a trade-off between inflation and unemployment, they had little ammunition for responding.

However, there is a less sanguine judgement to be made about Friedman's enterprise by pointing out that his ineffectiveness claim suffers from the basic flaw of having been constructed in reference to a case where hardly any stimulation policy is needed. From the start, Friedman hypothesises that the (unique) natural rate of unemployment is already realised. 'Let us assume that the monetary authority tries to peg the "market" rate of unemployment at a level below the "natural" rate' (1968: 9). As soon as this hypothesis is made, the issue is sealed, and Friedman's conclusion becomes compelling. Friedman's argument consists of asserting that demand stimulation policies will have no lasting effects whenever the natural rate of employment is realised. In other words, it is declared that *overemployment* cannot persist. But who would oppose such a statement? To undertake demand stimulation in this context is absurd, since all defects that such a policy might correct are conspicuous by their absence. The success of Keynesian policy should only be assessed in a context in which it has some *raison d'être.*

Oddly enough, this flaw was hardly perceived at the time – perhaps because it was too obvious, like Edgar Poe's stolen letter. It was voiced only later, when the rational expectations revolution was already well on its way.[23] Keynesians should not have accepted Friedman's way of positing the issue. Their lack of reaction was possibly due to the fact they had no alternative model to offer, where a really Keynesian result was obtained – a model featuring, if not involuntary unemployment in the reservation wage sense, at the least dominated underemployment.

The Marshallian character of Friedman's model

Friedman a Walrasian economist?

In his Presidential Address, Friedman seemed to give the natural rate of unemployment notion a Walrasian lineage by defining it in the following way:

> The 'natural rate of unemployment' is the level that would be ground out by the Walrasian system of general equilibrium equations, provided there is embedded in them the actual structural characteristics of the labor and commodities markets, including market imperfections, stochastic variability in demands and supplies, the cost of gathering information about job vacancies and labor availability's, the cost of mobility, and so on.
>
> (Friedman 1968: 8)

Several authors have taken this definition in earnest – the last of them being Leeson who writes that 'the natural rate of unemployment is a Walrasian concept' (2002: 10) – with the result of ranking Friedman within the Walrasian approach. To me, there is little grounds for such a point of view. As many commentators have noticed (Hall 1979: 154; Dixon 1995: 64; Rogerson 1997: 76), Friedman provides no real definition. For example, Hall states 'this definition is hardly more than a list of things to think about' (1979: 154). Moreover, as seen above, there is no room in the Walrasian framework for notions such as jobs or unemployment. Finally, such an interpretation runs counter to the several assessments of Walrasian theory made by Friedman both before and after he wrote his address.[24]

In sum, little credit should be given to Friedman's definition. The latter should be viewed as a mere ecumenical gesture, a rhetorical strategy serving the purpose of rallying as many people as possible around his views.

A return to the Marshallian conception of equilibrium

Friedman's model marks a return to the Marshallian conception of equilibrium on two scores. First, as the following quotation makes clear, he shares the view defended in Chapter 4 that the market-day should be viewed as operating instantaneously:

> Alfred Marshall's distinction among market equilibrium, short-period equilibrium, and long-period equilibrium was a device for analysing the dynamic adjustment in a particular market to a change in demand or supply. The device had two key characteristics . . . The second is the assumption that prices adjust more rapidly than quantities, indeed so rapidly that the price adjustment can be regarded as instantaneously.
>
> (Friedman 1974a: 17)

Second, Keynes and Hicks departed from Marshall by concatenating the market-day and the short-period, on the one hand, and by cutting off this new short-period from the long-period (the market equilibrium from normal equilibrium), on the other. This is a mistake Friedman is aware of.[25] The inner connection between the market-day and the normal equilibrium dimensions is restored in his model. As shown above, the natural rate of employment is understood as a normal magnitude, the quantity counterpart of the real normal equilibrium wage. Market-day outcomes can witness to disequilibrium – a departure from the natural rate of employment – yet this co-exists with market clearing. Moreover, as ought to be the case in Marshallian analysis, this state of affairs triggers a re-equilibrating process resulting in the eventual disappearance of the disequilibrium. As stated by Rogerson:

> Reading Friedman's Presidential Address, I think he also is describing an economy in which at any moment actual unemployment may be either above or below its natural rate, but it is continually gravitating towards its natural rate.
>
> (Rogerson 1997: 90)

Perfect information

In Chapter 4, I emphasised the pivotal role played by perfect information, as implying agents' ability to reconstruct equilibrium values, in the Marshall approach. It constitutes, I have argued, the *deus ex machina* underpinning the formation of market equilibrium. Marshallian economists never admitted to this, putting instead (incorrectly) the burden of the price-setting mechanism on the bargaining process. Friedman is treading in Marshall's footsteps. Although he fails to mention perfect information, his explanation of the working of the labour market makes no sense without it.

The snag is whether demand and function can be considered directly observable phenomena. Friedman takes it for granted that this is the case. Yet there is nothing on which this view can be grounded. Again this shows how much a Marshallian he is, since he implicitly assumes that workers are able to mentally reconstruct market functions. Equilibrium is virtually determined before the effective opening of markets, as it already exists in the market participants' minds. The agents' omniscience assumption, mitigated with workers' mistakes in assessing the demand for labour function, is as much required in Friedman's model as it is in Marshall's corn model.

However, Friedman's reasoning faces a problem of consistency that is absent from the standard Marshallian model based on perfect information. It bears on what triggers workers' conjecture that a shift in the demand curve has occurred. The spontaneous answer is that workers observe that a higher wage is announced and rationalise it by conjecturing that a shift in demand must have occurred. However, this answer cannot suffice. As stated above, in the Marshallian analysis of market equilibrium there are neither price nor quantity signals. Any conjectured change in price results from a conjectured change in supply or demand. Hence, the idea, that a change in supply or demand schedule is drawn from an observed change in price, is unacceptable. This anomaly is interesting for my purpose because it suggests that Friedman mingles the Walrasian conception of the functioning of markets – where prices function as a signal announced by the auctioneer – with the Marshallian view, where agents need to reconstruct these functions and derive the market equilibrium price as a result.

What arises when Friedman's reasoning is recast to conform with Marshallian principles? Figure 13.2 helps to answer this question.

The vertical axis now indicates the nominal wage. Expectations about the goods price, assuming a single final good, enter the supply and demand functions as fixed parameters. That is:

$L_t^S = L_t^S\ (w;\ p_t^{ew})$

$L_t^D = L_t^D\ (w;\ p_t^{ef})$, where p_t^{ew} (p_t^{ef}) stands for workers' (firms') expectations about p_t held before the opening of the trade round.

It is assumed: that $p_t^{ew} = p_{t-1}$, $p_t^{ef} = p_t$, that $p_t > p_{t-1}$ and that $w_t / w_{t-1} < p_t / p_{t-1}$. It is furthermore assumed that the natural rate prevails at t_0, with disequilibrium arising at t_1. In Friedman's scenario, firms hold perfect foresight of the price in the goods market and thus are aware that it will increase. As a result, the labour demand schedule shifts to the right (from L_0^D to L_1^D). In contrast, since workers hold adaptive expectations, the

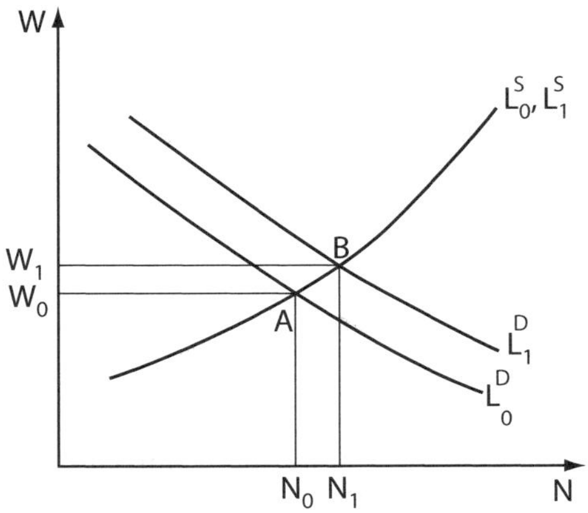

Figure 13.2 An alternative account of Friedman's reasoning.

labour supply schedule remains constant (L_0^S to L_1^S). At t_1, the labour market market-day equilibrium is W_1, N_1. This result features market clearing and disequilibrium at one and the same time (disequilibrium exists because the market values (W_1, N_1) depart from normal values (W_0, N_0)).

Figure 13.2 is based on the Marshallian premise that participants in the market are able to calculate the market-day equilibrium values (point *B*) before the starting of the market. Still, the argument remains wanting. If workers are able to reconstruct the market result, they must correctly conjecture the market demand, which implies that they are aware that firms' behaviour is based on price-expectations different from theirs. In fact, they are supposed to be able to reconstruct these expectations. But then, why should they stick to their own misleading adaptive expectations?

14

LUCAS

While Friedman paved the way, the decisive role in the dismissal of Keynesian economics was played by Lucas.[1] Put crudely, the standard view is that 'Keynesianism' was overthrown in a two-step revolution, the first stage of which is associated with monetarism and the second with new classical macroeconomics. Such a formulation suggests a line of continuity between monetarism and new classicism. On the contrary, I argue that the watershed should be located between Friedman and Lucas. In other words, the real divide separates an era of 'Marshallian macroeconomics' from one of 'Walrasian macroeconomics'.[2] The first era was a period where the IS-LM apparatus was the cornerstone of macroeconomic thinking, shared by both friends and foes of Keynes, Friedman being the best example of the latter group. The second era marks the dethroning of IS-LM and its replacement by a new theoretical apparatus, the dynamic macro model.

Lucas' contribution to the object of my investigation is threefold. First, he finalised Friedman's attempt at demonstrating the inefficiency of monetary policy. Second, he criticised Keynesian theory on the grounds of first economic principles. Third, he claimed that the concept of involuntary unemployment was non-intelligible.

Clinching Friedman's claim

Lucas' motivation for writing his 'Expectations and the Neutrality of Money' (1981) article was to strengthen Friedman's policy ineffectiveness claim by giving it stronger micro-foundations and casting it in an explicit general equilibrium framework.[3]

Lucas' model is an overlapping generations model with agents living for two periods. There is one perishable good, produced by the young generation yet consumed by both young and old agents. The young are self-employed. They acquire fiat money, which does not enter the utility function, by selling the good to the members of the old generation, and spend it to purchase goods when old. The overall size of the population is fixed with an equal proportion of young and old people. Production decisions depend on the relative price of the good across the two periods. As the substitution effect is supposed to outweigh the wealth effect, young agents will plan to consume more when old if they expect the next period price to be relatively low with respect to today's, and *vice versa*.

A decisive assumption of the model, marking a break with both Friedman and Lucas' earlier work with Rapping, is the adoption of the assumption of rational expectations. That is, agents are assumed to hold expectations which are consistent with the predictions of the theoretical model. A rational expectations equilibrium is a market equilibrium in which traders use equilibrium market prices to draw inferences about their uncertain environment.

The set-up of Lucas' reasoning is explicitly stochastic with two types of stochastic shocks being introduced – a real and a nominal shock (whereas in Friedman's model only a nominal shock was needed). The nominal disturbance follows from the fact that the members of the older generation receive a beginning-of-period money transfer proportional to their pre-transfer holdings of money. The real shock results from the fact that trade is supposed to take place in two physically separate places, each of them organised under the auspices of an auctioneer. It is assumed that young agents are allocated stochastically across the two trading places, whereas old agents are equally distributed across them. Whenever a young agent happens to be in a market with a proportionally low young population, thus facing a higher per capita demand, he will produce more and consume less in his young age, in order to consume more when old. The young are supposed to know the density functions of the two stochastic variables yet to ignore their drawing at the present period. As a result, they face a signal extraction problem, as they need to sort out whether the changes in price they observe follow from either a nominal or a real shock.

Three results are obtained. First, whenever the shock is exclusively monetary, young agents will be able to interpret it correctly. Consequently, no real effects are elicited. Second, an exclusive real shock is likely to generate changes in output. Young agents finding themselves in the market with a less-than-average number of suppliers will increase their production and hold higher real balances. The reverse will be true for those finding themselves in the thicker market. However, the two opposite movements will not necessarily balance each other. Finally, in the general case when the two shocks occur concurrently, agents are unable to separate them out, since the available information bears on their joint effect. Under certain conditions put on the densities of the two shocks, Lucas' result is that 'monetary changes have real consequences only because agents cannot discriminate perfectly between real and monetary demand shifts' (1981: 78). Like Friedman's, Lucas' model deals with variations in employment going along with market clearing. The bottom line is that Friedman was right. A positive relationship between the rate of inflation and the rate of employment can be observed yet cannot be used as a policy tool.

Beyond doubt, Lucas' model shows tremendous progress compared to Friedman's. It is a rigorous and elegant model, and succeeds in realising Friedman's initial aim. As Lucas writes in the paper's conclusion, 'the Phillips Curve emerges not as an unexplained empirical fact, but as a central feature of the solution to a general equilibrium system' (1981a: 84). Introducing rational expectations has a far-reaching impact. On the one hand, workers' unintelligent behaviour, which the adaptive expectations amounted to, is now swept way. On the other hand, the rational expectations hypothesis provides an operational solution to the difficult problem of modelling expectations. In short, as Sargent claims (1996), Lucas' contribution has mainly been methodological. It blazed the trail for real business cycle theory and dynamic macroeconomics.

This being stated, it must be remarked that the criticism levelled against Friedman's argumentation, that it justifies policy ineffectiveness only in cases where policy is blatantly unnecessary, applies to Lucas' model as well. In its framework, policy interventions have no *raison d'être.*

Lucas' rejection of Keynesian theory

Criticism of Keynesian theory can be undertaken from several angles. Friedman's consisted of using the Keynesian apparatus while subverting it by drawing anti-Keynesian conclusions from it. I, for one, have entered into an internal criticism of Keynes' concepts and theory. For his part, Lucas refuses to enter into any substantive discussion of the Keynesian model because he believes that its dismissal is a matter of first principles.

Lucas' negative judgement goes beyond Keynes' own contribution as it relates to the general state of economic theory at his time. In effect, he is prone to draw a divide between pre-scientific economics, as consisting of verbal discussions, and scientific economics, consisting of model-building. To Lucas, Keynes' *General Theory* is definitely on the side of the former. He views it as a rambling verbal exposition, eliciting endless hermeneutic discussions – 'disconnected qualitative talk' as stated in Lucas and Sargent ([1979] 1994: 6).[4] The problem that existed at the time of Keynes – and, of course, before – was that economists lacked the technical (i.e. mathematical and econometric) apparatus needed to move discussions to a more productive level (Lucas 1981: 275).

> While Keynes and the other founders of what we now call macroeconomics were obliged to rely on Marshallian ingenuity to tease some useful dynamics out of purely static theory, the modern the-

> orist is much better equipped to state exactly the problem he wants to study and then to study it.
>
> (Lucas 1987: 2)[5]

Lucas' indictment

According to Lucas, Keynes intended initially to construct a theory of the business cycle – massive unemployment being then associated with depression – yet ended up in redirecting his project to the apparently simpler issue of explaining the logical existence of involuntary unemployment at any given point in time. This is a move that Lucas regrets.

> The onset of the Great Depression did nothing to improve Keynes's equipment for understanding the business cycle, viewed as a recurrent sequence of booms and depressions. Instead, it permitted him to reformulate the problem itself as one of accounting for the level of output and employment at one point in time, as opposed to one of accounting for a particular pattern repeated in the time series. So reformulated, the problem could productively be studied simply by discarding an equation of static equilibrium (the labour supply curve) in contrast to the much more difficult task, undertaken in the *Treatise*, of supplementing this static theory with suitable short-run dynamics.
>
> (1981: 275)[6]

Lucas' remark can be related to my argument in Chapter 5. There, I emphasised the divide that existed at Keynes' time between value theory (i.e. price theory), on the one hand, and business cycle and monetary theory, on the other. To Marshallian economists, from Marshall until Keynes, a phenomenon such as unemployment was considered a market failure. Its qualification as involuntary raised no eyebrows. Yet, to all intents and purposes there was room for it only within business cycle theory. Hence my reconstruction of Keynes' project as an attempt to transfer involuntary unemployment from the field of business cycle to that of value theory. The contrast between Keynes' project, on the one hand, and that of Lucas and real business cycle theorists, on the other, can then be captured in the following way. While Keynes' project amounted to wanting to import involuntary unemployment from the field of business cycle into value theory, Lucas and real business cycle theorists aimed at merging these two fields while extending the exclusion of unemployment (and hence of involuntary unemployment), already present in value theory, to the new wider field.[7]

Turning now to Lucas's main argument, a striking point is that, contrary to Friedman, he engages in no substantive analysis of Keynes' theory. Its dismissal follows exclusively from a matter of principles. At stake is the equilibrium 'discipline' – a metaphor dear to Lucas – by which economists should abide when constructing theories. Its gist is simple: two postulates ought to be adhered to, that markets clear and that agents act in their own self-interest (Lucas and Sargent [1979] 1994: 15).[8] Moreover, to Lucas and Sargent these two postulates are linked by a relationship of implication. Economic rationality, they claim, implies market clearing. These postulates are not viewed as circumstantial, i.e. linked to particular models in view of their specific purpose. On the contrary, they are deemed to constitute a universal requirement. This claim pervades all of Lucas' methodological papers. It has been taken up, not only by new classical economists, to whom it has become a dogma, but also by a wider range of economists – with hardly any justification, as though the matter were so obvious that none was needed.

According to Lucas, Keynes' basic flaw is to have betrayed this equilibrium discipline. Keynes, he states, gives us an example of 'bad social science: an attempt to explain important aspects of human behaviour without reference either to what people like or what they are capable of doing' (1981: 4). The following two excerpts bring the point home:

> After freeing himself of the straightjacket (or discipline) imposed by the classical postulates, Keynes described a model in which rules of thumb, such as the consumption function and liquidity preference schedule, took the place of decision functions that a classical economist would insist be derived from the theory of choice. And rather than require that wages and prices be determined by the postulate that markets clear – which for the labour market seemed patently contradicted by the severity of business depressions – Keynes took as an unexamined postulate that money wages are sticky, meaning that they are set at a level or by a process that could be taken as uninfluenced by the macroeconomic forces he proposed to analyse.
>
> (Lucas and Sargent [1979] 1994: 15)

> Keynes chose to begin the *General Theory* with the declaration (for Chapter II is no more than this) that an equilibrium theory was unattainable: that unemployment was not explainable as a consequence of individual choices and that the failure of wages to move as predicted by the classical theory was to be treated as due to forces beyond the power of economic theory to illuminate.
>
> (1981: 219)

The counterpart of Lucas' claim that optimising behaviour is a postulate is his rejection of the disequilibrium notion on the grounds that it lacks micro-foundations (1981: 221) or is 'unintelligent behaviour' (1981: 225).

In sum, Lucas' indictment is not that Keynes offered his readers a flawed economic explanation of unemployment but rather that the gave them a non-economic explanation of it. Keynes's lapse from the equilibrium discipline, Lucas is ready to admit, was understandable in view of the apparent contradiction between cyclical phenomena and economic equilibrium, yet *ex post* it turns out to have been a dramatic mistake that prompted a long detour in the progress of economic theory.

A critique of Lucas' indictment

My objection to Lucas' claim bears on his central assertion that the presence of optimising behaviour and market clearing are two *sine qua non* requirements for any theoretically correct argumentation. To me, he is at fault by making this claim because of a failure to note the distinction, which I introduced in Chapter 2, between optimal choice or optimal plan, on the one hand, and observable optimising behaviour, on the other.[9]

The notion of optimal plan refers to agents' intentions as existing before the opening of trading. Optimising behaviour refers to what is observable after trading has started. Thus, optimising behaviour implies that the optimal plan has been realised. These two phenomena must be separated because conceiving a solution to a choice problem and having it implemented are not the same thing. Whenever optimising behaviour is the sole concept used, the possibility of a wedge between them is discarded by definition. My very introduction of the notion of individual disequilibrium serves the purpose of capturing the possibility that agents find themselves unable to transform their optimal plans into optimising behaviour.

If my claim that a distinction must be drawn between optimal planning and optimising behaviour is accepted, Lucas' view must be recast as stating that the economists' discipline rests on two distinct postulates, optimal planning and market clearing. These are not two faces of the same coin. Their validity must be assessed independently. Nor can it be taken for granted that the former implies the latter.

No objection will be levelled against adopting optimal planning as a postulate. The assumption that agents have the ability to solve optimally any decision problem they are facing is certainly an exaggeration. Nonetheless, it is acceptable as it is probably better, and certainly more tractable, than alternative assumptions. But what about market clearing?

As stated in Chapter 4, market clearing is the consequence of some prior assumption related to trade technology, the institutional set-up that is needed to make the realisation of equilibrium possible. Like other Walrasian models, Lucas' models are based on the auctioneer hypothesis. The latter is a theoretical scenario explaining how the equilibrium values calculated by the economist when studying the logical existence of a general equilibrium could effectively come into existence in the artificial economy described by the model. As soon as this hypothesis is made, market clearing is always present. But then market clearing is the direct consequence of the auctioneer hypothesis rather than the implication of agents construing their plans of action in an optimising way.

Two intertwined aspects must be disentangled. The first is the extent of what can be conceptualised taking market clearing as a postulate. The merit of authors like Lucas and other new classicists is to have demonstrated that this scope for theories resting on this postulate is wider than was previously believed. In effect, prior to them it was taken for granted that no theory of the business cycle could be based on it. They have proved the contrary. However, and this is the second aspect, this success does not justify the view that the aim of demonstrating market non-clearing, as a particular type of pathology of the functioning of market economies – Keynes's very project – is theoretically illegitimate. Why would this be the case? Lucas' view to the contrary notwithstanding, no objections of principles should be levelled against such a project. The individual disequilibrium notion does not run counter to the view that agents are rational and develop optimal plans. It just points to their incapacity to transform the individual optimal plan into optimising behaviour

In other words, Lucas' claim that market non-clearing should be rejected because of its lacking a motivation in individual rationality is ill-grounded. Unfortunately enough, this view has been widely endorsed, even by such a lucid mind as Woodford's (1999: 25). I readily admit that market non-clearing has no room in neo-Walrasian models, yet this is due to a trade technology rather than to an individual rationality reason.

The problem with the auctioneer hypothesis is that it runs counter to the deep nature of the theoretical *explanandum* as it amounts to picturing a decentralised system under the traits of a centralised organisation of trade.[10] Moreover, if axioms mark the stage beyond which one does not seek to explain, as aptly put by Hahn (1985: 6), it is unacceptable to exclude the very basic issue that political economy has been supposed to address from Adam Smith onwards.[11] In effect, the auctioneer hypothesis can be justified only on the grounds of an argument of expediency – the admission that any alternative scenario about the making of equilibrium is lacking. The change induced by Lucas then becomes no small matter. It amounts to transforming expediency into methodological virtue.

To conclude, I have taken on Lucas because he declares that Keynes betrays the equilibrium discipline. Contrary to him, I believe that attempting to demonstrate individual disequilibrium does not fall outside the scope of the equilibrium method. The fact that neither Keynes nor Keynesian economists have succeeded in demonstrating individual disequilibrium, their real target, cannot be equated with the proposition that such an aim ought be rejected as a matter of first principles. Had Lucas simply stated that Keynes and his successors have been unable to achieve their program, I would have been in agreement with him. It is the claim of the illegitimacy of Keynes' project that is unacceptable to me.

Lucas' critique of the involuntary unemployment concept

On top of his main indictment, bearing on Keynes's alleged abandonment of the equilibrium discipline, Lucas also criticises Keynes for having introduced the messy involuntary unemployment concept into macroeconomic thinking:

> What is the excuse for letting his [Keynes's] carelessly drawn distinction between voluntary and involuntary unemployment dominate aggregative thinking on labour markets for the forty years following?
>
> (1981: 242)

Small wonder, he claims, that trying to assess involuntary unemployment or to measure full employment has led to confusion, since 'the "thing" to be measured does not exist' (1981: 244). The sooner involuntary unemployment is disposed with, the better:

> This misses the point: involuntary unemployment is not a fact or a phenomenon which it is the task of theorists to explain. It is, on the contrary, a theoretical construct which Keynes introduced in the hope it would be helpful in discovering a correct explanation for a genuine phenomenon: large-scale fluctuations in measured, total unemployment. Is it the task of modern theoretical economics to 'explain' the theoretical constructs of our predecessor, whether or not they have proved fruitful? I hope not, for a surer route to sterility could scarcely be imagined.
>
> In summary, it does not appear possible, even in principle, to classify individual unemployed people as either voluntarily or involuntarily unemployed depending on the characteristics of the decision problem they face. One cannot, even conceptually, arrive at a usable definition of full employment.
>
> (1981: 243).

This conclusion results from three separate arguments. First, Lucas claims that Keynes should not have opposed two sorts of unemployment, frictional and involuntary unemployment. Second, he argues that every economic outcome features voluntarity and involuntarity jointly. Third, he argues that unemployment, viewed as an activity amongst others, should be considered voluntary since alternative activities are always present.

Why separate two sorts of unemployment?

The first question Lucas raises concerns Keynes' separation of two types of unemployment:

> [Keynes made] the prior assumption that measured employment can be decomposed into two distinct components: 'voluntary' (or frictional) and 'involuntary', with full employment then identified as the level prevailing when involuntary employment equals zero.
> (Lucas 1981: 241)

> Accepting the necessity of a distinction between explanations for normal and cyclical unemployment does not, however, compel one to identify the first as voluntary and the second as involuntary, as Keynes goes on to do. This terminology suggests that the key to the distinction lies in some difference in the way two different types of unemployment are *perceived by workers.* Now in the first place, the distinction we are after concerns *sources* of unemployment, not differentiated types . . . The recognition that one needs to distinguish among sources of unemployment does not in any way imply that one needs to distinguish among types.
> (Lucas 1981: 241–242)

I agree with Lucas on this point. Whenever the concern is value theory – i.e. the issue of the existence and formation of equilibrium – either market clearing exists, in which case unemployment is absent, or there is market non-clearing, in which case unemployment (or forced leisure) is effectively present. But then no other unemployment category should be introduced.

The mixed presence of voluntarity and involuntarity in any economic outcome

The second argument put forward by Lucas runs as follows:

> The worker who loses a good job in prosperous time does not *volunteer* to be in this situation: he has suffered a capital loss. Similarly, the firm which loses an experienced employee in depressed times suffers an undesirable capital loss. Nevertheless the unemployed worker at any time can always find *some* job at once, and a firm can always fill a vacancy instantaneously. That neither typically does so *by choice* is not difficult to understand given the quality of the jobs and the employees which are easiest to find. Thus there is an involuntary element in *all* unemployment, in the sense that no one chooses bad luck over good; there is also a

> voluntary element in all unemployment, in the sense that however miserable one's current work options, one can always choose to accept them.
>
> (1981: 242)

At stake is the meaning of voluntarity in general, an issue that is directly related to a much larger philosophical problem bearing on freedom. On this matter, Lucas has illustrious predecessors, the foremost being Aristotle, who devoted several passages of *The Nicomachean Ethics* to the voluntarity-involuntarity divide. The following is worth quoting:

> Those things, then, are thought involuntary, which took place by force or owing to ignorance . . . With regards to the things that are done from fear of greater evils or for some noble object (e.g. if a tyrant were to order one to do something base, having one's parents and children in his power, and if one did the action they were to be saved, but otherwise would be put to death), it may be debated whether such actions are involuntary or involuntary. Something of the sort happens also with regards to the throwing of goods overboard in a storm; for in the abstract no one throws goods away voluntarily, but on condition of its securing the security of himself and his crew any sensible man does so. Such actions, then, are mixed, but are more like voluntary actions; for they are worthy of choice at the time they are done, and the end of an action is relative to the occasion. Both the terms, then, 'voluntary' and 'involuntary', must be used with the reference to the moment of action. Now the man acts voluntarily; for the principle that moves the instrumental parts of the body in such actions is in him, and the things of which the moving principle is in a man himself are in his power to do or not to do. Such actions, therefore, are voluntary, but in the abstract perhaps involuntary; for no one would choose any such act in itself.
>
> (Aristotle 1980: 48–49)

Ought individuals, the underlying question runs, be considered responsible for their present condition? Whenever this question receives a straightforward 'yes' answer, the rejection of any involuntary outcome ensues automatically. All consequences of actions ought to be seen as voluntary. Think, for example, of a thief caught after a robbery and sent to jail. According to the strong acceptance of voluntarity, he is behind prison bars voluntarily. Before committing the robbery, he knew the odds of being caught. Likewise, a heavy smoker who ends up with lung cancer ought to be qualified as 'voluntarily ill'. However, as underlined by Aristotle, at least two factors run counter to such an affirmative answer: first, force – 'and that is compulsory of which the moving principle is outside, being a principle in which nothing is contributed by the persons who acts' ((1980: 48) – and, second, ignorance (going along with regret) – 'of people, then, who act by reason of ignorance he who regrets is thought an involuntary agent' (1980: 50). The 'full responsibility' view has a polar opposite, wherein, on the contrary, individuals are seen as socially determined, e.g. because of their class membership. As a result, they are depicted as mere 'products of the social structure' rather than as free choosers.

Neither of these two extreme views is satisfactory. Nonetheless, the involuntary unemployment category may still make sense in so far as it is accepted that some 'responsibility boundary' can be drawn. Placing this limit at a high or a low level would mean that one bends towards or away from the full responsibility viewpoint. By studying the occupational trajectory of individual unemployed people and by knowing the configuration of their choice sets, it should be possible, in principle, to assess whether or not an individual could be qualified as involuntarily unemployed. To put some flesh on this, think of the following case: a highly-skilled person, yet one who is already aged, has lost his job because the firm where he used to work went bankrupt. Assume, moreover, that the branch in which he was working is declining. Whereas his age is an handicap to getting a lower-skilled job, he lacks the means to become self-employed. Suppose also that the emigration solution is precluded. The question at hand is whether his unemployment qualifies for the 'involuntary' modifier. The answer to this question hinges on where to put the responsibility boundary. When younger, this person could have anticipated the frailty of the firm employing him and quit it immediately, in which case he would have found a job. Placing the responsibility boundary at a high pitch amounts to judging whether it was in his reach to make such a judgment and his responsibility to take the consequences. Hence the conclusion would be that he should be considered voluntarily unemployed. On the contrary, placing the boundary lower amounts to considering that expecting people to be able make such judgments and decisions amounts to overtaxing their rationality. Hence he should be classified as involuntarily unemployed. Significantly, in such a framework, nobody could be '100 per cent involuntarily unemployed', because some responsibility is always involved. It should come as no surprise that the proportion of the involuntarily unemployed within the pool of the unemployed would be higher in a context of depression. Therefore, the association made by Keynes between involuntary and mass unemployment is quite plausible.

To conclude on this point, Lucas is right when stating that all unemployment situations comprises a mix of voluntarity and involuntarity. However, it must be remarked that this statement bites as much at the new classical conception of economic theory as to that of Keynesians. If it is accepted that the assertion 'Mr. X is 100 per cent involuntarily unemployed' is too extreme, the opposite assertion, that 'Mr. X's unemployment is 100 per cent voluntarily', is just as wanting. Now this, it may be argued, is the very conception of freedom that underpins rational expectations models.

The existence of alternatives

To Lucas, unemployment should be viewed as an activity among others that, like them, should be tackled in choice-theoretical terms. If agents are observed as being unemployed, they must have chosen this activity over other ones:

> Workers who lose jobs, for whatever reason, typically pass through a period of unemployment instead of taking temporary work on the 'spot' labour market jobs that are readily available in any economy ... To explain why people allocate time to a particular *activity* – like unemployment – we need to know why they prefer it to *all* other available activities.
>
> (1987: 54)[12]

This claim can be addressed in terms of the distinction between labour rationing and unemployment as an activity that was presented in Chapter 3. There, I brought out the conditions necessary to assess the existence of involuntary unemployment. If my analysis is accepted, Lucas' claim, that it is impossible, even in principle, to construct the category of involuntary unemployment, is refuted.

This being stated, it must be admitted that eliciting the conditions making a phenomenon possible is only a preliminary step. Their plausibility must furthermore be assessed. One of them is that market non-clearing must exist in the unskilled labour. This brings us back to square one, demonstrating involuntary unemployment in the individual disequilibrium sense. The stumbling block to the realisation of the Keynesian project, it turns out, lies less in bringing out involuntary unemployment in the activity sense (that is, that rationing may end up in agents being involuntarily unemployed) than in generating involuntary unemployment as meant by Keynes (that is, that a market ends up with agents for whom the reservation wage principle is breached and who, on top, turn out to be in a state of individual disequilibrium).

Concluding remarks

In this chapter, I have critically examined the validity of Lucas' indictment of Keynes that he freed himself from the equilibrium discipline. I have argued that it is flawed because of Lucas' failure in drawing a wedge between optimal planning and optimising behaviour, to which earlier economists, whom he seems to hold in high esteem, like Hayek and Patinkin, were sensitive. Against this background, I have defended the view that there is no reason to claim that Keynes' involuntary unemployment project – in fact a project of demonstrating a case of individual disequilibrium – falls outside the equilibrium method. I repeat that what is at stake is theoretical legitimacy rather than success, for I readily admit that, more than half a century after having been launched, Keynes' project has hardly been implemented.

The second theme that I have tackled is Lucas' critical remarks on the involuntary unemployment concept. They are, I find, salutary. Lucas' merit is to have assessed this, and shown how messy the concept is, while it had long been taken for granted that its content was obvious. I have agreed with his first criticism that Keynes has no reasons for separating forms of unemployment. As for his other two criticisms – the mixed presence of voluntarity and involuntarity and the ever-presence of alternatives to unemployment – I find them interesting yet less compelling than he seems to believe.

In this chapter, my reflection has focused on a narrow aspect of Lucas' contribution to economic theory, and for that matter its negative part. I have not broached his positive contribution (as well as that of related authors such as Sargent, Kydland and Prescott, and many others), pertaining to the development of a conceptual framework enabling economists to come to grips with a subject that before had eluded them, namely dynamics. This contribution can be characterised in a twofold way – first as a shift from Marshallian to Walrasian macroeconomics and, second, as the introduction of the business cycle phenomenon within the field of value theory. On both scores, the intellectual achievement is impressive.

Beyond doubt, the attack led by Lucas and the other new classicists against Keynesian economics was a tremendous success. The latter was partially due to the strength of their theoretical criticism. It was also due to the empirical breaking down of the Phillips Curve relation. But the main cause of their success lay in their methodological breakthrough and its ensuing change in theoretical agenda. I am amazed that this dramatic shift from standard IS-LM macroeconomics to the new dynamic-stochastic macroeconomics has scarcely been accounted for as a Kuhnian scientific revolution because it perfectly fits such a characterisation.[13] Both the purpose and the programme of macroeconomics changed radically. Before the new classical revolution, macroeconomics was geared towards discussing the possibility of the malfunctioning of the market system – after all, it was born in the aftermath of the Great Depression. This is a perspective that new classicists have swept away, as aptly perceived by Hahn and Solow:

> The irony is that macroeconomics began as the study of large-scale economic pathologies: prolonged depressions, mass unemployment, persistent, inflation, etc. This focus was not invented by Keynes (although the depression of the 1930s did not pass without notice). After all, most of Haberler's classic *Prosperity and Depression* is about ideas that were in circulation before *The General Theory*. Now, at last, macroeconomic theory has as its central conception a model in which such pathologies are, strictly speaking, unmentionable. There is no legal way to talk about them.
>
> (Hahn and Solow 1995: 2–3)

The hallmark of new macroeconomics is to take for granted that the market system is functioning well. Thereby a return is made not only to Keynes' direct predecessors but also to themes that were dear to the founders of political economy, the explanation of the 'wealth of nations', growth, differences in growth patterns, etc. Both the ancient and the new classicists dodge the issue of the formation of trade round equilibrium prices. The great difference with respect to classicists, as Lucas has recurrently insisted, lies in the tools available. Now at last, dynamic theory can be made in a rigorous way.

As always with scientific revolutions, the earlier central themes have become old-fashioned. To return to the object of my inquiry, Lucas and his co-writers have succeeded in removing involuntary unemployment from the agenda. After initially strenuously defending it, most Keynesian economists have gradually ceased to feel the need of keeping fighting for it. To wit, the term has almost disappeared from macroeconomic textbooks.

However, the new classical attack on Keynesian economics did not put an end to the debate. On the contrary, by a standard dialectical effect, it stirred up a revival of Keynesian thought, known as 'New Keynesian economics'. It is examined in Part VI.

Part VI

THE NEW KEYNESIAN COUNTER-ATTACK

15

IMPLICIT CONTRACT THEORY

The theory of implicit contracts constitutes one of the first Keynesian attempts at retorting to Lucas while accepting his microfoundations requirement. An interesting example of 'simultaneous discovery', it was developed independently at more or less the same time by different authors, Azariadis (1975), Baily (1974) and Gordon (1974). My analysis will be limited to Azariadis' model as it is probably the most influential of these three papers.

Motivations and sources of inspiration

Although implicit contracts models have a definite microeconomic character, macroeconomic issues provided the impetus for their emergence (Azariadis 1987: 735). Azariadis wanted to vindicate the Keynesian cause against Lucas' criticism by putting forward a claim, which at first looked typically Keynesian, bearing on the existence of involuntary unemployment and the disengagement of the real wage from the marginal productivity of labour. Azariadis wanted to beat Lucas on his home turf, as it were – 'Oh, you want optimising behaviour', he might have said, 'then you'll get it, and it will lead to a Keynesian result!'.

This endeavour arose against a twofold background, the looming demise of the disequilibrium approach, on the one hand, and the arising of search models around the famous Phelps' volume, *Microeconomic Foundations of Employment and Inflation Theory* (1970), on the other. According to the disequilibrium approach, involuntary unemployment resulted from the fact that price rigidity impeded the attainment of Walrasian magnitudes. Wage rigidity was considered both an important fact of reality and a basic tenet of Keynesian macroeconomics. Yet Keynesians were well aware that its vindication was urgently needed. Implicit contracts, it was claimed, could do the job. Search theory arose as a serious theoretical rival to standard Keynesian theory. Its explanation relied exclusively on frictional unemployment, leaving no space for the additional category, involuntary unemployment, that Keynes wanted to bring to the fore. A theory as to redundancy, of which involuntariness seemed a natural feature, appeared as an appealing alternative to search models.

Against this background, what triggered Azariadis and his co-inventors was the long-standing insight that the labour market cannot be put on the same footing as the other markets. As stated by Azariadis:

> The drift of the preceding arguments points to a more complex view of the labour market than is customary in conventional short-run analyses: in uncertainty, labour services are not auctioned off in quite the same way fresh fruit is. Rather they are exchanged for some implicit set of commitments, hereinafter called an implicit labour contract, on the part of the firm to employ the owner of those labour services for a 'reasonable' period of time and on terms mutually agreed upon in advance.
>
> (Azariadis 1975: 1185)[1]

In order to substantiate the idea that the labour market is different from others, the founders of implicit contract theory took a rather roundabout path as they drew their inspiration from an outwardly remote source, Arrow's insurance theory, rather than from any direct observation of the working of real world labour markets.

> One can, for analytical purposes, regard a cost-plus contract (e.g. the government contracting for military procurement) as being made of two contracts, one a fixed-price contract of the usual commercial type, and one an insurance contract by which the government agrees to reimburse the manufacturer for his unexpected costs.
>
> (Arrow 1971: 136)

The central hunch of implicit contract models follows: the labour contract ought to be viewed as bearing on a wider package than the spot determination of a wage-hours pair. On top of serving the purpose of exchanging labour services, it comprises an insurance component. In Baily's terms:

> In deciding what wage-employment strategy to set, the firm will be willing to reduce worker risk. By doing so, the firm is offering a joint product, employment plus an insurance of financial intermediation service.
>
> (Baily 1974: 37)

Azariadis' model

Contract theory, in Azariadis' initial format, is a one-period, partial equilibrium model revolving around the relationship between a firm and its labour pool. Uncertainty exists as to the level of demand faced by the firm. To simplify, it can be assumed that two states are possible, a favourable and an unfavourable one, corresponding to a high or a low demand (and hence to a high or a low price). Technology being of the standard type, two levels of marginal value product of labour exist accordingly. It is assumed that the firm is risk neutral – its utility function is linear in profits – while workers are risk averse. As a result, firms and workers have a mutual interest in fixing a wage and employment contract contingent on the states of the world.

A two-tier process is present. Its first stage concerns the distribution of workers across the firms. It occurs through an auction market bearing on contracts and giving workers a given utility level, $\bar{v}$. The value of the contract offered plays the same role as the price in a competitive market. In equilibrium it must be equal for all firms. It is assumed that every worker gets an employment contract. Nobody is formally jobless. The second process, the very subject matter of the model, bears on the contents of the contract between a firm and its labour pool. Here, $\bar{v}$ acts as a constraint on the firm's objective function. At stake is whether the wage and the employment level – i.e. the rate of utilisation of the members of the labour pool – will be identical or vary across the states of the world. That is, is it optimal to have a wage equal to the marginal productivity of labour? Is the full employment contract optimal? Azariadis defines full employment as a state where the number of workers that the firm will put at work (n) is equal to the size of the firm's workforce (m), and underemployment as any state where $n < m$.

The model is based on a series of precise assumptions that I shall not detail, except for two crucial ones. The first is labour-time indivisibility: it is assumed that workers are endowed with one unit of time that must be used fully either as labour or as leisure. Second, the class of admissible contracts is restricted in that firms can insure volatility in wage yet not volatility in employment, i.e. provide severance payments to redundant workers.

A twofold result is obtained. First, the firm and it workers have a mutual interest in having the same wage across states of nature. This is Azariadis' 'rigidity' result. It is the straightforward consequence of their different attitudes towards risk. As a result, the wage will be higher than the marginal value product in the unfavourable state since workers receive an insurance benefit, and lower in the favourable state since an insurance premium is now deducted from the marginal value product. Thus, the employment contract is coupled with an insurance contract. To Azariadis, this disengagement of wages from the marginal-revenue product of labour amounts to a validation of Keynesian theory:

> There is indeed among macroeconomists a shared impression that, over a typical business cycle, average real compensation per hour fluctuates considerably less than does the marginal revenue-product of labour or, for that matter, the total volume of employment. One consequence is that wage and price rigidity are among the key assumptions of Keynesian macroeconomics both in the Hicksian IS-LM framework and in the concept of quantity-constrained equilibrium developed by Clower and formalised by Benassy and Drèze ... Involuntary unemployment is for many economists the *sine qua non* of modern economics.
>
> (Azariadis 1987: 734)

Azariadis' second result is that full employment is not necessarily optimal. Redundancies can be in the mutual interest of the firm and the workers in the unfavourable state of the world. They are more likely the lower the revenue marginal productivity in the unfavourable state, the smaller workers' risk premium and the higher the opportunity cost of leisure. Layoffs, which go along with a nil wage, are decided randomly. Those who lose out in this draw are worse-off than those who are put to work. Therefore, according to Azariadis, they must be considered involuntarily unemployed: 'The employed workers ... are to be envied by their laid-off colleagues – a situation that many economists would call "involuntary unemployment"' (Azariadis 1987: 734).[2]

So, Azariadis thought that he had provided a new impetus for the Keynesian cause. This new line of research also appealed to those authors who wanted to abandon the disequilibrium approach. Grossman's following statement illustrates:

> At that time, the observation that markets chronically failed to clear appeared to me so obviously correct that an effort to fill the missing link in the micro-economic foundations of the non-market-clearing paradigm seemed to me the only defensible research strategy. More recently, however, a theoretical innovation based on the idea that labour market transactions involve largely implicit contractual arrangements for shifting risk from workers to employers has led to models that rationalise the observed stickiness of measured real wage rates and explain the alleged symptom of non-wage rationing of employment without invoking the failure of markets to clear.
>
> (Grossman 1979: 65)

Misleading semantics

Two objections can be addressed to Azariadis' model. The first is that it is based on *ad hoc* assumptions. It did not take long to realise that its involuntary unemployment result was fragile. As soon as the assumption that firms cannot pay indemnities to the laid-off workers is removed, they are no longer worse-off. A mixed broader judgement eventually ensued. It was admitted that his model had made a breakthrough for a new field of research, contract theory, yet it was considered a failure for what concerned its initial purpose of justifying Keynesian claims. As stated by Rosen:

> Contract theory neither resolves nor illuminates questions of Keynesian unemployment based on nominal wage and price rigidities, money illusion and non-market clearing.
>
> (Rosen 1985: 1145)

While agreeing with this criticism, I also want to add a second one, more in keeping with the subject of my inquiry and bearing on Azariadis' distortion of the meaning of the concepts of rigidity, unemployment, involuntarity and full employment.

Rigidity

Implicit contract models were motivated by the aim of justifying rigidity as existing in fixprice models. Yet, during the process of theoretical construction, a shift occurred from rigidity, understood as an impediment to the formation of equilibrium, to a totally different object of analysis, rigidity across states of the world. Rigidity *à la* Azariadis is present whenever the optimal contract turns out to feature the same wage across the states of the goods market. Does this mean that, to Azariadis, flexibility is present whenever the contract comprises different wages contingent on the states of the world? Merely raising this question shows that the shoe fits. Azariadis' conception of rigidity has nothing to do with rigidity and flexibility as understood in the earlier chapters. In no way has rigidity *à la* Azariadis been an impediment to the normal working of markets. On the contrary, it is associated with efficiency. Azariadis' model must thus be characterised as a flexible wage model in spite of his claims to the contrary.

Unemployment or labour hoarding?

Azariadis' model provides a distinction between two allocative processes bearing on jobs or contracts, on the one hand, and on labour, on the other. The former concerns the distribution of workers across firms, the latter the rate of utilisation of the labour pool. The highest level of utilisation may be called 'full utilisation', all the others 'labour hoarding'. According to the assumption made about labour divisibility, a given total labour hoarding may be obtained either by an equal or by an unequal distribution.

The problem with Azariadis' model is then as follows. The generic notion of employment can designate either the fact of having a job, i.e. belonging to a peculiar labour pool, or the fact of belonging to that fraction of the labour pool that is effectively put at work. These two states should not be considered equivalent. The same is true for the unemployment notion, which can designate either joblessness or labour hoarding. While Azariadis' effective object of analysis is labour hoarding, his statement of purpose, his meta-theoretical commentaries suggest that it is, instead, unemployment in the joblessness sense.

Involuntarity

Keynes provided a plausible definition of involuntary unemployment – a state where agents are unable to participate in the labour market in spite of their readiness to work at a wage lower than the existing wage. As pointed out in Chapter 2, a breaching of the reservation wage must be involved. However, as seen in previous chapters, there is a gulf between defining a phenomenon and demonstrating its existence. Except for the wage floor factor, no theory of involuntary unemployment in the reservation wage sense has been put forward in the four decades that followed the publication of *General Theory*. Azariadis' model is the first to have succeeded in this respect, an undeniable feat.

Yet the main question to be addressed is whether any progress in the realisation of Keynes' programme has thereby been achieved. Keynes saw involuntary unemployment as an non-chosen result. Beyond doubt, this makes its insertion within neoclassical theory problematic – in short how can one conceive of obtaining a non-chosen result from the premise that people are free-choosers? Implicit contract theory resolves the dilemma in an ingenious manner, thanks to the inclusion of uncertainty and the lottery device. In the above simplified version of the theory, the representative agent must choose between two lotteries. The first leads to working with certainty at a given wage, whatever the prevailing state of the world. The second results in work at a higher wage if the state of the world is favourable yet in incurring a risk of no work and no pay, if it is unfavourable. Azariadis demonstrates that under certain conditions it is optimising to prefer the second lottery over the first. As a result, some agents will find themselves out of work if the state of the world is unfavourable. Keynes' reservation wage criterion for involuntary unemployment is met: at the going wage, the 'unemployed' would like to be working, since the wage is higher than their reservation wage. But should they be put in the involuntary unemployment pigeonhole? No, if the 'involuntary' modifier is understood in its individual disequilibrium meaning. Keynes understood involuntary unemployment as a manifestation of individual disequilibrium. This is hardly verified in Azariadis' model. The link made implicitly by Keynes between the breaching of the reservation wage principle and individual disequilibrium no longer holds.

Thus the meaning of involuntary unemployment is dramatically narrowed. Its exclusive import is now that the involuntarily unemployed are frustrated and envious of their employed colleagues. The connotation that it buttresses a restriction on freedom and that the unemployed are not responsible for their fate, is now discarded.[3]

Moreover, the involuntary unemployment result that Azariadis derives is efficient. The fact that involuntary unemployment dominates full employment in terms of agents' utility strongly suggests that semantics have gone astray! As noted by Bryant (1978), the letter of Keynes' project may be saved yet its spirit is sacrificed.

Full employment

In Chapter 2, I underlined the ambiguities surrounding the full employment notion. Azariadis' model illustrates what happens when semantic confusion reigns. In his model, full employment means full utilisation of the labour force. This amounts to defining full employment as equal to maximum employment. As pointed out above, it is quite conceivable that full employment so understood is sub-optimal. Azariadis' model is a case in point. But why make a fuss about the lack of realisation of full employment if this term is understood in a trivial and uninteresting way? Azariadis' semantics is misleading, because he suggests that his model supports lack of full employment in some Keynesian sense, i.e. the non-attainment of the optimal level of employment, while this is not the case.

Concluding remarks

When Azariadis' model is assessed against Keynes' programme, the following result comes out. First, it succeeds in demonstrating the existence of involuntary unemployment in the reservation wage sense. Yet, the individual disequilibrium connotation is not met. Second, while Azariadis' model was motivated by the aim of giving a foundation to wage rigidity, upon scrutiny, it turns out that it should be considered a flexible wage model. Thus, paradoxically enough, Keynes' criterion of exonerating wage rigidity is verified. In contrast, the remaining two criteria are not fulfilled: there is no general equilibrium perspective, and no justification of demand stimulation is offered.

16

EFFICIENCY WAGE THEORY

Efficiency wage theory refers to different types of models that have flourished since the 1980s and focus on issues of information and incentives.[1] According to Akerlof and Yellen, 'they have in common that in equilibrium an individual firm's production costs are reduced if it pays a wage in excess of market clearing, and, thus, there is equilibrium involuntary unemployment' (1986: 1). Different reasons, such as asymmetric information, morale, fairness or inside power, may explain such behaviour.

As before, my examination will be limited to the issue of the meaning and place of the involuntary unemployment concept within this theory.[2] Moreover, I will mainly be interested in a single (yet probably the most popular) model: Shapiro and Stiglitz's shirking model (Shapiro and Stiglitz 1984).

The shirking model

According to Akerlof and Yellen (1986), the gist of the shirking model is as follows:

> In the simplest model, due to Shapiro-Stiglitz, workers can decide whether to work or to shirk. Workers who shirk have some chance of getting caught, with the penalty of being fired . . . Equilibrium then entails unemployment. If all firms pay an identical wage and if there is full employment, there would be no cost to shirking and it would pay all workers, assuming that they get pleasure from loafing on the job, to shirk. Under these circumstances, it pays each firm to raise its wage to eliminate shirking. When all firms do this, average wages rise and employment falls. In equilibrium, all firms pay the same wage above market-clearing, and unemployment, which makes job losses costly, serves as a worker discipline device. Unemployed workers cannot bid for jobs by offering to work at lower wages. If the firm were to hire a worker at a lower

> wage, it would be in the worker's interest to shirk on the job. The firm knows this and the worker has no credible way of promising to work if he is hired.
>
> (Akerlof and Yellen 1986: 5)

In short, work is disagreeable. Left to themselves, workers will shirk rather than exert effort. Individual workers cannot be adequately monitored. As a result, to get them working requires both a carrot and a stick. The carrot is a wage higher than the market-clearing wage. The stick is the fear of being unemployed. To avoid shirking, the wage must be equal or higher than a given value determined by a series of parameters. Shapiro and Stiglitz call this the non-shirking condition.[3] Labour market equilibrium is determined by the intersection of aggregate labour demand with the aggregate non-shirking condition rather than with the aggregate labour supply. Figure 16.1, drawn from Shapiro and Stiglitz (1984), illustrates.

Full employment is inconsistent with non-shirking, since workers would fail to exert effort if it were realised. Involuntary unemployment is equal to the horizontal distance between E and the vertical labour supply. 'Those without jobs would be happy to work at w^* or lower, but cannot make a credible promise not to shirk at such wages' (Shapiro and Stiglitz 1984: 438).

This model shares several features with the implicit contract model. First, it explains involuntary unemployment as an equilibrium phenomenon (Shapiro and Stiglitz 1984: 433). That is, equilibrium is no longer associated with market clearing. As stated by Stiglitz in his Nobel lecture:

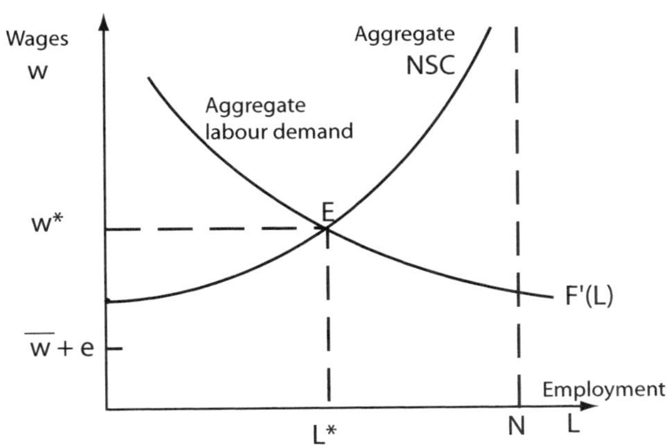

Figure 16.1 Involuntary unemployment in the shirking model.

> The efficiency wage theory explained the existence of unemployment in *equilibrium*. It was thus clear that the notion that underlay much of traditional competitive equilibrium analysis – that markets *had* to clear – was simply not true if information was imperfect.
>
> (Stiglitz 2002: 464; his emphasis)

Second, like in the implicit contract model, the wage serves a twofold function, 'to allocate labour and to provide incentives for adequate employee performance' (Katz 1986: 242). Third, frustration is considered the core element of involuntary unemployment. In Katz's words, 'Equilibrium unemployment is involuntary in this model since identical workers are treated differently and since the unemployed strictly prefer to be employed' (Katz 1986: 242).

What about efficiency? As seen in Chapter 15, lack of full employment is efficient in Azariadis' model. In the efficiency wage model, things are less clear. Shapiro and Stiglitz claim that 'the equilibrium is not in general Pareto optimal' (1984: 439). However, this claim is true only in the special case where the owners of the firm are the same individuals as the workers, and ownership is equally distributed among workers – i.e. the firm is self-managed. In this case, if profits are taxed away and wages subsidised, employment increases, and a Pareto improvement takes place. Otherwise, when the workers and the owners are distinct individuals, the equilibrium level of unemployment is Pareto optimal in spite of its failing to maximise net national product. Thus, Shapiro and Stiglitz are exaggerrating when claiming that it is in general inefficient. But they also make another claim related to the two fundamental theorems of welfare economics. According to them, the standard result that the issue of distribution can be separated from the issue of efficiency is no longer valid whenever imperfect information enters the picture. 'Externality-like effects are pervasive whenever information is imperfect or market incomplete – that is always – and as a result, markets are essentially never constrained Pareto-efficient' (Stiglitz 2002: 478).

An assessment

The main criticism levelled against the shirking model is that alternative mutually advantageous contracts, involving no unemployment – in particular, posting bonds (Carmichael 1985) – can be devised.[4] Another criticism bears on its relevance for modern industrial economies. It pertains, the criticism runs, only to menial jobs and hence to the secondary unskilled sector.[5] In spite of these criticisms, the efficiency wage explanation of involuntary unemployment has not been met with the same blunt dismissal as the implicit contract explanation. Twenty years after its introduction, it remains alive and well, having found its place in textbooks while being still present in research papers.[6]

Let me now gauge its contribution with respect to Keynes' programme. Its first component is the demonstration of involuntary unemployment in the reservation wage sense. In this respect, it should be stated at once that the shirking model succeeds in generating such a result. However, I have a lot more to say on this matter, and will return to it shortly.

The second element of Keynes' programme is the discharge of wage rigidity. Keynes wanted to exonerate wage rigidity as the cause of involuntary unemployment. Yet we have seen that neither him nor the first generation of Keynesian economists were able to deliver on this score. How does the efficiency wage model fare in this respect? The answer is close to what was concluded apropos implicit contracts. In his Nobel lecture, Stiglitz observes that 'standard interpretations of Keynesian economics emphasised the importance of wage and price rigidities, but without a convincing explanation of how those rigidities arise' (2002: 481). This remark suggests that that efficiency wage model may be credited for having filled the gap. But, if this is true, it departs from Keynes' programme. The irony, however, is that characterising the shirking model as a rigidity model is misleading – as it was the case for the implicit contract model. The motivation underlying Shapiro and Stiglitz's model may well have been to achieve the programme that followed from the criticism addressed to disequilibrium models – since these models postulated wage rigidity, the task to be addressed is to give rigidity a foundation. Yet, motivations and end results may diverge. We have here a case in point: the shirking model ends up with a totally different result where market non-clearing goes hand in hand with flexibility. The market non-clearing situation described in Shapiro and Stiglitz's model ought to be stamped as an equilibrium (agents have no incentives to change their behaviour), whereas market-clearing positions would represent disequilibrium. No impediment to the attainment of equilibrium is present. The erroneous view that the shirking model is about real rigidity follows from, first, its motivation and, second, the mistaken view that only rigidity can generate market non-clearing.

The third objective in Keynes' programme is to bring to the fore a system failure related to the interdependency across markets. In contrast, the concern of shirking model is a labour market flaw rather than a system failure. Thus, Keynes was wrong when believing that involuntary unemployment and an interdependency perspective were part and parcel.

In regard to the fourth element, the justification of demand stimulation, the shirking model fares no better. Its policy recommendation, if any, is taxation and subsidisation, a far cry from demand policy.

A final remark relates to my earlier discussion of the notion of the natural rate of unemployment. In Chapter 13, I have argued that no positive rate of unemployment is present in Friedman's perception model.

This criticism cannot be levelled against Shapiro and Stiglitz. Theirs is a theory of the determination of the natural rate of unemployment. Yet it is hardly a contribution to Keynes' project. To serve the latter, it is necessary for unemployment to be in excess of the natural rate. In the same line, their theory cannot challenge Friedman's and Lucas' policy ineffectiveness claims.

Meta-theoretical interpretations of the shirking model

Keynes took it for granted that involuntary unemployment was occurring against agents' will – they were forced into leisure. The conclusion reached in the previous chapter is that such a characterisation is absent from the implicit contract model. In the latter, involuntarity means frustration and jealousy, and nothing more. I now want to assess whether the same conclusion must be drawn about the shirking model.

According to the standard description of the shirking model, firms play the active role in eliciting the efficiency wage result.[7] Two aspects are present. First, the firms are deemed to call the shots. Second, they seem to be the villains of the piece. The efficiency wage comes into existence, the story runs, because it is in firms' interest. Profit maximisation then seems to be the ultimate cause of unemployment. Firms hold the power, unilaterally decide to fix the wage according to the efficiency wage principle, and impose the efficiency wage and its involuntary unemployment corollary on the workers. According to Stiglitz, 'unemployment is the discipline device that forces workers to work hard' (2002: 465). Lindbeck and Snower make a similar statement:

> In the efficiency-wage theories, all labour market power rests with the firms, who make the wage and employment decisions under asymmetric information ... In this case, the unemployment must be understood in terms of a conflict of interest between the firms and the unemployed workers.
>
> (Lindbeck and Snower 1988: 77)

Workers are rendered as passive, as victims, in the shirking model, which gives it a left-wing tone.[8] Their powerlessness is manifested by their inability to bid down wages (and thereby gain jobs). In Stiglitz's terms:

> An unemployed worker goes to a firm and offers to work for a wage less than it is currently paying its employees; but now the firm rejects this offer, since it believes that were it to hire this worker his productivity would be lower than that of current employees, lower enough that its total labour total costs would actually increase.
>
> (Stiglitz 1975: 29)[9]

My claim is that the above considerations belong to the domain of the meta-theoretical comments made about the shirking model rather than to the model itself. Moreover, they are not the only conceivable story, and another story, lacking these connotations, is more appropriate. To make my point, I need to delve into two issues, first, the formation of equilibrium and, second, the rationing scheme.

The formation of equilibrium

My starting point is the distinction between the issues of the determination and the formation of equilibrium introduced in Chapter 4. These two aspects must be present in every model, and thus also in the shirking model. When Shapiro and Stiglitz comment on the graph shown in Figure 16.1, and claim that point E represents the equilibrium of the model, this claim pertains to the issue of the logical existence of equilibrium. When in turn they state that firms are offering workers the wage rate corresponding to E, they are concerned with the formation of equilibrium. Instead of assuming, as they could have, that prices are announced by an outside auctioneer, they state that firms are setting the wage. We are thus in a Marshallian framework.

At this juncture, three features from the Marshallian analysis of the formation of market-day analysis are worth recalling. First, the Marshallian price formation process is based on a deus ex machina, perfect information *à la* Marshall, which is stronger than perfect information *à la* Walras and implies that agents are as knowledgeable about the data of the market as the outside model-builder. They are supposed to know the market supply and demand functions, and hence to be able to calculate the equilibrium values. Second, while imperfect competition is often characterised by the fact that agents are price-setters, the Marshallian corn market invalidates this view, as it combines price-setting agents and perfect competition. Third, in this context it matters little whether either suppliers or demanders set the price. Since the members of the two groups know the equilibrium price, no deviation favourable to the two sides of the market will ever emerge.

The hallmark of the shirking model is imperfect information. Therefore, it may look odd to put it under the banner of perfect information *à la* Marshall. The truth is that Shapiro and Stiglitz's is a *quasi*-perfect information model. It comprises only a drop of non-information in an ocean of perfect information. Firms' information may well be defective for what goes on in the workshop, yet this should not hide the tremendous amount of information that they are supposedly holding. To wit, they must be able to read the minds and hearts of workers, to know their preferences and every element on which their decision-making process is based. These are workers' most private data and yet they are perfectly transparent to firms.[10] Workers are hardly left out for what concerns perfect information. In order to be make their optimising choices they must be cognoscenti of all the data of the market, the probability of being detected, the exogenous quit rate, the flows out of unemployment, the unemployment rate.

Shapiro and Stiglitz seem to be unaware that perfect information in the Marshallian sense underpins their entire model. The information dimension is acknowledged on only two scores. First, they note that workers hold perfect information about job availability (1984: 433, 439). This assertion is misleading – why emphasise this particular object of knowledge while leaving unmentioned the fact that the domain over which workers hold perfect information is immensely wider? Second, they note that the information problem present in their model is that 'firms are assumed (quite reasonably, in our view) not to be able to monitor the activities of their employees costlessly and perfectly' (1984: 439). This information imperfection may well be reasonable, yet it should not hide the less reasonable high pitch of firms' perfect information over every other domain.

Next, let me investigate the implication of the fact that firms are setting wages. Whenever being a price-maker is associated with imperfect competition, as it is usually the case, the characteristics of market power and rent-capturing ensue at once. Yet, as stated above, this implication is invalid for the Marshallian corn model. The same is true, I think, for the shirking model. The latter is not a model of a monopsonistic firm. Its difference from the standard account lies elsewhere, in the replacement of the traditional supply schedule by the non-shirking condition schedule. What Shapiro and Stiglitz call the non-shirking condition is actually workers' supply of effective labour input, as distinct from their supply of time to be spent on the job. In other words, the generic concept of supply of labour needs to be separated into two distinct concepts. What they keep calling the labour supply has actually become the maximum level of employment, without any optimising behaviour contents, while what they call the non-shirking condition should be considered the effective labour schedule, expressing agents' optimal plans. In other words, as soon as lack of monitoring and workers' shirking tendencies enter the picture, the standard supply schedule ceases to play a role, and the modified supply schedule – i.e. the non-shirking condition – takes over. Equilibrium then consists of the intersection between the demand for labour curve and this modified labour supply schedule.

As to the mechanism of formation of equilibrium, it is like in Marshall's model: firms set the wage and employment at the level corresponding to this intersection, the constituting elements of which they are supposed to know perfectly. The correct account of the working of Shapiro and Stiglitz's labour market is thus that it hinges on the foreknowledge on the part of all transactors. The question can be raised of why workers accept this wage and employment level. The answer is plain: they have made the same calculation as the firm and come to the same result about the equilibrium values. Hence it does not matter whether it is the firm or the workers who set the wage. The same result would be obtained by assuming that workers do so.

The rationing scheme

Shapiro and Stiglitz have put forward what sociologists call a functionalist explanation of involuntary unemployment. Its existence is justified by the function it plays. But a further question arises: on whom will the burden of unemployment fall? What, in other words, will determine that Mr A is employed whereas Mr B is unemployed? The standard account is that

> The unemployed are a rotating pool of individuals who have quit jobs for personal reasons, who are new entrants to the labor market, or who have been laid off by firms with decline in demand.
>
> (Akerlof and Yellen 1986: 5)

Yet such a statement is unsatisfactory because it is too vague and fails to make clear the underlying allocative mechanism. The more precise explanation to be found in the literature – yet not in Shapiro and Stiglitz's paper, for they do not consider the issue – is that this distribution occurs through a lottery. The firm, it is stated, chooses its workers randomly from its applicant pool, every applicant having an equal probability of employment. While most commentators have felt no need to investigate the matter any further, it is necessary for my purpose to delve into it.

Consider the first trading round in the history of the labour market under consideration. A lottery is established that distributes the workers across the two employment positions. The winners get employment. Because of the wage setting process, they will avoid shirking. The only way they can lose their job in subsequent trading rounds is through what Shapiro and Stiglitz call exogenous separation, i.e. for other reasons than the detection of shirking. At each subsequent trading round, vacancies, owing either to the need to replace the workers who left for these exogenous reasons or to factors such as increases in demand, etc. will be allocated through a new lottery among the unemployed. This process will then go on over time.[11]

Thus, we have to explore how the initial lottery becomes established. That is, who has decided to resort to this precise rationing scheme instead of any other? Is it a decision made unilaterally by firms and imposed on workers without their assent, as the subtext of Shapiro and Stiglitz article suggests?

The need for the lottery institution springs from the shirking tendency. Both firms and workers know about it and recognise it as a universal, unfortunate yet irredeemable, feature of human nature. If everybody were shirking, as would be the case if the wage was lower than the non-shirking wage, nothing would be produced! It may then be conjectured that in the face of the shirking threat, all participants in the market, both firms and workers, come together and agree that unemployment is the solution to the problem – all this assuming that it is impossible to write contracts that ensure that the workers bear all the consequences of their actions. Any conflict of interest vanishes, both firms and workers having a common interest in checking the shirking tendency. Recall that the only case where Pareto inefficiency is demonstrated by Shapiro and Stiglitz is when the workers are the owners of the firm they are working for. In this case the lottery device will certainly be a joint decision by firms and workers. Even otherwise, it is quite plausible to have workers accepting it on the grounds of their wanting to avoid the paralysis of the economy.

In sum, Shapiro and Stiglitz's meta-theoretical commentary proves to be misleading. Being unemployed amounts only to suffering from bad luck, like in the implicit contract model. No individual disequilibrium connotation should be attached to it. Recall Stiglitz's passage quoted above about workers knocking at the doors of firms to underbid the wage yet being turned down. It suggests that the unemployed have not been in contact with the firm or other workers before and that they just happen to come into the game late. They are, as it were, outsiders. But then, the underlying rationing scheme must be different from the lottery device, for example a first-arrived, first-served rule. In contrast, the formation of equilibrium device underpinning Shapiro and Stiglitz's model implies that all the participants in the market are present together. Hence Stiglitz's comment is beside the point.

In the light of the above considerations, the spontaneous reading of the shirking model according to which firms are responsible for the existence of involuntary unemployment while workers are its victims can no longer be held.[12] No conflict of interest is present. The efficiency wage may well be a discipline device, but then it is self-inflicted discipline.

A radical change in perspective ensues. In the type of universe assumed by the shirking model, involuntary unemployment should not be viewed as a problem about which some action should be taken. Instead, it is the solution to a problem, namely shirking and moral hazard. Unemployment must now be viewed as a necessary evil. No idea of market failure should be associated with its existence. If there is a failure, it is a human nature failure of which unemployment is the solution.[13]

Only a few authors seem to be aware of this, most commentators having endorsed Shapiro and Stiglitz's meta-theoretical interpretation without qualms. Phelps and Kolm are among the exceptions:

> There is no doubt, then, that this involuntary unemployment is bad. It is an unfortunate side effect, or third-party effect, that the employers in trying to guard against the shirking and quitting of their own employees *inflict on others* – the workers whom they would otherwise have employed in addition. The result is a failure of labour markets to achieve ideal efficiency. But what as a practical matter can be done about it? What can be done to shrink the pool of involuntarily unemployed workers – the pool that young would-be workers must swim in until fished out by an employer – without making employed workers (who may have swum in that pool) and owners of firms (who may have once been unemployed also) worse off? There is not necessarily much or anything that can be done that would work and not harm anyone. Some things are regrettable but are not genuine *problems*, because they have no solutions!
>
> (Phelps 1985: 421)

> But above all, the theory of efficiency wages by itself leads to the exact opposite conclusions of the one it wishes to demonstrate *in fine*. The original intention was to find a base from which to counter the 'new classical' assertion that the government should not intervene (with Keynesian policies) because the labour market is in competitive equilibrium and is thus Pareto-efficient. The 'efficiency wage' does yield a labour market in disequilibrium and involuntary unemployment. But the situation it describes is Pareto-efficient since it corresponds to an unconstrained profit-maximisation in the labour market by the firms choosing both employment and wages. This theory does not justify therefore government intervention to improve the efficiency of the economy.
>
> (Kolm 1990: 230)[14]

Beyond the shirking model

Hitherto my analysis has focused on the shirking model because it is the best-known efficiency wage model. The conclusion reached about it is that it succeeds in demonstrating involuntary unemployment in the reservation sense while failing for what concerns the individual disequilibrium aspect. My next task is to investigate whether this conclusion is valid for other types of efficiency wage models. Without engaging in a systematic study, I will show that there exists at least one model in which the individual disequilibrium component is present, Dasgupta and Ray's malnutrition model (1986).[15] This model returns to the initial efficiency wage tradition where emphasis was placed on the link between nutrition and effort. Thus, the moral hazard dimension is absent from it.

The economy described in Dasgupta and Ray's model comprises a continuum of agents along the unit interval [0, 1], each with a landownership label, n. The higher n, the larger the amounts of land the agent owns. Figure 16.2, drawn from Dasgupta and Ray (1986: 1017), illustrates. All agents ranking from 0 to $\bar{n}$ are landless.

μ being the wage paid to an unit of labour power, define μ^* as the minimum cost of buying an efficiency unit of labour. This cost is relatively high for landless peasants, due to the link between food intake and work capability. Effort is a function of the food intake, the latter resulting from a linear combination of wage income and land ownership. Landless people cost more because their consumption is exclusively wage-financed. That is, it is necessary to pay a landless agent above his reservation wage because at this wage he is malnourished and hence his efficiency is low. In contrast, the small landed peasants have access to some income from cultivation or rental. Hence they cost less per efficiency unit of effort than landless labourers. The more people own land, the higher their reservation wage. Hence μ^* is shaped as in Figure 16.3, also drawn from Dasgupta and Ray, where its horizontal part coincides with what they call the food-adequacy standard, i.e. 'the cut-off consumption level below which a person will be said to be undernourished' (1986: 1017).

Let the $\bar{\mu}$ line represent the wage that is equal to the aggregate marginal product of effective labour. For workers whose cost exceeds this wage, the demand will be nil. Consider the case where the $\bar{\mu}$ line is below

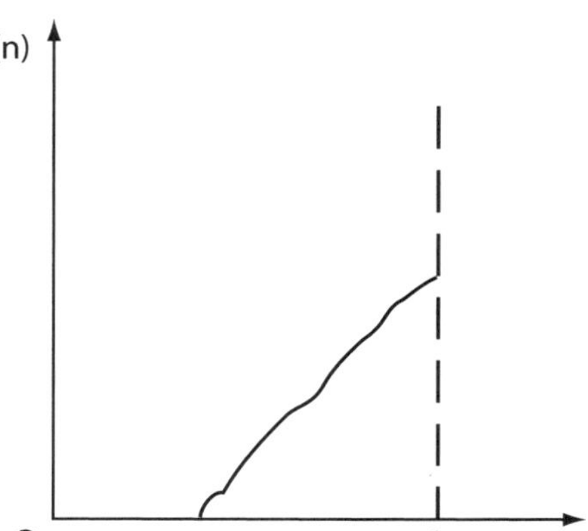

Figure 16.2 The distribution of land in Dasgupta and Ray's model.

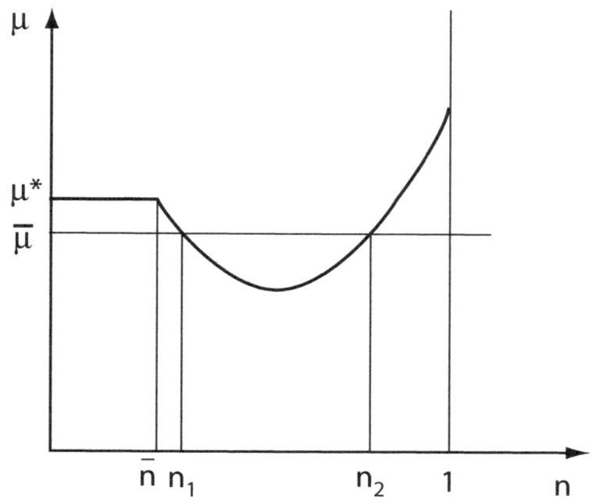

Figure 16.3 Involuntary unemployment in Dasgupta and Ray's model.

the horizontal section of the minimum cost. All persons between n_1 and n_2 are employed. In contrast, 'all n-persons below n_1 and above n_1 are out of the market: the former because their labour power is too expensive, the latter because their reservation wages are too high – they are too rich' (Dasgupta and Ray 1986: 1024).

In Dasgupta and Ray's model, the landless people's reservation wage is lower than the food-adequacy standard. As a result, if the difference between the horizontal section of μ^* and the $\bar{\mu}$ line is sufficiently large, the reservation wage criterion will be fulfilled for the landless agents. It will also be realised for the landed small peasants who are on the left of n_1. Thus involuntary unemployment in the reservation wage sense is present. In the shirking model individual disequilibrium was declared absent because of the lottery rationing scheme. The latter is missing here. If some agents are out of work, it is due to their lack of endowment. Their responsibility is not involved. Therefore the connotation of individual disequilibrium or encroachment on freedom is also present. Keynes' aim of a model as to involuntary unemployment embedding individual disequilibrium is achieved, yet in the totally different context of a subsistence economy.

Efficiency wages and the dual labour market

Involuntary unemployment as present in implicit contract and efficiency wage models ought to be understood in a narrow, technical meaning, different from its common-sense meaning. Nonetheless, it is difficult to cling to a such a narrow definition, especially when the motivation that triggered the interest for the involuntary unemployment concept was real-world unemployment and the conviction that, in large part, it is involuntary in the common-sense meaning.

The definitional issue is compounded whenever more than a single labour market is considered, a case that some efficiency wage theorists have considered while associating their models with the dual labour market literature. In a nutshell, the latter claims that the primary sector has the 'good jobs' and the secondary the 'bad' ones. According to these authors, two propositions can be formulated:

Proposition 1: certain unemployed agents must be characterised both as involuntarily and voluntarily unemployed. The following two quotations illustrate.

> In such a world an individual could, at the same time, be both voluntarily and involuntarily unemployed. That is, he could have applied for a number of jobs for which he was perfectly well qualified (i.e. as qualified as the individuals who obtain the jobs) and not obtained them, and in this sense his unemployment would be due not to his choice but to the random selection of the market; but at the same time, he could have chosen not to apply for a job that he might have obtained, and in this sense he would be voluntarily unemployed.
>
> (Stiglitz 1992: 54)

> With a secondary sector all workers can get a job. Does that not imply that all unemployment is *voluntary*? In some sense that it is true ... And, although it is true that every unemployed worker might be able to get a secondary sector job (so that in *one sense* there is no *involuntary* unemployment), it is also true that unemployed workers would be more than willing to work in primary sector jobs at prevailing wage rates. *In that sense* such workers are *involuntarily* unemployed.
>
> (Akerlof and Yellen 1986: 10)[16]

Proposition 2: an involuntarily unemployed agent can end up being employed! In Akerlof and Yellen's and Hahn's words:

> Dual labour markets can be explained by the assumption that the wage-productivity nexus is important in some sectors of the economy but not in others. For sectors where the efficiency wage hypothesis is relevant – the primary sector – we find job rationing and voluntary payment by firms of wages in excess of market-clearing; in the secondary sector, where the wage-productivity

> relationship is weak or non-existent we should observe fully neo-classical behaviour. The market for secondary sector jobs clears, and anyone can obtain a job in this sector, although it may be at lower pay.
>
> (Akerlof and Yellen 1986: 3)

> [Involuntary unemployment] denotes a state in which the market wage of 'labour' exceeds its shadow price. In a more agreeable context it means that there individuals for whom the expected utility of some jobs which it is known that they can do, exceeds their expected utility from their present position. That need not be one of unemployment. Thus, imagine Professor Lucas dismissed from his post because of serious malinvestment by his university. We find him washing up in a hamburger parlour. He is likely to be involuntarily unemployed as an economist.
>
> (Hahn 1983: 225)

For all their awkwardness, these two propositions make sense. However, they gain by being recast against the distinction between rationing and unemployment, presented in Chapter 3. Recall that rationing denoted the outcome of a given labour market trade round, and unemployment a specific post-rationing activity. Hitherto I have abided by standard terminology by calling 'unemployment' what, strictly speaking, should be termed 'rationing'. Let me now return to the first of the above propositions in the light of the strict terminology. A given agent, the story runs, is rationed in the primary sector for an efficiency wage reason. While he could subsequently have been employed in the secondary market, this has not happened. Whether his unemployment is or not involuntary depends on the conditions that I have analysed in Chapter 3. A necessary condition for involuntary unemployment is that the secondary market fails to clear. Oddly enough, this very condition is discarded by the authors quoted above without justification. According to them, the efficiency wage factor plays only in the primary sector. As a result, any observed unemployment must be declared voluntary – in view of the wage that is prevailing in the secondary market, the unemployed agents have opted for leisure (or search) instead of labour market participation. Hence proposition 1 pertains to people who are first rationed and subsequently become voluntarily unemployed.

The situation addressed in proposition 2 differs from the previous one only because rationed agents are now characterised as having accepted a job in the secondary sector. Yet, despite their employment, efficiency wage theoreticians want to call them involuntarily unemployed in reference to their initial rationing situation. In contrast, my taxonomy permits to recast this proposition as describing a situation that combines rationing in the primary market and market clearing in the secondary market. In other words, market rationing here results in no unemployment at all.

Propositions 1 and 2 have in common the exclusion of the possibility of involuntary unemployment in the activity sense. This is the direct implication of the view that secondary markets always clear, thus absorbing any labour force that has been rationed in primary markets. Efficiency wage authors seem unaware of how much they are yielding by taking such a stance. In effect, any ambition of explaining real-world unemployment must be forgone since the explanatory power of efficiency wage theory is admittedly restricted to the phenomenon of labour rationing, involuntary unemployment in the activity sense falling out of its scope.

In the light of these remarks, it turns out that the difference between the efficiency wage and the new classical standpoint is smaller than it first appears. To make this point, let me confront the view of the two towering figures of New Classicism and New Keynesianism, Lucas and Stiglitz.

In an interview by Klamer, Lucas calls Steinbeck to the rescue of his views:

> Did you ever look at Steinbeck's book *The Grapes of Wrath*? It's a kind of protest pamphlet from the '30s about migrant farmers in California. There's one passage in there that is a better anecdote that I could have written for the kind of models I like. It illustrates the auction characteristic of the labour market for migrant farm workers. He writes about a hundred guys who show up at a farm where there are only ten jobs available. The farmer will let the wage fall until ten people are willing to work for that wage and ninety people say 'the hell with it', and just go on down the road.
> (Klamer 1984: 46)

Lucas' fondness for Steinbeck's story is not-surprising. Here is a renowned left-wing novelist offering him on a silver platter an illustration of his own views. Market clearing prevails in Steinbeck's story. Those workers who say 'the hell with it!' are actually choosing leisure, however shocking the term may be in this context. For his part, Stiglitz's reaction against Lucas' observation is outwardly vehement, suggesting that their views are poles apart:

> At one level, the issue here is just a matter of semantics. It is little different from the old story that so long as there is a competitive labour market anywhere in the economy (grape picking in California) all unemployment must be voluntary, since any individual could have moved to California ('purchased a job'). To us, the fact that during the Great Depression 20 or 25 percent of the labour force in Chicago, workers who were once gainfully employed, were sitting idle at home, willing to work at the going

> wage in Chicago suggests a massive market failure, regardless of whether one says that, because of their decision not to migrate to California, they were voluntarily unemployed.
>
> (Shapiro and Stiglitz 1985: 1215)[17]

However, for all Stiglitz's strong overtones, the difference between Lucas' standpoint and his own is small. It cannot bear on the outcome of the grape picking market in view of Stiglitz' acceptance that the secondary market always clears. As stated above, in this case, the issue of voluntarity is sealed at once; any agent who is observed as not working must be so by choice. Thus, Stiglitz agrees with Lucas on the central point that those people who say 'the hell with it' are voluntarily unemployed. Both of them concur on the non-existence of involuntary unemployment in the activity sense.

Thus, their disagreement is limited to what happened earlier on in the primary market. In this respect, Stiglitz's claim is that even if the welders had remained in Chicago and were eventually observed as unemployed after their initial rationing, they should be classified as involuntarily unemployed in the activity sense, despite their refusal to emigrate to California. Recall my earlier discussion on choice sets, and the possibility of drawing their boundaries in a broad or in a narrow way. When a broad definition is taken, actions such as moving down the skill-ladder or emigrating are considered as belonging to the choice set. So, if an agent refuses to emigrate, he will be classified as voluntarily unemployed, no blame being attached to this label. On the contrary, such options will be considered as falling outside the choice set, if the choice set is defined more narrowly. Hence an agent who refuses to emigrate or to accept an under-skilled job could still be classified as involuntarily unemployed. Thus, Stiglitz implicitly defends a restricted definition of an agent's choice set, excluding emigration from the number of acceptable solutions. This stance is perfectly defensible. Yet, be this what it may, once these workers have moved to California and entered in an auction market there, their ultimate joblessness must be considered voluntary.[18]

A stronger difference would have emerged had Stiglitz admitted that the efficiency wages phenomenon could also arise in the secondary market. Assume that grape picking is the sort of activity that prompts shirking tendencies. Wages will then be fixed at their efficiency wage value with labour rationing ensuing. Thus, some agents will have been rationed twice, in their normal Chicago welder market and in the secondary grape picking market. Involuntary unemployment would become possible, even if the choice set was defined in a broad way. Some ex-Chicago welders may be amongst the rationed agents. If it is moreover assumed that they lack non-wage alternatives – if they had any valid alternative, they would not have moved to California – the conclusion can be drawn that they are involuntarily unemployed in the activity sense.

Concluding remarks

Both the efficiency wages and the implicit contract models have played a pioneering role and paved the way for a thriving research programme – contract theory on the one hand, and the information paradigm, on the other. However, their success is mitigated on the score of what was their initial motivation, namely their will to achieve Keynes' programme. True, they have succeeded in demonstrating the existence of involuntary unemployment in the reservation wage sense, which is a real feat – after all, it has taken several decades to get such a result. Yet, this is a Pyrrhic victory: when, at last, Keynes' aim of demonstrating involuntary unemployment is achieved, it turns out that this realisation hardly serves the purpose that Keynes himself had in mind!

17

INSIDER–OUTSIDER THEORY

Efficiency wage models can hardly be considered as having given a theoretical embodiment to ideas on the causes of unemployment that were widespread among commentators of the economic scene. The contrary is true for the model that will be examined in this section, the insider–outsider model. The fact that unemployment might be caused by the powerful position of insiders has been a recurrent theme, often associated with the existence of unions. The merit of Lindbeck and Snower is to have translated such an opinion into a theoretical model while at the same time driving a wedge between the insider–outsider phenomenon and the presence of unions.[1] Contrary to the authors examined in previous chapters, they do not claim a Keynesian lineage, so that, strictly speaking, their work should not be included within the New Keynesian tradition. Yet, it will seen that important affinities exist between their models and those I have studied in the previous two chapters.

The point that I want to make about Lindbeck and Snower's theory relates to the appropriateness of their definition of involuntary unemployment. At first, it is engaging – in particular because it incorporates the limited choice set aspect that I discussed in Chapter 3 – yet, upon scrutiny, it leads to an absurd situation where some agents need to be classified as involuntarily unemployed in spite of their having a job!

The basic idea underlying the insider–outsider theory is that the source of unemployment lies in the phenomenon of labour turnover costs (Lindbeck and Snower 1988: 72). Two types of these need to be separated, 'production-related' and 'rent-related' turnover costs. The former relate to technical differences in the costs of employment between insiders and entrants. For example, the hiring, screening and training of new recruits is costly. The second follow from insiders' ability to capture a rent. For example, they can get severance payments, they can refuse to cooperate with insiders or they can harass them, to the effect that their productivity is lowered.

In the insider–outsider model, the workforce is sub-divided into two categories: the incumbents or insiders and the non-incumbents or outsiders. Insiders are active in the wage setting process. According to the context, they will remain insiders or lose their employment. Outsiders are passive or voiceless, to borrow Hirschman's term. At the end of the wage setting process, they will either become entrants or remain outsiders.[2] Insiders are the villains of the piece. They are able to capture some rent from the firm, forcing their wage above the reservation wage level before it becomes profitable for the firm to replace them. The outsiders' exclusion from participation in the labour market ensues.

> The crucial assumption [of insider–outsider] is that it is costly to exchange a firm's current, full-fledged employees (the insiders) for unemployed workers (the outsiders), and that the rent associated with this turnover cost can be tapped by the insiders in the process of wage negotiation ... Accordingly, involuntary unemployment arises out of a conflict of interest between the insiders and the outsiders.
>
> (Lindbeck and Snower 1988: 77)

Lindbeck and Snower's is not a pure market power theory. While it comprises some market power, prompting rent-related turnover costs, this power is grafted onto objective differences in the costs of employment between insiders and outsiders, the production-related turnover costs. Moreover, they are keen to insists that their theory stands up independently from the existence of unions. Actually, the latter are absent from their main models.

Lindbeck and Snower's richest model is the cooperation–harassment model (Lindbeck and Snower 1988, Chapter 5). However, the point I am interested in can be made in reference to their simpler hiring–firing model. The latter will therefore be my main object of analysis.

The hiring–firing model

In the hiring-firing model, it is assumed that hiring costs, such as search, screening and training are production-related, whereas firing costs – for example, job security legislation or severance pay – are rent-related.[3] On account of these differentiated turnover costs, a distinction ought to be drawn between two demand functions, one for insiders, the other for entrants. The demand for insiders is determined as the marginal product of labour plus the marginal cost of firing labour, the demand for outsiders is equal to the marginal product of labour minus the marginal cost of hiring workers (Lindbeck 1993: 39).

The first step in Lindbeck and Snower's reasoning is to draw a distinction between three alternative occurrences, which they call the *retention*, the *hiring* and the *firing* scenarios. The first designates the case where it is in the firm's interest to keep all its incumbent workforce without hiring new recruits, the second the case where the firm will expand its workforce, the third when it will fire a fraction of its workforce. The hiring scenario is associated with a small incumbent workforce, the firing scenario with a large one, and the retention scenario with an intermediate one. The benchmarks between these scenarios are determined by intersections of the two labour demand functions with the reservation wage, supposedly identical for insiders and outsiders. Figure 17.1 illustrates.

There exists a lower bond ($\underline{m}$), set at the intersection of the demand for entrant labour schedule with the reservation wage and an upper bound ($\overline{m}$), set at the intersection of the demand for insider labour schedule with the reservation wage. The hiring scenario refers to a case where the incumbent workforce (m) is small with respect to demand, i.e. when $\underline{m} > m$ (for example, m_1 in Figure 17.1). The retention scenario prevails whenever $\underline{m} < m < \overline{m}$ (for example, m_2), the firing scenario whenever $m > \overline{m}$ (for example, m_3).

Equilibrium values are supposed to be formed in two steps. First, the nominal wage is fixed by the insiders in an 'individualistic' way (Lindbeck and Snower 1988: 69). Each insider sets his wage as high as possible, consistent with his continued employment. Production and employment decisions are made by the firm in a second stage, taking the nominal wage as given. The insiders' opportunity of capturing a rent will vary according to the scenario that is prevailing. The underlying general principle is that 'the insider wage is the smaller of the insider marginal product (net of firing costs) and the sum of the entrant wage and the marginal turnover costs' (Lindbeck and Snower 1988: 69). That is:

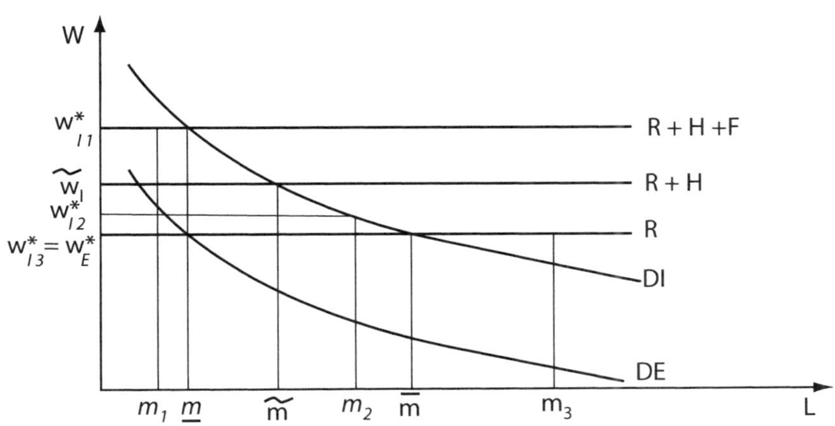

Figure 17.1 The hiring–firing model.

$w_I^* = \min\,[(f(m)+F), (R+F+H)]$, where the asterisk indicates the equilibrium value, w_I^* is insiders' equilibrium wage, $f'(m)$ is the marginal product of labour, F the marginal firing cost, R the reservation wage and H the marginal hiring cost.

In the hiring scenario, when the incumbent work force is small (m_1 in Figure 17.1), insiders' equilibrium values are:

$w_{I1}^* = R + F + H$,
$w_E^* = R$ [where w_E is entrants' wage],
$L_I^* = m_1$ [where L_I is the number of insiders who remain employed],
$L_E^* = \underline{m} - m_1$ [where L_E is the number of outsiders who are hired].

In the retention scenario, where the incumbent workforce is intermediate, i.e. m_2 in Figure 17.1, insiders will set the wage at the point of the insiders' demand function corresponding to the incumbent workforce. The smaller the incumbent workforce (within the range $\underline{m} - \overline{m}$) the higher the insiders' wage.

$w_{I2}^* = f'(m_2)$,
$L_I^* = m_2$,
$L_E^* = 0$.

Finally, in the firing scenario, where the incumbent workforce is large (m_3 in Figure 17.1), the insiders are unable to capture any rent and fix the wage at the competitive level, at which point they are actually indifferent to being either employed or unemployed.[4] Still, some incumbents are fired. A fortiori, no outsider is hired.

$w_{I3}^* = R$,
$L_I^* = \overline{m}$
$L_E^* = 0$.

Lindbeck and Snower's definition of involuntary unemployment

Contrary to other authors, Lindbeck and Snower cannot be accused of eschewing conceptual and definitional issues. Here is their definition of involuntary unemployment:

> At prevailing current wages and future expected wages, some workers are unsuccessful in finding jobs because, at no fault of their own, they face a more limited choice set between work and leisure than employed workers, even if the wage demands of the

> former are adjusted for productivity differences, including unavoidable (production-related) resource costs in connection with hiring and firing of workers.
>
> (Lindbeck 1993: 47–48)

It must be noted that this definition does not coincide with the reservation wage definition. Looking at the retention and firing scenarios as depicted in Figure 17.1, the wage which the firm is able to pay to entrants (in the hiring scenario, outsiders are hired up to the intersection between the demand for outsiders and the reservation wage) is lower than the reservation wage.[5] Moreover, Lindbeck and Snower characterise involuntary unemployment in two intertwined ways, first by noting that it is a matter of outsiders enjoying a more limited choice set than insiders, and, second, by stating that it constitutes a phenomenon of discrimination, the existence of which hinges on the passing of a threshold. The limited choice set idea is appealing. As argued in Chapter 3, it can play an important role in the analysis of post-rationing trajectories. The problem with Lindbeck and Snower in this respect is that, for all their recurrent references to it, they hardly elucidate its meaning. For example, they write on p. 7 that 'the outsiders have a smaller choice set – in terms of wages received and productive services offered – than the insiders', but then what does the expression 'in terms of wages received and productive services offered' exactly mean? Does the limited choice set idea convey something more than the discrimination idea? Put bluntly, my impression is that it belongs to Lindbeck and Snower's meta-theoretical discourse while playing no effective role in their model. As to the latter, its central tenet is the idea of discrimination, the existence of which hinges whether a precise threshold is passed.

> Whenever this wage differential exceeds the insider–outsider productivity differential minus the production related turnover cost, there is unemployment, which we have argued may be characterised as 'involuntary' in a well defined sense.
>
> (Lindbeck and Snower 1998: 75)

Envy is central to involuntarity *à la* Lindbeck-Snower is envy. Outsiders are not envious of insiders as long as the differential between the insiders' wage and their reservation wage encompasses only production-related costs (and productivity differences in more complicated models). Envy arises when this differential is larger because it includes a rent-related element. It can then be concluded that, to them, envy and involuntary unemployment amount to the same, what brings them close to the frustration aspect characterising implicit contract and efficiency wage models. In reference to the simple hiring–firing model, where no difference in productivity between insiders and entrants is present, the envy threshold is passed whenever $w_I^* > R + H$. This condition in turn hinges on the size of the incumbent workforce. The latter ought to be relatively small. More precisely, the threshold is passed as soon as $m < \widetilde{m}$, where $\widetilde{m}$ is the incumbent work force size prompting insiders to fix a wage equal to $\widetilde{w}_I$. Thus, outsiders will be envious of insiders only if $w_I^* > \widetilde{w}_I$. In contrast, if $m \geq \widetilde{m}$, the outsiders have no reason to envy the insiders. According to Lindbeck and Snower's definition, they ought to be considered as voluntarily unemployed.

Lindbeck and Snower do not use the envy threshold term. Rather they call it the 'involuntary unemployment constraint' (1998: 102 ff.). Moreover and oddly enough, this constraint is made explicit only in their cooperation–harassment model. It should however be introduced in the hiring–firing model as well because otherwise no way of sorting out voluntary from involuntary unemployment exists.

Finally, it should be noted that, while Lindbeck and Snower's definition of involuntary unemployment fails to incorporate the reservation wage aspect that was present in Keynes, it takes up Keynes' lack of freedom dimension, with its connotation of exclusion, discrimination and injustice:

> By no fault of their own, outsiders are exposed to social discrimination as compared to those who already have a job, and therefore they have a smaller choice set than incumbent workers, in addition to what can be explained by differences in intrinsic productivity ... This notion of the involuntariness of unemployment in the insider–outsider theory probably captures what laypeople consider to be its most distinguished feature: The social injustice of being unemployed due to the discriminatory job rationing associated with the unequal opportunities caused by social factors rather than by intrinsic differences between individuals.
>
> (Lindbeck 1993: 50)

Beyond doubt, these views are appealing. What Lindbeck and Snower are pointing at is exactly what the succession of authors who ventured into demonstrating involuntary unemployment had in mind. The question is whether their model delivers on such a claim.

The existence of involuntary unemployment

The possibility of involuntary unemployment *à la* Lindbeck and Snower varies according to the prevailing scenario. Let me start with the retention scenario, where any new hiring is absent. Here, the unemployed and the outsiders group coincide. However, involuntary unemployment is not necessarily present. Its existence depends on the size of the incumbent workforce relative to the envy threshold. For example, in Figure 17.1 with incumbents numbering m_2, the unemployed are voluntarily unemployed since $m_2 < \tilde{m}$.

Consider now the firing scenario. Here, the envy threshold is never passed. Though unemployment is more important in this scenario than in the other two, it ought to be considered as voluntary unemployment. Fired incumbents are no worse-off than those who keep their jobs. Outsiders have no reason to envy insiders, as the latter are unable to capture any rent. In fact, the employed and the unemployed are on the same footing, as they all get their reservation wage.

Turning to the hiring scenario, a distinction ought to be drawn between two categories of employed workers, the insiders (m_1) and the entrants ($\underline{m} - m_1$). They do not receive the same wage. While insiders' wage is equal to the total turnover costs, entrants' wage equals their reservation wage. In Figure 17.1, $w^*_{I1} = \text{R} + \text{F} + \text{H}$. In this scenario, the envy threshold ($\tilde{\underline{w}}_I = \text{R} + \text{H}$) is always passed. Surprisingly enough, however, the entrants are not better off than those outsiders who remain unemployed, as both of them gain their reservation wage.

We now witness the odd situation where, in spite of their opposite employment status, entrants and non-hired outsiders must be ranked in the same involuntary unemployment category, according to Lindbeck and Snower's criterion for the latter.

By now the oddity of Lindbeck and Snower's stance should become clear. In their view, passing the envy threshold is a sufficient condition for involuntary unemployment. The employment status does not need to be considered. Put differently, unemployment is not a necessary condition for involuntary unemployment. As a result, the set of the involuntarily unemployed people may be larger than that of the unemployed! At the limit, it may be imagined that all outsiders become entrants (if $\text{N}_\text{E} = \underline{m} - m_1$, where N_E is the total number of outsiders), to the effect that full employment and involuntary unemployment *à la* Lindbeck and Snower would co-exist.

Lindbeck and Snower cannot be accused of being unaware of the existence of such an odd case of 'employed involuntarily unemployed' agents. In their cooperation–harassment model, they coin the term 'job discrimination' to designate it (Lindbeck and Snower 1988: 107). However, they mention it in passing, as if it was an unimportant *curiosium*. After all, it arises only in one of their three scenarios and then it affects barely a fraction of the outsiders. Hence, they could argue, there is no point making a fuss about it. I totally disagree with this standpoint. The conclusion drawn in the hiring scenario has implications for the retention scenario – the only other one which matters since unemployment is voluntary in the firing scenario. True, the retention scenario features involuntary unemployment both in the envy and joblessness meanings. Yet, the combination of the two criteria, it now turns out, is just a coincidence. In particular, frustration is not caused by unemployment, since the outsiders' frustration would not disappear were they getting a job (assuming for example that an increase in demand for labour triggers a shift from the retention to the hiring scenario).

The lesson to be drawn is that the real subject-matter of Lindbeck and Snower's investigation is not what they claim, unemployment or people's failure to find a job. More rightly, they study the issue of the conditions under which members of an unprivileged group will effectively become jealous of those of a privileged group. This, it turns out, never hinges on the employment status per se. In still other words, if the criterion they use for assessing the existence of what they call 'involuntary unemployment' generates cases of either 'job discrimination' or 'jobless discrimination', it is misleading to state that joblessness is the specific subject-matter of their analysis. Discrimination is the subject-matter.

A discrepancy exists between what I believe is Lindbeck and Snower's real definition of involuntary unemployment and the several definitions of it they give in their essays. One of them has been given above, but similar ones abound in their book. In these definitions, the discrimination and the jobless characteristics are always mixed, which inevitably induces the reader to think that, to them, involuntary unemployment means joblessness *and* its ensuing frustration while actually it exclusively means frustration. Let me give two examples.

> Their [outsiders] unemployment is 'involuntary' in the sense that they would like to be in the 'shoes' of the current insiders but are unable to find jobs on account of the *discrimination* they face in the labour market.
>
> (Lindbeck and Snower 1988: 7)

This proposition would be better if rephrased as: 'Their unemployment is "involuntary" in the sense that they would like to be in the "shoes" of the current insiders, point blank, this being the case whether or not they have got a job'. Now consider this other statement:

> According to our definition, workers are involuntarily unemployed when they are unable to find work on the same terms as insiders.
>
> (Lindbeck and Snower 1988: 8)

Where should the emphasis be put? On 'finding work' or on 'the same terms'? The statement suggests that what is central for being involuntarily unemployed is the inability to get a job – and indeed, this is what one should expect – yet this is not what ensues from their threshold definition of involuntary unemployment. According to the latter, people can be involuntarily unemployed even if they have found a job as long as discrimination is present (and whenever entrants will be hired, terms will be discriminatory).

Underlying Lindbeck and Snower's awkward classification, we have an interesting case of backfiring, a subtle and only half-acknowledged shift in theoretical *explanandum.* Whereas their initial intention must certainly have been to study unemployment, they have ended up tackling a different subject-matter, namely the issue of envy. A sharp contrast then emerges between the use of the involuntary unemployment concept in efficiency wage and insider–outsider models (besides the difference about breaching the reservation wage). Whereas, in the former, frustration is the result of unemployment – to the effect that they disappear concomitantly – in the latter theory, it becomes an autonomous feature, liable to exist on its own, i.e. without unemployment. This is why Lindbeck and Snower's view recalls an image of Lewis Carroll's Cheshire Cat. We may have the grin (frustration) without the cat (unemployment)!

18

COORDINATION FAILURE MODELS

The primary aim of the models studied in the three previous chapters was to rehabilitate the involuntary unemployment concept after Lucas' blunt attack against it. To this end, the authors adopted a partial equilibrium framework. Coordination models, the subject-matter of the present chapter, take a different route. Returning to a general equilibrium perspective, they aim at highlighting cases where the economy is stuck in an inefficient equilibrium, their main thrust being the idea of multiple equilibria. Dominated underemployment comes to the forefront. As far as involuntary unemployment in the reservation wage meaning is concerned, while a few models still purport to demonstrate it, most have, to all intents and purposes, foregone it. The gain from such a renunciation is that the other elements of Keynes' programme, which the earlier New Keynesian models were unable to cover, now receive pride of place. My analysis of coordination failures will be limited to three articles that I have selected for their representativeness and seminal character: Diamond ([1982] 1991), Howitt (1985) and Roberts (1987).[1]

Diamond's search equilibrium model

Description of the model

The parable underpinning Diamond's model runs as follows:

> It is common in theoretical economics to use a tropical island metaphor to describe the working of a model. The island described here has many individuals, not one. When employed, they stroll along the beach examining palm trees. Some trees have coconuts. All bunches have the same number of nuts but differ in the height above the ground. Having spotted a bunch, the individual decides whether to climb the tree. There is a taboo against eating nuts one has picked oneself. Having climbed a tree, the

> worker goes searching for a trade – nuts for nuts – which will result in consumption.
>
> (Diamond [1982] 1991: 42)[2]

The economy comprises only self-employed agents. They fall into two classes. Either they are searching for a productive activity, i.e. for a tree that is worth climbing, or they are looking for a trading partner after having found a suitable tree. Agents who are searching for a production opportunity are called the 'unemployed', those who are searching for a trading opportunity, the 'employed' ([1982] 1991: 33). Every coconut tree bears the same number of coconuts yet trees vary in terms of the effort needed to reach and pick up the coconuts. The arrival of production possibilities is stochastic. The effort must be below some threshold pertaining to the individual willingness to act on production opportunities (the cut-off cost c^*). Once agents are in possession of coconuts, they must find somebody also in possession of coconuts with whom they can trade.[3] This is the second searching process. When it is over, trade takes place on a one-for-one basis, and the good is consumed.

Diamond's central assumption is that the arrival rate of trading partners is a strictly increasing function of the level of activity, i.e. the number of agents holding coconuts to trade. Thus, trade technology exhibits increasing returns to scale: an increase in the level of activity makes trade easier.

The time derivative of the employment rate satisfies:

$$\dot{e} = a(1 - e)\ G(c^*) - eb(e)$$

where e is the level of activity, a the arrival rate of production possibilities, $(1 - e)$ is the unemployment rate, G the distribution of costs and b the arrival rate of trading partners.

The first element of the right-hand expression is the rate of inflow in tradable goods, the second the rate of outflow, i.e. the decrease in the stock of inventories.

As illustrated in Figure 18.1, drawn from Diamond (1982), the steady-state employment rate, $\dot{e} = 0$, is an upward sloping function of b, 'since a greater willingness to invest goes with a greater number of traders if the flows into and out of inventories are to match' (Diamond 1984: 11). It starts from a positive lower bound of possible production costs, $\underline{c}$, and is bounded above by the employment level reached if all production opportunities are accepted.

The next step in Diamond's analysis is to consider the determination of c^*, the cut-off cost. Individuals, who are supposed to know a and b, choose c^* to maximise their expected lifetime utility. c^* is shown to be a positive concave function of e, starting from the origin.

As Figure 18.1 shows, Diamond's model features multiple Pareto-rankable equilibria:

> As long as the economy has an equilibrium with a positive level of production, it will have multiple equilibria ... Thus, I have demonstrated that an active economy with this trading technology has multiple equilibria.
>
> (Diamond 1984: 17)

After a shock, the economy can get stuck in a 'wrong' steady state equilibrium, even if the shock has gone away. Thus the way is paved for exogenous interventions.

> With multiple equilibria there is an important potential role for government. The government can attempt to influence beliefs by suggesting that there is nothing to fear but fear itself. More important, the government can take fiscal action to increase aggregate demand and so launch the economy on the optimistic path. In this way we can model pump-priming while being completely consisted with individual maximisation and rational expectations.
>
> (Diamond 1984: 26)

An assessment

Diamond uses the 'employed' and 'unemployed' terms in a particular way. As stated, to him, somebody is unemployed whenever he is searching for a production opportunity, while an employed person is somebody who is

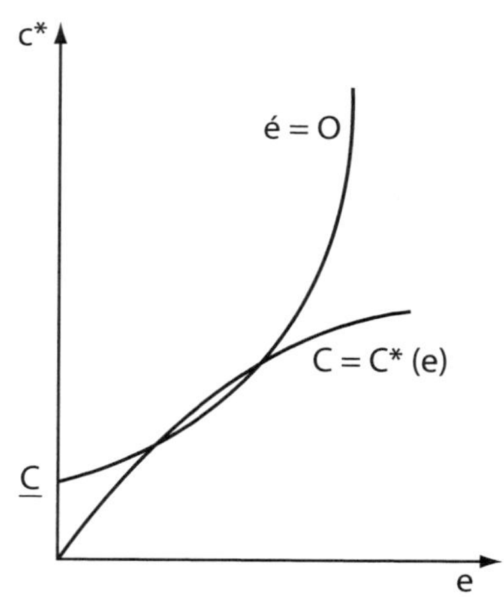

Figure 18.1 Underemployment in Diamond's search model.

searching for a trading opportunity. My own definition is narrower. According to it, an agent is unemployed if he is attempting to participate in the labour market. Although there is something in common between the self-employed person who happens to be without clients and the jobless person, I believe that they should be viewed as belonging to distinct types of activities. In other words, without the existence of a labour market, the unemployment notion is irrelevant.[5] As a result, the involuntary unemployment concept in its reservation wage definition makes no sense in Diamond's model. Hence, the first point of Keynes' programme is not met. In reference to my Chapter 2 taxonomy, I would rather characterise his model as pertaining to dominated underemployment.

In contrast, Diamond's model wins the day as far as the other three items on Keynes' agenda are concerned. First, it exhibits a system failure. Second, demand activation is the proper policy to be undertaken to counteract this. Third and finally, wage rigidity is discharged from any responsibility in the underemployment phenomenon.

Howitt's transaction costs model

Howitt has been more keen than other authors to draw a connection between modern models and Keynes' own conceptions – probably because of his close link to Clower and Leijonhufvud.[6] One of his strong beliefs about the Keynesian programme is that fixed prices should have no place within it. Keynesian economists, he argues, ought to be criticised for their failure to follow suit with this principle.

> Keynes was a great success in many respects. But in his main objective, that of freeing the theoretical explanation of unemployment from depending upon sticky wages and prices, he was a failure. The Keynesian revolution soon settled on the conclusion that Keynes's system made sense, and resulted in unemployment, only under the assumption of a sticky money wage rate.
>
> (Howitt 1990: 7)[7]

As seen, Keynes himself proved unable to dispense with wage rigidity. Therefore any theoretical development that might succeed in this enterprise should be warmly welcomed. According to Howitt, getting rid of the standard claim 'that people are unemployed because they are asking too much' is what coordination failures models have contributed.

Howitt's model

Howitt's model (1985) has a twofold lineage – first, the disequilibrium tradition and, second, Diamond's model. From the former, Howitt retains the presence of quantity signals, while abandoning its fixprice feature. From Diamond, he borrows the trade externality idea.

The auctioneer is present in Howitt's model yet he exerts only his price announcing function without arranging trade. Agents have to find traders in a costly way, i.e. they must use resources in order to execute transactions. Firms have to use up a fraction of the produced good to this end, households a fraction of their time. The thrust of Howitt's model is that the per unit cost of selling decreases with the quantity traded. Hence the 'thin-market externality': the thinner the market, the higher the transaction cost, and vice versa. The existence of these costs changes agents' decision-making process, as they need to be alert to quantity signals. Hence, the demand for labour is a function not only of the real wage but also of the quantity of labour traded, the same being true for labour supply.

> An increase in aggregate demand for output raises the demand for labour even with no change in the real wage, not because it raises the maximum amount a firm can sell, but because it makes any given amount of output easier to sell.
>
> (Howitt 1985: 93–94)

To Howitt, labour trading costs is a sort of unproductive labour, to use classical economists' parlance. This unproductive labour is 'unemployment'.

> I shall interpret unemployment as labour services used up in the selling of labour services ... The rate of unemployment is the fraction of all labour services used in selling labour.
>
> (Howitt 1985: 93)

Increases in trade reduce the unit selling cost. More precisely, there are two markets, labour (n) and output (y). Call s the total sale effort per capita (of either a firm or a household), s_y the total sale effort per firm and s_n total sale effort per worker. Call $\bar{y}$ total output, $\bar{n}$ total labour traded, $\bar{s}$ the aggregate total sale effort, $\bar{s}_y$ firms' total sale effort and $\bar{s}_n$ workers' total sale effort. The unitary sale effort per firm is σ, the unitary sale effort per worker is τ. Howitt's claim is that σ and τ are a function respectively of $\bar{y}$ and $\bar{n}$, with $\sigma'(\bar{y}) < 0$ and $\tau'(\bar{n}) < 0$.

The eventual effect of such transaction costs is that equilibrium will not generally be unique.

> [Without externalities] equilibrium would be unique because the assumptions of declining marginal product and rising marginal disutility of labour would guarantee that the demand price was

> decreasing and the supply price increasing in n . . . But with externality, D [the demand for labour] can be upward sloping because as employment increases, the unit cost of selling output decreases, which tends to increase the demand price. Likewise, S [the supply of labour] can be downwards sloping because as employment increases, the unit cost of selling labour decreases which tends to lower the supply price. These effects of externalities make it possible for D and S to intersect more than once in non-pathological cases.
>
> (Howitt 1985: 95–96)

Figure 18.2 below, drawn from Howitt (1985: 95), illustrates.

The welfare implication of multiple equilibria is that households' utility will be greater whenever employment is greater. This result, Howitt claims, must be interpreted as a case of involuntary unemployment, the latter being equal to the fraction of labour services used up in the selling of labour services.

> There is a sense in which at least some of the unemployment in a low-level equilibrium (n_L in Figure 18.2) fits Patinkin's criterion of involuntariness. For, in this equilibrium, the transaction-cost constraint could be regarded as 'unusually severe'. In order to sell n_L units of labour, the household is required to spend the amount $n_L\tau(n_L)$ in unemployment instead of the smaller amount $n_L\tau(n_H)$ that would be required to sell that much if the economy were at its high-level equilibrium. Thus, the amount $n_L(\tau(n_L) - \tau(n_H))$ might be regarded as involuntary.
>
> (Howitt 1985: 98)

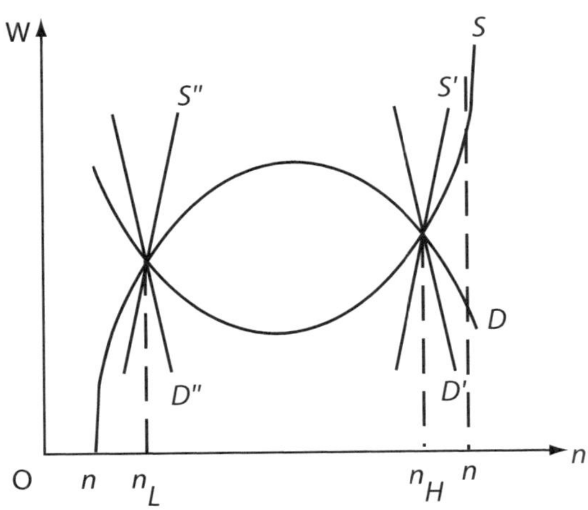

Figure 18.2 Underemployment in Howitt's model.

An assessment

In discussing Diamond's model, I have argued that it cannot be considered having unemployment as its proper object because it comprises no labour market. Although the labour market is present in Howitt's model, I still find it inappropriate to characterise it as having demonstrated unemployment. What Howitt calls unemployment does not fit what I consider to be its appropriate definition. In his model there is market clearing, everybody who wants to work is working, and the loss in employment is equally distributed across agents. Thus, like Diamond's model, its real object of analysis is dominated underemployment. Since unemployment is absent, the 'involuntary' modifier is disqualified as well.

Howitt asserts that he is just borrowing Patinkin's definition of involuntary unemployment, yet this claim is unconvincing. In Chapter XIII of *Money, Interest and Prices*, Patinkin states that any element of involuntariness which may be present must result from a confrontation between ideal circumstances, taken as the norm, and some given circumstances. Such a statement is too general, yet, fortunately enough, Patinkin makes it clearer by asserting that the norm consists of being on the supply or demand curves, while the deviation from it amounts to being off these curves. It is then quite logical to see Patinkin's earlier statement as just an introduction to his narrow definition. Howitt on the contrary, views Patinkin's introductory remark as forming a definition on its own, therefore stating that by 'involuntary' Patinkin meant 'chosen subject to an unusually severe constraint' (1965: 98). Thereby he leaves in the shadow the fact that his model features no involuntary unemployment against Patinkin's criterion of being off the supply curve.

Howitt is a good example of modern Keynesian economists' ambiguous stance with respect to involuntary unemployment. On the one hand, as just seen, he claims to have demonstrated it – although, it seems to me, at the price of a semantic twist. On the other hand, in another essay we find him stating that the voluntary/involuntary unemployment distinction is of little interest.

> The above discussion suggests that the distinction between voluntary and involuntary behaviour is not a useful one for macroeconomic theory. The misery of unemployment is as great if it is voluntary or involuntary, the behaviour of the unemployed does not depend upon whether they quit or were fired, and the reaction of a firm to an accumulation of inventories does not depend upon whether the accumulation was voluntary or whether it is a result of voluntary speculation.
>
> (Howitt 1990: 31)

Howitt is on firmer ground for what concerns the other elements of Keynes' programme. First, his result belongs to the system failure type. Any demand boast will result in decreasing the unitary transaction cost. Hence agents' welfare will be improved. Moreover, no objection should be levelled against Howitt's claim that price rigidity plays no part in his model.

Roberts' coordination failures model

As seen, authors like Clower, Leijonfvud and Benassy had realised that the trade organisation assumption, i.e. in the auctioneer hypothesis, constituted the decisive obstacle to introducing market rationing in Walrasian or neo-Walrasian theory. The difficulty, however, was how to operationalise this insight that one should dispose of it. Roberts' model (1987) marks an important progress in this respect.

According to Roberts, his model formally captures Clower's idea of self-confirming conjectures. He also claims to be heir to authors such as Barro-Grossman, Drèze and Benassy in emphasising perceived quantity constraints as well as the idea that demand constrains employment. Yet the fixprice assumption is disposed with.

The following two quotations bring home the gist of Roberts' model:

> Equilibrium with full employment exists, with all agents transacting their Walrasian quantities. Simultaneously there are also equilibria at the same prices and wages in which markets fail to clear. In particular, some price-taking and wage-taking workers are rationed in their labour market transactions and are unable to sell as much of their labour as they desire at the given wage. This involuntary unemployment arises despite the model's incorporating markets for all commodities . . . and in equilibrium no such agent finds it worthwhile, for example, to reduce wages in the face of involuntary unemployment.
>
> (Roberts 1987: 856)

> The economy and institutions together define a game in extensive form. We then examine the subgame perfect equilibria of the game. These have the crucial property indicated above that equilibrium in this strong sense does not imply market clearing. Subgame perfection implies that consumers are price-takers. However, they may be subject to quantity rationing and thus be unable to buy and sell their Walrasian utility-maximising quantities at a given vector of prices. This rationing arises because other consumers' output orders are inadequate to justify firms hiring the Walrasian input quantities, even if they are offered, or

> because others' input supply offers will not allow firms to meet the Walrasian demands.
>
> (Roberts 1989: 149)

Roberts' claim is stronger than Howitt's since he is unambiguously striving at demonstrating involuntary unemployment in its reservation wage definition where 'workers facing given prices and wages are off their supply curves in equilibrium' (Roberts 1987: 858). Coming after decades of failures, such a result, if vindicated, cannot but be good news for the Keynesian camp.

In line with the conclusion reached in Chapter 4, the possibility of such a result stems from the radically non-Walrasian trade technology adopted: 'the key is in the modelling of the processes determining prices and individual transactions' (1987: 856). Roberts assumes a separation and specialisation in production and consumption. There are two types of producers (A and B), two types of worker-consumers (J and K), two types of labour (r and s) and two flows of goods (x and y). In total the economy comprises five commodities, money (m), which is non-produced, being the fifth. The model is based on a generalised absence of a 'Ford effect'. No worker can supply inputs to a producer from whom he might buy outputs. Symmetrically, a worker buys output only from the type of producer to whom he supplies no labour. As shown in Figure 18.3, the Js can supply input only to A's while they can purchase output only from B.

All agents are endowed with money. Only producers have the technical knowledge to produce goods. Labour is the only factor of production. Returns to scale are constant. The input–output coefficient is set at unity. Production is made to order. No inventories are present. Prices and wages are flexible, in that each producer may set the price and wage it controls at any level it wishes.

A more formal account is as follows. Producers of type A care only about money, i.e. $V_A = (m, r, s, x, y) = U_A(m)$. Their endowment is $e_A = (\overline{m}_A, 0, 0, 0, 0)$. Producers of type B care only about money, i.e. $V_B = (m, r, s, x, y) = U_B(m)$. Their endowment is $e_B = (\overline{m}_B, 0, 0, 0, 0)$. Workers of type J care about m, r and y, i.e., $V_J = (m, r, s, x, y) = U_J(m, r, y)$. Their endowment is $e_J = (\overline{m}_J, \overline{r}_J, 0, 0, 0)$. Finally, workers of type K care about m, s and x, i.e. $V_K = (m, r, s, x, y) = U_K(m, s, x)$. Their endowment is $e_K = (\overline{m}_K\, 0, \overline{s}_K, 0, 0)$.

There are n agents of each type. Assume that $n = 2$. The production functions are: $x = f_A(r) = r$ and $y = f_B(s) = s$.

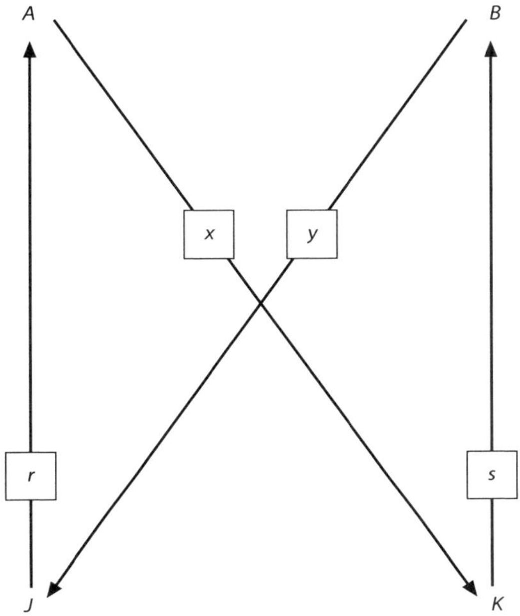

Figure 18.3 The trade structure in Roberts' model.

Three stages in the formation of equilibrium prices and quantities are separated:

Stage 1: price announcements by producers

A producers announce p_x^1, p_x^2 and w_r^1, w_r^2, B producers announce p_y^1, p_y^2 and w_s^1, w_s^2, where the subscript identifies the producer.

Stage 2: workers react by making a trading proposal

Each J worker proposes simultaneously r_J^1, r_J^2, subject to $r_J^1 + r_J^2 \leq \bar{r}_J$, and y_J^1, y_J^2, subject to $m_J + p_y^1\, y_j^1 + p_y^2\, y_j^2 \leq \overline{m}_J + w_r^1\, r_j^1 + w_r^2\, r_j^2$. Each K worker proposes simultaneously s_k^1 s_K^2, subject to $s_k^1 + s_K^2 \leq \bar{s}_K$, and x_K^1, x_K^2, subject to $s + p_x^1\, x_K^1 + p_y^2\, x_K^2 \leq \overline{m}_K + w_s^1\, s_K^1 + w_s^2\, s_K^2$. The subscript indicates the producer to whom the worker makes his trading proposal.

Stage 3: producers make their quantity decisions

Each A-producer selects $x_A^1 \leq x_K^1$, $x_A^2 \leq x_K^2$ and $r_A^1 \leq r_J^1$, $r_A^2 \leq r_J^2$, where x_A^1 is the sale of x by the concerned A-producer to K-agent 1, r_A^1 its hiring of r from

J-agent 1, etc. Each *B*-firm selects $y_B^1 \leq y_J^1 \leq y_J^2$ and $s_B^1 \leq s_K^1$, $s_B^2 \leq s_K^2$, where y_B^1 is the sale of *y* by the concerned *B*-producer to *J*-agent 1, s_B^1 its hiring of *s* from *K*-agent 1, etc.

The economy and institutions together define a game in extensive form. Examining its subgame perfect equilibria, Roberts shows that a continuity of equilibrium is possible. Walrasian equilibrium is one of them. In this case, in spite of the special trade technology assumption made, the observed price and wage and quantities traded are the same as those which would have been obtained had the price formation process been auctioneer-led. Another possible equilibrium is when agents do not trade at all. Keynesian equilibria can also exist, where some of the consumers trade their Walrasian quantities at the Walrasian price and wage while a subset of consumers consume their initial endowments. They can be observed as supplying no labour and demanding no output.

As for the explanation of such a result, it has to do with the non-cooperative character of the game coupled with its institutional arrangement, on the one hand, and with the presence of the non-produced good, on the other. Involuntary unemployment will result from households of one type developing self-fulfilling pessimist conjectures about the quantity choices made by households of the other type (Roberts 1987: 868). As a result, some agents may become stuck in

> Zero-activity level equilibria that involve each consumer ordering zero because the person expects no labour to be supplied and thus no output to be available, and simultaneously offering no labour because he or she expects zero output demand and hiring.
>
> (Roberts 1987: 869)

Such pessimist conjectures arise for example when a K-consumer, whose optimising plan is to sell labour and purchase output, conjectures that their 'correspondent' J-agent decides to consume their endowment and make a zero labour and output offer. Agent J makes the same conjecture about agent K. As a result, none of them will supply labour and demand output, against their optimising plan. In this case, the state of involuntary unemployment of some agents results from their conjecture of a voluntary unemployment choice (i.e. the decision to use the total time endowment as leisure) of others. Another example is the case where a K-household, whose optimising plan is to trade *s* and *x*, conjectures that the correspondent agent-J chooses to supply *r* while expressing no demand for *y*. They further conjecture that the firm B to whom they were intending to propose their labour will end up refusing their offer for lack of demand for *y* while in contrast the firm A, from whom he or she was intending to buy *x*, will accept the trade offer. Realising that they therefore might end up with negative money holdings, they will refrain from trading (Roberts 1987: 868).

An assessment

Two main criticisms have been levelled against Roberts' model. The first is that it comprises too many equilibria. The second is that its result is ad hoc because it follows from the special trade arrangement made. In particular, Jones and Manuelli (1992) show that Robert's conclusion no longer holds if inventories are introduced, replacing made-to-order production. That is, Roberts' three-stage price and quantity formation process is replaced by a four-stage process, where firms set prices in the first stage, workers make an offer to work at the announced prices and wages in the second stage, firms hire workers, production takes place, workers are paid and output goes into inventories in the third stage, and finally workers go shopping in the fourth stage (Jones and Manuelli 1992: 453). As these authors argue, 'what seems like only small changes in the economic structure can give rise to altogether different conclusions about the qualitative properties of equilibrium' (1992: 466).

Should this 'ad hoc' criticism be accepted? The borderline between what is and what is not ad hoc is difficult to draw. There are cases where the ad hoc indictment is valid. For example in Azariadis' model, the fact that the firm is able to insure workers against wage fluctuations yet not against employment fluctuations is definitely ad hoc. Yet, the case at hand here is less clear-cut. Economists construct models with a precise intention in mind. Roberts aimed at getting an involuntary unemployment result and shaped his assumptions to this end. Jones and Manuelli want to produce the opposite result and therefore modify some of Roberts' assumption to this purpose. In this way, every model is ad hoc!

Be that as it may, Roberts should be hailed for having succeeded in developing a theory about involuntary unemployment in the reservation wage sense. Does it also feature individual disequilibrium? Roberts, himself, does not make such a claim. His paper is based on Selten's notion of subgame equilibrium. This leads to the result that 'the unemployed workers correctly perceive that there is nothing that anyone of them can do that will lead to gainful employment' (1987: 857). Roberts wants his agents to exhibit optimality and rationality, two features which he views selfsame to their being in equilibrium. It then seems unwarranted to refer to individual disequilibrium. However, such a definitional stance rests on equating optimality, rationality and equilibrium. As a result, individual equilibrium is axiomatic. My viewpoint is different. As claimed in Chapter 2, and in my Chapter 14 discussion of Lucas, I believe that a distinction should be drawn between individual planning and effective or observable behaviour – it is not because an agent has rationally conceived an optimal plan that the latter will necessarily be realised. Roberts' model bears witness to this. My very definition of individual disequilibrium refers to the case where an agent is unable to make his optimal plan come through. Thus, individual disequilibrium does not exclude rationality and optimising planning. If my distinction and definition are accepted, Roberts' rationed agents ought to be considered as being in a state of individual disequilibrium since they are stuck in forced leisure through no fault of their own.

Finally, let me turn to the other features of the Keynesian programme. The framework adopted by Roberts is general equilibrium. The involuntary unemployment result co-exists with the Walrasian wage, so that wage rigidity cannot be incriminated as its cause. Unfortunately Roberts' paper misses the full realisation of Keynes' programme for it fails to properly tackle the policy dimension.

Concluding remarks

Table 18.1 summarises the results of my investigation as to how the three models fare with respect to the Keynesian programme.

Two main conclusions stand out. First, all three models mark an undeniable progress with respect to the type of new Keynesian models studied in the previous chapters for what concerns the realisation of Keynes' programme (even if it is at the price of foregoing the involuntary unemployment claim). My second, less sanguine, conclusion is that these models do not make the cut in spite of the progress they have brought about. Take Roberts' model. In my opinion, it marks a victory on the front of demonstrating involuntary unemployment. But then, it turns out to be a one-shot victory – yes involuntary unemployment has been demonstrated, yet so what? On the one hand, no research programme ensues. Roberts just provides an example of involuntary unemployment – and for that matter, it rests on particular assumptions. On the other hand, the victory may have

Table 18.1 The realisation of Keynes' programme

	Diamond	*Howitt*	*Roberts*
Involuntary unemployment In the reservation wage sense	no	no	yes
Involuntary unemployment in the reservation wage definition plus individual disequilibrium	no	no	yes
System failure	yes	yes	yes
Price and wage flexibility	yes	yes	yes
Demand activation as the proper remedial policy	yes	yes	no

come too late. At least in the United Sates, the problem of unemployment was about to cease to be a central topic for research. Moreover, on the theoretical front, the works of Lucas and Kydland and Frescott had sparked off a change in the agenda of macroeconomics away from the study of market failures.

19

IMPERFECTLY COMPETITIVE GENERAL EQUILIBRIUM MODELS

In this chapter, I examine another strand of literature, imperfect competition models. While Keynes aimed at reaching his results within a perfect competition framework, the authors whom I will now study base their models on the view that a departure from this framework is needed in order to vindicate Keynes' insights. As in earlier chapters, my analysis will be limited to a few seminal works – first, Hart's model ([1982] 1991) and, second, Blanchard and Kiyotaki's model ([1987] 1991).[1] Hart's paper played a pioneering role in promoting the idea that imperfect competition had Keynesian features, as indicated by its title, 'A Model of Imperfect Competition with Keynesian Features'. However, it soon appeared that imperfect competition alone was insufficient for getting strong Keynesian results. A supplementary ingredient, such as nominal rigidity, had to be brought into the picture. This led to a second generation of models of which Blanchard and Kiyotaki's work is emblematic.

Hart's model

According to Hart, his model displays the following Keynesian features: in equilibrium, the economy operates at too low a level of activity and features underemployment; government policy can increase employment; exogenous demand shocks have a multiplier effect greater than one. Moreover, he claims that his model shows that '"depressions" occur when the demand shifts from the produced good to the non-produced good' ([1982] 1991: 334). This is reminiscent of Keynes' insight that the ultimate cause of involuntary unemployment is to be found in financial factors, which led Hicks to emphasise the preference for liquidity.

The model

Hart's model is a static general equilibrium model with imperfect competition, based on a Cournot-Nash conception of equilibrium. The economy comprises three goods, a produced commodity, a non-produced commodity and labour. The non-produced good serves as *numéraire*.[2]

There is a given large number of firms (N) producing a single good. The number of individuals is a multiple of that of firms (mN, where m is large). Agents are endowed with $\bar{k}$ units of the non-produced good and T units of labour. Each agent is assumed to own a fraction $1/mN$ of every firm. Agents' utility function is $U(k,y)$, where k is the consumption of the nonproduced good and y the consumption of the produced good. Preferences are homothetic. Leisure does not enter the utility function – i.e. labour is inelastically supplied.[3] mNT is the fixed total labour supply. The demand addressed to the market for the produced good is $h(p)I$, where I indicates the joined wealth (or income) of consumers in the market in point. It is formed from wages and profits as having accrued in the other markets and their endowment in the non-produced good. Although I is taken as given in every market, it is endogenously determined at the level of the economy as a whole.

Different market structures are considered. Consider first the output market. At one extreme, all firms may belong to the same market. In the other cases, it is assumed that this single market is sub-divided into separated entities, each of them being a reduced version of the economy, with the same ratio of firms to consumers. Since the total number of firms is given, the higher the number of separate markets the higher the prevailing degree of monopoly. The latter is measured by parameter ϑ, with $1>\vartheta>0$. The limiting cases ($\vartheta=0$ and $\vartheta=1$) indicate perfect competition and monopoly. Hart is interested in the case of oligopoly. Each goods market thus comprises $1/\vartheta$ firms and m/ϑ agents. There are N/q separate and identical labour markets. Each of them has a large number of firms (q) and a still larger number of individuals (mq). It is assumed that workers form syndicates, whose objective function is to maximise total receipts. The smaller the number of unions per market, the higher their market power. Call ρ the degree of monopoly in the labour market, with $1>\rho>0$. Each union has $mq\rho$ members. It is assumed that oligopolists know the objective demand functions.

This setting enables economic actors to be of significant size relative to the market they operate in, yet negligible with respect to the aggregate economy. Thereby, it can be assumed that only a negligible fraction of workers purchase output in a market served by the firms they work for. Similarly, it is assumed that a negligible fraction of workers' income comes from holding shares in the firms they work for.

The existence of oligopoly results in the economic activity being lower than under perfect competition. Efficiency is equated with the latter. More precisely, efficiency exists only if all labour is employed (in view of the fact that labour is supplied inelastically). In this context, full employment means the level of employment prevailing in perfect competition, which is both the maximum and the optimal level of employment.[4]

Hart's reasoning proceeds in four stages.

First stage: firms' optimal decisions

In every output market, firms act as Cournot oligopolists. An individual firm chooses its output level in order to maximise profits, taking as given the amount of output sold by other firms (as well as the wealth of the buyers and the wage rate). In equilibrium marginal revenue equals marginal cost. That is:

$$p(1 + \vartheta/\eta(p)) = wC'(\vartheta h(p)I)$$

where η is the elasticity of market demand and C' the marginal cost.

Second stage: unions' optimal decisions in a partial equilibrium context

Unions know the solution to the firm's optimal decision, $\tilde{p}$(w, I). Therefore, they are aware that the demand for labour in each labour market is:

$$L(w, I) = qC(\vartheta h(\tilde{p}(w, I))I).$$

In a partial equilibrium analysis, the choice-problem of an oligopolistic syndicate simply consists of picking up the point on its residual demand for labour curve that maximises its objective function, taking as given the quantity of labour traded by other unions. This leads to the following first order condition:

$$w(1 + \rho/\varepsilon(w, I)) \geq 0$$

where ε is the elasticity of demand for labour with respect to the wage, with equality there is underemployment.[5]

Third stage: unions' optimal decisions in a general equilibrium context

In a general equilibrium context, syndicates must take into account the fact that any reduction in labour traded will drive the wage rate up, which in turn will generate a higher price and lower output and employment. Therefore, Hart re-expresses ε(w,I), the elasticity of demand for labour, in terms of $\eta(p)$, the elasticity of demand for output. With a few additional conditions, he arrives at the following result:

> If there is underemployment in equilibrium, syndicates will choose the wage rate so that the price of the produced good in output markets is $\hat{p}$; i.e., they will set w so that $\gamma(\hat{p}) = wC'(\vartheta h(\hat{p})I)$ [where γ is the marginal revenue of the firm]. That is, it is as if the syndicates controlled the price of the produced good directly.
>
> (Hart [1982] 1991: 325)

Fourth stage: making wealth endogenous

The joint wealth of the buyers in an output market at the Cournot equilibrium price, $\tilde{p}$, must be the same level of wealth $\tilde{I}$ that determines the demand curve faced by firms.[6]

Hart's model nicely captures the interdependency between the labour and the goods markets, i.e. that the degree of competition existing in the product market is an integral element in the determination of the equilibrium quantity in the labour market. Silvestre (1993: 112) has proposed the notion of the 'eventual demand-for-labour curve' to designate this linkage.[7] Figure 19.1, drawn from Silvestre (1993: 113), illustrates.

Figure 19.1 describes the labour market result conditionally to the output market competitive structure. It features two eventual demand-for-labour curves. The upper curve assumes that the output market exhibits perfect competition, the lower that it is oligopolistic. Point A corresponds to the situation where both the output and the labour market are competitive ($\vartheta = 0$ and $\rho = 0$). When $\vartheta = 0$ and $\rho > 0$, the equilibrium point is on the upper curve, either at A or some interior point, as B. When

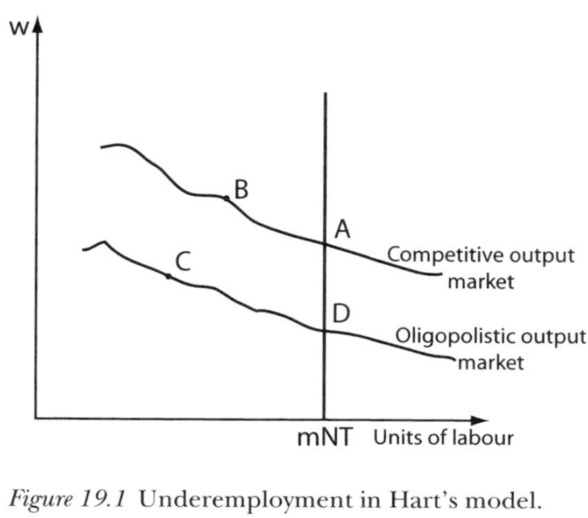

Figure 19.1 Underemployment in Hart's model.

$\vartheta = 0$, the equilibrium point is on the lower curve. If the labour market is competitive, D will prevail. Otherwise, the equilibrium point will be D or a point on its left, as C. A and D are full employment outcomes while B and C are states of underemployment. To get the Keynesian result – i.e. trade on the left of mNT – a necessary yet insufficient condition is that oligopolistic conditions prevail in the labour market. Put differently, as soon as the labour market is competitive, there is full employment whether or not the output market is competitive.

The occurrence of B or C, rather than of A or B, depends on the relationship between $\hat{p}$, the price of output that is optimal to unions, and another benchmark, p^*, the price of the produced good relative to the non-produced good generating the level of demand consistent with full employment. The equilibrium is $\tilde{p} = \max(\hat{p}, p^*)$. If $\hat{p} > p^*$, underemployment exists. If $\hat{p} < p^*$, there is full employment, and the union raises the wage until p^* prevails.

To conclude, the existence of underemployment hinges on two factors, the market power of the syndicates, on the one hand, and the way in which income is spent across the produced and the non-produced good, on the other. This is turn depends on $\bar{k}$ and p^*. The higher the price of the produced good, the higher the income spent on the non-produced good and the lower the demand for labour.

Hart lucidly recognises that his model comprises no unemployment result – i.e. an unequal allocation of the total number of hours worked across agents. Its exclusive concern is underemployment. 'Each member is underemployed to the extent of $T - L/mq\rho$ – in our analysis there will be underemployment but no unemployment' (Hart [1982] 1991: 317). Unfortunately, commentators of Hart have not always been as cautious as him concerning terminology.[8]

The fact that in Hart's model the cause of unemployment lies in the oligopolistic structure of the labour market may suggest that unions, rather than the firms or the 'system', are the culprit. Clearly, this was not what Keynes had in mind. D'Aspremont, Dos Santos Ferreira and Gérard-Varet (1989, 1990) have tried to turn this conclusion upside down. Generalising Hart's result, they specify the conditions under which underemployment is possible with a perfectly competitive labour market going along with an oligopolistic output market. Competition in the labour market may then result in the equilibrium wage being equal to zero.[9] Figure 19.2, also drawn from Silvestre (1993), illustrates.

Now an oligopolistic labour market is no longer a necessary condition for underemployment. Its cause lies instead in the goods markets and in firms' monopolistic position. Thereby, workers responsibility for underemployment is lifted. Too high a wage cannot be responsible for unemployment since the latter can exist even when competition drives the wage to zero. In Silvestre's words:

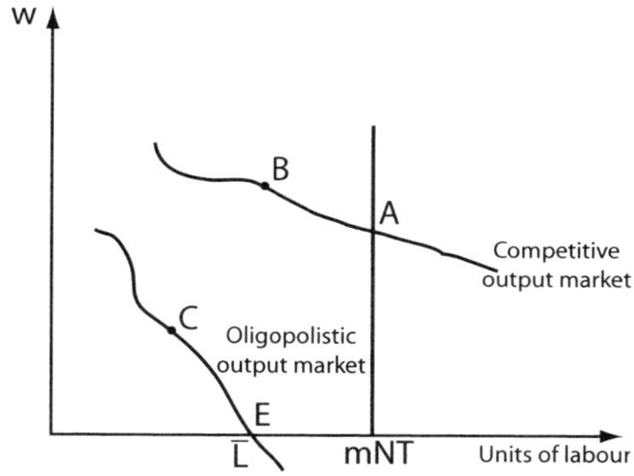

Figure 19.2 Involuntary unemployment according to d'Aspremont, Gérard-Varet and Dos Santos Ferreira.

> The quantity of labour demanded reaches a finite number $\overline{L}$ at zero wage, which may well be lower than the labour supply *mNT*. In that case, there is unemployment at any wage, even at zero wage . . . If the labour market is perfectly competitive, then equilibrium means excess supply at zero wages, that is to say, labour becomes a free good, yet there is still excess supply, as in point E.
>
> (Silvestre 1993: 114)

Moreover, d'Aspremont *et al.* claim that the change they introduce into Hart's model results in justifying the existence of involuntary unemployment:

> This we have called a situation of 'involuntary unemployment' in the spirit of Keynes, according to whom unemployment is involuntary when there is 'no method available to labour as a whole for attaining full employment' by making revised money bargains with the entrepreneurs.
>
> (d'Aspremont, Dos Santos Ferreira and Gérard-Varet 1990: 896)

An assessment

In Chapter 2, I insisted on the need to draw a distinction between unemployment and underemployment and remarked that many authors were unaware of this distinction, and used the two terms indistinctly. Such a criticism cannot be levelled against Hart since he explicitly asserts that his model is concerned with underemployment rather than unemployment. If there is no unemployment, there can be no involuntary unemployment. A fortiori, Keynes' idea of individual disequilibrium can play no part.

Thus, the case at hand is one of dominated underemployment, to refer to my Chapter 2 typology. As such, it features an inefficiency or loss of social welfare.

What about d'Aspremont, Dos Santos Ferreira and Gérard-Varet's claim that their result deserves the involuntary unemployment label? I cannot agree with them. The exclusion of labour from the utility function must be interpreted as meaning that leisure is considered a neutral good, in which case agents' indifferent curves are horizontal lines, with the lowest line coinciding with the abscissa. As soon as the wage is positive, a corner solution will prevail and the total time endowment will be devoted to labour market participation. However, if the wage is zero, agents are indifferent between working or consuming leisure. Thus, the supply function is not a vertical line, as it first appears. It has rather an inverse-L-shape, its horizontal section coinciding with the abscissa. On any point of this horizontal section, agents are indifferent between leisure and work. Their reservation wage is zero, there is no infringement of the reservation wage principle. No grounds exist for invoking involuntary unemployment.

I now turn to the other items of Keynes' programme. On the score of the exoneration of the price and wage rigidity explanation, Hart's fits. In his model, prices and wages are fully flexible. If they fail to decrease in the presence of underemployment, it is because the consequent increase in demand would not offset the loss in revenue of the price-making agent. The same positive conclusion can be drawn about the general equilibrium character of his type of analysis. But evidently, Hart departs from Keynes for what concerns the choice between a perfect or imperfect competition line of research. As far as the vindication of demand stimulation is concerned, his model is less convincing. The increase in demand that Hart's is considering amounts to changing the data of the economy, either the per capita endowment in the non-produced good or agents' tastes. Likewise, the fiscal policy he is proposing is inconclusive because of its sensitivity to assumptions about technology and preferences. All in all, the Keynesian features of Hart's model are secondary.

Blanchard and Kiyotaki's model

The model

Hart considered his model as non-monetary. Other imperfect competition theorists had less qualms about introducing money in similar models, in spite of their being as static as Hart's. An important paper taking this stance is Blanchard and Kiyotaki ([1987] 1991).[10]

Theirs is a model of monopolistic competition. Every seller, be it a firm or a household, has a monopoly over the good that they sell yet their monopoly power is limited by the existence of imperfect substitutes. I will not enter into a detailed description of firms' and households' optimising behaviour. Equilibrium consists of a relationship between the aggregate demand for goods and real money balances, the demand functions for goods and labour, and the price and wage rules. These refer to the way in which monopolistic firms (households) set prices (wages). In equilibrium, symmetry will prevail and all relative prices and wages will be equal to unity.

The 'aggregate price rule' is summarised by the following equation:

$$(P/W) = (\vartheta/(\vartheta - 1))\ K_p\ Y^{\alpha-1}$$

where P is the price of the output, W the wage, $\vartheta/(\vartheta-1)$ the degree of monopoly power of firms in the goods market, K_p a constant that depends on the technology and the number of firms, Y the aggregate demand for goods, α is the inverse of the degree of returns to scale, $\alpha-1$ the elasticity of marginal cost with respect to output.

If firms operate under decreasing returns, the price wage ratio is an increasing function of the level of output.

The 'aggregate wage rule' consists of the following equation:

$$(W/P) = (\sigma/(\sigma - 1))\ K_w\ Y^{\alpha(\beta-1)}$$

where $\sigma/(\sigma-1)$ is the degree of monopoly power of workers in the labour market, K_w a constant depending on the parameters of the utility function and the number of households, $\beta-1$ the elasticity of marginal disutility of labour.

The real wage is a positive function of output:

> If β is strictly greater than unity, that is, if workers have increasing marginal disutility of work, an increase in output that leads to an increase in the derived demand for labour, requires an increase in the real wage.
>
> (Blanchard and Kiyotaki [1987] 1991: 351)

In a competitive set-up, the same equations remain valid except that, at any level of output, the price-wage ratio consistent with firms' behaviour is lower by $\vartheta/(\vartheta-1)$, the real wage consistent with households' behaviour by $\sigma/(\sigma-1)$.

Figure 19.3, drawn from Blanchard and Kiyotaki ([1987] 1991: 354) and where A' is the competitive equilibrium and A the monopolistically competitive equilibrium, illustrates.

The view that monopolistic competition leads to a sub-optimal level of employment is a staple of economic analysis. Yet Blanchard and Kiyotaki re-interpret this feature as an externality, bringing thereby a system failure

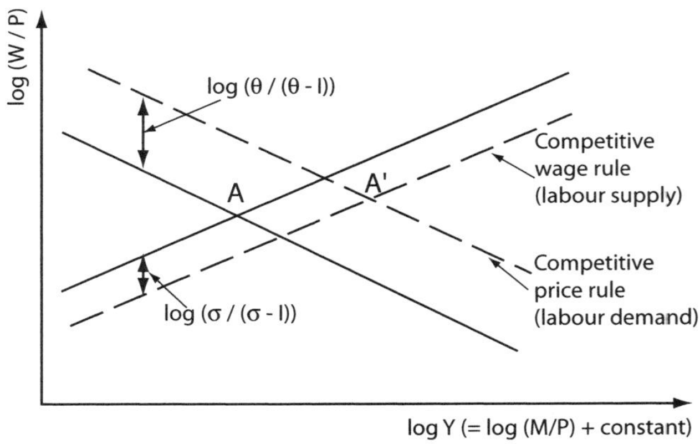

Figure 19.3 Underemployment in Blanchard and Kiyotaki's model.

flavour to their model. The economy is viewed as stuck in a state from which agents have no incentive to depart in spite of the fact that all agents would benefit from a symmetric departure.

> In the monopolistically competitive equilibrium, each price (wage) setter has, given other prices, no incentives to decrease its own price (wage) and increase its output (labour). Suppose however that price setters decrease their prices simultaneously; this increases real money balances and aggregate demand. The increase in output reduces the initial distortion of underproduction and underemployment and increases social welfare.
>
> (Blanchard and Kiyotaki [1987] 1991: 354)

In Hart's model an increase in the existing quantity of the non-produced good directly raises the level of activity. In Blanchard and Kiyotaki's model the matter is slightly more complicated, because the aggregate price rule and the aggregate wage rule are homogenous of degree zero in *P*, *W* and *M*. As a result, 'nominal money is neutral, affecting all nominal prices and wages proportionately and leaving output and employment unchanged. Thus something else is needed to obtain real effects of nominal money' ([1987] 1991: 356).[11]

The additional element is nominal rigidity. In their model, it is justified by 'menu costs' – changing nominal prices, it is assumed, implies a fixed cost.[12] Assume an increase in the aggregate demand triggered by an increase in money supply. Because of the price-setting cost, firms and workers may judge it profitable not to adjust the price of the output and the wage while accepting to meet the increase in demand. This acceptance is due to the fact that price exceeds marginal cost and wage exceeds marginal disutility in the initial equilibrium. As a result, under certain conditions, firms and unions will satisfy the extra-demand. While menu costs are second-order (i.e. small), the increase in real money balances resulting from monetary expansion has first-order (i.e. significant) effects on welfare.[13]

> The results of this paper are tantalisingly close to those of traditional Keynesian models: under monopolistic competition, output is too low because of an aggregate demand externality. This externality, together with small menu costs, implies that movements in demand can affect output and welfare. In particular, increases in nominal money can increase both output and welfare.
>
> (Blanchard and Kiyotaki [1987] 1991: 368)[14]

An assessment

Assessing Blanchard and Kiyotaki's model against Keynes' programme is easy. First of all, they do not seem to be interested in involuntary unemployment. They avoid using the this term and take a position similar to Hart's. No household is unemployed in their model. Thus, their result pertains to dominated underemployment. Obviously, they also depart from Keynes' programme on the matter of exonerating wage rigidity from any responsibility in explaining the underemployment outcome. To them, nominal rigidity is an essential ingredient of Keynesian theory. For what concerns the remaining two items, Blanchard and Kiyotaki are more in line with Keynes' programme. They take up the interdependency claim, as they insist on their model being about a system failure. Finally, demand stimulation is an effective remedy against the externality. In this respect, their model is more convincing than Hart's.

But the main contribution of Blanchard and Kiyotaki's model is to have strengthened the case for the effectiveness of monetary policy against Friedman and Lucas' claim to the contrary.[15]

Benassy on imperfect competition models

Benassy, who on top of his contributions to the disequilibrium approach, has also played an important role in the development of imperfect competition theory – his first paper on imperfect competition goes back to 1976 (Benassy 1976) – claims that imperfect competition and fixprice models are two parallel branches of the same broader non-Walrasian framework (1990, 1993). Hence he feels that no breach is involved when moving from perfect to imperfect competition models – imperfect competition amounts to generalising the fixprice approach by making its price formation process endogenous. According to him, the quantity-constrained agents encountered in disequilibrium theory and the monopolist are in a similar position. Both exhibit the same phenomenon of perceived constraint and rationing. The following quotation summarises his claim:

> Each seller sells only one good and, we shall see below, sets its price high enough so as to be willing to satisfy all demand for that good. In equilibrium each agent thus will be constrained only on his sales, and we shall somehow have a situation of 'general excess supply' . . . This boils down to finding total demand for goods *i* and *j* as a fix-price K-equilibrium.
>
> (Benassy 1990: 153)

To assess Benassy's point of view, which is not shared by other imperfect competition theorists, let me proceed in two steps. First, Table 19.1 draws a contrast between the two approaches on a series of scores.

Table 19.1 shows that the differences between the two approaches are significant. The main point, however, is to see whether we can follow Benassy when he is asserting that monopolistic sellers are rationed. To him, this assertion is based on the fact that they are trading off their supply curve. According to the definitional stance that I have adopted in Chapter 2, I should agree with him. In effect, in this chapter, I have claimed that involuntary unemployment in the reservation wage sense can be viewed from two angles: from the individual's point of view, it amounts to a state of individual disequilibrium while, from the interactive point of view, it gives rises to a phenomenon that can be captured through the synonyms 'terms of market rationing', 'market non-clearing' and 'off the supply curve trading'.

But this characterisation ceases to be valid when it comes to imperfectly competitive general equilibrium models. As far as the first of these two aspects (individual disequilibrium) is concerned, the matter is clear:

Table 19.1 A comparison between the fixprice and the imperfect competition approaches

	Fixprice models	*Imperfect competition models*
Market structure	perfect competition	imperfect competition
Prices and wages	real rigidity	nominal rigidity
Foundation of the possible rigidity	none	menu costs
Market outcome	involuntary unemployment and market non-clearing	underemployment

imperfect competition models do feature optimising behaviour. Evidently, the seller chooses an optimising point. The same is true for purchasers. At the risk of stating the obvious, a monopolist cannot impose upon his customers any economic outcome they are unwilling to accept. He just picks up the element of their optimising plan that is the most favourable to him. So, both the seller and the demanders are in an optimising situation. The second aspect, the interactive point of view, is more troublesome. It is admitted that trade takes place off the supply curve under imperfect competition. Should it then be concluded that imperfect competition models exhibit market non-clearing or is it the case that the earlier coincidence between market non-clearing and trading off the supply curve ceases to be valid for such models (market rationing and market non-clearing still remaining synonymous)?

While Benassy adopts the first option, I prefer the second. For a start, note that the matching of supply and demand should be seen as an immediate definition of market clearing. Its ultimate meaning is to be a state where the plans of the agents participating in the market (or the economy) have become compatible, at least for what concerns the specific trade round under consideration. If market clearing means the matching of supply and demand, it is not realised in the case of monopoly. However, if its ultimate, instead of its immediate, meaning is taken in consideration, i.e. the compatibility of agents plans, market clearing should be considered verified. The criterion of compatibility of plans dominating the equality between demand and supply criterion, monopolistic competition models should be viewed as featuring market clearing, in spite of their exhibiting a mismatch between supply and demand.[16]

In my opinion, Benassy's mistake consists of amalgamating things that should be kept separate. An agent should be considered rationed whenever he is impeded to trade the quantity that is optimising to him at some outside-determined price. When looking at the imperfect competition case against this definition, it turns out that it departs from it on two scores. On the one hand, the ongoing trade allows for the realisation of the seller's optimising plan. On the other hand, the seller chooses the price-quantity mix at which trade occurs. Therefore, trading off the curves cannot have the same meaning as in a perfectly competitive one. Deciding to move off the supply curve because it is optimising is not the same as being forced from it![17]

To trace the lineage of the imperfect competition approach, I would rather look in a direction different from the Walrasian approach, namely the Keynesian models of the first generation, and more precisely Modigliani's 1944 model. Like Modigliani's, Blanchard and Kiyotaki's model is based on nominal wage rigidity, and on the insight that monetary expansion increases social welfare. However, two changes are introduced – first, the shift from perfect to imperfect competition and, second, an allegedly better foundation for the rigidity premise. Another feature worth emphasising is the turning upside-down of the significance of rigidity. While before rigidity was considered as an unmitigated evil, now it plays a virtuous role. Under perfect competition, rigidity is a 'source of alarm', to borrow Modigliani's expression (Modigliani 2002) since it constitutes an impediment towards the realisation of Walrasian equilibrium, resulting in a loss of social welfare. In contrast, under imperfect competition it is a 'source of optimism' as it provides a positive opportunity allowing for a gain in social welfare as compared to the outcome prevailing when imperfect competition goes along with flexible prices.[18]

20

EPILOGUE

Two tasks are undertaken in this concluding chapter. First, I synthesise the results of my survey of Keynesian models with respect to their success in achieving Keynes' programme. Second, I consider the issue of whether Keynesian authors should keep fighting for the involuntary unemployment concept.

The achievement of Keynes' programme

Involuntary unemployment has been defined as a breaching of the reservation wage principle, and as being tantamount to a labour market rationing. Moreover, two meanings of involuntary unemployment have been separated, the individual disequilibrium and the frustration meanings. To the question, 'are there models which have succeeded in demonstrating involuntary unemployment so defined?', the answer is 'yes'. The shirking model demonstrates involuntary unemployment – yet only in the frustration meaning. Some particular types of efficiency wage models, such as Dasgupta and Ray's model, feature involuntary unemployment in the individual disequilibrium sense, due to their consideration of the existence of objective differences between agents. The same is true for Roberts' model, where involuntary unemployment in the individual disequilibrium sense occurs as a result of an alteration in trade technology. In contrast, the other models that I have studied fail to demonstrate involuntary unemployment in the reservation wage definition, yet several of them succeed in demonstrating dominate underemployment.

However, involuntary unemployment should not be considered in isolation from Keynes' broader programme of which it is only one element. This programme has been defined as consisting of four principal items, plus two subsidiary ones:

1 the phenomenon to be explained is involuntary unemployment in the reservation wage sense;
   (1a) with the additional individual disequilibrium characteristic;

2 demonstrating that wage rigidity can be exonerated as a cause of the phenomenon;
3 giving a general equilibrium explanation of the phenomenon;
 (3a) within perfect competition framework;
4 demonstrating that that demand stimulation is the proper remedy to be taken for solving the problem.

I argued in Chapter 6 that Keynes was unable to fulfil his programme in *The General Theory*. True, immediately after its publication and for many years afterwards, the contrary opinion prevailed. This early positive impression was made possible because of a confusion between involuntary unemployment and lack of full employment. While in Chapter 2 of *The General Theory*, Keynes defined involuntary unemployment according to the reservation wage criterion, in Chapter 3, he shifted to the lack of full employment concept. At one point, full employment was defined as the absence of involuntary unemployment, at another as maximum employment. The two definitions were declared to be selfsame. The same then applies for their opposite, lack of full employment as meaning involuntary unemployment and lack of full employment as meaning less than maximum employment. Yet, this claim of selfsameness is invalid. The conclusion to be drawn is that Keynes may have succeeded in making a point about the existence of lack of full employment in the most general (and trivial) sense of lack of maximum employment without making it clear whether it was sub-optimal. Yet, he failed in demonstrating involuntary unemployment. *General Theory* was sufficiently opaque to allow readers to be unaware of the flaw.

From Chapter 7 onwards, I have examined whether Keynesian economists have been able to improve on Keynes. To this end, I have studied the works of the first interpreters of Keynes, such as Hicks and Modigliani, some textbook versions of the IS-LM model, the Walrasian disequilibrium school and, finally, different brands of New Keynesian theory, the implicit contract model, efficiency wage models, the insider–outsider model, coordination failure models and imperfect competition models. Table 20.1 summarises how they fare with respect to the different elements composing Keynes' programme. The assessment is either positive (+) or negative (−). (. . .) indicates that the question is irrelevant (e.g. if a model does not aim at explaining involuntary unemployment in the reservation wage sense, it cannot be considered as aiming at explaining it in its individual disequilibrium dimension).

Rather than providing a thorough commentary of Table 20.1, I will point out a few salient traits. Starting with Hicks, his seminal 'Mr Keynes and the "Classics"' paper aimed at identifying more precisely Keynes' programme, an essential task in view of *The General Theory* readers' perplexity as to the exact nature of its contribution. To Hicks, Keynes' real target was the neutrality of money view, coming down all the way from Ricardo. Hicks' reasoning started from the premise that the money wage was rigid at a level such that employment has potential to increase. This was true both for his classical and his Keynesian systems. Their difference rather bore on another point, namely persistence and policy effectiveness. In the classical system a monetary expansion would necessarily increase employment (at least, in the short term), whereas, in the Keynesian system, this result might fail to arise as soon as preference for liquidity exhibited perfect interest elasticity over a certain domain. In Hicks' paper, no attempt was made at explaining the cause of the false nominal wage (and hence of unemployment). An exogenous wage floor was implicitly assumed to be present. This explained involuntary unemployment but only in a trivial way.

Moving on to disequilibrium authors, the aim of most of them was to develop their analysis within the framework of Walrasian general equilibrium. While in Patinkin's opinion the only way to give room to involuntary unemployment was to conceive of its existence as limited to the adjustment process, most subsequent disequilibrium authors based their analysis on the fixprice assumption. This led them to bring out the 'Keynesian Unemployment' regime, which fared well with Keynes' programme, except for the rigidity factor. The general lesson that I have drawn from the disequilibrium episode is a stronger realisation that no place exists in Walrasian and neo-Walrasian models for the phenomenon of rationing and hence for involuntary unemployment because of the centralised character of its trade technology.

New Keynesian models arose as a reaction against Friedman's and Lucas' anti-Keynesian offensive. Their aim was to take up the Keynesian banner while accepting Lucas' way of positing issues, especially the equilibrium requirement. Three sub-schools of New Keynesian theory have been separated. The first, regrouping implicit contract and efficiency wage models, adopts a partial equilibrium approach. While these models succeed in demonstrating involuntary unemployment in the reservation wage sense, this goes along with its meaning being narrowed down to frustration. The individual disequilibrium connotation is thus lost. Moreover, no support for demand stimulation is given. The second group of New Keynesian models is coordination failures models. To all intents and purposes, Diamond's and Howitt's papers renounce to demonstrate involuntary unemployment in the reservation wage sense. But they succeed, first, in exonerating wage rigidity and, second, in modelling a state of dominated underemployment equilibrium that can be remedied by demand stimulation. While no foregoing of the involuntary unemployment programme is to be found in Roberts' model, the latter is wanting on the matter of justifying demand stimulation. The last group of New Keynesian models is imperfectly competitive general equilibrium models.

Table 20.1 Achieving Keynes' programme

		First generation models			*Disequilibrium theory (Patinkin, Barro-Grossman, Drèze, Benassy)*	*New Keynesian models*						
		Hicks	*Modigliani*	*Standard IS-LM models, Ackley)*		*Implicit contract models*	*Efficiency wages*	*Insider–Outsider*	*Coordination*		*Imperfect Competition*	
									Diamond, Howitt	*Roberts*	*Hart*	*Blanchard and Kiyotaki*
1	Demonstrating involuntary unemployment in the reservation wage meaning	+	–	+	+	+	+	–	–	+	–	–
1a	With the additional individual disequilibrium connotation	. . .	. . .	+	+	–	–	. . .	. . .	+	. . .	. . .
2	Exonerating wage-rigidity	–	–	–	–	+	+	+	+	+	+	–
3	A general equilibrium perspective	+	+	+	+	–	–	–	+	+	+	+
3a	With perfect competition	+	+	+	+	. . .	. . .	. . .	+	+	–	–
4	Demand stimulation as the proper remedy	+	. . .	+	+	–	–	–	+	–	–	+

In Blanchard and Kiyotaki's model, two items of Keynes' programme are sacrificed, involuntary unemployment and flexibility. On the positive side, these authors are able to give a foundation to the non-neutrality of money and thus to offer a rebuttal of Friedman's and Lucas' claims. Moreover, in their model, wage rigidity becomes a positive factor allowing to trim the inefficiency due to the existence of monopolies.

My investigation leads to the conclusion that no model fully succeeds in achieving Keynes' programme. While several achieve all of its items but one, none reaches complete success. How should this failure be interpreted? My opinion is that, seven decades after the publication of *General Theory*, the most plausible explanation is that Keynes' programme must be unfeasible; at least, one of its elements is always too much.

None of the authors studied have cast their standpoint in reference to Keynes' programme as I defined it. Otherwise, they could have stated that their departure from this programme stemmed from such a realisation of its non-implementability and from their feeling the need to replace it by a more implementable programme. If this viewpoint is accepted, my analysis resolves two standard enigmas in the history of Keynesian economics. The first is why Keynesian theories, departing from Keynes' own way of putting issues, have emerged. They did so, it can now be asserted, because Keynes' programme is unfeasible. The second conundrum is why, if Keynes's programme had to be amended, has it not been replaced by a single alternative programme, rallying the views of all Keynesian economists? Why, in other words, are there competing Keynesian theories? Here again, the answer is simple. Once it is admitted that some departure from Keynes' programme is necessary, several alternatives present themselves, according to which aspect of the programme is shelved. It is then a small surprise that different Keynesian theories co-exist. They have all a lineage in Keynes' programme and there is no reason to argue that one particular departure is superior to the others.[1]

Still the models studied can be regrouped according to where they put the priority. First, we have a group of models – disequilibrium theory, implicit contract theory and efficiency wage theory – emphasising the aim of demonstrating involuntary unemployment in the reservation wage sense. Models that give a priority to exonerating wage rigidity as crucial – implicit contract, efficiency wage and coordination failure – form a second group, partially overlapping with the first.[2] Third, there is the group of models whose authors view the Keynesian project as based on the nominal rigidity/non-neutrality of money couple: Hicks' model, Modigliani's model, textbook IS-LM models, imperfect competition *à la* Blanchard-Kiyotaki (not *à la* Hart). This is probably the dominant stream. All in all, the main divide is between models giving the priority to the demonstration of involuntary unemployment, at the price of abandoning the demand stimulation aim, and models based on the opposite choice.

Thus, we have implicit contract and efficiency wage models on one side and all the rest on the other.[3]

The realisation that Keynes' programme has not been fulfilled should not be interpreted as meaning that Keynesian theory made no headway. The contrary is true. However, progress has been far from uniform. It went through ups and downs, with incessant shifts from one line of research (i.e. a specific combination of the items on Keynes' programme) to another. New models came and went, as in fashion. Interestingly enough, their dismissal has been founded on conceptual rather than empirical grounds. This is obvious, for example, for what concerns the dismissal of fixprice theory or implicit contract theory. The discussion about the validity of efficiency wage theory also bears witness to this. Claims to the contrary notwithstanding, Friedman's contribution is no exception. His criticism of the Phillips Curve was mainly conceptual. True, Friedman's views gained a lot of success because of his prediction about the arising of stagflation, but I would argue that the two are not organically linked, as implicitly acknowledged by Lucas in his introduction to the volume *Studies in Business Cycle Theory* (1981: 8). Thus, the effective theoretical practice to be found in the literature surveyed here comes on a collision course with the explicit empiricist methodological stance taken by most participants in the debate.

Should Keynesian economists keep fighting for the involuntary unemployment concept?

What explains the difficulty of constructing a theory as to involuntary unemployment? Is it, as argued by Lucas, that the 'thing' to be explained is non-existing or is it due to some deeply built-in premise of economic theory?

To many of the authors whom I have studied the main motivation for their defence of involuntary unemployment is that they believe that it is an important fact of life. For example, Shapiro and Stiglitz write 'To us, involuntary unemployment is a real and important phenomenon with grave social consequences that needs to be explained and understood' (Shapiro and Stiglitz 1985: 1217). This belief is shared by most Keynesian economists. They are convinced that out there in the real world something exists which deserves to be called involuntary unemployment, and bears the connotations mentioned above, especially that people are unemployed through no fault of their own.[4] Hence their will to introduce this concept in the theoretical discourse. Yet, every time they tried to do it, they stumbled on daunting obstacles, as my analysis has amply testified.

My view as to the basic reason explaining this failure can be summarised as follows. Economic theory is an abstract language. The premises upon which it is based have the advantage of allowing tractable rigorous theorising yet with the drawback of excluding important facts of life from the theoretical universe. Non-chosen outcomes is one of them. The underlying reason lies in the trade technology and perfect information assumptions upon which both the Walrasian (and neo-Walrasian) and the Marshallian (and neo-Marshallian) theories of value are based. Put differently, as soon as the centralised market hypothesis is adopted, the democratic character of the market becomes a compelling conclusion: no non-optimal solution can be imposed upon any agent or, in other terms, interactive equilibrium implies individual equilibrium. The exclusion of non-chosen outcomes ensues.

As far as the real world existence of involuntary unemployment is concerned, I am unaware of the existence of studies aiming at assessing it. Such studies should tackle two tasks. The first is to settle the taxonomic issues that I have evoked in Chapter 3. In particular, some convention must be established as to what enters or is excluded from agents' choice sets. The second task is an empirical assessment, possibly through experiments. One might, for example, interview people on the dole and suggest to them a job they are qualified for at the existing, or at a slightly lower, wage. If they accept, they could be considered as involuntarily unemployed. I strongly suspect that a significant fraction of people would qualify for such a classification.

Assume that such an experiment was made and that its result was positive. Facts of life and economic theory would be shown to be on a collision course. One straightforward way out would consist of stating that, if the neoclassical paradigm has proved unable to generate an involuntary unemployment result over so many years, this must mean that there is something wrong with it. Among others, Coddington and Kregel are of this opinion.[5]

> The difficulty of the task of giving a coherent and convincing choice-theoretic account of involuntary unemployment, however, may be taken in either of two ways: it may be taken as reflecting on the concept to be clarified or on the method by which clarification is sought. Thus, taking the latter alternative, if the idea of involuntary unemployment cannot be made to emerge from the logic of choice in the labour market, then that may be seen as a deficiency of the choice-logic approach to the problem. On this view, we should simply hold fast to the concept of involuntary unemployment, and disregard any framework that cannot accommodate it.
>
> (Coddington 1983: 29)
>
> Modern labour markets theories which find that voluntary unemployment is 'not the best account of employment fluctuations but

> rather the *only* account' (Lucas) cannot then imply that involuntary unemployment does not exist, but only, as Keynes suggested, that it cannot be expressed within the choice-theoretic set of axioms.
>
> (Kregel 1987: 135)

We fall back on the dilemma, which Keynes faced when starting to write *The General Theory*, between opting for a radical departure from standard theory, implying the creation of a totally new paradigm, or 'working within the system'. Keynes himself, I have argued in Chapter 5, gradually retreated from the radical in favour of the reformist strategy. Two facts suggests that this choice is still justified for what concerns the present state of affairs. The first is the failure of alternative paradigms, based on a more heterodox reading of *The General Theory*, to take off. The second is the impressive resilience of the neoclassical apparatus and its capacity to tackle issues that were earlier thought to be beyond its grasp.

In a brilliant and often quoted passage of the *The General Theory*, Keynes wrote:

> Obviously, however, if the classical theory is only applicable to the case of full employment, it is fallacious to apply it to the problems of involuntary unemployment – if there is such a thing (and who would deny it?). The classical theorists resemble Euclidean geometers in a non-Euclidean world who, discovering that in experiences straight lines apparently parallel often meet, rebuke the line for not keeping straight – as the only remedy for the unfortunate collisions which are occurring. Yet, in truth, there is no remedy except to throw over the axiom of parallels and to work out a non-Euclidean geometry.
>
> (Keynes 1936: 16)

Let it be accepted that Keynes is right in his diagnosis. Still, this does not bring us very far. The fact that a non-Euclidean geometry may be something one might pray for is hardly the same as bringing it about. And if it proves so difficult to construct, what should be done in the meantime? With the exception of Clower and Leijonhufvud, on the one hand, and of defenders of the radical interpretation of Keynes, on the other, Keynesian economists can be seen as geometricians who have opted for continuing to use traditional Euclidean geometry for want of a strong alternative.

Euclidean geometry means economic theory without involuntary unemployment. However, the dismissal of the latter would concern only the theoretical sphere. Drawing conclusions from it concerning real world existence would be a mistake. That is, one should not deny the existence of real world involuntary unemployment on the mere ground that the concept of involuntary unemployment can find no room in the theoretical discourse. As a counterpart, the fact that solid arguments can be put forward as to real world existence cannot be a sufficient condition to give it theoretical legitimacy. But this position makes sense only if one accepts the separation between the real world and the fictitious theoretical universe, that I have sketched out in Chapter 5. Unfortunately enough, the principle of such a separation is scarcely accepted either by Keynesians or by new classicists. The latter have hardly hesitated to transpose to the real world the non-existence of involuntary unemployment statement that is valid only in the special construct of the theoretical parable. The flaw of Keynesians such as Stiglitz is overdoing their achievements: while their models demonstrate involuntary unemployment only in the narrow frustration meaning, they proceed as if they had succeeded in giving an explanation of involuntary unemployment in its common-sense meaning.

To forego the involuntary unemployment claim may look too high a price to pay, since the existence of mass unemployment, interpreted as having an important involuntarity component, was the real world phenomenon that triggered the whole Keynesian enterprise. Yet in fine, would its abandonment be so dramatic? Not necessarily. First of all, as stated above, this theoretical abandonment should have no impact on assessments made about reality, in as far as the principle of a separation between the two levels of discourse is accepted.

Second, the reasons for its dismissal should be taken into account. There is the hypothesis of an extremely strong rationality, as existing in neoclassical theory – and its corollary, an extremely strong viewpoint about freedom. This assumption is defensible, in particular on the grounds of tractability and lack of better alternatives. Furthermore, there is the trade technology dimension. Market clearing is the corollary of the assumption that markets function in a centralised way with either the auctioneer or perfect information serving as the driving force of the formation of market equilibrium. There is nothing to boast about the adoption of these two hypotheses. Their only justification is expediency. If involuntary unemployment is deemed to be theoretically unacceptable only on such grounds, there is no reason to make a fuss of its dismissal. The latter is a matter of methodological convention.

Third, the issue is less that involuntary unemployment in the reservation wage meaning result cannot be demonstrated (since the contrary is true) than to judge whether it is the best path to take. As my investigation has revealed, the involuntary unemployment objective may turn out to be an obstacle against the vindication of the other points on Keynes' programme. To him, the concept of involuntary unemployment was instrumental in the realisation of a larger cause, namely the denunciation of a system failure and the vindication of state interventions in the economy. If this concept has been an object of controversy, it is mainly because it was a metaphor for the wider judgement to be made on the efficiency of a competitive market system, and of the opportunities for state intervention in it. Wanting to defend the involuntary unemployment concept then amounts to taking up a sceptical stance about the virtues of laissez faire, and to defending the view that outside interference in the market can be beneficial. Similarly, the opposition to involuntary unemployment would stem from the fact that one supports full laissez faire. This is the real issue in the dispute. But this debate does not necessarily need the involuntary unemployment concept. Therefore, one should not stick to Azariadis' statement, evoked above, that involuntary unemployment is the sine qua non of Keynesian theory.

NOTES

1 INTRODUCTION

1 As aptly recounted by Lindbeck and Snower,

> Strange as it may seem to the layman, economists have found it difficult to agree on what should be meant by involuntary unemployment and to pose coherent arguments that show why people who are willing and able to work at the prevailing wages in market economies cannot find jobs when they seek them ... Economists have had a difficult time explaining how involuntary unemployment comes about and why it may persist for substantial periods of time. They appear to have gone through all the various behaviours that doctors exhibit in the face of unresponsive patients: scepticism, diagnosis, refinement of the diagnosis, finding reasons for doubt, retracting the diagnosis, pronouncing the problem non-existent, formulating a new diagnosis, and so on.
>
> (Lindbeck and Snower 1988: 19)

2 A further restriction of the scope of my work is that I will only consider models that stand in a Keynesian lineage (and the criticism put forward against such models). Therefore, for all their interest, unemployment models belonging to other traditions, especially search models, will not be tackled.

3 In particular, I would have expected defenders of the involuntary unemployment concept to have undertaken the task of resolving any conceptual muddle besetting it. Instead they have often been the first to dodge the issue. The following quote from Stiglitz illustrates: 'Critics might say at this juncture, "Aha, so unemployment is really voluntary". We think little is gained from a semantic debate over whether unemployment is, in this sense, voluntary or involuntary' (Stiglitz 1987a: 35).

4 Beaud and Dostaler (1995) pursue the same aim.

2 DEFINING INVOLUNTARY UNEMPLOYMENT

1 A standard definition of the reservation wage, drawn from Pencavel is as follows

> 'the real reservation wage, w^*/p, is the slope of an indifference curve between consumption and hours at work evaluated at $h=0$ [i.e. the corner solution at which total time is allocated to leisure, MDV] ... Equivalently, the real reservation wage is the individual's implicit

> valuation of his time when at the margin between participating in the labour market and not participating. If, at that margin, the market's valuation of his time, *w*, exceeds the individual's implicit value of his time, *w**, then he will participate in the labour market and supply a positive number of market work'.
>
> (1986: 28–29)

2 In Coddington's terms: 'To say that someone is involuntarily unemployed is to relieve him of the responsibility for his condition; it is to suggest that he is unemployed "through no fault of his own"' (1983: 27).

3 The market rationing effect of a price or wage floor is, for example, acknowledged by Walras (1954: 432–433).

4 The shift from the first narrow definition to the second broad definition can be captured in reference to Dworkin's distinction between 'brute bad luck' (the former case) and 'option bad luck' (the latter case):

> 'Option luck is a matter of how a deliberate and calculated gamble turns out – whether someone gains or loses through accepting an isolated risk he or she should have anticipated and might have declined. Brute luck is a matter of how risks fall out that are not in that sense deliberate gambles. If I buy a stock on the exchange that rises, then my option luck is good. If I am hit by a falling meteorite whose course could not have been predicted, then my bad luck is brute.
>
> (1981: 293)

5 To Lucas' remark that 'Keynes wanted to get labour markets out of the way in Chapter Two so that he could get to the demand theory which really interested him' ([1978] 1981: 242), they react by stating the following:

> In contrast to Lucas, we appreciate Keynes' desire 'to get labour markets out of the way'. Why not have an analytical scheme that permits the level of employment (and the extent of involuntary unemployment) to be determined independent of the labour market? Keynes' aggregate demand and supply price model from Chapter 3 of *The General Theory* provides such an apparatus.
>
> (Darity and Horn 1987–1988: 220)

6 This point will be taken up again in Chapter 8 in my discussion of Modigliani.

7 This stronger definition is also to be found under Hawtrey's pen in his correspondence with Keynes (letter dated 29 April 1936), wherein he criticises Keynes' conception of involuntary unemployment. In his words: 'My point was that if unemployment is to be regarded as "involuntary", it must be such that a reduction of wages would not remedy it. If the requisite reduction is within the power of wage policy, then wage policy is responsible for not making it, and the unemployment is voluntary' (Keynes 1973: 30).

8

> As long as workers are on their 'supply curve' – that is, as long as they succeed in selling all the labour they want at the prevailing real wage rate – a state of full employment will be said to exist in the economy . . . It also follows that the benchmark of full employment is not an absolute constant, but something which itself varies with every change in the real wage rate or in the subjective or objective determinants of the labour supply curve.
>
> (Patinkin 1965: 314–315)

9
> The point of full employment is defined by the point of intersection of the supply curve and the demand curve. When effective demand is such that actual employment stands at this level, then every unit of available labour at the corresponding level of real wages is bespoken and one entrepreneur can increase the amount of labour he employs only by reducing the amount employed by someone else.
>
> (Robinson 1947: 126)

10 The use of the notion of a natural rate of employment rather than a natural rate of unemployment is justified in my discussion of Friedman in Chapter 13.
11 This will be demonstrated in Chapter 8.
12 Cf. For example Mortensen (1970), Okun (1981: Chapter II), Pissarides (1990) and Mortensen and Pissarides (1999).

3 FROM LABOUR RATIONING TO (INVOLUNTARY) UNEMPLOYMENT

1 Some occurrences have been discarded because of their lack of plausibility. The first one is the case of the exclusive supply participation in goods markets (it is assumed that in order to supply goods or services other inputs than labor ought to be purchased). The second one is the case of joint supply and demand participation in the labor market.
2 Since rationing is excluded, unemployment ought to be left aside.
3 Thus there is no empty choice set.
4 The existence of the wage-dependency category implies the existence of barriers to entry for self-employed jobs. As stated by Lindbeck and Snower, 'If workers were always able to achieve self-employment, then there could be no involuntary unemployment. Whoever could not work for someone else, would work for himself' (Lindbeck and Snower 1988: 51).
5 Moreover, mobility across social forms of activities will also be assumed possible.
6 It is unnecessary to delve into what may motivate agents to prefer unemployment against taking their chances in lower-skill markets. Just to give a hint, they may for example assume that taking a lower job prejudices the chances of getting a job in their normal market in the future (which amounts to believing that the risk of human capital loss is higher with downwards mobility than with unemployment).
7 The 'misemployment' term ought thus to be understood widely, as it may encompass the rentier activity.
8 Agents of the second type could be called 'disguised rentiers'.
9 In the same vein, in an essay on unemployment in Britain in the inter-war years, Whiteside and Gillepsie note that a possible rationale behind the rise of unemployment as a distinct category was the need to differentiate it from poverty:

> 'Unemployment' as originally conceived in the late nineteenth century had no uniform or self-evident meaning. The 'unemployed' were distinguished from the rest of the pauper host by their moral superiority: made evident in their previous regular working habits, their independence, thrift, sobriety, and honesty. Policies for the unemployed therefore aimed to save these stout fellows from the horrors of a punitive poor law, on whose tender mercies they might be thrown in hard times, through no fault of their own. Such policies, however, excluded the 'residuum' – those surplus to labor market

> requirements whose physical and mental weaknesses rendered them incapable of regular work.
>
> [1991: 674–675]

10 As stated by Whiteside and Gillepsie: 'The survey [New Survey of London, carried out at the London School of Economics between 1928 and 1931] concluded that the loss of six weeks wages in the course of six months would be enough to place the average unskilled worker in poverty. At the beginning of 1929, a relatively prosperous year, almost 14 percent of the adult male workforce fell within this category' (1991: 671).

4 TRADE ORGANISATION

1 Sometimes this distinction, which does not coincide with the distinction between existence and stability of equilibrium, is made under a different terminology. For example, in his translator's commentary in the English version of Walras' *Elements*, Jaffé calls 'emergence' or 'establishment' what I suggest calling 'formation':

> The laws of the *emergence* or *establishment* of equilibrium prices refer to the laws of those operations of the market that result in equilibrium, whereas the laws of the *determination* of equilibrium price take into account 'the ultimate facts and forces which *constitute* that price.
>
> (1954: 501)

2 While the formation of equilibrium is the task that the economic agents need to achieve, establishing the logical existence of equilibrium is the job of the outside supposedly ominicient theorist.

3 The notion of trade round will play a central role throughout my book. In the literature it is sometimes referred to as the 'market period'.

4 'Simultaneous assembly is replaced by arrangements whereby one market side, buyer or seller, stands ready to serve at irregular arrival times. The bazaar or a system of posted prices emerges' (Brunner and Meltzer 1993: 136).

5 In Clower and Due's words: 'Strictly speaking, therefore, the term "market price" is a misnomer; the typical commodity has no market price, only market prices . . . In virtually all cases, the term will refer to some kind of *index* of prices rather than a single figure associated with all trades in a particular market' (1972: 80).

6 The Marshallian approach is less easily reconstructed than the Walrasian. Hence more time will be devoted to it.

7 Cf. De Vroey (1998).

8 Lucas is an exception. See Lucas (1986).

9 Cf. De Vroey (2000). For a comparison with the Walrasian conception, see De Vroey (1999a) and De Vroey (2002).

10 In modern parlance a distinction is drawn between short and the long period equilibrium. I prefer to stick to Marshall's terminology, which is less equivocal, and use the market/normal equilibrium divide.

11 The central reference is Marshall's corn model, to be found in Book V, Chapter 2 of his *Principles.*

12 This point that has scarcely been perceived, with a few exceptions. Hayek was one of them:

> In the usual presentations of equilibrium analysis it is generally made to appear as if these questions of how the equilibrium comes about

> were solved. But, if we look closer, it soon becomes evident that these apparent demonstrations amount to no more than the apparent proof of what is already assumed. The device generally adopted for this purpose is the assumption of a perfect market where every event becomes known instantaneously to every member ... The whole economic system must be assumed to be one perfect market in which everybody knows everything. The assumption of a perfect market, then, means nothing else than that all the members of the community, even if they are not supposed to be strictly omniscient, are at least supposed to know automatically all that is relevant for their decisions.
>
> (Hayek [1937] 1948: 45–46)

Brown (1994) makes the same point: 'The process of "haggling and bargaining" referred to in Marshall's account is strictly redundant, as it is not haggling that results in the final price, but a foreknowledge on the part of transactors' (1994: 78).

13 On this difference, see De Vroey (2003).

14 Marshall also stressed the possibility of false trading. Here, his argument was based on the assumption of a constant marginal utility of money. The latter permits the elimination of income effects yet requires that an agent's expenditure in every market is small with respect to his total expenditure. However – and this is what counts for my purpose – market clearing remains present in this false trading context, in the sense that the total quantity traded is equal to the quantity that would have been traded without false trading while the last transaction takes place at the 'true equilibrium' price.

15 For an analysis of Marshall's views on the labour market, see Matthews (1990).

16 Stating that market clearing becomes an irrelevant concept when it comes to the decentralised market organisation does not amount to altogether abandoning an equilibrium perspective. First, the notion of individual equilibrium remains relevant. Moreover, the notion of normal equilibrium, although no longer being underpinned by that of market equilibrium, is still operative.

17 Often, authors take rigidity as an extreme form of stickiness, in which case a rigid price is also sticky. I believe that this way of putting things is misleading and prefer to have three non-overlapping categories, rigid prices (or fixprices), flexible prices and sticky (or sluggish or slowly adjusting) prices.

18 At stake are prices expressed in terms of a *numéraire*, which should not be confused with monetary prices.

19 The same view is to be found under Tobin's and Blanchard's pens: 'I shall argue that Keynesian macroeconomics neither asserts nor requires nominal wage and/or price rigidity. It does assert and require that markets not be instantaneously and continuously cleared by prices. That is a much less restrictive assumption, and much less controversial' (Tobin [1993] 1997: 136). 'In retrospect, the post-war consensus was a consensus about two main beliefs ... The second main belief was indeed that prices and wages did not adjust very quickly to clear markets' (Blanchard 1987: 634).

20 A further line, fitting only the Marshallian approach, consists of trying to give a foundation to the wage rigidity notion, thereby releasing the otherwise contrived character of this assumption. Onne might have believed that perfect competition was another stumbling block. Yet, it will be shown below that

substituting imperfect for perfect competition allows a dominated underemployment result yet no involuntary unemployment.

5 KEYNES' PROGRAMME: A RECONSTRUCTION

1 As stated by Keynes: 'A classical economist may sympathise with labour in refusing to accept a cut in its money-wage, and he will admit that it may not be wise to make it to meet conditions which are temporary; but scientific integrity forces him to declare that this refusal is, nevertheless, at the bottom of the trouble' (1936: 16).

2 For an alternative interpretation, see Gerrard (1995).

3 On their contents, see, amongst others, Tarshis (1989).

4 The analysis presented here is a rational reconstruction of Keynes' project. A study along the same lines yet different in style is Laidler (1999). For more historiographical studies, see, e.g. Bateman (1996), Clarke (1990), Dimand (1988), Moggridge (1992), Skidelsky (1983, 1992, 2000).

5 In Leijonhufvud's terms: 'Keynes was concerned with a *systemic* problem that could be defined neither in terms of individual decision situations nor in terms of interactions between buyers and sellers in a single market' (Leijonhufvud 1983: 195–196). Or as stated by Coddington: 'Involuntary unemployment arises because of a malfunctioning of the economic *system*: it is not that individuals lack the willingness or ability to work but rather that the economy is failing to provide them with the opportunity to do so' (Coddington 1983: 27). See also Kregel (1987: 135).

6 For example, in his Appendix to Chapter 19, where he criticises Pigou, Keynes writes the following: 'I maintain that the real wage ... is not primarily determined by "wage adjustment" ... but by other forces of the system ... in particular the relation between the schedule of the marginal efficiency of capital and the rate of interest' (1936: 278).

7 Cf. Patinkin (1987a: 27, 35) and Weintraub (1979: 39).

8 Clower (1975) quotes an extract of a letter from Keynes to Georgescu-Rodan, dated December 1934 and running as follows: 'All the same, I shall hope to convince you some day that Walras' theory and all the others along those lines are little better than nonsense!' (1975, reprinted in Walker 1984: 190).

9 On Keynes' Marshallian roots, see Clower (1979, reprinted in Walker 1984), Clower (1989, reprinted in Clower, 1995) and Leijonhufvud (1968, 1999).

10 The fact that Keynes saw no connection between unemployment and imperfect competition has puzzled many commentators. For example, Tobin notes that:

> By assuming that firms are price takers in auction markets rather than price setters in monopolistic competition or oligopoly, he [Keynes] made it harder to sustain his vision of persistent disequilibrium, with failures of coordination, communication, and adjustment. Imperfect competition was the other revolution in economics in the 1930s; one of its sites was Keynes' Cambridge, and two of its agents, Joan Robinson and Sraffa, were in his group. Yet for some mysterious reason the two revolutions were never meshed.
>
> (Tobin 1981: 207)

However, Tobin is wrong in asserting that Keynes' reasoning supposes that firms are price-takers in auction markets. As seen in Chapter 4, price-setting agents and perfect competition are compatible in a Marshallian framework. On the subject of Keynes' attitude towards imperfect competition, see Feiwel (1989: 32 and seq.), from which Tobin's quotation is drawn, Marris (1991) and Keppler (1994).

11 For an opposite view, see Meltzer (1988).

12 On this see Hutchison (1978) and Laidler (1999).

13 As the French philosopher Louis Althusser used to say, 'the concept of dog will never bark'!

6 INVOLUNTARY UNEMPLOYMENT IN KEYNES' *THE GENERAL THEORY*

1 Cf. Kahn (1976: 19) and Corry (1996: 12–15). Boianovsky and Trautwein (2001) analyse the use of the involuntary unemployment concept in English literature before Keynes as well as in non-published lectures by Cassel and Wicksell where this concept is to be found. For an analysis of Pigou's theory of unemployment, see Klausinger (1998) and Ambrosi (2002).

2 Leontief emphasised this point long ago:

> Keynes by analogy refers to it as a fundamental postulate, which it obviously is not . . . Far from being directly assumed, the real supply curve of labour is derived by the modern non-Keynesian theory from a set of other much more general propositions. The truly fundamental postulates of orthodox theory deal with the general nature of economic choice.
>
> (Leontief 1947: 233–234)

Keynes must have had in mind that the cause lying behind the violation of the second postulate was the insufficiency of effective demand, yet, as will be seen below, he was unable to clinch the argument.

3 'Nor should we regard as "involuntary" unemployment the withdrawal of their labour by a body of workers because they do not choose to work for less than a certain real reward' (Keynes 1936: 15).

4 For a more standard account of Keynes' analysis of the labour market, see e.g. Snowdon and Vane (1994: 68, *seq.*)

5 Or also:

> But the other, more fundamental objection, which we shall develop in the ensuing chapters, flows from our disputing the assumption that the general level of real wages is directly determined by the character of the wage bargain. In assuming that the wage bargain determines the real wage the classical school have slipped in an illicit assumption. For there may be *no* method available to labour as a whole whereby it can bring the wage-good equivalent of the general level of money-wages into conformity with the marginal disutility of the current volume of employment. There may exist no expedient by which labour as a whole can reduce its *real* wage to a given figure by making revised *money* bargains with the entrepreneurs. This will be our contention.
>
> (1936: 13)

6 Only a few economists seem to have been aware of this point. Lipsey is one of them. He writes:

> Shortly after I published my first Phillips Curve article, Milton Friedman visited me at the London School of Economics. He argued that I was perpetrating money illusion by putting a nominal wage variable on the vertical axis of my figures rather than using some variant of the rate of change of real wages. My answer to him then was the same as my response now. The variable that workers bargain over is the nominal not the real wage (with rare exceptions). If workers care abut the real wage, then their expectation of how the nominal rate and the real wage may differ should enter the wage formation equation as an independent variable. But the dependent variable should be the true behavioural variable, the nominal wage change.
>
> (Lipsey 2000: 70)

Branson (1972, Chapter 6) is another exception.

7 In this case, the two above formulations of the labour supply function – $L^s = f(w/p)$ and $L^s = f(w; p^e_w)$ – amount to the same. The fact that in Marshallian and neo-Marshallian theory reasoning usually proceeds in terms of the first of these formulations can be viewed as an evidence of it being based on the assumption of perfect foresight.

8 This point was already noticed by Harrod ([1937] 1947: 598).

9 Keynes' statement would have been clearer had he written that 'Men are involuntarily unemployed if, in the event of a small rise in the price of wage-goods relatively to the money-wage, the new volume of employment would be higher than the existing volume'.

10 Contrary to me, Hoover (1995) claims that Keynes' concern for relative wage is fundamental.

11 To be more specific, rigidity cannot be captured under the form of a specially shaped supply of labour, like the inverse-L-shaped supply of labour. This point will be taken up in Chapter 8.

12 The 'effective-demand deficiency' expression is introduced on p. 30 of *The General Theory*. An effective-demand deficiency can also be characterised as an aggregate-demand deficiency, as it is the insufficiency of aggregate demand which explains the gap in effective demand.

13 De Vroey (1999c) defends the view that, for all its non-acceptability in a Walrasian context, the claim that rationing can exist in a single market raises no problems in a Marshallian general equilibrium framework.

14 'These three assumptions, however, *all amount to the same thing in the sense that they all stand and fall together, any of them logically involving the other two*' (1936: 21–22; my emphasis).

15 More generally it is the labour market itself which seems to have been put aside, a point which hardly escaped Lucas' sharp eye: 'The fact is, I think, that Keynes wanted to get labour markets out of the way in Chapter Two so that he could get to the demand theory which really interested him'. ([1978] 1981: 242).

16 Were one considering that normal equilibrium values are never realised, but act just as centres of attraction, it should still be assumed that a firms' conjectures are not too false, as cumulative disequilibria processes would otherwise arise.

17 This statement runs counter to what Keynes wrote in Chapter 12 of *The General Theory* as well as in his *Quarterly Journal of Economics* 1937 article. But then, this is testimony to the co-existence in his writings of the radical and the reformist strategy.

18 Some solace may be found by returning to Schumpeter's appraisal of the relative contributions of Malthus and Ricardo to economic theory:

> It is perfectly compatible with recognition of these facts that much less ingenuity went into Malthus's than into Ricardo's analytic schema, and that the former was throughout in the most unenviable position an economist can be in, namely, in the position of having to defend plain sense against another man's futile but clever pirouettes.
>
> ([1954] 1994: 483)

19 On this distinction, see Blaug (1997).

20 Several interpreters have taken it up this interpretation. To give just two examples: 'Also it is clear that Keynes did not rely upon the fixity of nominal (or real, for that matter) wage in characterising his system. In fact, he devoted an entire chapter, Chapter 19, to examining the effects of "*changes* in money wages"' (Lawlor, Darity and Horn 1987: 321; their emphasis). 'It is true that Keynes assumed a fixed money wage for the first eighteen chapters of the book, but this, as he explained, was just "to facilitate the exposition" (p. 27). In Chapter 19, entitled 'Changes in Money Wages' he relaxed the assumption and argued that it made no difference to the conclusions of the previous eighteen chapters' (Howitt 1990: 72). See also Trevithick (1992).

7 HICKS' 'MR KEYNES AND THE "CLASSICS"'

1 Samuelson's testimony is worth recalling:

> I think I am giving away no secrets when I solemnly aver – upon the basis of vivid personal recollections – that no one else in Cambridge Massachusetts really knew what is was about for some twelve to eighteen months after its publication. Indeed, until the appearance of the mathematical models of Meade, Lange, Hicks, and Harrod, there is reason to believe that Keynes himself did not truly understand his own analysis.
>
> (1947: 146)

2 Of interest in this respect are Hicks' following papers: 'The "Classics" Again' (1967), 'Monetary Theory and History – An Attempt at Perspective' (1967), 'Recollections and Documents' (1977), 'The Formation of an Economist' (1983), 'IS-LM. An Explanation' (1982), *A Market Theory of Money* (1989) and Klamer's 'An Accountant Among Economists: Conversations with Sir John R. Hicks' (1989). For a broader appraisal of the relationship between Keynes and Hicks, see Coddington (1983), Leijonhufvud (1984), Hamouda (1993), Hagemann and Hamouda (1994), McKenzie and Zamagni (1991).

3 Notice that a change in opinion is discernible in his *Market Theory of Money*, where Hicks comes closer to the view that I am defending. 'I have nevertheless come to feel sure that when Keynes spoke of "classical" theory it was Marshall's he had in mind' (1989: 72). In the accompanying footnote, Hicks adds the following commentary:

> So it was that when Keynes saw it ['Mr Keynes and the "Classics"'], though he found my version of his own theory fairly acceptable . . .,

> he insisted that I had got the 'classics' all wrong. My 'classical' was much more primitive than his 'classical' theory. I now regard this as evidence that his 'classic' was Marshall.
>
> (1989: 72)

4 Quite a number of things will fit into place if we suppose that the classical economists, of this important and in so many ways constructive period, did have some such short-period theory, somewhere at the back of their minds, though they preferred not to emphasise it . . . They were afraid that if too much weight were given to short-period effects, it would play into the hands of crude inflationists. The long-period, it would be said, is just a succession of short-periods. Why not keep the stimulus going, when the first dose is exhausted, by another dose? They were afraid of that question, for they did not know the answer to it. Yet they felt in their bones that the suggestion in it was wrong.

> (1967: 162)

5 The model [the 'dynamic' model of *Value and Capital*] was already in my mind before I met that of Keynes. When I did read him, I recognised at once that my model and Keynes' had some things in common. Both of us fixed our attention on the behaviour of an economy *during a period* – a period that had a past, which nothing that was done during the period could alter, and a future, which during the period was unknown.

> (1982: 319)

6 Other critical studies of Hicks' article are Darity and Young (1995) and Barens and Caspari (1999).
7 The fact that Hicks wrote his 'Mr Keynes and the Classics' while he was working on *Value and Capital* may also explain why he did not bother to justify the wage rigidity assumption in his article, since he was doing it in the book. Cf. Young (1987: 98). The fairness theme is also present in his *Theory of Wages* (1963: 69–74) and in *The Crisis in Keynesian Economics* (1974: 64–66).
8 Except for scattered remarks, no explicit reason for this absence is given. In his new commentary in the second edition of the *Theory of Wages*, Hicks remarks that he finds Keynes' distinction between voluntary and involuntary unemployment awkward (1963: 318) without further elaboration. The same opinion is expressed in Hicks (1983: 127).
9 To Hicks the fact that monetary expansion can have real effects does not necessarily justify it being undertaken:

> It follows from this theory that you may be able to increase employment by direct inflation; but whether or not you decide to favour that policy depends upon your judgement about the probable reaction on wages, and also – in a national area – upon your views about the international standard.
>
> (1967: 130)

10 Labour will be employed more in the investment trades, less in the consumption trades; this will increase total employment if the elastic-

> ity of supply in the investment trades is greater than that in the consumption-goods trades – diminish it if vice versa.
>
> (1957: 129)

11 The 'liquidity trap' terminology is not due to Hicks but to Robertson.

12

> In a world where the interest-rate mechanism can always operate – where the rate of interest is flexible, and sufficiently flexible, in either directions, for its movements to have a significant effect on (saving or) investment – the Keynes theory is true and the 'classical theory' is true; they lead to the same results. Though the paths of analysis are different, the end-results, achieved when all the same things have been taken into account, are the same. And either analysis can be put into a general equilibrium form in which it is directly apparent, that they come to the same thing.
>
> (Hicks 1967: 144)

13 Hicks labelled his curves SI and LL respectively.
14 Other differences between the Hicksian and the textbook versions of IS-LM exist, bearing on the change in labelling of the model, the abandonment of Hicks' two sectors perspective and the shift from money to real income. Yet in comparison to the two above central differences, they look benign.

8 IS-LM *À LA* MODIGLIANI

1 Cf. Patinkin ([1948] 1951, 1987).
2 Modigliani also seems to think that another characteristic of the Keynesian labour supply is money illusion – that is, its argument is the nominal rather than the real wage. However, this factor plays no effective role in his argumentation. On the one hand, money illusion can co-exist with a standard upwards sloping supply of labour. On the other, with an inverse-L supply of labour, money illusion is not needed in order to have less than full employment.
3 The inverse-L labour supply curve mentioned in Chapter 2 is thus an extreme form of Modigliani assumption, as it supposes in addition that from the kink onwards labour supply becomes perfectly inelastic. To be simple, in the subsequent discussion I will reason in terms of the inverse-L case.
4 Patinkin (1965: 342) and Stiglitz (1992: 73) are among them.
5 This point is made by Rubin in his doctoral dissertation (Rubin 2002b, Chapter 2).

9 LANGE, LEONTIEF, TOBIN, KLEIN AND HANSEN

1 For a similar critical survey, see Darity and Young (1995).
2 In his earlier 1936 review of *The General Theory* Leontief ([1936] 1990) had proposed a different interpretation, namely that Keynes' theory rested exclusively on the money illusion assumption. Keynes, he claimed, assumed a non-homogeneous supply of labour – that is to say, he abandoned the general postulate that demand and supply is homogeneous of degree zero in uniform changes in its arguments. This homogeneity postulate was criticised by Patinkin (1965: 174, seq.) on the grounds that the complete separation between the theories of relative and absolute prices, which it implied, was invalid.

3 On the notion of hysteresis, see Cross (1995).

4 This being stated, at one point Leontief falls prey to the mistake of believing that, due to the wage floor, a new supply of labour schedule replaces the normal upwards sloping labour supply curve (Leontief 1947: 236).

5 'Involuntary unemployment could thus always be eliminated through an upward shift of the classical monetary supply and demand curves, a shift which necessarily would follow a general rise of all prices (excluding the price of labour)' (Leontief 1947: 237).

6 I have argued above that putting the nominal wage as the argument of the labour supply function does not necessarily imply money illusion, as long as a price-expectation parameter is introduced in this function.

7 However, Hoover (1995) claims that this money illusion interpretation of Keynes' message still retains some currency in textbooks.

8 Klein (1947) is a precursor of this book.

9

> Again, as in the *Treatise*, Keynes did not really understand what he had written, and chose the wrong thing to publicize as his innovation. The Keynesian supply curve of labour and definition of involuntary unemployment were no more important to *The General Theory* than the 'fundamental equations' were to the *Treatise*.
>
> (Klein 1948: 83)

10 At the time Klein was writing the pieces discussed here, he was, in effect, defending Marxian views.

10 INVOLUNTARY UNEMPLOYMENT IN MACROECONOMIC TEXTBOOKS

1

> It is in the specification of the supply function that the Keynesian analysis diverges from that of the classical system, and in two respects. First, the supply of labour is made to depend, not on the real wage w, but on the money wage rate W. This takes account of the institutional aspects of wage negotiations and it allows for the fact that workers may be subject to the 'money illusion' that higher money wages are always a good thing, without regards to what may happen to prices. Second, whereas the real wage rate of the classics is completely flexible up and down, the money wage rate of the Keynesian system is limited in its flexibility in the downwards direction . . . The Keynesian supply function is a truncated one, cut off below at certain level at which the wage rate becomes inflexible.
>
> (Allen 1967: 124)

11 THE FORERUNNERS: PATINKIN, CLOWER, LEIJONHUFVUD

1 For a methodological appraisal of the disequilibrium approach, see Backhouse (1995, Chapter 10).

2 As will be seen, Leijonhufvud stands as an exception with respect to several of these traits.

3 Semantics is treacherous here because these so-called non-Walrasian models still largely belong to the Walrasian research programme rather than being antinomic to it, as the modifier 'non' suggests. In other words, they are non-

Walrasian in a radically different way from other types of models that might be called so, in fact more deservedly, such as Marxian theory, Sraffian theory or, for that matter, Marshallian theory.

4 For a study of the evolution of Patinkin's ideas on involuntary unemployment from his doctorate to *Money, Interest and Prices*, see Rubin (2002a).

5 Patinkin has recurrently claimed, e.g. Patinkin (1987, 1990), that Keynes was his precursor in conceiving involuntary unemployment as a disequilibrium phenomenon. Yet his argumentation in this respect seems unconvincing to me.

6 *Money, Interest and Prices* comprises two parts, entitled respectively Microeconomics and Macroeconomics. The only difference between them signalled by Patinkin is that the idiosyncrasies of individuals' demand function are still reflected in the microeconomics part, while the market demand functions assume the aggregative forms familiar from Keynesian theory in the macro part (1965: XXV).

7 See pp. 532 and 534.

8 In reference to his champagne example, Clower writes: 'For the moment let us imagine ourselves to be involuntarily unemployed in the sense of Keynes' ([1965] 1984: 48). Likewise, in his formal argumentation, Clower starts by evoking the case where households' effective and notional income coincide. He then goes on by noting that: 'in the contrary case, however, i.e. if $\sum_{j}^{n} \mathbf{p}_j s_j < \sum_{j}^{n} \mathbf{p}_j \bar{s}_j$, a second round of decision making is indicated, namely maximise [utility] subject to the modified budget constraint', where $\boldsymbol{s}$ indicates traded quantity, a parameter to the agent and $\bar{s}$ his notional optimal trading offer at the given wage ([1965] 1984: 49–50). The same statement is made on p. 53: 'suppose that the notional aggregate demand for factors is less than aggregate supply (in the sense indicated). Then involuntary unemployment may be said to exist'.

9 As he states in his Afterthoughts to the Walker volume (1984), 'this paper does not take issue with the price adjustment rules of established theory, nor with the presumption that all prices (including wage rates) are freely flexible' (1984: 262).

10 In Clower's example, there is no *numéraire* since it comprises a single relative price. Yet my main point – that it happens that the auctioneer is discarding one of the markets – is still verified.

11 Cf. De Vroey (1998: 208).

12 The eventual result is paradoxical, however. Clower may well have castigated Keynesian theory as it stood in the 1960s as being too Walrasian yet, actually, its full Walrasation came only afterwards in the works of Barro and Grossman and subsequent authors, who took their lead from him!

13 When speaking of Keynesian economics or the 'income-expenditure model', Leijonhuvfud has in mind the IS-LM apparatus (1968: 4).

14 The fact that later on Clower and Leijonhufvud jointly wrote the programmatic piece evoked above ([1975] 1984) may then suggest that it is Clower who made the step towards Leijonhufvud.

15 See also Leijonhufvud (1968: 53, 333).

16 See also Leijonhufvud (1968: 85).

17 At present, Leijonhufvud formulates the matter differently by accepting a difference in behaviour between wages, supposed to be sluggish, and prices,

supposed to be fast adjusting. 'The correct statement is that, in Keynes' theory, wages adjust less rapidly than output rates and that prices adjust either as fast or faster than output rates' (1998: 226). As will be seen, this reformulation has no impact on my assessment.

18 Note, however, that the attainment of the new equilibrium price has also to wait until t_3.

19 For a different assessment of Leijonhufvud's claim, see Backhouse (1980, 1982).

12 THE SECOND GENERATION: BARRO AND GROSSMAN, DRÈZE, BENASSY AND MALINVAUD

1 Barro and Grossman's 1971 paper and 1976 book present the same basic claim, the only difference between them being that the argumentation is significantly more complete in the book – in particular, some dynamic perspective is introduced.

2 I would nonetheless classify Drèze's model as Walrasian because it belongs to the Walrasian research programme.

3 Benassy's contribution to the debates on unemployment has not been limited to the type of models examined here, i.e. perfectly competitive models. He was also among the initiators of the imperfect competition approach to the problem. More on this in Chapter 19.

4 'Effective demand (or supply) on one particular market is the trade which maximizes the agent's criterion subject to the usual constraints *and* the quantity constraints on the *other* markets' (Benassy 1993: 739; his emphasis).

5 Amongst others, d'Autume (1985) and Silvestre (1982) have demonstrated that Drèze's and Benassy's equilibrium concepts result in similar allocations.

6 Benassy's case will be discussed later.

7 Of course, Lucas has hardly been alone in highlighting the incongruity between Walras and Keynes. See for example the following statements made by Negishi and Leijonhufvud: 'Walrasian economics cannot explain Keynesian equilibrium with involuntary unemployment since tâtonnement always results in a general equilibrium with full employment in the labour market' (Negishi 1979: 17). 'It is a silly endeavour to insist on trying, by hook or crook, to produce some sort of "involuntary unemployment" which could be called "Keynesian" and which could at the same time obey all the strictures of the neo-Walrasian code' (Leijonhufvud 1998: 234).

8 The short-side rule was first introduced by Marschak. Cf. Boianovsky (2002: 235).

9 According to the disequilibrium viewpoint, he or she should accept the deal, because receiving half the amount gives a higher utility than receiving nothing does. Yet it is more plausible to assume that this person, feeling that the contract has been breached and his rights encroached, will prefer to block the whole decisional process rather than receiving the smaller amount.

10 As seen, Clower and Leijonhufvud made their mind rather early on the conclusion that this programme could not succeed. Hence, they must be put aside from the others.

11 The same point had been made earlier by Weintraub:

> This symposium provided additional examples of such argumentations: the discussions generated by McCallum's paper, and Grandmont's, contained various appeals to the 'Principle' that the world either was or

> was not in equilibrium. The commentators in this audience seemed to think that they had a way of discussing the truth of the idea that observed states were equilibria without committing themselves to any particular theory of macroeconomics. This is, of course, an illusion: equilibrium states, or disequilibria are characteristics of our theories, and are thus imposed on the world
>
> (1990: 273)

12 Many interpreters have followed Malinvaud by assuming that Lucas was making a claim as to the real-world existence of market clearing. 'The "new classical macroeconomists" claim that markets do clear at every instant – in the Walrasian sense – in actual economies' (Grandmont 1983: 2). 'I have probably to remind you that an important school of thought in modern economics chooses to deny everything. Its members argue that supply and demand actually do balance in the labour market as they do in the fish market' (Solow 1990: 28). 'If we are to make empirically interesting statements about disequilibrium and equilibrium, statements that have potential empirical contents, we must define these two terms so that both are meaningful and both can be observed – in order to say that in fact we do not observe one of them' (Lipsey 2000: 72).

13 Clower was hardly enthusiastic about Benassy's enterprise, as the following extract from his Afterthoughts to the Walker volume witnesses.

> As for the dual-decision hypothesis, I gave it up, for the reasons indicated, before the 'Reconsideration' appeared (and also before the 'Counter-revolution' was published). Imagine my astonishment when a virtually distinct branch of economic theory began to develop from the dual-decision hypothesis and from the surprisingly similar (but, to my mind, even less coherent) Patinkin model of constrained supply. I refer, of course, to the fix-price models of Barro and Grossman, Drèze, Negishi, Grandmont, Benassy, Malinvaud, Varian and other writers. Although I am an acknowledged 'grandfather' of all these 'babies', I disowned them at the 1980 Aix-en-Provence World Conference of the Econometric Society as 'monsters' begotten by a father (the dual-decision process) whose paternity I admitted but whose character I deplored. I then gave my blessing to other babies – a motley lot, excepts for their distinctively Marshallian grins – describing them as well-formed off-springs of a fraternal twin of the father whose babies I just disowned.
>
> (Walker 1984: 266)

Clower, however, is wrong when stating that the above mentioned authors adopted his dual-decision hypothesis. Only Benassy did.

14 It took some time for the need for such a shift to be perceived. For example, Benassy entitled his 1982 survey *The Economics of Market Disequilibrium* (1982) while his 1990 piece received the title 'Non-Walrasian Equilibrium, Money and Macroeconomics' (1990).

13 FRIEDMAN

1 For a broader methodological assessment of Friedman's views, see Hammond (1996).

2 Its importance has been admitted even by Friedman's opponents, as Tobin's following statement illustrates: 'In retrospect, Friedman's 1967 Presidential Address to the American Economic Association was the opening shot of the new classical macroeconomics, the precursor of Lucas's misperceptions' explanation of Phillips curve observations and of the "policy ineffectiveness proposition"' (Tobin 1995: 32).

3 The paper was first published as a NBER occasional paper. Afterwards, it was published as a book, edited by R.J. Gordon, jointly with critical comments from opponents of different boards. Finally, it was included in Friedman and Schwartz's book *Monetary Trends in the United States and the United Kingdom* (1982) as its general theoretical framework.

4 See, for example, his contribution to Stein's volume on monetarism (Friedman 1976b).

5 The reason why I find it more appropriate to refer to the natural rate of employment rather than to the natural rate of unemployment will be explained shortly.

6 Recall my Chapter 6 analysis of Keynes' second observation where I claimed that the proposition as to the real wage being formed at the closure of the labor market is admissible if perfect information is assumed yet becomes unacceptable whenever it is removed. Friedman's model is a testimony to this point.

7 In other words, the default lies in the construction of the optimising plan rather than in its implementation.

8 This definition comes up again and again in the literature. For example, it is to be found in Santomero and Seater's *Journal of Economic Literature* survey: 'Because of market frictions and structural changes, unemployment always is positive. By implication, then, there will be unemployment even when the economy is in general equilibrium, defined as the absence of excess demand in each market' (1978: 515). To take another, more recent, example, in their *Macroeconomics* textbook, Hall and Taylor (1991) define the natural rate of unemployment as 'the amount of unemployment when the labor market is in equilibrium' (1991: 71) while they define equilibrium employment as 'the volume of employment at the intersection of supply and demand' (1991: 85).

9 In Marshallian theory, the non-instantaneous attainment of *normal* equilibrium can be explained in terms of frictions (i.e. the fact that adjustment is slow, e.g. because of a time-to-build factor). However, frictions play no role in the attainment of *market* equilibrium (i.e. market clearing).

10 See also Rogerson (1997) who confronts Friedman's categories with the search approach and makes it clear that his model is far from being a search model.

11 My point is not that a theory as to the natural rate of unemployment (i.e. a theory where unemployment in positive at equilibrium) is inconceivable. To restrain myself to the models analysed in this book, the efficiency wage model is a contribution to such a theory. My claim is rather that no such contribution is to be found in Friedman's misperception model.

12 A further sign of the existence of an anomaly in Friedman's reasoning is his resorting to the awkward notion of 'overfull employment' (1976a: 223).

13 Tobin has admitted to have fallen prey to the same mistake: 'until I re-read

Friedman's Presidential Address in order to write this chapter, I had the impression that Friedman accepted a Keynesian non-market clearing explanation of unemployment in excess of the natural rate' (Tobin 1995: 40).

14 Later in an interview with Snowdon and Vane Friedman characterised *The General Theory* as a 'remarkable intellectual achievement' and the 'right kind of theory' even if it eventually proved to be an 'unsuccessful argument' (Snowdon and Vane 1999: 127).

15 The following anecdote told by Mark Skousen is instructive:

> On December 31, 1965, Time magazine put John Maynard Keynes on the cover and quoted Friedman as saying, 'We are all Keynesians now'. Later, Friedman said he was quoted out of context. 'In one sense, we are all Keynesians now; in another, no one is a Keynesian any longer. We all use Keynesian language and apparatus, none of us any longer accepts the initial Keynesian conclusions.
>
> (Skousen 1988)

As will be seen, this is a type of statement that Lucas would never make.

16 On this see Hirsch and de Marchi (1990), Dostaler (1998) and Hammond (1992).

17 The following excerpt from his 'Marshallian Demand Curve' illustrates:

> Of course, it would be an overstatement to characterise all modern economic theory as 'Walrasian' in this sense. For example, Keynes' theory of employment, whatever its merits or demerits on other grounds, is Marshallian in method. It is a general equilibrium theory containing important empirical content and constructed to facilitate meaningful predictions.
>
> (Friedman [1949] 1953: 92)

18 Friedman suggests that Keynes' mistake was due to the exceptional quantity disruptions that characterised the Great Depression:

> However rationalized, the basic reason for the assumption was undoubtedly the lack of concordance between observed behavior and the implications of a literal application of Marshall's assumptions to aggregate magnitudes ... If anything, at least in the decades and a half between the end of World War I and the writing of *The General Theory*, economic fluctuations were manifested to a greater degree in output and employment than in prices. It therefore seemed highly plausible that, at least for aggregate phenomena, relative speeds of adjustment were just the reverse of those assumed by Marshall. Keynes explored this penetrating insight by carrying it tot he extreme: all adjustment in quantity, none in price.
>
> (Friedman 1974a: 19)

19 Asked by Snowdon and Vane 'Do you think that the distinction made by Keynes between voluntary and involuntary unemployment has been a useful one for the development of macroeconomics?', Friedman's answer is typically subdued: 'I have not myself found it a terribly useful distinction, but I cannot speak for others' (1994: 173).

20 As stated by Hoover:

> Friedman's analysis seemed remarkably prescient. Phillips curves estimated in the early 1960s continued to fit well until the early 1970s – a few years after Friedman's address. But this was a period of moderate inflation and so in line with his prediction. When inflation accelerated in the early 1970s, the Phillips curve broke down, just as Friedman said they would.
>
> (1988: 26)

21 For a more general assessment, see Leeson (1997a; 1997b).
22 See, e.g. Lipsey 1978.

23

> It is puzzling to find it [the short-run Lucasian Phillips curve] put forward as a discovery that a higher inflation rate will not increase the full-employment level of employment: Keynes and the Keynesians would not have claimed otherwise ... In fact, the world that they [the Lucasians] describe quite plainly needs no macro-policy. Keynesians were concerned with the problem of pushing the economy to its natural rate, not beyond it. If the economy is already there, we can all go home.
>
> (Hahn, 1982: 74–75)
>
> When the rational expectations people describe policy they have always a nice trick: they start from full employment where there is no need for anything, then the government stupidly does something and that ends up being completely ineffective in real terms, because you start at 'full employment' and eventually you end up at full employment.
>
> (Modigliani in Feiwel 1989: 570).

24 Several pieces of evidence exist in this respect. The first is Friedman's endorsement of the Marshallian approach against the Walrasian is his article on demand theory ([1949] 1953: 90), a viewpoint which he re-asserted in Friedman (1974b). Second is his interview with Snowdon and Vane (1997: 202).

25

> Even his [Keynes'] steps were essentially Marshall's, his short-run being distinguished from his long-run by the fixity of the aggregate capital stock. However, he tended to merge the market period and the short-run period, and, true to his own misleading dictum 'in the long run we are all dead', he concentrated almost exclusively on the short run.
>
> (Friedman 1974a: 18).

14 LUCAS

1 An interesting yet unfortunately unpublished paper on the genesis of Lucas' ideas is de Marchi (1990). For an investigation of the methodological and epistemological foundations of his theory, see Vercelli (1991).
2 Cf. De Vroey (2004).

3 See Snowdon and Vane (1998: 126) and Lucas' introduction to *Studies in Business Cycle Theory* (1981).
4 Nonetheless, Lucas recognises that the shift towards modern, scientific economic theory arose with the first macroeconomic models constructed in the aftermath of the Keynesian revolution, a development that Keynes hardly encouraged yet that was often made in his name (1981: 219).
5 See also his Nobel lecture (1996: 669).
6 See also Lucas (1981: 215).
7 One of the hallmarks of the initial business cycle models (Lucas 1979, Kydland and Prescott 1982), which sprung from Lucas' neutrality of money model, was that they require no unemployment concept, their object of analysis being fluctuations in *employment* rather than variations in *unemployment*.

> In most such models [of the business-cycle] unemployment as a distinct activity plays no role whatever. For many other economists, explaining business cycle is taken to *mean* accounting for recurrent episodes of widespread unemployment. From this alternative viewpoint, a model with cleared markets seems necessarily to miss the main point, however successful it may be accounting for other phenomena, and the work of 'equilibrium"' macroeconomists is often criticized as though it were a failed attempt to explain unemployment (which it surely does fail to) instead of as an attempt to explain something else.
>
> (Lucas 1987: 48)

Unemployment *per se*, Lucas goes onto argue, should be studied 'as an individual problem, identical in character in business cycle peaks and troughs (though more people have this problem in troughs)' (1987: 67), an investigation to be undertaken under the distinct banner of search theory rather than that of the business cycle.
8 For a more in-depth analysis of Lucas' conception of equilibrium, see De Vroey (2002).
9 Vercelli (1991: 20 ff.) offers a more methodological criticism of Lucas' equilibrium method.
10 Cf. De Vroey (1998).
11 In Hahn's terms, 'Imposing the axiom that the economy is at every instant in competitive equilibrium simply removes the actual operation of the invisible hand from the analysis. By postulating that all perceived Pareto-improving moves are instantaneously carried out, all problems of co-ordination between agents are ruled out' (1985: 4).
12 Lucas' stance has, in fact, a long lineage. To wit, it was voiced by von Mises in his 1949 *Human Action* book: 'Unemployment in the unhampered market is always voluntary. In the eyes of the unemployed man, unemployment is the minor of two evils between which he has to choose' (1949: 596).
13 Cf. De Vroey (2004).

15 IMPLICIT CONTRACT THEORY

1 The 'implicit contract' term is an evocative coinage. Unfortunately, it is misleading, at least for what concerns Azariadis' model where the contract bears only on a given trade round, is perfectly explicit, and is simple rather than complex. The implicit contract notion is more apposite for other works, e.g. Okun (1981), where the idea of a long-standing relationship is more central and

which are concerned with 'arrangements that are not legally binding but that give both sides incentives to maintain the relationship' (1981: 49).

2 An alternative definition is Ito's: 'After the revelation of states of nature, if unemployed workers have lower utility than retained workers in some states of nature, they are said to be unemployed involuntarily' (1991: 10).

3 As stated by Hahn and Solow, 'Involuntary unemployment has nothing to do with any metaphysical conundrum about "free will"'. (Hahn 1983: 225). 'The key point here is that the notion of "involuntary unemployment" is not metaphysical or psychological; it has little or nothing to do with free will.' (Solow 1986: S 33).

16 EFFICIENCY WAGE THEORY

1 Cf. Lazear and Moore (1984), Salop (1979), Shapiro and Stiglitz (1984), Weiss (1980), Yellen (1984).

2 For broader surveys of these models see Katz (1986), Riley (2001) as well as Akerlof and Stiglitz's Nobel lectures (Akerlof 2002, Stiglitz 2002).

3

> The critical wage for nonshirking is greater: (a) the smaller the detection probability; (b) the larger the effort; (c) the higher the quit rate; (d) the higher the interest rate; (e) the higher the unemployment benefit; and (f) the higher the flow out of unemployment.
>
> (Shapiro and Stiglitz 1984: 438)

4 Cf. MacLeod and Malcomson (1998).

5 Cf. Weiss' comments on Katz (Katz 1986: 285–286).

6 A possible explanation for this success is tractability. Introducing the efficiency wage assumption in a standard model is an easy task, as it just consists of replacing a traditional production function, $y = f(k, l)$, with the function $y = f(k, e(w)l)$.

7 See, e.g. Akerlof and Yellen (1986).

8 Bowles' Marxian recasting of Shapiro and Stiglitz's basic insights (1985) thus appears a natural extension of the initial model.

9 See also Akerlof and Yellen (1986: 5).

10 This is a point that, to the best of my knowledge has hardly been underlined. It definitely contradicts a remark that Stiglitz voiced years later in his Nobel lecture, that 'there are incentives on the part of individuals for information not to be revealed, for secrecy' (2002: 463).

11 An all-round lottery at each trading round, involving a total reshuffling of workers – the assumption made by Solow (Solow 1990: 44 ff.) – cannot do because workers would have no incentives to work in such a framework.

12 Moreover, why should the firms be the villains? After all, the workers are at fault, since they fail to respect the hiring contract.

13 I am not claiming that this conclusion is valid for every type of efficiency model.

14 Both Phelps and Kolm seem to adopt the unilateral decision assumption that I have criticised above.

15 For a pedagogical account of the Dasgupta-Ray model, see e.g. Bardhan and Udry (1999: 35–36).

16 Similar statements can be found in Bullow and Summers (1986: 405), Hahn (1987: 3) and Layard, Nickel and Jackman (1991: 41), Akerlof (2002: 415).

17 The same point is repeated in Stiglitz:

> To most economists, and to almost all non economists, pinning the label 'voluntary' on unemployment simply because an unemployed worker has foregone the option of moving to California to pick grapes is semantic quibbling. The trained welder living in Chicago who is unemployed, while other welders are working, considers himself involuntarily unemployed as a welder. He would be willing to work at the going wage for welders (or perhaps even at somewhat lower wages). But he is justifiably unwilling to relocate to California to become a grape picker.
>
> (Stiglitz 1993: 712)

18 As far as Lucas is concerned, he expresses no opinion on what happened to those people before they went to California. My guess is that while he might admit that they experienced rationing in their normal Chicago market, he surely would prefer to explain it in terms of a standard search model than of efficiency wages.

17 INSIDER–OUTSIDER THEORY

1 Their main articles have been collected in Lindbeck and Snower (1988). See also Lindbeck (1993) and Lindbeck and Snower (2002). These authors have also written an excellent survey of the unfolding of involuntary unemployment theory (it became Chapter 1 of Lindbeck and Snower (1988)).
2 The transition from the outsider to the insider status, as well as the inverse move, depends on membership rules or the length of the initiation period. Lindbeck and Snower usually make the simplifying assumption that the initiation period amounts to the unitary period of time considered in their model. As a result, the status of incumbents and insiders coincide.
3 Cf. Lindbeck and Snower (1988: 70). The advantage of the cooperation–harassment model is that rent-related costs follow more directly from insiders' behaviour.
4 Lindbeck and Snower assume that, whenever turnover costs have no impact and as long as a reserve of unemployment is existing, competition leads the wage rate to be equal to the reservation wage rate.
5 In their cooperation–harassment model, Lindbeck and Snower consider the possibility of the reservation wage criterion being met, yet it remains a minor and rather contrived element of their model.

18 COORDINATION FAILURE MODELS

1 Cooper and John (1988) is probably the best-known paper on coordination failures. It shows how an outwardly disparate stream of literature can be unified by pointing out their common two traits, the existence of spillovers and strategic complementary. However, it will not be discussed here, because its aim is not to offer a specific unemployment or underemployment model. Other interesting coordination failures articles are Bryant (1983), Drazen (1987), Heller (1986) and Weitzman (1982).
2 In my eyes, the third sentence of Diamond's quotation should read 'when unemployed' in view of what he writes on p. 33, 'Individuals have 0 or *y* units for sale. The former are looking for production opportunities and are referred to as unemployed'.
3 On top of the assumption that agents cannot consume the product of their own

investment, it is also assumed that they cannot undertake a production before having exchanged the coconuts they hold.

4 Drawn from Diamond ([1982] 1991: 36).

5 Therefore, the remark that I made above about Friedman should be extended to Diamond. While he claims that his model exhibits multiple natural rates of unemployment, it would be more correct to state that it is concerned with multiple natural rates of employment, each of them being an equilibrium state.

6 See in particular Howitt (1990).

7 In the same vein, Howitt notes that 'from Modigliani to Taylor the modern Keynesian position has been the classical one that Keynes was attacking: that sticky wages are to blame' (1990: 75). However, when reading his review of Bewley's 1999 book (Howitt 2002), one gets the impression that he may have changed his mind.

19 IMPERFECTLY COMPETITIVE GENERAL EQUILIBRIUM MODELS

1 Survey papers are Benassy (1993), Dixon and Rankin (1995), Gordon (1990) and Silvestre (1993).

2 Hart recognises that it should not be considered as money, since agents have no reason to hold money, due to the static character of the model.

3 In section 5 of his model Hart removes the assumption that work has no disutility. This, he claims, compounds the conclusions of his model without radically modifying them.

4 I.e. the fifth definition of full employment pointed out in Chapter 2. In this chapter, I also observed that full employment will be different from the maximum feasible level of employment, as long as it is optimising behaviour for agents to consume some leisure. Since this is not the case in Hart's model, the socially optimal and the maximum levels of employment coincide.

5 The right-hand side zero stems from the assumption that labour has no disutility.

6 That is, $\tilde{l} = \dfrac{m\bar{k}/\theta}{1 - \tilde{p}h(\tilde{p})}$. Cf. Silvestre (1990: 10).

7

> *Define an amount of labour eventually demanded at a given wage* to be a number of units of labour for which there exists a price of output a quantity of output per firm and a level of buyer's wealth per market satisfying: (i) the price and the quantity of output solves the profit maximisation problem of a Cournotian firm that faces the given wage rate and the market demand curve defined by the level of buyer's wealth when each other firm in its market produces that quantity of output; (ii) the level of buyer's wealth is the one determined by those prices, wages and quantity of output; (ii) the amount of labour equals the economywide input requirement when each firm is producing that quantity of input.
>
> (Silvestre 1990: 902)

8 For example, Dixon and Rankin write that "Some of these possibilities were realised in Oliver Hart's study, which thus had as part of its title' . . . with Keynesian features', the Keynesian Features being a multiplier and involuntary unemployment" (Dixon and Ranking 1995: 4).

9 D'Aspremont, Dos Santos Ferreira and Gérard-Varet depart from Hart by ques-

tioning his hypothesis that firms' marginal revenue – i.e. $p(1 + \vartheta/\eta(p))$ – is always positive, an assumption that Hart vindicates on the grounds of analytical simplicity. Since $\eta(p) < 0$, Hart's assumption requires that $\vartheta/\eta(p) > -1$, which will be true only for certain values of η and ϑ. In particular, ϑ (which, I recall, is the degree of monopoly) must be small. Instead, they assume that the marginal revenue of a firm with significant market power becomes negative for large quantities (i.e. when prices are low).

10 Benassy (1987), which appeared simultaneously, is close to Blanchard and Kiyotaki's model.

11 As noted by Benassy, 'If one wants to obtain less "classical" results, one has to add other "imperfections" than imperfect competition such as imperfect information or costly price changes, to quote only two' (Benassy 1995: 16).

12 Cf. Akerlof and Yellen (1985) and Mankiw (1985).

13 As explained by Dixon and Rankin, 'If we take a Taylor's approximation to firm *i*'s forgone profits of not increasing P_i, or to union *h*'s forgone utility of not increasing W_h, it will contain no term in ΔM_0, only in $(\Delta M_0)^2$ and higher powers of ΔM_0. By comparison, the increase in output is first order, i.e. proportional to ΔM_0.' (Dixon and Rankin 1995: 45).

14 Blanchard and Kiyotaki admit that, although an increase in nominal money increases output and employment, it cannot succeed in attaining the competitive equilibrium ([1987] 1991: 365).

15 Blanchard and Kiyotaki have not been the first authors to have counterattacked on the ineffectiveness claim. Staggering contract models (Fischer [1977] 1991, Taylor [1979] 1991), aiming at justifying wage rigidity by the fact that labour contracts extended over several trade rounds, paved the way. I have not retained them for examination because they put little emphasis on the unemployment aspect.

16 Hart's following remark goes in my direction:

> In an imperfectly competitive equilibrium an agent will generally want to buy or sell more at the going price. It is inappropriate, however, to describe this as 'rationing' or to associate it with the non-clearing of markets.
>
> (Hart [1982] 1991: 337)

17 At one juncture, at least, Benassy has conceded to my view:

> We see first that at equilibrium there is both underemployment and underproduction: equation (27) shows that the firm would by happy to produce and sell more if the demand for its product was forthcoming. Similarly equation (29) shows that the household would like to sell more of its labor if the demand was present. We should point out however that this underemployment of resources is not really 'involuntary' as each agent himself chooses a price or wage high enough for him to be rationed.
>
> (Benassy 1991: 130)

This is the very point I want to make: unemployment cannot be equated to underemployment.

18 Of course, this is true only if it is assumed that abolishing the monopolistic situation is not possible.

20 EPILOGUE

1 This conclusion runs on a collision course with Patinkin (1990), who argues that the only possible reason for differences in interpretation of *The General Theory* resides in political motivations.
2 Recall that I have criticised the view that implicit contract and efficiency wage models are rigidity models.
3 As stated in Chapter 17, the insider–outsider model should be put aside.
4 As once stated by Solow, 'I believe that what looks like involuntary unemployment is involuntary unemployment' (1980: 3).
5 This was also Leontief's opinion, as seen in Chapter 9.

BIBLIOGRAPHY

Ackley, G. (1961) *Macroeconomic Theory*, New York: Macmillan.

Akerlof, G. (2002) 'Behavioral Macroeconomics and Macroeconomic Behavior', *American Economic Review*, vol. 92, pp. 411–433.

Akerlof, G. and J. Yellen (1985) 'A Near-Rational Model of the Business Cycle, with Wage and Price Inertia', *Quarterly Journal of Economics*, supplement. vol. 100, pp. 823–835.

Akerlof, G. and J. Yellen (eds) (1986) *Efficiency Wage. Models of the Labor Market*, Cambridge: Cambridge University Press.

Allen, R. G. D. (1967) *Macroeconomic Theory. A Mathematical Treatment*, London: Macmillan.

Ambrosi, G. (2002) *Keynes, Pigou and Cambridge Keynesians: Authenticity and Analytical Perspective in the Keynes-Classics Debate*, London: Palgrave.

Aristotle (1980) *The Nichomachean Ethics*, Oxford: Oxford University Press (second edition).

Arrow, K. (1971) *Essays in the Theory of Risk-Bearing*, Amsterdam: North-Holland.

Ashenfelter, O. (1978) 'What is Involuntary Unemployment?', *Proceedings of the American Philosophical Society*, vol. 122, pp. 135–138.

Azariadis, C. (1975) 'Implicit Contracts and Underemployment Equilibria', *Journal of Political Economy*, vol. 83, pp. 1183–2002.

Azariadis, C. (1981) 'Implicit Contracts and Related Topics: A Survey', in Hornstein *et al.* (eds) *The Economics of the Labour Market*, London: HMSO, pp. 221–248.

Azariadis, C. (1987) 'Implicit Contracts', in Eatwell, J., M. Milgate and P. Newman (eds) *The New Palgrave. A Dictionary of Economics*, London: Macmillan, vol. 2, pp. 733–736.

Backhouse, R. (1980) 'Fix-Price Versus Flex-Price Models of Macroeconomic Equilibrium With Rationing', *Oxford Economic Papers*, vol. 30, pp. 210–223.

Backhouse, R. (1982) 'Price Flexibility and Keynesian Unemployment in a Macroeconomic Model With Quantity Rationing', *Oxford Economic Papers*, vol. 32, pp. 292–304.

Backhouse, R. (1995) *Interpreting Macroeconomics. Explorations in the History of Macroeconomic Thought*, London: Routledge.

Baily, M. (1974) 'Wages and Employment Under Uncertain Demand', *Review of Economic Studies*, vol. 41, pp. 37–50.

Bardhan, P. and C. Udry (1999) *Development Microeconomics*, Oxford: Oxford University Press.

Barens, I. and V. Caspari (1999) 'Old Views and New Perspectives: On Re-Reading Hicks' 'Mr. Keynes and the "Classics"', *The European Journal of the History of Economic Thought,* vol. 6, pp. 216–241.

Barro, R. and H. Grossman (1971), 'A General Disequilibrium Model of Income and Employment', *American Economic Review,* vol. 61, pp. 82–93.

Barro, R. and H. Grossman (1976) *Money, Employment and Inflation,* Cambridge: Cambridge University Press.

Bateman, B. W. (1996) *Keynes' Uncertain Revolution,* Ann Arbor: The University of Michigan Press.

Beggs, D., S. Fischer and R. Dornbusch (1997) *Economics,* London: McGraw-Hill (fifth edition).

Benassy, J. P. (1975) 'Neo-Keynesian Disequilibrium Theory in a Monetary Economy', *Review of Economics Studies,* vol. 13, pp. 503–523.

Benassy, J. P. (1976) 'The Disequilibrium Approach to Monopolistic Price Setting and General Monopolistic Equilibrium', *Review of Economic Studies,* vol. 43, pp. 69–81.

Benassy, J. P. (1982) *The Economics of Market Disequilibrium,* New York: Academic Press.

Benassy, J. P. (1987) 'Imperfect Competition, Unemployment and Policy', *European Economic Review,* vol. 31, pp. 417–426.

Benassy, J. P. (1990) 'Non-Walrasian Equilibria, Money, and Macroeconomics' in Friedman, B. M. and F. Hahn (eds) *Handbook of Monetary Economics,* vol. I, Amsterdam: Elseviers Science Publishers B.V., pp. 108–169.

Benassy, J. P. (1991) 'Microeconomic Foundations and Properties of a Macroeconomic Model with Imperfect Competition' in Arrow, K. (ed.) *Issues in Contemporary Economics,* vol. 1: Markets and Welfare, International Economic Association Conference vol. 98, London: Macmillan, pp. 121–138.

Benassy, J. P. (1993) 'Nonclearing Markets: Microeconomic Concepts and Macroeconomic Applications', *Journal of Economic Literature,* vol. XXXI, pp. 736–761.

Benassy, J. P. (1995) 'Classical and Keynesian Features in Macroeconomic Models with Imperfect Competiton' in Dixon, H. and N. Rankin (eds) *The New Macroeconomics. Imperfect Markets and Policy Effectiveness,* Cambridge: Cambridge University Press, pp. 15–33.

Benetti, C. (1998) 'La structure logique de la Theorie générale de Keynes', *Cahiers d'économie politique,* no. 30–31, pp. 11–48.

Beaud, M. and G. Dostaler (1995) *Economic Thought Since Keynes. A History and Dictionary of Major Economists,* Edward Elgar.

Bewley, T. (1999) *Why Wages Don't Fall During a Recession?,* Cambridge: Cambridge University Press.

Blanchard, O. (1987) 'Neoclassical Synthesis', in Eatwell, J., M. Milgate and P. Newman (eds) *The New Palgrave. A Dictionary of Economics,* London: Macmillan, vol. 3, pp. 634–636.

Blanchard, O. and S. Fischer (1989) *Lectures on Macroeconomics,* Cambridge, MA: The M.I.T. Press.

Blanchard, O. and N. Kiyotaki ([1987] 1991) 'Monopolistic Competition and the Effects of Aggregate Demand' in Mankiw, G. and D. Romer (eds) *New Keynesian Economics, Imperfect Competition and Sticky Prices,* vol. 1, Cambridge, MA: The M.I.T. Press, pp. 345–375.

Blaug, M. (1997) 'Competition as an End-State and Competition as a Process' in

Eaton, B. C. and R. G. Harris (eds) *Trade, Technology and Economics*, Cheltenham: Edward Elgar.

Blinder, A. ([1988] 1997) 'The Fall and Rise of Keynesian Economics' in Snowdon, B. and H. Vane (eds) *A Macroeconomics Reader*, London: Routledge, pp. 109–134.

Boianovsky, M. (2002) 'Patinkin, the Cowles Commission, and the Theory of Unemployment and Aggregate Supply', *The European Journal of the History of Economic Thought*, vol. 9, pp. 226–259.

Boianovsky, M. and H. M. Trautwein (2001) 'Wicksell, Cassel and the Idea of Involuntary Unemployment', *History of Political Economy*, vol. 35, pp. 385–436.

Bowles, S. (1985) 'The Production Process in a Competitive Economy: Walrasian, Neo-Hobbesian and Marxian Models', *American Economic Review*, vol. 75, pp. 16–36.

Bowles, S. and H. Gintis (1988) 'Contested Exchange, Political Economy and Modern Economic Theory', *American Economic Review*, vol. 78, pp. 145–150.

Branson, W. (1972) *Macroeconomic Theory and Policy*, New York: Harper and Row (third edition).

Brown, V. (1994) 'Higgling: The Language of Markets in Economic Discourse' in de Marchi, N. and M. Morgan (eds) 'Higgling. Transactors and Their Markets in the History of Economics', *History of Political Economy*, annual supplement, vol. 26, Durham: Duke University Press, pp. 66–93.

Brunner, K. and A. Meltzer (1993) *Money and the Economy. Issues in Monetary Analysis*, Cambridge: Cambrige University Press.

Bryant, J. (1978) 'An Annotation of 'Implicit Contracts and Underemployment Equilibria'', *Journal of Political Economy*, vol. 86, pp. 1159–1160.

Bryant, J. (1983) 'A Simple Rational Expectations Keynesian-Type Model', *Quarterly Journal of Economics*, vol. 98, pp. 525–528.

Bulow, J. and L. Summers (1986) 'A Theory of Dual Labor markets with Application to Industrial Policy, Discrimination and Keynesian Unemployment', *Journal of Labor Economics*, vol. 4, pp. 376–414.

Carlin, W. and D. Soskice (1990) *Macroeconomics and the Wage Bargain*, Oxford: Oxford University Press.

Carmichael, L. (1985) 'Can Unemployment be Involuntary? A Comment', *American Economic Review*, vol. 75, pp. 1213–1214.

Cartelier, J. (1993) 'Récursivité et monnaie: un autre point de vue sur "Keynes and the Classics"', *Revue d'économie politique*, vol. 103, pp. 527–549.

Cartelier, J. (1995) *L'économie de Keynes*, Bruxelles: De Boeck.

Clarke, P. (1990) *The Keynesian Revolution in the Making 1924–1936*, Oxford: Clarendon Press.

Clower, R. ([1965] 1984) 'The Keynesian Counter-revolution: A Theoretical Appraisal', in Walker (ed.) pp. 34–58.

Clower, R. ([1975] 1984) 'Reflections on the Keynesian Perplex', in Walker, D. (ed.) *Money and Markets. Essays by Robert Clower*, Cambridge: Cambridge University Press, pp. 187–208.

Clower, R. (1984) 'Afterword' in Walker, D. (ed.) *Money and Markets. Essays by Robert Clower*, Cambridge: Cambridge University Press, pp. 259–272.

Clower, R. (1989) 'Keynes' General Theory: The Marshall Connection', in Walker, D. (ed.) *Perspectives on the History of Economic Thought*, vol. II, London: Edward Elgar, pp. 133–147.

Clower, R. (1995) *Economic Doctrine and Method. Selected Papers of R.W. Clower*, London: Edward Elgar.

Clower, R. and J. Due (1972) *Microeconomics*, Homewood: R. D. Irwin.

Clower, R. and A. Leijonhufvud ([1975] 1984) 'The Coordination of Economic Activities: A Keynesian Perspective', in Walker, D. (ed.) *Money and Markets. Essays by Robert Clower*, Cambridge: Cambridge University Press, pp. 209–217.

Coddington, A. (1983) *Keynesian Economics. The Search for First Principles*, London: Allen and Unwin.

Collard, D. (1990) 'Unemployment', in Creedy, J. (ed.), *Foundations of Economic Thought*, Oxford: Blackwell, pp. 331–355.

Cooper, R. and A. John (1988) 'Coordinating Coordination Failures in Keynesian Models', *Quarterly Journal of Economics*, vol. 103, pp. 441–463.

Corry, B. (1996) 'Unemployment in the History of Economic Thought: An Overview and some Reflections' in Corry, B. (ed.) *Unemployment and the Economists*, Cheltenham: Edgar Elgar, pp. 1–30.

Cross, R. (ed.) (1995) *The Natural Rate of Unemployment. Reflections on 25 Years of the Hypothesis*, Cambridge: Cambridge University Press.

Darity, W. Jr. and A. H. Goldsmith (1995) 'Mr. Keynes, the New Keynesians, and the Concept of Full Employment' in Wells, P. (ed.) *Post-Keynesian Economic Theory*, Boston: Kluwer, pp. 73–93.

Darity, W. Jr. and B. Horn (1983) 'Involuntary Unemployment Reconsidered', *Southern Economic Journal*, pp. 717–733.

Darity, W. Jr. and B. Horn (1987–1988) 'Involuntary Unemployment Independent from the Labour Market', *Journal of Post-Keynesian Economics*, vol. X, pp. 216–224.

Darity, W. Jr. and W. Young (1995) 'IS-LM: An Inquest', *History of Political Economy*, vol. 27, pp. 1–41.

Dasgupta, P. and D. Ray (1986) 'Inequality as a Determinant of Malnutrition and Unemployment Theory', *Economic Journal*, vol. 96, pp. 1011–1034.

d'Aspremont, C., R. Dos Santos Ferreira and L. A. Gérard-Varet (1988) 'On Monopolistic Competition and Involuntary Unemployment', *Quarterly Journal of Economics*, vol. 105, pp. 895–919.

d'Aspremont, C., R. Dos Santos Ferreira and L. A. Gérard-Varet (1990) 'Unemployment in an Extended Cournot Oligopoly Model', *Oxford Economic Papers*, vol. 41, pp. 490–505.

d'Autume, A. (1985) *Monnaie, croissance et déséquilibre*, Paris: Economica.

Davidson, P. (1984) 'Reviving Keynes's Revolution', *Journal of Post Keynesian Economics*, vol. VI, pp. 561–575.

de Marchi, N. (1990) '"Discovery" and the Unimportance of Lucas' Test of the Natural Rate Hypothesis', mimeo.

De Vroey, M. (1998) 'Is the Tâtonnement Hypothesis a Good Caricature of Market Forces?', *The Journal of Economic Methodology*, vol. 5, pp. 201–221.

De Vroey, M. (1999a) 'Equilibrium and Disequilibrium in Economic Theory: A Confrontation of the Classical, Marshallian and Walras-Hicksian Conceptions', *Economics and Philosophy*, vol. 15, pp. 161–185.

De Vroey, M. (1999b) 'The Marshallian Market and the Walrasian Economy. Two Incompatible Bedfellows', *The Scottish Journal of Political Economy*, vol. 46, pp. 319–338.

De Vroey, M. (1999c) 'Keynes and the Marshall-Walras Divide', *Journal of the History of Economic Thought*, vol. 21, pp. 117–136.

De Vroey, M. (2000) 'Marshall on Equilibrium and Time. A Reconstruction', *The European Journal of the History of Economic Thought*, vol. 7, pp. 20–44.

De Vroey, M. (2001a) 'Price Rigidity and Market Clearing: A Conceptual Clarification', *Cambridge Journal of Economics*, vol. 25, pp. 639–656.

De Vroey, M. (2001b) 'Friedman and Lucas on the Phillips Curve: From a Disequilibrium to an Equilibrium Approach', *Eastern Economic Journal*, vol. 27, pp. 127–148.

De Vroey, M. (2002) 'Equilibrium and Disequilibrium in Walrasian and Neo-Walrasian Economics', *Journal of the History of Economic Thought*, vol. 24, pp. 405–426.

De Vroey M. (2003) 'Perfect Information *à la* Marshall versus Perfect Information *à la* Walras' *Journal of Economic Methodology*, vol. 10, pp. 465–492.

De Vroey, M. (2004) 'The History of Macroeconomics Viewed Against the Background of the Marshall–Walras Divide', in De Vroey, M. and K. Hoover (eds), *The IS-LM Model. Its Rise, Fall and Strange Persistence*, Durham, N.C.: Duke University Press.

Dernburg, T. and D. McDougall (1960), *Macroeconomics*, New York: McGraw-Hill.

Diamond, P. ([1982] 1991) 'Aggregate Demand Management in Search Equilibrium', in Mankiw, N. G. and D. Romer (eds) *New Keynesian Economics, Volume 2, Coordination Failures and Real Rigidities*, Cambridge, MA: The M.I.T. Press, pp. 31–46.

Diamond, P. (1984) *A Search-Equilibrium Approach to the Micro-Foundations of Macroeconomics*, Cambridge, MA: The M.I.T. Press.

Dimand, R. (1988) *The Origins of the Keynesian Revolution*, Aldershot, Hampshire: Edward Elgar.

Dixon, H. (1995) 'Of Coconuts, Decomposition, and a Jackass: the Genealogy of the Natural Rate' in Cross, R. *The Natural Rate of Unemployment. Reflections on 25 Years of the Hypothesis*, Cambridge: Cambridge University Press, pp. 57–74.

Dixon, H. and N. Rankin (eds) (1995) *The New Macroeconomics. Imperfect Markets and Policy Effectiveness*, Cambridge: Cambridge University Press.

Donzelli, F. (1989) *The Concept of Equilibrium in Neoclassical Economic Theory. An Inquiry into the Evolution of General Competitive Analysis from Walras to the Neo-Walrasian Research Programme*, Ph.D. Dissertation, University of Cambridge.

Dos Santos Ferreira, R. (2000) 'Keynes et le développement de la théorie l'emploi dans une économie monétaire' in Béraud, A. and G. Facarello (eds) *Nouvelle histoire de la pensée économique*, vol. III, Paris: La Découverte, pp. 236–293.

Dostaler, G. (1998) 'Friedman and Keynes: Divergences and Convergences', *The European Journal of the History of Economic Thought*, vol. 5, pp. 317–347.

Drazen, A. (1987) 'Reciprocal Externality Models of Low Employment', *European Economic Review*, vol. 31, pp. 436–443.

Drèze, J. H. 1975, 'Existence of Equilibrium Under Price Rigidities', *International Economic Review*, vol. 16, pp. 301–320.

Dworkin, R. (1981) 'What is Equality? Part 2: Equality of Resources', *Philosophy and Public Affairs*, vol. 10, pp. 283–345.

Farmer, R. (1993) *The Macroeconomics of Self-Fulfilling Prophecies*, Cambridge, MA: The M.I.T. Press.

Favereau, O. (1985) 'L'incertain dans la révolution keynésienne: l'hypothèse Wittgenstein', *Economies et Sociétés*, série Oeconomia, vol. 3, pp. 29–72.

Feiwel, G. R. (1989) 'Towards an Integration of Imperfect Competition and Macrodynamics: Kalecki, Keynes, Joan Robinson' in Feiwel, G. R. (ed.) *The Economics of Imperfect Competition and Employment. Joan Robinson and Beyond*, London: Macmillan, pp. 3–145.

Fischer, S. ([1977] 1991) 'Long-term Contracts, Rational Expectations, and the Optimal Money Supply Rule' in Mankiw, G. and D. Romer (eds) *New Keynesian Economics*, vol. 1, *Imperfect Competition and Sticky Prices*, Cambridge, MA: The M.I.T. Press, pp. 215–231.

Fischer, S. (1987) '1944, 1963, and 1985', in Dornbusch R., S. Fischer and J. Bossons, *Macroeconomics and Finance. Essays in Honor of Franco Modigliani*, Cambridge, MA: The M.I.T. Press, pp. 229–256.

Friedman, M. ([1949] 1953) 'The Marshallian Demand Curve' in *Essays in Positive Economics*, Chicago: The University of Chicago Press, pp. 47–99.

Friedman, M. (1968) 'The Role of Monetary Policy', *American Economic Review*, vol. 58, pp. 1–17.

Friedman, M. (1974a) 'A Theoretical Framework for Monetary Analysis' in Gordon, R. J. (ed.) *Milton Friedman's Monetary Framework*, Chicago: Chicago University Press, pp. 1–62.

Friedman, M. (1974b) 'Comments on the Critics', in Gordon R. J. (ed.) *Milton Friedman's Monetary Framework*, Chicago: Chicago University Press, pp. 132–177.

Friedman, M. (1976a) *Price Theory*, Chicago: Aldine Publishers.

Friedman, M. (1976b) 'Comments on Tobin and Buiter' in Stein J. L. (ed.) *Monetarism*, Amsterdam: North-Holland, pp. 310–317.

Friedman, M. (1977) 'Nobel Lecture: Inflation and Unemployment', *Occasional Paper 51*, London: Institute for Economic Affairs.

Friedman, M. and A. J. Schwartz (1982) *Monetary Trends in the United States and the United Kingdom. Their Relationship to Income, Prices and Interest Rates. 1867–1975*, Chicago: The University of Chicago Press.

Frisch, R. (1950) 'Alfred Marshall's Theory of Value', *The Quarterly Journal of Economics*, vol. 64, pp. 495–524.

Gerrard, B. (1995) 'Keynes, the Keynesian and the Classics: A Suggested Interpretation', *The Economic Journal*, vol. 105, pp. 445–458.

Gordon, D. F. (1974) 'A Neoclassical Theory of Keynesian Unemployment', *Economic Inquiry*, vol. 12, pp. 431–449.

Gordon, R. J. (1990) 'What is New Keynesian Economics?', *Journal of Economic Literature*, vol. 28, pp. 1115–1171.

Grandmont, J. M. (1977) 'Temporary General Equilibrium Theory', *Econometrica*, vol. 45, pp. 535–572.

Grandmont, J. M. (1983) *Money and Value: A Reconsideration of Classical and Neoclassical Monetary Theory*, Cambridge: Cambridge University Press.

Grandmont, J. M. and G. Laroque (1976) 'On Keynesian Temporary Equilibria', *Review of Economic Studies*, vol. 43, pp. 53–67.

Greenwald, B. and J. Stiglitz (1987) 'Keynesian, New Keynesian and New Classical Macroeconomics', *Oxford Economic Papers*, vol. 39, pp. 119–133.

Grossman, H. (1979) 'Why Does Aggregate Employment Fluctuate?', *American Economic Review*, vol. 69, pp. 64–69.

Guerrien, B. (1989) *Concurrence, flexibilité et stabilité*, Paris: Economica.

Haavelmo, T. (1950) 'The Notion of Involuntary Economic Decisions', *Econometrica*, vol. 18, pp. 1–8.

Hagemann, H. and O. F. Hamouda, (1994) (eds) *The Legacy of Hicks. His Contribution to Economic Analysis*, London: Routledge.

Hahn, F. (1982) *Money and Inflation*, Oxford: Basil Blackwell.

Hahn, F. (1983) 'Comment on Axel Leijonhufvud's "Keynesianism, Monetarism and Rational Expectations: some Reflections and Conjectures"' in Frydman, R. and E. Phelps (eds) *Individual Forecasting and Aggregate Outcomes, Rational Expectations Explained*, Cambridge: Cambridge University Press, pp. 223–230.

Hahn F. (1985) 'Introduction', *Equilibrium and Macroeconomics*, Oxford: Blackwell, pp. 1–19.

Hahn, F. (1987) 'On Involuntary Unemployment', *The Economic Journal*, vol. 97, pp. 1–17.

Hahn, F. (1995) 'Theoretical Reflections on the "Natural Rate of Unemployment"', in Cross, R. (ed.) *The Natural Rate of Unemployment. Reflections on 25 Years of the Hypothesis*, Cambridge: Cambridge University Press. pp. 43–56.

Hahn, F. and R. Solow (1986) 'Is Wage Flexibility a Good Thing?' in Beckerman W. (ed.) *Wage Rigidity and Unemployment*, Baltimore: John Hopkins University Press, pp. 1–19.

Hahn, F. and R. Solow (1995) *A Critical Essay on Modern Macroeconomic Theory*, Oxford: Basil Blackwell.

Hall, R. (1979) 'A Theory of the Natural Unemployment Rate and the Duration of Employment', *Journal of Monetary Economics*, vol. 5, pp. 153–169.

Hall, R. and J. Taylor (1991) *Macroeconomics. Theory, Performance, and Policy*, New York: Norton.

Hammond, J. D. (1992) 'An Interview with Milton Friedman on Methodology' in Caldwell, B. (ed.) *The Philosophy and Methodology of Economics*, vol. I. Cheltenham: Edgar Elegar, pp. 216–238.

Hammond, J. D. (1996) *Theory and Measurement. Causality Issues in Milton Friedman's Monetary Economics*, Cambridge: Cambridge University Press.

Hamouda, O. F. (1993) *John R. Hicks. The Economist's Economist*, Oxford: Basil Blackwell.

Hansen, A. (1949) *Monetary Theory and Fiscal Policy*, New York: McGraw-Hill.

Hansen, A. (1953) *A Guide to Keynes*, New York: McGraw-Hill.

Harris, S. (ed.) (1947) *The New Economics. Keynes' Influence on Theory and Public Policy*, New York: A. A. Knopf.

Harrod, R. F. ([1937] 1947) 'Mr Keynes and Traditional Theory', in Harris, S. E. (ed.) *The New Economics. Keynes' Influence on Theory and Public Policy*, New York: A. A. Knopf, pp. 591–605.

Hart, O. (1979) 'Monopolistic Competition in a Large Economy with Differentiated Commodities', *Review of Economic Studies*, vol. 46, pp. 1–30.

Hart, O. ([1982] 1991) 'A Model of Imperfect Competition with Keynesian Features' in Mankiw, G. and D. Romer (eds) *New Keynesian Economics*, vol. 1, *Imperfect Competition and Sticky Prices*, Cambridge, MA: The M.I.T. Press, pp. 313–344.

Hayek, F.A. von ([1937)] 1948) 'Economics and Knowledge', in *Individualism and Economic Order*, Chicago: The University of Chicago Press, pp. 33–55.

Heller, W. P. (1986) 'Coordination failures under Complete Markets with Applications to Effective demand', in Heller, W., R. Starr and D. Starret (eds)

Equilibrium Analysis: Essays in Honor of Kenneth J. Arrow, vol. II, Cambridge: Cambridge University Press, pp. 155–175.
Hicks, J. R. (1946) *Value and Capital*, Oxford: Clarendon Press (second edition).
Hicks, J. R. (1963) *The Theory of Wages*, London: Macmillan (second edition).
Hicks, J. R. (1965) *Capital and Growth*, Oxford: Clarendon Press.
Hicks, J. R. (1967) *Critical Essays in Monetary Theory*, Oxford: Clarendon Press.
Hicks, J. R. (1974) *The Crisis in Keynesian Economics*, Oxford: Basil Blackwell.
Hicks, J. R. (1977) 'Recollections and Documents' in *Economic Perspectives. Further Essays on Money and Growth*, Oxford: Clarendon Press, pp. 143–148.
Hicks, J. R. (1982) *Money, Interest and Wages. Collected Essays on Economic Theory*, vol. II, Oxford: Basil Blackwell.
Hicks, J. R. (1983) *Classics and Moderns. Collected Essays on Economic Theory*, vol. III, Oxford: Basil Blackwell.
Hicks, J. R. (1989) *A Market Theory of Money*, Oxford: Clarendon Press.
Hines, B. (1980) 'Involuntary Unemployment' in Malinvaud, E. and J. P. Fitoussi (eds) *Unemployment in Western Europe*, London: Macmillan, pp. 141–164.
Hirsch, A. and N. de Marchi (1990) *Milton Friedman. Economics in Theory and Practice*, Ann Arbor: The University of Michigan Press.
Hoover, K. D. (1988) *The New Classical Macroeconomics: A Sceptical Inquiry*, Oxford: Basil Blackwell.
Hoover, K. D. (1995) 'Relative Wages, Rationality, and Involuntary Unemployment in Keynes' Labor market', *History of Political Economy*, vol. 27, pp. 653–685.
Howitt, P. (1985) 'Transactions Costs and the Theory of Unemployment', *American Economic Review*, vol. 75, pp. 88–100.
Howitt, P. (1990) *The Keynesian Recovery and Other Essays*, New York: Philip Allan.
Howitt, P. (2002) 'Looking Inside the Labor Market: A Review Article', *Journal of Economic Literature*, vol. XL, pp. 125–138.
Hutchison, T. W. (1978) *On Revolution and Progress in Economic Knowledge*, Cambridge: Cambridge University Press.
Ito, T. (1982) 'Implicit Contract Theory: A Critical Survey', Discusssion Paper no. 82, Center for Economic Research, Department of Economics, University of Minnesota.
Kahn, R. (1976) 'Unemployment as seen by the Keynesians', in Worswick, G. D. N. (ed.) *The Concept and Measurement of Involuntary Unemployment*, London: Allen and Unwin.
Katz, L. (1986) 'Efficiency Wage Theories: A Partial Evaluation' *National Bureau of Economic Research Macroeconomics Annual*, pp. 235–276.
Keppler, J. (1994) *Monopolistic Competition Theory. Origins, Results and Implications*, Baltimore and London: The Johns Hopkins University Press.
Keynes J. M. (1936) *The General Theory of Employment, Interest and Money*, London: Macmillan.
Keynes J. M. (1973) *The Collected Writings of John Maynard Keynes*, vol. XIII, *The General Theory and After, Part I, Preparation*, Moggridge, D. (ed.) London: Macmillan, for The Royal Economic Society.
Keyssar, A. (1986) *Out of Work: The First Century of Unemployment in Massachusetts*, Cambridge: Cambridge University Press.
King, R. G. (1993) 'Will the New Keynesian Macroeconomics Resurrect the IS-LM Model?', *Journal of Economic Perspectives*, vol. 7, pp. 67–82.

Klamer, A. (1984) *The New Classical Macroeconomics. Conversations with the New Classical Economists and their Opponents*, Brighton: Harvester Press.

Klamer, A. (1989) 'An Accountant Among Economists: Conversations with Sir John R. Hicks', *Journal of Economic Perspectives*, vol. 3, pp. 167–180.

Klausinger, H. (1998) 'Pigou on Unemployment', in Fontaine, P. and A. Jolink (eds), *Historical Perspectives on Macroeconomics, Sixty Years after the General Theory*, London: Routledge, pp. 51–71.

Klein, L. (1947) 'Theories of Effective Demand and Employment', *Journal of Political Economy*, vol. 55, pp. 108–131.

Klein, L. (1948) *The Keynesian Revolution*, New York: Macmillan.

Kolm, S. C. (1990) 'Employment and Fiscal Policy with a Realistic View of the Role of Wages', in Champsaur, P., M. Deleau (eds) *Essays in Honour of Edmond Malinvaud, vol. 2, Macroeconomics*, Cambridge, MA: The M.I.T. Press, pp. 226–281.

Kregel, J. A. (1987) 'The Effective Demand Approach to Employment and Inflation Analysis', *Journal of Post-Keynesian Economics*, vol. 10, pp. 133–145.

Kydland, F. and E. Prescott (1982) 'Time to Build and Aggregate Fluctuations', *Econometrica*, vol. 50, pp. 1345–1370.

Laidler, D. (1996) 'Wage and Price Stickiness in Macroeconomics: Historical Perspective' in Forrest, C. and G. Wood (eds) *Monetary Theories in the 1930s. The Henry Thornton Lectures*, London: Macmillan, pp. 92–121.

Laidler, D. (1999) *Fabricating the Keynesian Revolution. Studies of the Inter-war Literature on Money, the Cycle, and Unemployment*, Cambridge: Cambridge University Press.

Lange, O. (1944) *Price Flexibility and Employment*, Bloomington: The Principia Press.

Lawlor M., W. A. Darity Jr. and B. Horn (1987) 'Was Keynes a Chapter Two Keynesian?' *Journal of Post-Keynesian Economics*, pp. 516–528.

Layard, R. S. Nickell and R. Jackman (1991) *Unemployment. Macroeconomic Performance and the Labour Market*, Oxford: Oxford University Press.

Lazear, E. and R. Moore (1984) 'Incentives, Productivity and Labor Contracts', *Quarterly Journal of Economics*, vol. 101, pp. 275–296.

Leeson, R. (1997a) 'The Political Economy of the Inflation-Unemployment Trade-Off', *History of Political Economy*, vol. 29, pp. 117–156.

Leeson, R. (1997b) 'The Trade-Off Interpretation of Phillips' Dynamic Stabilisation Exercise', *Economica*, vol. 64, pp. 155–173.

Leeson, R. (2000) *The Eclipse of Keynesianism. The Political Economy of the Chicago Counter-Revolution*, Basingstoke, Hampshire: Palgrave.

Leijonhufvud, A. (1967) 'Keynes and the Keynesians: A Suggested Interpretation', *American Economic Review*, vol. 57, pp. 401–410.

Leijonhufvud, A. (1968) *On Keynesian Economics and the Economics of Keynes*, Oxford: Oxford University Press.

Leijonhufvud, A. (1969) *Keynes and the Classics. Two Lectures on Keynes' Contributions to Economic Theory*, London: The Institute of Economic Affairs.

Leijonhufvud, A. (1983) 'What would Keynes have thought of Rational Expectations?' in Worswick, D. and J. Trevithick (eds) *Keynes and the Modern World*, Cambridge: Cambridge University Press, pp. 179–203.

Leijonhufvud, A. (1984) 'Hicks on Time and Money', *Oxford Economic Papers*, Supplement, pp. 26–46.

Leijonhufvud, A. (1998) 'Comments on De Vroey: Involuntary Unemployment

One More Time' in Backhouse, R., D. Hausman, U. Mäki and A. Salanti (eds) *Economics and Methodology: Crossing Boundaries*, London: Macmillan, pp. 225–235.

Leijonhufvud, A. (1999) 'Mr. Keynes and the Moderns' in Pasinetti, L. and B. Schefold (eds) *The Impact of Keynes on Economics in the 20th Century*, Cheltenham: Edward Elgar, pp. 16–35.

Leontief, W. (1947) 'Postulates: Keynes' *General Theory* and the Classicist' *The New Economics. Keynes' Influence on Theory and Public Policy*, New York: A. A. Knopf, in Harris (ed.) pp. 232–242.

Leontief, W. ([1936] 1990) 'The Fundamental Assumption of Mr. Keynes' Monetary Theory of Unemployment', *Quarterly Journal of Economics*, as in Wood, J. C. (ed.) vol. II, pp. 115–119.

Lindbeck, A. and D. Snower (1988) *The Insider–Outsider Theory of Employment and Unemployment*, Cambridge, MA: The M.I.T. Press:

Lindbeck, A. (1993) *Unemployment and Macroeconomics*, Cambridge, MA: M.I.T. Press.

Lindbeck, A. and D. Snower (2002) 'The Insider–Outsider Theory: A survey', *IZA Discussions Papers*, no. 534.

Lipsey, R. G. (2000) 'IS-LM, Keynesianism, and the New Classicism', in Backhouse, R. and A. Salanti (eds) *Macroeconomics and the Real World, vol. 2 Keynesian Economics, Unemployment and Policy*, Oxford: Oxford University Press, pp. 57–82.

Lipsey, R. G. (1978) 'The Place of the Phillips Curve in Macroeconomic Models', in Bergstrom, A., A. J. L. Catt, M. H. Peston and B. D. J. Silverston (eds) *Stability and Inflation: A Volume of Essays to Honour the Memory of A. W. H. Phillips*, New York: John Wiley and Sons.

Lucas, R. E. Jr. ([1979] 1981) 'An Equilibrium Model of the Business Cycle', in *Studies in Business Cycle Theory*, Cambridge, MA: The M. I. T. Press, pp. 179–213.

Lucas, R. E. Jr. (1981) *Studies in Business Cycle Theory*, Cambridge, MA: The M. I. T. Press.

Lucas, R. E. Jr. (1986) 'Adaptative Behavior and Economic Theory', *Journal of Business*, vol 59, pp. S401–S426.

Lucas, R. E. Jr. (1987) *Models of Business Cycle*, Oxford: Basil Blackwell.

Lucas, R. E. Jr. (1996) 'Nobel Lecture: Monetary Neutrality', *Journal of Political Economy*, vol. 104, pp. 661–681.

Lucas, R. E. Jr. and T. Sargent ([1978] 1994) 'After Keynesian Macroeconomics' in Miller, P. R. (ed.) *The Rational Expectations Revolution. Readings from the Front Line*, Cambridge, MA: The M.I.T. Press, pp. 5–30.

McCombie, J. (1987–1988) 'Keynes and the Nature of Involuntary Unemployment', *Journal of Post-Keynesian Economics*, vol. X, pp. 202–215.

McKenzie, L. W. and S. Zamagni (eds) (1991) *Value and Capital Fifty Years Later*, London: Macmillan.

MacLeod, W. and J. Malcomson (1998) 'Motivations and Markets', *American Economic Review*, vol. 88, pp. 606–620.

Malinvaud, E. (1977) *The Theory of Unemployment Reconsidered*, Oxford: Basil Blackwell.

Malinvaud, E. (1984) *Mass Unemployment*, Oxford: Basil Blackwell.

Mankiw, N. G. (1985) 'Small Menu Costs and Large Business Cycles: A Macroeconomic Model of Monopoly', *Quarterly Journal of Economics*, vol. 100, pp. 529–539.

Marris, R. (1991) *Reconstructing Keynesian Economics with Imperfect Competition. A Desk-top Simulation*, London: Edward Elgar.

Marshall, A. (1920) *Principles of Economics*, London: Macmillan, (eighth edition).

Matthews, R. (1990) 'Marshall and the Labour Market' in Whitaker, J. (ed.) *Centenary Essays on Alfred Marshall*, Cambridge: Cambridge University Press, pp. 14–43.

Meade J. ([1937] 1947) 'A Simplified Model of Keynes's System', in Harris, S. E. (ed.) *The New Economics. Keynes' Influence on Theory and Public Policy*, New York: A. A. Knopf, pp. 606–618.

Meltzer, A. (1988) *Keynes's Monetary Theory. A Different Interpretation* Cambridge: Cambridge University Press.

Modigliani, F. (1944) 'Liquidity Preference and the Theory of Interest and Money', *Econometrica*, vol. 12, pp. 44–88.

Modigliani, F. (1963) 'The Monetary Mechanism and Its Interaction with Real Phenomena', *Review of Economics and Statistics*, vol. 65, pp. 79–107.

Modigliani, F. (2002) 'The Keynesian Theory of Unemployment', mimeo.

Moggridge, D. E. (1992) *Maynard Keynes: An Economist's Biography*, London: Routledge.

Mortensen, D. (1970) 'A Theory of Wages and Employment Dynamics', in Phelps, E. S., A. Alchian and C. Holt (eds) *Microeconomic Foundations of Employment and Inflation Theory*, New York: Norton, pp. 167–211.

Mortensen, D. and C. Pissarides (1999) 'Job Reallocation, Employment Fluctuations and Unemployment', in Taylor, J. B. and M. Woodford (eds) *Handbook of Macroeconomics*, vol. I, Elsevier Science B.V., pp. 1171–1228.

Negishi, T., (1979) *Microeconomic Foundations of Keynesian Economics*, Amsterdam North-Holland.

Okun, A. (1981) *Prices and Quantities. A Macroeconomic Analysis*, Oxford: Basil Blackwell.

Olson, M. (1982) *The Rise and Decline of Nations, Economic Growth, Stagflation and Social Rigidities*, New Haven: Yale University Press.

Patinkin, D. ([1948] 1951) 'Price Flexibility and Full Employment', in American Economic Association, *Readings in Monetary Theory*, Philadelphia: Blakiston, pp. 252–283.

Patinkin, D. (1965) *Money, Interest and Prices*, New York: Harper and Row (second edition).

Patinkin, D. (1987a) 'Keynes, John Maynard', in Eatwell, J., M. Milgate and P. Newman (eds) *The New Palgrave. A Dictionary of Economics*, London: Macmillan, vol. 3, pp. 19–41.

Patinkin, D. (1987b) 'Real balances', in Eatwell, J., M. Milgate and P. Newman (eds) *The New Palgrave Dictionary of Economics*, London: Macmillan, vol. 4, pp. 98–101.

Patinkin, D. (1989) 'New Introduction', *Money, Interest and Prices*, Cambridge, MA: The M. I. T. Press, pp. XV–LXV.

Patinkin, D. (1990) 'On Different Interpretations of the *General Theory*', *Journal of Monetary Economics*, vol. 26, pp. 205–245.

Pencavel, J. (1986) 'Labour Supply of Men. A Survey' in Ashenfelter, O. and R. Layard (eds) *Handbook of Labor Economics*, vol I, Elsevier Science, pp. 3–102.

Phelps, E. (1985) *Political Economy*, New York: Norton.

Phelps, E. (1994) *Structural Slumps: The Modern Equilibrium Theory of Unemployment, Interest, and Assets*, Cambridge, MA: Harvard University Press.

Phelps, E., A. Alchian and C. Holt (eds) (1970) *Microeconomic Foundations of Employment and Inflation Theory*, New York: Norton.

Picard, P. (1993) *Wages and Unemployment. A Study in Non-Walrasian Macroeconomics*, Cambridge: Cambridge University Press.

Pigou, A. C. (1914) *Unemployment*, Williams and Norgate.

Pigou, A. C. ([1936] 1983) 'Mr J. M. Keynes' General Theory of Employment, Interest and Money', in Wood, J. C. (1983) *John Maynard Keynes. Critical Assessments*, vol. II, London: Routledge, pp. 18–31.

Pigou, A. C. (1943) 'The Classical Stationary State', *Economic Journal*, vol. 53, pp. 343–351.

Piore, M. J. (1987) 'Historical Perspectives and the Interpretation of Unemployment', *Journal of Economic Literature*, vol. XXV, pp. 1834–1850.

Pissarides, C. (1990) *Equilibrium Unemployment Theory*, Oxford: Basil Blackwell.

Riley, J. (2001) 'Silver Signals: Twenty-Five years of Screening and Signaling', *Journal of Economic Literature*, vol. 39, pp. 432–478.

Rivot, S. (2001) 'The Evolution of the Concept of Involuntary Unemployment: from Keynes to New Keynesians', *History of Economic Ideas*, vol. XI, pp. 121–144.

Roberts, J. (1987) 'An Equilibrium Model with Involuntary Unemployment at Flexible, Competitive Prices and Wages', *American Economic Review*, vol. 77, pp. 856–874.

Roberts, J. (1989) 'Equilibrium without Market Clearing' in Cornet, B. and H. Tulkens (eds) *Contributions to Operation Research and Economics*, Cambridge, MA: The M.I.T. Press.

Robertson, D. (1915) A *Study of Industrial Fluctuation: An Inquiry into the Character and Causes of the So-called Cyclical Movements of Trade*, London: London School of Economics.

Robinson, J. (1947) *Essays in the Theory of Employment*, Oxford: Basil Blackwell (second edition).

Rogerson, R. (1997) 'Theory Ahead of Language in the Economics of Unemployment', *Journal of Economic Perspectives*, vol. 11, pp. 73–92.

Rosen, S. (1985) 'Implicit Contracts: A Survey', *Journal of Economic Literature*, vol. XXIII, pp. 1144–1175.

Rosier, M. (2002) 'The Logic of Keynes' Criticism of the Classical Model', *The European Journal of the History of Economic Thought*, vol. 9, pp. 608–643.

Rubin, G. (2002a) 'From Equilibrium to Disequilibrium: the Genesis of Don Patinkin's Interpretation of the Keynesian Theory', *The European Journal of the History of Economic Thought*, vol. 9, pp. 205–225.

Rubin, G. (2002b) *La contribution de Don Patinkin à la 'synthèse néoclassique': genèse et portée*, Université de Paris X-Nanterre, thèse de doctorat.

Salais, R., N. Baverez and B. Reynaud (1986) *L'invention du chômage: histoire et transformation d'une catégorie en France des années 1890 aux années 1980*, Paris: Presses Universitaires de France.

Salop, S. (1979) 'A Model of the Natural Rate of Unemployment', *American Economic Review*, vol. 69, pp. 117–125.

Samuelson, P. A. (1947) 'The General Theory (3)', in Harris, S. E. (ed.) *The New Economics. Keynes' Influence on Theory and Public Policy*, New York: A. Knopf, pp. 145–160.

Samuelson, P. A. (1964) 'The General Theory', in Lekachman, R. (ed.) *Keynes's General Theory. Reports of Three Decades*, London: Macmillan.

Santomero, A. and J. Seater (1978) 'The Inflation-Unemployment Trade-off: A Critique of the Literature', *Journal of Economic Literature*, vol. 16, pp. 499–544.

Sargent, T. J. (1996) 'Expectations and the Nonneutrality of Money', *Journal of Monetary Economics*, vol. 37, pp. 535–548.

Schumpeter, J. ([1954] 1994) *History of Economic Analysis*, London: Routledge.

Sebastiani, M. (1994) *Kalecki and Unemployment Equilibrium*, London: Macmillan.

Shapiro, C. and J. Stiglitz (1984) 'Equilibrium Unemployment as Worker Discipline Device', *American Economic Review*, vol. 74, pp. 433–444.

Shapiro, C. and J. Stiglitz (1985) 'Can Unemployment Be Involuntary? Reply', *American Economic Review*, vol. 75, pp. 1215–1217.

Silvestre, J. (1982) 'Fixprice Analysis in Exchange Economies', *Journal of Economic Theory*, vol. 26, pp. 28–58.

Silvestre, J. (1990) 'There May be Unemployment When the Labour Market is Competitive and the Output Market is Not', *The Economic Journal*, vol. 100, pp. 899–913.

Silvestre, J. (1993) 'The Market-Power Foundations of Macroeconomic Policy', *Journal of Economic Literature*, vol. XXXI, pp. 105–141.

Skidelsky, R. (1983) *John Maynard Keynes: Hopes Betrayed, 1883–1920*, London: Macmillan

Skidelsky, R. (1992) *John Maynard Keynes: The Economist as Savior*, 1920–1937, London: Macmillan.

Skidelsky, R. (2000) *John Maynard Keynes: Fighting for Britain*, London: Macmillan.

Skousen, M. (1998) 'Milton Friedman, Ex-Keynesian', http://www.mskousen.com/books/articles.exkeynes.html.

Smith, A. ([1776] 1976), *An Inquiry into the Nature and Causes of the Wealth of Nations*, Oxford: Oxford University Press.

Snowdon, B. and H. R. Vane (1994) *A Modern Guide to Macroeconomics. An Introduction to Competing Schools of Thought*, Aldershot: Edward Elgar.

Snowdon, B. and H. R. Vane (1997) 'Modern Macroeconomics and its Evolution from a Monetarist Perspective: an Interview with Professor Milton Friedman', *Journal of Economic Studies*, vol. 24, pp. 192–221.

Snowdon, B. and H. R. Vane (1998) 'Transforming Macroeconomics: an Interview with Robert E Lucas Jr.', *Journal of Economic Methodology*, vol. 5, pp. 115–145.

Snowdon, B. and H. R. Vane (1999) *Conversations with Leading Economists. Interpreting Modern Macreoconomics*, Cheltenham: Edward Elgar.

Solow, R. (1980) 'On Theories of Unemployment', *American Economic Review*, vol. 70, pp. 1–11.

Solow, R. (1986) 'Unemployment: Getting the Question Right', *Economica*, vol. 47, supplement, pp. 23–34.

Solow, R. (1990) *The Labour Market as a Social Institution*, Cambridge: Blackwell.

Stigler, G. ([1965] 1957) 'Perfect Competition, Historically Contemplated', in *Essays in the History of Economics*, Chicago: The University of Chicago Press, pp. 234–267.

Stiglitz, J. (1975) 'Information and Economic Analysis: a Perspective', *The Economic Journal*, vol. 85, pp. 22–39.

Stiglitz, J. (1987) 'The Causes and Consequences of the Dependency of Quality on Price', *Journal of Economic Literature*, vol. 25, pp. 1–48.

Stiglitz, J. (1992) 'Methodological Issues and the New Keynesian Economics' in Vercelli, A. and N. Dimitri (eds) *Macroeconomics. A Survey of Research Strategies*, Oxford: Oxford University Press, pp. 38–85.

Stiglitz, J. (1993) *Economics*, New York: Norton.

Stiglitz, J. (2002) 'Information and the Change in Paradigms in Economics', *American Economic Review*, vol. 92, pp. 460–501.

Tarshis, L. (1989) 'Keynes's Co-operative Economy and the Aggregate Supply Function', in Pheby, J. (ed.) *New Directions in Post-Keynesian Economics*, Edwar Elgar: London, pp. 35–58.

Taylor, J. ([1979] 1991) 'Staggered Wage Setting in a Macro Model' in Mankiw, G. and D. Romer (eds) *New Keynesian Economics*, vol. 1, *Imperfect Competition and Sticky Prices*, Cambridge, MA: The M.I.T. Press, pp. 233–241.

Tobin, J. (1947) 'Money Wage Rates and Employment', in Harris, S. E. (ed.) *The New Economics. Keynes' Influence on Theory and Public Policy*, New York: A. A. Knopf, pp. 572–587.

Tobin, J. (1972) 'Inflation and Unemployment', *American Economic Review*, vol. 62, pp. 1–19.

Tobin, J. (1981) 'Review of Patinkin's *Keynes' Monetary Thought*', *Journal of Political Economy*, vol. 89, pp. 204–207.

Tobin, J. ([1993] 1997) 'Price Flexibility and Output Stability. An Old Keynesian View' in Snowdon, B. and H. Vane (eds) *A Macroeconomics Reader*, London: Routledge, pp. 135–155.

Tobin, J. (1995) 'The Natural Rate as New Classical Macroeconomics', in Cross, R. (ed.) *The National Rate of Unemployment. Reflections on 25 Years of the Hypothesis*, Cambridge: Cambridge University Press, pp. 32–42.

Trevithick, J. A. (1992) *Involuntary Unemployment. Macroeconomics from a Keynesian Perspective*, London: Harvester Wheatsheaf.

Vercelli, A. (1991) *Methodological Foundations of Macroeconomics: Keynes and Lucas*, Cambridge: Cambridge University Press.

von Mises, L. (1949) *Human Action: A Treatise on Economics*, New Haven: Yale University Press.

Walker, D. (ed.) (1984) *Money and Markets. Essays by Robert Clower*, Cambridge: Cambridge University Press.

Walras, L. (1954) *Elements of Pure Economics*, translated by Jaffé W., London: Allen and Unwin.

Weintraub, E. R. (1979) *Microfoundations. The Compatibility of Microeconomics and Macroeconomics*, Cambridge: Cambridge University Press.

Weintraub, E. R. (1990) 'Methodology Does not Matter, But the History of Thought Might', in Honkepohja, S. (ed.) *The State of Macroeconomics. Proceedings of the Symposium, Whiter Macreoeconomics?*, Oxford: Oxford University Press, pp. 263–280.

Weiss, A. (1980) 'Job Queues and Layoffs in Labor Markets with Flexible Wages', *Journal of Political Economy*, vol. 88, pp. 526–538.

Weiss, L. (1986) 'Comments on Katz', *National Bureau of Economic Research Macroeconomics Annual*, pp. 285–287.

Weitzman, M. (1982) 'Increasing Returns and the Foundations of Unemployment Theory', *The Economic Journal*, vol. 92, pp. 787–804.

Whiteside, N. and J. Gillepsie (1991) 'Deconstructing Unemployment: Developments in Britain in the Interwar Years', *Economic History Review*, vol. XLIV, pp. 665–682.

Wood, J. C. (1990) (ed.) *John Maynard Keynes. Critical Assessments*, four volumes, London: Routledge.

Woodford, M. (1999) 'Revolution and Evolution in Twentieth-Century Macroeconomics', mimeo, to be published in Gifford, P. (ed.) *Frontiers of the Mind in the Twenty-First Century*, Cambridge, MA: Harvard University Press.

Yeager, L. (1960) 'Methodenstreit Over Demand Curves', *Journal of Political Economy*, vol. 68, pp. 53–64.

Yellen, J. (1984) 'Efficience Wage Models of Unemployment', *American Economic Review*, vol. 74, pp. 200–205.

Young, W. (1987) *Interpreting Mr Keynes. The IS-LM Enigma*, London: Polity Press.

INDEX

Figures and Tables are indicated by *italic* page numbers